GLOBAL MISSION

Endorsements for Global Mission

Evangelical faith has two complementary emphases: the eternal, universal truth revealed in Jesus Christ and the Bible as its written testimony, and the need of a very personal trust in God—the truth adapted into everyone's everyday life. Thus local theology is as true as global theology, bringing the gospel tradition truthfully and contextualized to every place and every generation. This book is a great tool to help you to achieve this and should be used in any theological training worldwide.

Thomas Schirrmacher, Executive Chair, Theological Commission, World Evangelical Alliance and Editor, Evangelical Review of Theology, Germany

The more I work in cross-cultural contexts, the more I am amazed by the variety of God's people and at the same time just how much my faith is dominated by an English mind-set. This excellent book encourages us to take the time to learn, observe, and understand what it means to follow Christ in different contexts. There are no easy answers, but it is challenging to read of the journeys made by many.

Martin Lee, Executive Director, Global Connections, United Kingdom

Both church and mission movements have desperately recognized and discussed the need to be contextual with the gospel, but very few have spelled out "how to do it." In today's paradoxical scenario, with many challenges to bring the gospel to all peoples, nurture followers, and establish witnessing clusters, this book of case studies is a welcome effort. I am delighted that it attempts to spell out models for contextualizing the gospel in various aspects to current followers of Christ. I am pleased that these are not just theories but practices from practitioners to be followed in diverse settings. May these case studies bring new brands of Christ disciples, building a mosaic of Jesus followers across the world. I am grateful for the worldwide voices in this book that suggest contextualizing paths and solutions, especially in the Global South. May we all be inspired to move forward to establish the new faces of Jesus followers.

K. Rajendran, Chairman, World Evangelical Alliance Mission Commission, India

The many authors of the books of our Scriptures lived and experienced God in their different contexts, generations, and ages. They were faithful to convey to us the reality and various expressions of the words, ways, and works of God from their respective understanding and perspectives. This in turn formed the BODY of the revelation of God we have in the Scriptures. I am convinced similarly that the authors and contributors of the insights and wisdom contained in the pages of this book have also demonstrated a level of faithfulness, understanding, and appreciation of the diverse ways in which the Triune God reveals himself through the ages and in our contemporary times, locations, and contexts. For these reasons I commend this book to the generation of "God-seekers" as a veritable compass and road map as we "seek him and perhaps reach out for him, and find him, though he is not far from each one of us" (Acts 17:27 NIV).

Reuben Ezemadu, International Director CMF, INC; Ministry Center Director, DAI Nigeria; Continental Coordinator, Movement of African National Initiatives, Nigeria

This new book represents the best of contemporary evangelical reflection on and practice of contextualization. Built on solid biblical foundations and packed with insight, illustrations, and thought-provoking discussion questions, the essays carefully balance text and context, the local and the global, theology as both universal and "at-home" in every culture. The mature thinking and global breadth of the authors is refreshing evidence that evangelicals have come of age in their contribution to global theologizing. No reader will agree with everything, but the chapters are never dull and will consistently sow seeds of fresh thought and creative approaches for ministry.

Steve Strauss, Professor of World Missions and Intercultural Studies, Dallas Theological Seminary, USA

We welcome this companion volume to the Theological Commission's *Local Theology for the Global Church*. It is packed full of practical and realistic examples of contextualization which are sensitive and effective. They are well based in the experience of the writers and grounded in careful missiological thinking, making it a vital contribution to one of the most important aspects of mission today. We highly commend both books.

David Parker, Former Executive Director, World Evangelical Alliance Theological Commission, Australia

This book is indeed the fruit of Spirit-led reflections from local mission practitioners who sustain the momentum of global mission, in tune with the timeless Lord's commission. I highly commend the reading and usage of this book to everyone to mobilize both the local and global church to carry on the noble task of reaching people for Christ with new insights and strategies in various contexts. Understanding and correctly interpreting the contextual worldviews will greatly help to firmly establish believers in the faith in Christ, which in turn bears fruit of change. Rose Dowsett and the writers have produced a great work for the task of the church.

Abel Laondoye Ndjerareou, TEN-RTF Bureau Afrique, Chad

'Why has contextualization become such a pressing—and contentious—issue?' asks the editor in her opening essay. This excellent book unfolds part of the answer, but it does so not by offering the reader a bird's-eye view of global missions. Rather, the essays gathered in this volume take us on a journey through contextual theology into the messiness, the challenges, and the joys of people who try to "live in faith, obedience, and authentic discipleship in whichever setting the sovereign Lord has given" them (Introduction, p. 4). What does contextualization look like? Well, it depends. But when you read this book, you will glimpse the patchwork of God's saving plan for creation in the particularities of each experience, each mission, and each life narrated in these pages.

C. Rosalee Velloso Ewell, Executive Director of World Evangelical Alliance Theological Commission and New Testament Editor for the Latin American Bible Commentary Project, Brazil

This is a fascinating collection of articles and case studies by evangelicals drawn from mission frontiers all over the world. It will serve as an excellent reader on contextual theology and culturally sensitive mission approaches. And it may just convert the most intransigent anti-contextualist!

Hwa Yung, Bishop, The Methodist Church, Malaysia

In missiology we have worked on contextualization issues for a long time. Didn't we figure out "how to do it"? Why another book? The reason is clear: because contextualization is closely related to the ongoing incarnational nature of God's mission. Taking part in God's mission therefore calls us to take part in all the fascinating and changing issues that continue to arise when gospel meets culture. This book demonstrates how Christian mission in all parts of the world is profoundly responding to important contextualization issues. You gain a deeper sense of the nature of God by studying the richness of the world he has created.

Birger Nygaard, Areopagos, National Evangelical Alliance, Denmark

Since New Testament times, the Christian church has struggled with the challenge of understanding how the one, universal gospel may be incarnated in multiple, particular contexts. More recently, the concerns expressed by the cross-cultural missionary writers of Cultural Anthropology in the 1950s and 1960s were taken up by Shoki Coe and others in the 1970s, seeking to explore the mystery of contextualization. This volume continues that search. Of the five paradigms of contextualization that have developed in the past fifty years (communication, indigenization, translatability, local theologizing, and epistemology), this volume is centered in the classic communication paradigm of contextualization. This collection of essays is a refreshing kaleidoscope of portraits of careful attempts to understand how the unchanging gospel of Jesus Christ may be incarnated in always-changing cultural contexts around the globe. This book is globally extended, locally focused, practice oriented, biblically careful, and culturally aware.

Charles (Chuck) Van Engen, Arthur F. Glasser Professor of Biblical Theology of Mission, School of Intercultural Studies, Fuller Theological Seminary

GLOBAL MISSION

REFLECTIONS AND CASE STUDIES IN CONTEXTUALIZATION FOR THE WHOLE CHURCH

Rose Dowsett

Editor

WILLIAM CAREY
LIBRARY

Global Mission: Reflections and Case Studies in Contextualization for the Whole Church

All scripture quotations, unless otherwise indicated, are taken from the Holy Bible, New International Version. © 1973, 1978, 1984 by the International Bible Society.
Used by permission of Zondervan Publishing House. | www.zondervan.com

Published by William Carey Library
1605 E. Elizabeth St.
Pasadena, CA 91104 | www.missionbooks.org

William Carey Library is a ministry of the
US Center for World Mission
Pasadena, California | www.uscwm.org
Printed in the United States of America.
15 14 13 12 11   5 4 3 2 1 BP1200

Koe Pahlka, copyeditor, interior design, indexing
Kalun Lau, cover design

Library of Congress Cataloging-in-Publication Data
Global mission : reflections and case studies in contextualization for the
whole church / Rose Dowsett, editor.
    p. cm.
 ISBN 978-0-87808-532-3
 1. Christianity and culture. 2. Missions. I. Dowsett, Rose.
 BR115.C8G586 2011
 261--dc23
                        2011030186

CONTENTS

REFLECTIONS ON A NEW BOOK ON CONTEXTUALIZATION

William D. Taylor

We welcome you to another WEA Mission Commission publication, the twelfth of our "Globalization of Mission" series. Our books owe a primary debt to the 1999 Iguassu missiological consultation that gathered in a missiologically meaningful setting for a seminal encounter. Out of those rich discussions came specific challenges for the Mission Commission leadership. This book is birthed out of that gathering, and it has taken a long time gestating.

This book is a partner publication to *Local Theology for the Global Church: Principles for an Evangelical Approach to Contextualization*, edited by Matthew Cook, Rob Haskell, Ruth Julian, and Natee Tanchanpongs. That book was generated by the WEA Theological Commission and this new one by the WEA Mission Commission. The teams worked separately from each other, but the reader will discover how they complement one another. We are thankful to William Carey Library for continuing to publish and promote these books.

This is a book presenting the evangelical challenges of contextualization, though the title does not easily give that away. We do not establish one definition of contextualization, but rather allow the rich facets of this term to emerge in each chapter by each author. However, the title does reflect our biblical commitment to the universal church and the local church, the gathered-scattered body of Christ on both the cutting edges as well as the maturing stages of Kingdom advance. We are passionately committed to the thoughtful spread of the gospel of Jesus to the less-reached people (individuals, families, clans, peoples, political nations) of our world, whoever and wherever they may be. And we are equally committed to the solid establishment of the church that leads to transformational discipleship. And both passions require serious contextualization.

This book is directed to the "reflective practitioners" of the global mission community. This concept, coined at the Iguassu consultation, speaks of those women and men who think well as they serve, who ask questions on the move, who prod our own ministry approach in the context of a commitment to action. We affirm this category because of the stereotyped extremes of the ivory tower academic and the enthusiastic activist. We place ourselves in the middle of these polarities. The MC has a diverse set of constituencies, all in arenas of leadership: the local church or denomination; mission agencies or sending structures; missionary training schools/programs; theology education institutions; field-based mission bodies that serve the field missionary in terms of strategizing, shepherding, supervising; and a wide spectrum of other global and national networks and teams. Thus our book serves the field-based leader as well as the academy in search for good books on contextualization.

Some other reflections on the publication: It was written by thirty-three authors from nineteen nations, on contextualization issues in many more countries and peoples. Their personal cross-cultural ministry expands the breadth and experience from which they write. It is truly a global book. Many of our authors have never published anything in their lives, and the MC is privileged to serve as publishing obstetricians for our friends around the world. Some of our writers crafted their original paper in their mother tongue and then it was translated to English. Others wrote in English, though it might have been their second or third language. Our editorial team has softly edited the manuscripts, thus allowing the writer's style and wording to trump any attempt to produce "BBC English," or "American English."

A good number of our writers are field-based practitioners who are reflecting in written form in the middle of their contextual ministries. That also produces a diverse style of documentation. And here we thank our readers for exercising grace to allow a more flexible perspective on footnotes or references. Rose Dowsett, our lead editor, and I are very confident that no writers are guilty of plagiarizing, but some did not have all the scholarly primary sources on hand while writing, especially in another language and country without those resources at hand.

Finally, I want to thank three people. Rose Dowsett is our lead editor, though at the start of the project there were to have been two other co-editors who were then unable to continue. So Rose handled it by herself. She and I worked together to scan our mission landscape to discover writers with something to say, many of whom would be first-time published writers. And that was another MC value and joy of the book: opening space for new writers that will help shape the mission landscape into the future. Rose shepherded the writers and had to cajole some of them to turn their assignment in, at least on the sixth deadline given. She personally scrutinized and edited each chapter. We would not have this book without her perseverance and dedication. Much of her work came in the context of a very heavy volunteer commitment to Lausanne III, especially serving on the team of eight that produced the key document, The Cape Town Commitment.

Rose, a simple though heartfelt word: thank you.

We are also grateful for our faithful copy editor, Koe Pahlka, who has now helped produce the fourth book in our series. Koe is the young mother of a small tribe of adopted children, and having visited her in her home-farm, I cannot imagine how she disciplines her schedule. Thank God for her husband and the children whose chores help the family!

Kalun Kau, living and working in Hong Kong, has produced the third cover for us. Thank you friend, for your keen creativity and willingness to work with our limited resources.

Good reader, may you find the creative Holy Spirit at work in your heart and mind as you engage with the writers and themes of this book. May you be encouraged; may your ministry be strengthened; may you be nurtured, prodded, challenged.

William D. Taylor, Publications Coordinator
WEA Mission Commission

TITLES OF THE "GLOBALIZATION OF MISSION" SERIES

William D. Taylor, ed., *Internationalising Missionary Training: A Global Perspective*, Paternoster Press, Baker Book House, 1991.

William D. Taylor, ed., *Kingdom Partners for Synergy in Missions*, William Carey Library, 1994.

Jonathan Lewis, ed., *Working Your Way to the Nations: A Guide to Effective Tentmaking*, InterVarsity Press, 1996.

William D. Taylor, ed., *Too Valuable to Lose: Exploring the Causes and Cures of Missionary Attrition*, William Carey Library, 1997.

William D. Taylor, ed., *Global Missiology for the 21st Century: The Iguassu Dialogue*, Baker Academic, 2000.

Kelly O'Donnell, ed., *Doing Member Care Well: Perspectives and Practices from Around the World*, William Carey Library, 2002.

Richard Tiplady, ed., *One World or Many: The Impact of Globalisation on Mission*, William Carey Library, 2003.

Robert Brynjolfson and Jonathan Lewis, eds., *Integral Ministry Training: Design and Evaluation*, William Carey Library, 2006.

Rob Hay, Valerie Lim, Detlef Blöcher, Japp Ketelaar, and Sarah Hay, *Worth Keeping: Global Perspectives on Best Practice in Missionary Retention*, William Carey Library, 2007.

Matthew Cook, Rob Haskell, Ruth Julian, and Natee Tanchanpongs, eds., *Local Theology for the Global Church: Principles for an Evangelical Approach to Contextualization*, William Carey Library, 2010.

Rose Dowsett, ed., *Global Mission: Reflections and Case Studies in Contextualization for the Whole Church*, William Carey Library, 2011.

William Taylor, Tonica van der Meer, and Reg Reimer, eds., *Sorrow and Blood: Christian Mission in Contexts of Suffering, Persecution, and Martyrdom*, William Carey Library, 2012.

THE SHAMAN MEETS THE MAN WITH THE BLACK BEARD

Bertil Ekström

"Who is that man in the long black beard?" asked the shaman as soon as he saw me coming together with the pastor on the path in the jungle. Although he had seen many non-Indians before, it was not every day that someone from outside the Guaraní tribe came to visit him.

The reason for my visit some years ago to the Guaraní tribe in the north of Paraguay had to do with contextualization. For several years, we had organized leadership training for the Guaraní among our partner churches in Paraguay, but the results were not satisfactory. The curriculum was good, the teachers well prepared, and the materials of best quality. Every year fifteen to twenty young Guaraní men and women came to the Bible schools and training seminars, and they always expressed their gratitude for the help from the neighboring country. However, after all these years we had not seen much result, and very few of the former students were engaged in local churches.

After one of these training events I was really frustrated and went to a local pastor for advice. Pastor Rojas told me about the importance of understanding the history and culture of the Guaraní, the main and original population of the country. It was an indispensable and extremely helpful lecture about the need for contextualization. The training methods and the models of leadership were certainly efficient in Brazil, but not necessarily adequate for this Paraguayan context. This conversation with Pastor Rojas led me to a journey to discover more about Paraguayan culture and particularly the view of leadership among the Guaraní.

Through some missionaries I heard about a single lady who had moved to a tribe that still lived in a jungle area where many of the Indians had converted. "Indian-Anna," as she was called, was happy to receive me and introduce me to the local leadership. So there I was, trying to learn from the "original" source about leadership in a traditional Guaraní tribe. The pastor of the congregation was himself a Guaraní, and everything in his church was conducted in the Tupi-Guaraní language. The pastor told me that almost the entire local population belonged to the church and only a few remained in their animistic beliefs.

I asked him who had not yet accepted the Christian faith. His answer was that there were just two or three who did not want to leave their addiction to alcohol as well as the shaman who still practiced traditional magic.

My desire to talk to the shaman was of course a surprise to my local colleague, but he agreed to introduce me to the shaman, certainly knowing that this was not what was expected of a foreigner visiting the tribal area. The house of the shaman was located several kilometers from the rest of the tribe. After the initial shock of our coming and some phrases of greetings, the shaman invited us to sit outside his house and an interesting conversation developed. The first thing I wanted to know was, "Why are you a medicine man and what does that mean to you?" My interpreter was not happy with the question but decided to cooperate and took the risk in asking him. For the next twenty minutes or so the shaman told us his story, how he as a young boy was walking in the jungle and heard a voice calling for his secret name. He thought initially that it was his father who was calling him but could not see anyone. Three times the voice called his name and he understood that it was Tupan, the creator, the main god of the Guaraní who was calling him. The voice continued challenging him to be the spiritual leader of the people and the one who should guide the tribe to paradise. He decided to accept the call to be a shaman, following the footsteps of his father and he had been faithful to Tupan during all the years. With the new religion and the conversion of almost the entire tribe to the Christian faith, he could not do much anymore. The tribe had stopped searching for paradise, and only a few came to him for help.

Suddenly the shaman stood up and asked us to leave his house, perhaps regretting that he had told us his life story. I had many more questions to ask him, but our time was up. The long walk back to the centre of the village was done in complete silence, and we were both reflecting about his testimony. Had he "contextualized" his story to our Christian ears? Was it really true? We knew that the description of his leadership role was right. For the rest of the day we discussed leadership issues and how to apply the tradition and the deeply rooted myths that people still believed as they dedicated themselves to the development of Christian leadership. The typical Guaraní leadership had a clear division of functions and the cacique and the shaman formed a team. The cacique was responsible when the tribe had settled in a place and the shaman was the leader when the nomadic tribe moved from one to another. Therefore the cacique was more the administrative leader while the shaman was the spiritual leader with a special task to lead the people to the ultimate and perfect place—paradise.

Our Bible schools and training seminars changed considerably after this experience. Pastor Rojas became my local mentor. Being a teacher in Guaraní history and culture, he was always invited to share about contextualization with the students. For some years we were able to develop and equip our national leadership with a different understanding of their tradition and the possibility of developing their own leadership models.

Contextualization has been one of the main challenges in the missionary work. Not just to adapt to local and national customs and religious expressions, but to know the beliefs and worldview behind these and, at the same time, respect biblical principles. Indian missiologist

Hrangkhuma, gives, in the case of India, five negative results of what he calls "the missionaries' failure to incarnate":

- A failure to communicate the gospel at the deepest level, through not knowing the worldview of the Indians;
- Changes imposed on the receiving people, rejecting their indigenous culture;
- Missionaries not contextualizing their theological teaching and not understanding that their own theology was conditioned by their own culture of origin;
- The formation of "exotic" churches as almost exact copies of denominational churches in the missionaries' homelands; and,
- The formation of a top-down leadership according to the model practiced by the missionaries (1998, 318-22).

This book that you hold in your hands is an invaluable tool to avoid these kinds of mistakes. The great variety of examples, combined with solid teaching on biblical principles and basic anthropological and cross-cultural rules, offer a precious source for all who are involved in missionary work and communication in other cultural contexts.

Bertil Ekström is the Executive Director of the WEA Mission Commission.

PART ONE

REFLECTIONS AND FOUNDATIONS

RAINBOW FAITH

Authentic Discipleship in Global Perspective
Rose Dowsett

In my attic, there is a pigtail: a long black plait of hair, attached to a Chinese skull cap, such as scholars and many others wore in late nineteenth-century China. I do not know the name of the person who wore it, though I do know he was a missionary with the China Inland Mission.

Every now and then I hold the cap and pigtail in my hands and remember my forebears who carried the gospel with such passion (literal suffering as well as commitment) to the interior of a vast, and even then, vastly populated land. And I also remember why that anonymous man chose to wear Chinese dress, despite being despised and taunted for it by most of his own countrymen. He did it to identify with the people he longed to reach with the gospel and to show respect for their culture. I honor him, this man unknown to me, but known to God and a brother in Christ.

As I write, I have beside me a reproduction of an etching—a detailed line drawing from before the days of photography—originally printed in a missionary magazine in the late 1860s. In the picture, the King of Yoruba in Nigeria, surrounded by hundreds of his subjects, welcomes three missionaries recently arrived from Scotland. The foreigners, two men and a woman, are dressed in full Western attire: long frock-coats, trousers and hats for the men, and floor-length heavy dress, shawl, and bonnet for the woman.

It's hard not to smile; it looks so exasperatingly silly. More seriously, it perhaps suggests a complete lack of adaptation to another culture, with all the likely failure in gospel contextualization that goes with it. And yet, these, too, I honor. They were part of a brave procession of men and women who knew full well as they left their homes that they were not likely to survive more than a year or two at most in "the white man's graveyard," yet even so believed the cause of the gospel more urgent and more precious than their own lives.

The history of the church in its mission is full of the good and the bad, the absurd and the tragic, the awful and the inspiring. As fallen human beings our motives are rarely pure and, whoever we are and of whichever generation or culture, our ministry will bear all the ambiguities of our humanity. Even though redeemed, we are still not perfected!

Because it is very fashionable to dismiss much of the modern Protestant mission movement since the early nineteenth century as cultural and/or political imperialism and therefore harmful, we can easily lose sight of God's amazing grace in choosing to use and work through flawed human beings and all the peculiarities of history. Yes, it is easy to spot many things which should have been done differently. But we need also to honor those who gave themselves in the cause of bringing the gospel to unreached and unevangelized people, often at tremendous cost. We need also to recognize that it is always easier to see the splinter in another's eye rather than the log in our own, as our Lord so graphically put it. How discerning are we about what we are doing in mission today? Nor is this a Western problem, though it is that. I also observe that many in the exciting, God-birthed new mission movements from Africa, Asia and Latin America, equally do not find it easy to contextualize, but assume that what they have been familiar with is equally transferable to their new setting.

In other words, contextualization is a challenge to us all.

AS OLD AS THE HUMAN RACE
Although the word "contextualization" is modern, the practice is as old as the human race.

In the Old Testament, over the centuries, God's people had to work out what authentic discipleship looked like in pilgrimage or settledness, in servitude or freedom, in exile or in homeland. In the midst of many contexts and cultures, what did faith and obedience consist in? How could they display the distinctiveness of their calling and of their message, and the uniqueness of the God whose they were? Of course, over and over again they failed or wrongly slipped into cultural legalisms. But on the other hand, over and over again they were renewed through the grace of God and, as Hebrews 11 celebrates, there are many shining examples of men and women of faith.

Although the word "contextualization" is modern, the practice is as old as the human race.

The New Testament illustrates the same journey of faith, though now wonderfully in the transforming light of the life, death and resurrection, and ascension of our Lord Jesus Christ. Repeatedly, the challenge is the same as it always was: how to live in faith, obedience, and authentic discipleship in whichever setting the sovereign Lord has given us. Character, word and deed—personally and in community—must all bear witness to the one and only living God so that the community of believers becomes a visual aid and shining beacon of light, communicating God's truth to the world and living a life of worship to God himself. You could be Jew or Gentile, slave or free, male or female, young or old, live in Jerusalem or Corinth or anywhere else, but you would have a visible, audible DNA in common, alongside all the enriching, complementary particularities.

It was the particularities that were to cause so much trouble down through the centuries. We all have an inbuilt tendency to reject or be suspicious of those who are different from ourselves. Difference can be unsettling and threatening. It challenges our security in our own identity. And, since Genesis 3, the consequence of fallenness is the constant pattern of the more powerful imposing their will upon the weaker. At the same time we are not very skilled at being able to critique our own cultures, and it's easy to have blind spots about values, beliefs, and behaviors with which we are familiar and comfortable, but which in some way or another are not compatible with biblical norms.

Painfully, as we study church and mission history, we see repeatedly the distortion that comes when the gospel is compromised by being linked to political, economic, military, or cultural power. Sadly, the same is true of ecclesiastical power, especially where that power is bound up with all the others. Further, conquering powers rarely show respect for, or real understanding of, the cultures to which they come. Even within the church, from early centuries, bitter splits occurred between those streams of the Christian community whose expression and understanding of their faith differed largely because of different cultures: hence, for example, the violent rupture between the Greek and Latin parts of the church, which was quite as much to do with culture and struggling for power as it was to do with theology.

At the same time, church and mission history is also mercifully lit up with examples of fine pioneers and groups who contextualized their precious message with sensitivity and creativity. The Nestorians and later the Jesuits in China; the Celtic missions in northwestern Europe; the Moravians; William Carey and his friends in Bengal: these and many more exemplify great respect for the cultures to which they came, a desire to share the gospel in terms that made sense to their particular audience, a willingness to learn the language and live long term alongside and among the people they wished to reach, and flexibility in thinking what the church might need to look like in this particular setting. This is all the more remarkable in that these people would rarely if ever have encountered people much different from themselves before setting out on their missionary journeys.

By the time we come to the past two centuries, alongside so much that was flawed, we also find ample evidence of careful study of particular cultures and much thoughtfulness about appropriate contextualization to meet the challenge of an alien religion, different thought forms, different customs and values and social organization. Yes, there are plenty of infuriating examples of totally inappropriate Western church buildings replicated in some tropical setting, or of pipe organs exported to Africa, or of hymns extolling the beauties of the snow in a place where the temperature rarely drops below 90 degrees Fahrenheit. But equally there are plenty of examples of early converts being encouraged to develop their own authentic patterns of worship in their own language and cultural idioms and of being helped to face-up to the particular issues in their context which would be incompatible with following Christ.

THE CONTEMPORARY CHALLENGE

Why has contextualization become such a pressing—and contentious—issue at the present time, both in the west/north and in the Global South? The reasons may be different in different places and among different communities, but there seem to be some widespread issues.

...IN THE WEST AND NORTH

In most places in the west/north (though not all) the church is declining and there is a widespread loss of confidence in the gospel and in the uniqueness of Christ in the face of other world religions. Even evangelicals are caught up in this. We have lost our Reformation understanding of truth, and with it the authority of Scripture is undermined. With the collapse of Christendom, not only has the church largely lost its credibility as a voice in public affairs (in Europe especially, now dominated by secularism), but also it faces an internal crisis of how to reach a generation increasingly totally alienated from traditional forms of church life and values. Further, there is an uncomfortable realization that much of our ecclesiology has itself been in cultural captivity to Christendom and Enlightenment structures. Too often it has mirrored rather than challenged the assumption that authority should be expressed through power; too often it has been preoccupied with structures and organizations rather than with the simple, flexible authentic life of the Spirit among God's people.

At the same time, mass immigration to the west/north means that, on the one hand, we find ourselves living for the first time face to face with people who are Muslim or Hindu or Buddhist and, on the other hand, also with Christians from other parts of the world who live out their Christian faith differently. Many of the latter have far more experience than we do of bearing witness to Christ in the context of another dominant world religion and are not subverted by the long shadows of Christendom in the same way.

All these factors disturb old ways and assumptions, challenge our identity, and raise profound questions (sometimes healthily as well as painfully) about what authentic discipleship, personal and communal, should look like in the twenty-first century. Here is a sobering reminder that the task of contextualization is never completed, never static; it needs to be sensitive and continuous, with ongoing critical reflection on the status quo. Change is hard but essential. But how can we ensure that change is not shaped by an increasingly pagan culture but rather by a faith-full re-reading of and re-living of God's Word?

To complicate matters, among evangelicals there are at least two polar opposite reactions, with many others uneasily somewhere inbetween. On the one hand, conservatives have often reacted with rigidity, believing their traditional theological formulations, (in some cases) a very literal reading of Scripture, and particular forms of church life and worship are essential for true orthodoxy. Any kind of change or adaptation is perceived as unfaithfulness. They see many fumbling attempts at contextualization driven, they believe, more by sociological analyses than theological ones, and so reject them out of hand. At the far opposite end of the spectrum, perhaps most strongly among those who embrace elements of postmodernism with the greatest enthusiasm, are those who see truth as in some sense evolving, with the Bible as a strong story written for particular contexts, and therefore offering guidelines rather than unchanging absolutes; this means that in a vastly different cultural climate one can be as flexible as one wishes about most things, provided people hear "the story of Jesus."

Is there a third way between these two extremes? The issue of contextualization is not one only for mission and church in the Majority World. It is of acute importance for the people of God in the north and west as well.

...IN THE GLOBAL SOUTH AND NON-WESTERN CHURCHES

In the Global South and non-Western churches, the issues are usually different, though not all Global South churches are growing vigorously—some of them, too, are declining, especially where they are unable to pass on the baton of faith to an upcoming generation. Also, among Global South churches there is not one uniform attitude to the Bible so that some of the tensions seen among northern churches are reflected in the south, too.

Many (but by no means all!) Global South churches are comparatively young, having come into being sometime during the past two centuries. There are, of course, some ancient churches of various streams in Asia, Africa, and Latin America. But Protestantism, and Charismatic and Pentecostal churches, are rarely older than a century. Many trace their roots to Western missionary work. They are no longer, quite rightly, willing to accept without question forms and formulations of Christian faith and behavior handed down to them by foreigners. There are inherent questions especially where evangelization was compromised by travelling alongside imperialism and colonialism; the form of Christian faith may be alien and alienating, impose cultural patterns which are unhelpful, and exclude cultural forms which would be very positive.

If the church was shaped by poorly contextualized missionary activity, there may be too little engagement with real questions in societies which did not have a long Christianized history, there will be specific questions (e.g., relating to pre-Christian ancestors, what can be salvaged from pre-Christian religion, etc.) which are not adequately addressed, and a high likelihood of too little transformation at a deep level—the deep level conversion to which the Lord calls us all. Where the latter does not take place, syncretism follows. Superficial contextualization may address—even helpfully address—external behavior, literal translation from one language to another, local stories that can be adapted, and so on. But if there is not a profound encounter between biblical truth and a person's or culture's worldview—the application of "Jesus is Lord" in every dimension—the foundations of faith will be shallow. It is further complicated by the fact that Western theology was shaped by long centuries of Greek and Latin logic and propositional thinking; this is not often the way that those in the Global South think, nor indeed is it any longer how many from the Global North think, but those who have struggled to recast theology in more acceptable forms that engage with worldview may have been misunderstood and criticized by traditional northerners. Most people in the Global South are much more naturally holistic, and much less individualistic, than northerners, who have been impacted by centuries of Enlightenment thinking.

These are not issues resolved speedily, indeed not at all without the gracious transforming ministry of the Holy Spirit. Nor is the lack of radical discipleship a problem for only some parts of the world church, largely based on geography. It is a problem for all of us.

PARTICULARITY, DIVERSITY, AND CONTEXTUALIZATION

So how do we move forward from here? How can we help one another, wherever we may be in the world, to live out the gospel more faithfully and to pursue the radical transformation which glorifies the Lord while also respecting and celebrating our differences? How can we live out the pattern of the Incarnation so that the world will see Christ, in terms that can be understood, and not just some alien philosophy?

One of the exciting privileges we have today is the opportunity for genuine encounter with brothers and sisters from around the world in order to help us identify our own cultural blind spots on the one hand, and on the other, to positively to recognize our commonalities. For this we need honesty, humility and integrity, a learning spirit, trust, a seeking of the other's highest good. We have the opportunity to listen to those of other cultures open the Scriptures so that we see things freshly. We can pray and worship together, opening ourselves to a variety of styles and traditions, and experiencing the dynamic touch of the Spirit in new ways. We can weep together as we struggle with failures and sin and painful history. We can rejoice that the Lord, who delighted in creating tens of thousands of species of trees and butterflies and flowers, does not ask us all to be the same either.

> One of the exciting privileges we have today is the opportunity for genuine encounter with brothers and sisters from around the world in order to help us identify our own cultural blind spots and to recognize our commonalities.

We will celebrate cultural diversity, but we will not let our cultures have the last word. In recent decades it has been fashionable for cultural anthropologists to assert that culture is neutral and we should not challenge or confront anything, simply accept and affirm the validity of whatever we observe. However, as Christians we need to affirm both grace and sin, so that we will recognize in every culture many traces of human beings made in the image of God and of God's merciful and gracious dealings with his creatures, but we will also sorrowfully but firmly recognize that our fallenness means that we are by nature pulled to subvert what is good and to reinforce rebellion. Thus, the cultures we develop will be marked by both beauty and ugliness, by both goodness and wickedness. In our diversity, different cultures will demonstrate sinfulness in different areas, and goodness in different areas. Part of our task as we interact with one another will be to help identify that which glorifies God and reflects his beauty, encouraging its reinforcement; and to help identify that which is the outworking of fallenness, finding ways to replace it with values, beliefs and behavior which are in keeping with God's nature and Word.

We will be more discerning about programs, methodologies, and training—developed in one place and transferred somewhere else. Although these have often been transported with good intentions, they rarely fit well in another context without considerable adaptation. Indeed, in cross-cultural situations it is far more effective for an outsider to be content to be a catalyst enabling local believers to develop their own. What "works" in Kenya may not work in France; what works in Korea may not work in Peru. Similarly, we will expect to see a growing resource of Christian literature and hymnody bubbling up freshly and with variety, all over the world. That does not mean that we will all worship in separate ethnic groups, except in contexts where there is genuinely only one ethnic group in a given location (increasingly rare in today's mobile world), or where language barriers are genuinely insurmountable. The coming together in reconciled fellowship of people of different ethnic backgrounds is one of the most powerful gospel signs in today's fragmented world and we should work hard at multicultural as well as monocultural worship and visibly shared life. But within that multiculturalism there needs to be space for diversity of expression so that we celebrate our diversity as well as our unity in Christ. Because of recent patterns of rapid migration, this will be one of the most exciting—and demanding—challenges in the near future.

Because contextualization often involves experimentation and dealing with the unfamiliar, it can be rather messy and unnerving. At present one area where this is clearly seen is in the debate about insider movements. These are not an entirely new phenomenon, but are being analyzed and discussed in a different way in some quarters today. Similarly, the now well-known C1-C6 scale is a particular way of assessing something that has been going on for centuries. It is important that these do not become "the latest fashion" but that we learn from past history the strengths and weaknesses of discipleship expressed and outworked in a variety of ways. As we look with heartache at the huge swathes of the world where there are few believers and acknowledge how few inroads the gospel seems to have made in the Muslim, Buddhist, and Hindu worlds, we will humbly and prayerfully support those who work in such contexts while also wanting to be watchful to live and work in ways that honor the Lord. That doesn't rule out new and unexpected things! Our God is not to be chained by our traditions and comfort zones.

Ironically, there has been a great deal of discussion and writing about contextualization in the past thirty years, but not necessarily any more informed practice of it. This is particularly true of the mission community, perhaps especially because of the huge increase in short-term mission as opposed to long-term mission. While there are many great values in short-term mission trips, especially for those who go on them and sometimes through them for their home churches and friends, short-termers by definition are not likely to be able to engage in sensitive, profound contextualization. They simply do not have the time to learn, observe, and understand beyond the superficial. This is the case even where there is a common language and it's true of short-termers from anywhere in the world, not just from the West. It is sobering to remember that the Lord Jesus spent thirty years learning and listening and watching before embarking on his three years of public ministry in his own home country. In an impatient age, we need to reaffirm the non-negotiability of "a long obedience in the same direction" and of being willing to invest a lifetime in the cause of the gospel.

SO, WELCOME TO THIS BOOK!

In the following pages, you will find many of the issues raised here, and more besides, being developed and reflected upon. Some of the chapters look at theological and biblical foundations, some look at generic issues, some home in on a very specific context or topic. You may find yourself saying "Amen!" to some contributions, being puzzled by others, and even disagreeing strongly with others again. That is part of our struggle together as we try to live and speak and apply God's Word, faithfully, creatively, relevantly, whether within the community of God's people or as we seek to witness to him among those who do not know him. It is no easy task, there are no easy answers, but we do know in quiet confidence that God himself longs to communicate and to display himself so that in every corner of our world people would become worshipping disciples, redeemed and being transformed and transforming.

The authors come from many different contexts and live and work with many different people groups. They are practitioners, and they write out of ministry, not untested theory. Many of their stories arise from specific contexts, but most have lessons applicable far more widely. Each chapter ends with a few suggested study questions to help us move from reading to understanding and application. We invite you to join us on our pilgrimages as we seek the fulfilment of the promise that every tribe and tongue and nation will be gathered round the throne of God, worshipping the Lamb.

CONCLUSION

The Scripture teaches us that we are to stand on tiptoe, in daily expectant readiness for the Lord's return. At the same time, and paradoxically, we are also to show the patience and long-term vision of the farmer, who knows there will be a long wait between the sowing of the seed and the harvest in due season. As we think about contextualization, we do not know where in the Lord's timetable we are; many have tried to guess, but the Lord himself tells us not to. We only know that we are somewhere between the now and the not yet; that is our context in history and eternity. In the here and now, we will have limited understanding, flawed ministry, lives shaped more than we realize by our own culture and heritage. Yet, despite all that, we have a priceless treasure, the treasure of the gospel. Paul tells us that we have that treasure in old clay pots, so that all the glory may be seen to be the Lord's. Let it be our prayer, and our life's work, to display the beauty of Jesus in whichever culture the Lord has set us, and by all means to make the gospel plain.

Rose Dowsett served forty years with OMF International in Asia and the UK. She is an international speaker and author, and the Vice-Chair of the Mission Commission of the World Evangelical Alliance.

CHAPTER 1

A BIBLICAL THEOLOGY OF CONTEXTUALIZATION

Ronaldo Lidório

The greatest challenge to the church when we think about contextualization is this: how do we communicate the gospel in a way that is theologically and biblically faithful, and at the same time humanly intelligible and relevant?

Historically, the absence of a biblical theology of contextualization has given birth to two disastrous consequences in the world missionary movement: religious syncretism and evangelical nominalism. An inadequate understanding of the Bible will leave some human questions open and stimulate a search for answers in traditional religion, thus giving birth to syncretism. So the newly converted animist worships God, preaches the Word and applies it in his home. But if he does not understand the biblical principles behind seeking God and worshiping God, he will look for a local healer to answer his questions when he faces illness in his family. Such syncretism arises from and also contributes to a deficient communication of God's Word, lacking the contextualization to make it readily understandable. This bad or weak understanding of the Bible can also produce people interested in the gospel but not genuinely converted—which is Christian nominalism.

I believe that no universal principle can be well communicated to a group or distinct social entity without being contextualized. Without doubt Jesus was the greatest model for delivering a contextualized message. To the Jews he spoke of subjects which belonged to their world: tax collectors, hypocrisy in worship, and wedding feasts. He speaks about fishermen, farmers, and candles which light up the house. He talks about crops, bread and wheat. He mentions Jerusalem several times and frequently talks about the patriarchs. His message was thus comprehensible and appropriate to the universe of those who heard it. It made a significant impact and called for human and social transformation. At the same time it was faithful to the Scriptures, God's revelation, and had a firm theological basis.

I would like to lead into the theme of contextualization by looking at Matthew 24.14.

THE RELEVANCE OF CONTEXTUALIZATION IN CHURCH PLANTING

In this scene in Matthew 24, Jesus was meeting with his disciples shortly before being taken up into heaven, and he answers their questions about the signs which will precede his second coming. After mentioning some historical signs (wars and rumors of wars) and ecclesiological signs (persecution and false prophets), Jesus gives a purely missiological sign when he says: "This gospel of the kingdom will be preached in the whole world as a testimony to all nations, and then the end will come" (Matt 24:14).

The Greek expression "will be preached" has as its root *kerygma*, an audible, intelligible proclamation of the gospel, in parallel with the "testimony" (*martyria*) whose meaning is more personal, that of witness through one's life.[1] This kerygmatic action emphasizes the fact that the gospel will be preached in a comprehensible way. The "world" in this text translates *oikoumene*, which means the inhabited world. So the idea of the text is not geographical or territorial but demographic, to do with people, telling us that this gospel of the Kingdom will be preached kerygmatically, intelligibly, in all the inhabited world.

According to the text, the way this happens is through witness to all nations. The Greek root of "testimony" here is *martyria*, which teaches us that this kerygmatic action of proclaiming the gospel will take place by means of a witnessing church which bears the character of Christ. That is, only the saved will preach this gospel of the Kingdom. The last part of the phrase says the witness will reach all nations, translating the term *ethnê* as "nations," that is, groups which are linguistically and culturally defined.

We could therefore paraphrase verse 14 as follows: "The gospel of the kingdom will be proclaimed in an intelligible, comprehensible way in all the inhabited world, by means of the martyr testimony of the life of the church, to all ethnic groups." The final phrase says that, "then the end will come," where "end" (*telos*) points to the return of the Lord Jesus, his parousia.

> The communication of the gospel involves both the life and witness of the church as well as the activity of proclaiming and explaining the gospel of Christ.

I would like to call attention to the biblical principle of communication. On several occasions Jesus teaches us that the transmission of the knowledge of the gospel will involve both the life and witness of the church as well as the activity of proclaiming and explaining the gospel of Christ.

This communication of the gospel, therefore, in a transcultural perspective needs a work of "translation" in two specific areas: language and culture. Languages have different cultural codes which make communication possible, and the same is true of culture. When you explain to an Inuit or Eskimo that the blood of Jesus makes us whiter than snow, he will ask about the shade of white, because in his cultural perception as that of someone who has lived with snow and ice for millennia, there are thirteen different

---

1   *"Martyria"* (testimony) indicates an informal style of action, while *"kerygma"* (proclamation) presupposes a more systematic preaching of the gospel.

shades of white. To ignore that cultural dimension is to end up with a shallow preaching or a confused distortion of the Word of God.

To sum up what we have learned from this text: the message must be transmitted in a way that makes it intelligible in each language and context, and this contextualization is a prerequisite for the fulfilling of the Great Commission, since we not only have to live Jesus, but to proclaim him in an understandable way. Only the redeemed church will complete this task: it is not Christendom that will evangelize the world, but the church, those who have been born again.

With these ideas in mind, I would like to present some presuppositions which underlie this chapter.

1. The Word is above culture and outside time, therefore a viable communication of it is possible to all men, in all cultures, in all generations. So I believe the Word defines humankind, not the other way round.
2. To contextualize the gospel is not to rewrite it or to remold it in the light of anthropology, but to translate it linguistically and culturally for a scenario which is different from the usual scenario of the one who transmits the Word, so that all people can understand the biblical and historical Christ.
3. To present Christ is the final goal of contextualization. The church must avoid presenting Jesus Christ only as an answer to the questions that missionaries ask, a message which is foreign to the target audience.

Contextualization evokes many reactions. On the one hand are those who defend its relevance on the basis of the general principles of communication between cultures; without contextualization there can be no true communication, and so they try to study the different possible approaches to this contextualized communication. On the other hand are those who would alert us to the dangers when contextualization is divorced from an essential biblical theology which directs and critiques it.

> Without contextualization there can be no true communication; on the other hand, contextualization must not be divorced from an essential biblical theology which directs and critiques it.

The term "contextualization" was widely used by Charles Kraft, working from the starting-point of Kierkegaardian relativism, and on the foundation of a liberal theology which did not believe in the Word of God in a strict sense. His school of thought believed that the Word of God applies only to contexts similar to those in which it was first revealed, that it is not above culture and time.

By contrast, I believe that, with a biblical basis to guide it, contextualization is not only possible, but necessary for the faithful transmission of biblical concepts. Martin Luther, believing in the wholeness of biblical truth, expounded a gospel which was communicable in the language of the people with their culturally defined symbols, but it was a scriptural gospel with no dilution of truth. On several occasions he said to Melanchthon, "Preach in such a way that they either hate sin or hate you."[2] Translate the Bible into the people's language, preach the Word in the context of that time, and have laypeople take part in the services, but make it clear that the content of the Word must not be truncated by the fear of a cultural confrontation. If his cultural sensitivity had been the defining factor of his theology and not the opposite, we would have had a Reformation which was purely humanistic, but not a reformation of the church. The Reformation would have been the beginning of a movement of liberation only in the sense of freedom of thought and expression, a cry for social justice which included neither God nor salvation, a mere appeal for the recovery of cultural identity but not a leading of the people into the Kingdom of God.

DANGERS IN THE PRESUPPOSITIONS OF CONTEXTUALIZATION

There are three basic dangers we need to avoid when we deal with contextualization in missionary work.

The first danger, which I will call *imposition*, has its roots in the natural human tendency to inflict on other peoples one's own forms of thought and interpretation, a practice carried out on a large scale by political movements in the past and in the present, as well as by missionary workers who understood the significance of the gospel only in terms of their own worldview, culture and language. So the tall towers in some churches, the color of the tablecloth for the Lord's supper, the correct height of the pulpit, and facial expressions of reverence become much more than the peculiarities of one people at one particular time: they become mixed up with the essence of the gospel, in the transmission of a message which does not set out to redeem the heart but only to produce conformity to a network of imposed elements which are culturally defined only for the one who is communicating the message, but without significance for those who receive the message.

The results of this imposition of a cultural gospel have been various, but the most common are nominalism on the one hand and almost irreversible syncretism on the other. David Bosch affirms that the effectiveness of any proclamation of the gospel can only be measured by the cultural comprehension of the people who receive it. George Hunsburger observes that it is not possible to preach an acultural gospel divorced from the comprehension and worldview of the culture which receives it, because the goal of Christ as he revealed himself in the Word was to reach people in their human condition. The danger of an impositional presentation of the gospel is that it does not present Christ but only the cultural clothing of the messenger.

A second danger, which we may call *pragmatic*, appears when we take a purely practical approach to contextualization. Because contextualization is a subject which is often associated with methodology and processes on the field, we are led to understand and evaluate it on the basis of its results rather than its theology. As a result, what is biblically and theologically evident becomes less important than what is functional and pragmatically effective.

---

2   See quotes in *Reformed Church Publications*, Toronto, 1937.

Among the most contextualized missionary initiatives we find a significant number of heretical movements, such as the church of the Holy Spirit in Ghana, whose founder proclaims himself to be the incarnation of the Holy Spirit of God. From a purely pragmatic point of view, however, this is a church which contextualizes its message and is sensitive to the nuances of a matriarchal culture which is also traditional, incarnational and mystic. We need to be reminded that *not everything which works is biblical*. Pragmatism leads us to overvalue the methodology of contextualization at the expense of the content which is being contextualized.

A third danger, which is *sociological*, is that of accepting contextualization as nothing more than a set of solutions for human needs, in an approach which is purely humanist. This growing danger should concern us because we live in a post-Christian, postmodern and hedonistic context. This danger appears when missionaries make decisions based purely on the sociological evaluation and interpretation of human needs and not on the instructions of the Scriptures. In this case, cultural issues and not the Scriptures determine the message and accommodate the theology which is to be applied to a certain group or segment. The desire for social justice ought not to make us forget the presentation of the gospel.

Some mission scholars say that only a profound biblical knowledge of the nature of the church (Eph 1:23) will equip missionaries to have attitudes which are rooted in the *missio Dei* and not merely in the demands of society. The defense of a holistic gospel and the desire to transmit a contextualized message must not lead us to forget doctrinal foundations and biblical theology. In fact, it is these biblical foundations that give us the real motives for a holistic understanding of the gospel, for sensitivity to human needs, and for the call for practical action which can transform society.

THEOLOGY AND CONTEXTUALIZATION

The current world impasse between theology and contextualization is possibly a reflection of a divorce between the teaching of missiology and of theology. Some see missiology as theologically simplistic and consequently it is given no space in centers of academic theological studies in many parts of the world, or sidelined as being of little value.

We have to see that this is a serious error, which often produces pastors with no vision, missionaries with no adequate preparation, and theologians who cannot always find the way to bring their insights to bear on the daily life of churches engaged in mission—insights which could be of great use. Lacking a healthy theology of biblical contextualization, many segments of the church have been influenced by a liberal theology, which has used the concept of contextualization as a "window dressing" for its own ideas.

Soren Kierkegaard,[3] with his pragmatic relativism, proposed that truth should be understood on an individual basis, without absolute dogmas. William James, in 1907 established the basis for a "movement of philosophical and theological contextualization," arguing that theology needed updating on sociocultural or linguistic grounds. In the same direction,

---

3   Soren Aabye Kierkegaard (1813-1855) was a Danish theologian and philosopher, who is known as the father of existentialism.

Rudolf Bultmann defended a philosophical contextualization of the gospel, discarding as myth everything that was not relevant to the context of modern man. These and other influential thinkers proposed a new conceptual basis for contextualization: there is no objective truth which is above culture and universally applicable. Truth is individual, and as such must be understood and applied after being molded to the receptor context.

These ideas have divided the evangelical world for decades, and their effects are still felt today, leading some groups to argue that the gospel can only be presented in ways that the receptor culture considers acceptable. In a brief discussion with an English team that was working among the Bassaris in Togo, I was made aware of their missionary strategy: to teach about Jesus as the one who purchased our salvation, but without personal sacrifice, since personal sacrifice is seen by the Bassaris as a sign of weakness. This is the sort of decision that results from a sociological theology, and it exemplifies this pragmatic tendency to reshape the Word in the interests of greater acceptance by the community.

At a more institutional level this current of thinking was clearly seen at the General Assembly of the World Council of Churches in Uppsala in 1968. The emphasis there on the humanization of the Church opened the way for a study of contextualization based more on anthropology than on theology. The conference on "Dialogue with Peoples with Living Religions and Ideologies" in 1977 in Chiang Mai Thailand also emphasized universalism and contextualization as a form of value relativization.

The theological counter-weight to this tendency only began to make itself felt in 1974 with the Lausanne Congress on World Evangelization;[4] there, while recognizing the cultural, linguistic and interpretative differences that exist between different races of the world, it was affirmed that the Word is the only generator of the truth to be proclaimed. On evangelism and culture, the Lausanne Covenant declares: "The development of strategies for world evangelization calls for imaginative pioneering methods…. Culture must always be tested and judged by Scripture. Because men and women are God's creatures, some of their culture is rich in beauty and goodness. Because they are fallen, all of it is tainted with sin and some is demonic…. [C]hurches must seek to transform and enrich culture, all for the glory of God (Mark 7:8,9,13; Gen 4:21,22; 1 Cor 9:19-23; Phil 2:5-7; 2 Cor 4:5)."

Bruce Nicholls highlights the danger of syncretism and nominalism as a consequence of an existential contextualization with no theological basis. He affirms that syncretism is a synthesis between Christian faith and other religions, in which the biblical message is gradually replaced by non-Christian dogmas and presuppositions, and Christian expressions of the religious life in worship, witness and ethics become more and more assimilated to the non-Christian partners in the dialogue. In the end, Christian mission is reduced to a so-called Christian presence and, at best, a social and humanitarian concern. Syncretism means the slow death of the church and the end of evangelization.

---

4   The Lausanne Covenant (Lausanne, Switzerland, 1974) is composed of fifteen declarations with biblical basis showing the sovereignty of God, his objective revelation and his purpose on earth. The whole text (in English and Portuguese) may be found at www.lausanne.org.

Others warn us that, if we believe that God is the Author of the Word, and the Creator who loves his creation, then we must also believe that the gospel is addressed to every human being. Minimizing the message when it touches on uncomfortable subjects such as polygamy, for instance, will not help people, in their culture, to enter the Kingdom of God, but will encourage treating the rest of Scripture with the same partiality. Paul Hiebert alerts us that, in the desire to enjoy the world's favor, we forget that the message of the Bible will confront cultures, reveal sin, and call for transformation through the Lamb. Hesselgrave warns us of the dangers of presenting Scripture selectively; the gospel is liberating even in the most unfavorable cultural situations.

> The message of the Bible will confront cultures, reveal sin, and call for transformation through the Lamb.

We may conclude that the theological liberalism of Kierkegaard, James and Bultmann is a threat to a biblical understanding of contextualization, since it leads us to believe in a presentation of the gospel which does not transform (because any cultural change would be negative) or confront (because truth is individual and not objective) or liberate (because the freedom it offers is merely social liberty).

If we believe that God is the Author of the Word, that the gospel "is the power of God for the salvation of everyone who believes" (Rom 1:16), and that "in the gospel a righteousness from God is revealed" (Rom 1:17), we shall care about how best to communicate this truth in an understandable and applicable way, sure in the knowledge that, in provoking confrontation and change, it is God's Truth that sets free everyone who believes.

BIBLICAL PRESUPPOSITIONS FOR CONTEXTUALIZATION

In his letter to the Romans (1:18-27) the apostle Paul introduces us to the idea of contextualization, as opposed to inculturation, bringing to light some truths that are crucial for the proclamation of the gospel, and he does so with scriptural and revelational presuppositions.

In verse 18 Paul shows God's wrath against the attitude of humankind, a wrath which comes out against all "godlessness" (when humans break their relationship with God and his divine values) and "wickedness" (when humans break their relationship with their neighbors and their human values). He shows us humankind corrupted by injustice and creating its own truth.

In verses 19-20, God shows himself through his creation, and here there is a universal element: a God who is sovereign, creator, controller of the universe, with all authority over his creation. The people mentioned in verse 18 are without excuse, since God is revealed in creation since the beginning of the world; both "his eternal power" and "his divine nature" have been revealed. Therefore, facing a fallen humankind caught up in its own injustice, godless, and wicked, Paul does not point to human solutions, be they ecclesiastical or social. He presents God. In Pauline theology, the solution for humankind is not humankind, but God and his revelation.

In verses 21-23, humankind tries to manipulate God and his truth: despite their natural knowledge of God through creation, "they neither glorified him as God nor gave thanks to him." They built altars and created their own gods following their own hearts' desires and anxieties, gods who could be manipulated or commanded, reflections of fallen human will. So "their thinking became futile," and they exchanged "the glory of the immortal God for images made to look like mortal man and birds and animals and reptiles." Therefore, people are not condemned for not knowing biblical history: they are condemned for not glorifying God. They are not condemned for not having heard the Word: each is condemned for his own sin.

In verses 24-27 these people, in their world re-created with the colors of sin and injustice, "exchanged the truth of God for a lie, and worshiped and served created things rather than the Creator." God's response was judgment, and the text tells us he gave them over "to sexual impurity" and "to shameful lusts."

Some basic principles for contextualization emerge from this text.
1. There is a universal truth above all cultures: God is sovereign and all glory belongs to him. This truth provides a base for the preaching of the gospel.
2. Intentional sin (godlessness and wickedness) separates us from God. There is no way to present a God who seeks to relate to humankind without also showing human sin and the total need of salvation.
3. Culturally, we are idolatrous beings. It is normal for fallen humankind to generate an idea of god which will satisfy needs without confronting sin. This attitude is found in all human history and prevents humankind from finding God's truth.
4. The message Paul preaches is *contextualized*, presenting God in relation to real life and human fallenness. It is not *inculturated*, preaching an acceptable or desirable God, but reveals the true God. If we soften the message about sin we will contribute to a misunderstanding of the gospel.

BIBLICAL MODELS OF CONTEXTUALIZATION

Let us look a bit closer at contextualization as we can see it practiced at three moments in Paul's experience. Although Paul was the apostle to the Gentiles (Gal 1:16), he was a devout Jew, so we can glean some guiding principles from his preaching and teaching: first, to a purely Jewish group, then to another Jewish group where gentile sympathizers are also present, and finally to Gentiles who have no connection with the Jewish world or Old Testament values. It will become clear, I believe, that Paul never compromises the authority of the biblical message, but he does communicate it in a culturally applicable manner.

In Acts 9:19-22 we find Paul in Damascus with the disciples, preaching Christ in the synagogues and presenting him as "the Son of God"; and he "baffled the Jews living in Damascus by proving that Jesus is the Christ." The Greek term behind "proving" in verse 22 implies a demonstration with objective, visible evidence, which gives us the impression that Paul was using the sacred text, the Scriptures. His manner of preaching was to be the same in all his ministry among Jews: showing by Scripture proofs that Jesus was the long-awaited Messiah (Acts 17:1-3). Paul knew well enough that if someone wanted to convince the Jews that a certain person was the Messiah, it would have to be done by the Scriptures. Paul here is speaking to the children of Israel, who saw themselves as "children of the Promise,"[5] so in all his preaching he appealed to the historical record of God's dealing with his chosen people.

In Acts 13:14-16 we find Paul on a Sabbath day entering the synagogue in Pisidian Antioch, and soon he is preaching Christ to them. In this text the group is the same as before in cultural terms, made up of Jews. However, there is also a Gentile presence, of some who are sympathetic to the Jewish faith. Paul begins with one of the key facts of Jewish history, the Exodus. Then he reminds them of the history of Israel up to David, when he deliberately brings in the promise of the Messiah (Acts 13:23) and links this to Jesus. It is interesting how Paul in this case preaches Christ starting from the "God of Israel" and bases his word on the Old Testament, because he knows that the Gentiles present are not only acquainted with the Old Testament but desire to follow it. But his preaching here also has a strong moral and eschatological note, which makes it different from that in Acts 9, and shows his sensitivity to a mixed audience, even though a primarily Jewish one. In verse 39 Paul uses an inclusive phrase ("everyone who") in contrast to the more exclusive way of speaking to Jews in the former scenario, saying now that everyone who believes would be saved. Certainly the gentile sympathizers, even with no biological connection with Israel, would see themselves included here: a Jewish Messiah for Jews *and* Gentiles.

In our third passage, Acts 17:16-31, Paul proclaims Christ to Gentiles who have no acquaintance with the Jewish Scriptures. Paul is in Athens, the philosophical capital of the world in those days, and is brought to the Areopagus by the Epicurean and Stoic philosophers. Now he is in a totally pagan scenario, with no Jewish presuppositions. This time his sermon does not begin with the Scriptures or even with the promise of a Messiah. Paul preaches God to them, starting from the evidence of creation and of the unknown god: "Now what you worship as something unknown I am going to proclaim to you." (Acts 17:23). He goes on to present the attributes of the "God who made the world" and who "is the Lord of heaven and earth" (v. 24), who "from one man…made every nation of men" (v. 26), "is not far from each one of us" (v. 27), "commands all people everywhere to repent" (v. 30), "by the man he has appointed…raising him from the dead" (v. 31). Note that in verse 24, Paul uses the word theos to refer to "the God who made the world," the same word used to mention the "unknown god." He uses the existing Greek word to present the God revealed in the Word, the Creator of all things. In his message he distinguishes clearly between god and God. The end of the message is the same: Jesus died and rose again.

To sum up, we note how to the Jews Paul spoke of the God of the promise, who brought them out of Egypt, since they knew the God of the Scripture and saw themselves as the children of the promise. To the second group Paul speaks of the God of the promises and of Israel's history, but as there were Gentiles present he also speaks of the Messiah who comes for the salvation of everyone who believes. We see here how Paul presents the gospel with

---

5   The Jews saw themselves, in the light of Old Testament prophecy, as children of the promise made by God to Abraham. In the New Testament, however, the whole church is identified as "children of the promise" (Rom 9:8; Gal 4:28), "children of the kingdom" (Matt 13:38) and "children of light" (Luke 16:8; Eph 5:8).

strong scriptural witness, for the Jews, as well as a strong moral and eschatological appeal, for the Gentile God-fearers.

For the third, purely gentile group, the coming Messiah is not an applicable message. This group did not see themselves as *children of the promise*, but as *children of the creation*. They were tremendously attracted to created things and fascinated by the figure of the Creator. They were looking for answers, students of any and every religion. So Paul preaches to them about the God of creation, he who existed before creation, who has power to cause things to exist, and who upholds humankind and the cosmos. He explains at length the attributes of this God who is unique, sovereign, near at hand and forgiving. Finally he speaks of Jesus as the center of God's saving plan, the Messiah for all humankind.

Now let us draw some conclusions about contextualization from this Pauline model of gospel preaching.

1. The message must never become diluted in the process of contextualization. Faithfulness to Scripture must be our priority, as it was for Paul when he spoke of the resurrection of Christ to those at the Areopagus, even though he knew it would be a controversial subject for the philosophers.

2. The target audience, with their cultural and linguistic presuppositions and ideas about God, are relevant factors in how we present the gospel. Paul did not preach Christ the same way to the three groups. His sensitivity to his hearers affected his approach.

3. Cultural symbols may be used to explain biblical truths providing they clearly show the gospel's relevance. This is how Paul used the "unknown god," taking as his starting point a sociocultural element in order to explain clearly the truth of the gospel. On other occasions he started from creation, from the contrast between God and the gods who were worshiped, or from the human feeling of lostness, of missing out on life.

4. The gospel has to be explained on its own terms, not those of the culture. The content of the gospel is not negotiable. When Paul speaks to Jews about the Messiah and presents Jesus to them, he is in a "safe" line of contextualized communication. However, his desire to create a suitable atmosphere does not make him minimize more confrontational truths, and he may end up being rejected, ignored, or questioned.

5. The ultimate aim of the presentation of the message is to bring the hearer to the knowledge of Christ, not simply to communicate. Paul's communication paves the way for the presentation of the truth, whether to the children of promise or to the children of creation.

6. The linguistic and cultural contextualization of the message is an instrument for successful communication, transmitting the gospel in a clear and understandable way. Paul makes good use of this instrument, speaking in different ways to Jews and Gentiles, to slaves and free, masters and servants. So too Jesus, when he talks of making "fishers of men," or when he uses in his sermons candles that give light, seed sown in different soils, wheat and tares in the same field, a lost coin, nets full of fish, does all this so that the essence of the Word can reach in an intelligible way the person, society and culture that hears it.

7. The result that is hoped for from the contextualized presentation of the gospel is repentance from sin and sincere conversion. Any presentation of the gospel that allows

the hearers to feel comfortable in their state of sin is definitely inconclusive and incomplete. This is clear from the way Paul sets forth a gospel that liberates and transforms.

BIBLICAL CRITERIA FOR CONTEXTUALIZATION

Tippett emphasizes that when a people comes to see Jesus as a personal Lord and not a foreign Christ, when they behave in accordance with Christian values applied to their own culture, living a gospel which makes sense within their worldview, when they worship the Lord in accordance with criteria that they themselves understand, then we will have a church present among them (Tippett 1971).

Although the gospel is above culture and timeless, for all peoples in all times, yet each individual culture will have its own way of raising questions to be answered by the Word. Sensuality is condemned by the Bible, but each people develops its own distinct cultural understanding of what is or is not sensual. Among the Bassaris in the north of Togo, the part of a woman's body that is seen as most sensual is her forearm, which therefore must be kept decently covered. But the same woman will go with her breasts uncovered, and this will not embarrass or provoke a sensual reaction in those who see her. The message must pass through the process of contextualization if it is to be transmitted faithfully.

Think, for example, of an urban Western man who is suffering from pneumonia. In the West, such a disease is treated in accordance with the sum of known facts about the disease and the prescribed way of treating it. The question that arises, therefore, is simply how to treat it. In an African context, the question to be decided is not how, but why. The cause of the disease is the most relevant question, and no action will be taken until an attempt is made to answer this question. The objective disease is the same, produced by the same biological mechanisms, but the cultural approaches are different. A knowledge of the questions that trouble people's hearts is fundamental if the gospel proclamation is to be "decoded" so as to produce transformation.

> The question is not simply *how* to contextualize, but especially *what* to contextualize.

So the question is not simply how to contextualize, but especially what to contextualize. What matters is the gospel; contextualization is only a tool.

We need to ask:
- Do people see the gospel as being a relevant message in their own universe?
- Do they understand Christian principles in relation to the local worldview?
- Do they apply gospel values as answers to their daily life conflicts?

Contextualizing the gospel means translating it in such a way that the lordship of Christ is not only an abstract principle or merely an imported doctrine, but a life-shaping factor, a basic criterion in every dimension, in relation to the cultural values that make up the stuff of human life as it is lived.

For this to happen, some criteria for the communication of the gospel have to be observed.
1. All communication of the gospel must be based on biblical principles, not held captive to cultural presuppositions, whether of the transmitting or receiving cultures. I understand

that God's Word is both cross-culturally applicable and supraculturally clear and relevant. Therefore, it is sufficient for every human being, urban or tribal, past or present, academic or layperson.

2. The communication of the gospel must always be done observing and evaluating the exposition of the message that is being communicated, so as to make sense for the day-to-day life of the hearers. The people must be brought to see that God speaks their language, in their culture, in their homes, in their daily life.

3. The rejection of the gospel does not necessarily mean that contextualization was not well done. The Word will always confront the local culture, which may lead to rejection of the biblical message.

4. When working out our approach in presenting the gospel, we must always work from the Bible to the culture, not the other way round.

A church planter has to preach the gospel, no matter what else he does. Social work, holistic ministry and cultural understanding will never take the place of clear gospel communication, nor can they justify the presence of the church. The content of the gospel set forth in any and every church-planting ministry must include: (a) God as Sovereign Creator (Eph 1:3-6); (b) sin as the cause of separation between humankind and God (Eph 2:5); (c) Jesus, his cross and resurrection as God's historical, central plan for human redemption (Heb 1:1-4); (d) the Holy Spirit as the fulfillment of the Promise, and he who leads the Church until the last day.

To sum up, we need to unite cultural sensitivity and interest to a biblical theology that underpins the ministry. We need to reevaluate our evangelistic and church activity in the light of its theological basis, not only looking at what works in practice; and this to include not only the communication of the message but also the formation of the church. At the same time, we must verify that the biblical message is being understood, linguistically and culturally, that it is being seen as something applicable and relevant to the hearers, God's word to real people.

Sadly, today we are reaping a bitter harvest all over the world of Christian nominalism and religious syncretism, springing from a failure to keep the Word central during the work of communicating the gospel. The historical factors used to justify this failure have almost always orbited around two points: an emphasis purely on social justice, and the search for a more culturally sensitive communication. However, if we believe that God is the Creator and Lord of history, of peoples, languages and cultures, then we must believe that his Word is not only true, but also promotes justice (liberating the weak and oppressed), and is communicable to the heart of every person, addressed to every human being.

Let us have confidence in God's Word, and keep it central to our contextualization. The power of the gospel can transform every context!

Ronaldo Lidório is a Brazilian Presbyterian pastor who has been a church planter in Ghana and in Brazil.

QUESTIONS FOR REFLECTION:

1. Ronaldo Lidório takes a strong stance on the priority of Scripture over culture, and says that we must always work from the Bible to the culture, not the other way round. What arguments does he use to support this? Why does he feel so strongly about this?

2. Almost at the end of his chapter, Lidório suggests four essential elements of the content of the gospel that must be included in any and every church-planting ministry. Do you think this is a helpful summary? Explain your reasons. In your context, are there other things you would wish to add as "essentials"? In your context, how would you communicate faithfully each of the elements Lidório cites?

3. Lidório lists three major dangers when engaging in contextualization: imposition, pragmatism, and a primarily sociological approach. How does each of these challenge your own engagement in mission, cross-culturally or among your own people?

CHAPTER 2

LOOKING, LEARNING, AND LIVING

Implications for Missionary Training from the Example of Jesus

Paul Woods

There is a story of two young men undergoing training in missions at a Christian college who were asked to go out separately and broaden their practical experience in street outreach. Both had an enjoyable time and saw fruit from the ministry. When they returned, they exchanged notes and experiences. One clearly thought he had emulated the Master more closely than his friend and summarized things thus: "We both worked hard for the gospel, you in your way and I in his."

This amusing anecdote highlights the issue of the extent to which ordinary servants of God can or even should attempt to "do things as Jesus did." Perhaps a more modest expectation is represented by the title of Roland Allen's mission classic *Missionary Methods: St. Paul's or Ours*. The fact remains, however, that there may be considerable merit in examining the life and ministry of Christ to discover insights and encouragements for cross-cultural mission, particularly as these relate to the tasks of familiarizing oneself with the culture and developing sensitivity to the situation on the ground. Here are some brief starting points.

THE WORD MADE FLESH AS OUR EXAMPLE

If we are to look at the life and ministry style of our Lord to discern useful ideas for training and equipping, then it is necessary at the outset to differentiate between those elements which we can hope in some way to adopt or emulate and those things which it is simply impossible for us to attempt. That is to say, there can only be one incarnate Son of God and he had certain factors in his earth-bound ministry which are clearly beyond us.

There is no way with our finite and sinful human minds that we can begin to comprehend the experience of the infinite God coming to be a limited human being. In a sense we are on holy ground and cannot speculate too much. We cannot assess how much of Jesus' ability to absorb culture and language was human and how much divine. Such an atomistic approach is not necessary. The task here is to derive broad principles, rather than point-by-point rules which must be followed slavishly. The broad brushstrokes of Jesus' earthly ministry and his use of local culture and everyday life, along with the strong principle of incarnational ministry (as we now understand it, rather than in the once-in-history original sense), furnish us with many helpful ideas which we can follow.

Firstly, we see in John 1 the idea of dwelling among the people, the pitching of a tent. Far from frequent visiting or an extended temporary stay, we see Jesus making the decision to come and live among those he sought to reach. Indeed the whole notion of God becoming man is tied up with a long-term commitment to, identification with, and residence among the lost. We should not rush too quickly to see the incarnation as purely the preparation for a sacrificial function. Jesus lived around three decades on this earth, with only the last three years in active ministry, as far as we know. His time on earth is longer than might be needed simply for the purpose of being a sacrifice; he also taught the masses and mentored those closer to him. In this area Jesus embodies a principle which is denied to most of us not ontologically (in that we are not divine), but practically: he was born and grew up in a ministry context to which he did not fully belong.

> Indeed the whole notion of God becoming man is tied up with a long-term commitment to, identification with, and residence among the lost.

That he who was divine spent approximately thirty years absorbing and reflecting on the lives, struggles, and understanding of the faith of the target people is certainly something to which we should pay attention. Jesus knew very well the background religion of those among whom he ministered, and yet he still underwent a long preparatory period of culture and worldview learning. We can think of this in two ways, perhaps. Jesus spent thirty years among working-class Jewish people in order to understand and identify with them. He also spent thirty years among finite human beings to understand them not only intellectually, but also experientially. Is the lesson for the missionary that rounded culture learning is a combination of academic and practical, theoretical and experiential?

At this point it is necessary to spend some time unpacking the implications of Jesus' thirty years of time and energy spent learning and understanding the ministry context of his target people. In this process we can distill several elements or approaches that are certainly as important for us as they were for him, while of course remaining mindful of the differences between an ordinary missionary and the incarnate Son of God. To put this point in a nutshell: what was good enough for him is surely good enough for us too.

JESUS' "SITZ IM LEBEN" (SETTING IN LIFE)

It is useful to consider the basic details of Jesus' early, pre-ministry life, as far as we can discern these from the gospels. It is interesting that in his magisterial presentation of the theology and history of mission, David Bosch discusses Luke's view of Jesus' ministry as one of breaking down barriers between Jewish people and showing the inclusivity of God (Bosch 2000, 27). For Luke, Jesus' ministry involved reconciliation between individuals and groups within the Jewish community, and specifically the inclusion of the hitherto marginalized. How appropriate then, that Jesus was born under dubious family circumstances and in a lowly environment. Later he was a refugee in Egypt and may have lost his earthly father before his public ministry began (Carson 1991). There is here a clear identification with the outcast, the poor, and the unloved and we see this flow out into his earthly ministry. While this might not normally be taken as part of ministry training, the fact remains that these experiences would have been very important in shaping elements of his worldview and later ministry praxis. Identification and personal experiences equip for ministry; it is one thing to read about social issues and deprivation and quite another to experience them firsthand.

As well as developing what might be called a low-level, emotional sense of belonging with those to whom he ministered, we also see an intense and practical learning environment in Jesus' early life. We know that the public ministry began when Jesus was roughly thirty years old, and that he was widely known as "the son of the carpenter" in his hometown (Mark 6:1-3); presumably he had worked at least for some time in the same trade as his earthly father. At first consideration, Jesus' years as a carpenter or around the carpenter's shop might not come across as the best setting for his training as a missionary in the context in which he later worked. That is to say, in Jesus' teaching we see many stories and illustrations from agricultural life, from the experiences of hired workers, from various domestic and family matters, and so on, but nothing from the world of carpentry or manufacturing, except perhaps the story of the piece of dust and the plank in the eye.

A moment's reflection, however, reminds us that a carpenter works in a service industry, presumably in an urban or semi-urban setting, close to or at the heart of the community, especially in a predominantly agricultural society. Yet he is not always out in the fields with animals and away from people. In other words, carpentry is a trade in which a person would meet and associate with people from all kinds of backgrounds, all of whom need his services. The physical location and nature of business of a carpenter mean that such a person is effectively "at the center of the action," hearing all of the latest happenings, gossip, and rumors, and thus building up a vast storehouse of stories, secondhand accounts, anecdotes, and worldly wisdom rooted in the context of everyday life.

This should inform any discussion of the need for missionaries to learn the local culture and learn from the local culture. It may not be possible for us to become carpenters in a small town among those whom we seek to reach for Christ, but the indirect lessons are there. Jesus sought to mix with a wide range of people and learn of their life issues and situations. He would have heard many stories of events and incidents in farming life, among hired workers, and in families of different socioeconomic status. Surely the foreign missionary coming into a cross-cultural context should endeavor to do the same. Apart from theological training concerning our own faith and reading high-level books about the religion and culture of the target people, we should actively encourage and facilitate experiential learning from and in the context. We can thus gain a good grasp of local issues and problems. We can develop a range of illustrations and "parables" from the everyday lives of those around us.

> Jesus was effectively "at the center of the action," hearing all of the latest happenings, gossip, and rumors, and thus building up a vast storehouse of stories, secondhand accounts, anecdotes, and worldly wisdom rooted in the context of everyday life.

Jesus' example also reveals to us that this process takes time; it cannot be rushed or condensed into a small book, Power Point, or multimedia presentation—valuable as these modern aids and tools are. No, there is no substitute for taking time and immersing oneself in the living, breathing, hurting society which our target people call home. There is a substantial investment of time and energy, and no doubt reflection also, in the commitment of Jesus to his time as a carpenter.

From a consideration of Jesus' "sitz im leben" (setting in life) as a means of cross-cultural training or a source of an ethos for such training, it is now appropriate to tease out further the actual lessons and insights which he seems to have applied in the three years of public ministry.

JESUS' UNDERSTANDING OF THE SOCIAL AND POLITICAL DYNAMIC OF THE DAY

Jesus seems to have been able to spend time at the lathe and the workbench not only with an eye open and an ear cocked for knowledge about the society in which he lived and would later minister, but also with a willingness to understand and empathize with it. We have mentioned Jesus' desire to remove barriers between God's people, later summarized by the radical statement that in Christ distinctions of race, social status, and gender are as nothing (Gal 3:28).

With this broad concern in mind, Jesus was also able to deal with issues of status and barriers carefully and with sensitivity. He seems to have known when to challenge the status quo and when to be more accommodating, with of course the proclamation of the Kingdom as his main objective. Jesus knew how to deal with the rich young ruler, the tax collectors Matthew and Zacchaeus, the sisters Mary and Martha, as well as a group of small children. He related well to outcast lepers and the demon possessed, and knew how and what to say to a senior political figure such as Nicodemus. Going beyond the strictly Jewish camp, Jesus also dealt with the Samaritan woman using a combination of concern, directness, and counter-cultural courage. He also interacted with a centurion, a symbol of the occupying Roman authorities. Later there is a powerful undermining of established social norms as Jesus washed the feet of his disciples. As we have already considered, in all of these situations the divine nature, which is not available to us, was clearly of no small benefit; yet at the same time his deftness and flexibility speaks of a deep knowledge of and reflection on the society in which he lived.

As the conflict with the Pharisees and teachers of the law intensifies and as this tension looks increasingly likely to attract the attention of the ruling Roman authorities, we see yet another area in which detailed local knowledge is applied. The sociopolitical, racial, and religious milieu of first-century Palestine was a cauldron in ferment, and into this volatile mixture was added the element of the Kingdom—Jewish and yet not Jewish, radical but not revolutionary, and powerful yet peaceful. What is fascinating is that Jesus was careful to avoid political and indirectly political themes in his ministry. We are reminded of Jesus' remarkable wisdom in answering the question about paying taxes to Caesar. His detailed knowledge of the society and culture of the people enabled him to be very focused in his message, and his handling of his increasingly difficult relationship with the Pharisees also suggests a mind deeply familiar with the broader social and political themes of the day. Jesus knew where to tread and how hard; again, foreign missionaries need to cultivate this kind of knowledge.

While we should avoid political action or involvement, we should, however, understand the local issues and difficulties and know how to function in their midst.

JESUS' MODE AND CONTENT OF TEACHING

Jesus spent three years as a travelling teacher, preaching a complex and challenging message of God's plan for mankind. From the gospel records we can learn something of Jesus' method of teaching, as well the nature of the material he taught. We can examine the content of his teaching as well as his mode of delivery. Both of these elements are derived from his preparatory time spent in the community as a learner in context.

Jesus used a variety of different methods of communication. In some contexts he used a fairly straight *proclamation* style to a passive audience, such as that at the edge of the Sea of Gennesaret (Luke 5) or the Sermon on the Mount (Matt 5-7). A variation on this is the more formal setting of the synagogue, as in Luke 5. We also note many occurrences of dialogue, almost in "question and answer" form. Then there are instances of enquirers coming to him (e.g., the rich young man of Matt 19), and meeting a friendly, affirming reception or perhaps a more robust challenge to repentance and action. Further, we find cases of brief teaching, taking advantage of a specific situation, often associated with a miraculous healing or other action, for example in the healing of the paralytic (Luke 5).

> In modern terms, Jesus knew the learning style of his listeners and was willing and able to adapt his presentation to suit this, as well as their educational level and life experience.

In modern terms, Jesus knew the learning style of his listeners and was willing and able to adapt his presentation to suit this, as well as their educational level and life experience. He knew what would work in a given context. This again speaks of a long-term commitment to being among the people and seeing how they learn and how they discuss and how they interact with new material. Such knowledge is again difficult to gain from academic study and there is no substitute for living among the people and observing them.

Related to this is the final matter of the content of the message or teaching given by Jesus. These days it is fashionable to talk of storytelling and oral learners and there is much value in these concepts. Jesus' use of story and metaphor is very important and is significant for cross-cultural missionaries and their training needs. Jesus seems to avoid propositional truth statements in his teaching of the masses, focusing on narrative and stories based on life experience. At the same time we do see more direct and pointed use of logic (in the broader sense) and reasoned argumentation when he deals with the Pharisees and the teachers of the law. Remember Jesus' powerful question to the Pharisees in Luke 5:23: "*Which is easier: to say, 'Your sins are forgiven,' or to say, 'Get up and walk'?*" (NIV). Again, the style Jesus employs with Nicodemus (John 3) would probably not be helpful to the ordinary peasant people to whom the Parable of the Sower was told (Matt 13).

Jesus was the man with a message *par excellence*: his whole life was for the purpose of fulfilling, proclaiming, modelling, and being God's Word to the people. Yet against this background of a definite and clear message, we see tremendous flexibility and willingness to make use of a wide range of material, particularly in the case of the parables.

The parables are often described as earthly stories with spiritual meanings. That is to say, it seems that Jesus took stories, rumors, and perhaps even elements of gossip that he had heard, together with conventional wisdom located and anchored in the society of the day and worked with it, weaving in spiritual content and baptizing them into powerful illustrations of the message of the Kingdom. The Master Teacher made use of ordinary life to render what is beyond man's understanding understandable to men and women.

We have already noted the significant amount of agriculture-related content in the parables. There is also a focus on masters and servants or workers. There are illustrations from family life. But Jesus also makes use of building and fishing, as well as the lives of the rich in order to flesh out his message. As we think over the range and type of the content here, we may conclude that some of these stories he made up himself, while the material for others came from his daily life. At any rate there are no parables about carpentry!

To use this kind of earthly story to make a spiritual point naturally requires insight and confidence, that the right message will be communicated, and in an appropriate manner. It may be argued that life in an agricultural society 2,000 years ago was simpler than that in modern societies today and that we now have a lot more distractions such as busy work schedules, family, and a whole host of electronic and communication tools which consume our time. That is true, but at the same time we have access to large numbers of comprehensive resources which can make our use of time more efficient.

To spend three decades in a location before beginning ministry is a luxury that few of us can afford in terms of our age and life situation, our families, visas, or even funding, let alone patience on the part of churches and supporters. Yet the message from Jesus' ministry is that long-term immersion, in the right place and with a high degree of focus, can be a powerful tool to help us function more and more as insiders, ministering from within, and less and less as friendly but foreign faces at the window to whom so many of the nuances of local culture and sociopolitics are opaque and confusing. In our age of desktop publishing, web pages, and multimedia tools, we should be able to adopt these same broad principles but make use of the experience of those who have gone before us, insights from secular anthropology and cultural studies to produce high-quality learning materials and motivational tools which will facilitate deeper and more powerful learning and identification.

CONCLUSION

This brief article has looked at elements of Jesus' life, location, and style of ministry. Without advocating a simplistic following of Jesus, an attempt has been made to draw out general principles which can be used by ordinary missionaries. The lessons from Jesus' preparation for ministry are clear. Missionaries need time to learn and experience the culture in which they aim to work. Head knowledge is complemented by that which is gained by immersion; academic study must be supplemented by exposure to the life of the real people on the ground. In addition, missionaries need to be in touch with the local people in order to be relevant in terms of interpersonal protocol, current issues, and sensitivity to the broader atmosphere of the society. These processes of exposure and learning clearly take time and effort, learning, and reflection. It is to be hoped that those engaged in training missionaries for serious long-term involvement can once more return to the feet of the Master and learn from his example.

Paul Woods teaches cross-cultural and mission studies at Singapore Bible College.

QUESTIONS FOR REFLECTION

1. Paul Woods emphasizes the importance of long immersion in a culture if we are to understand it and be able to minister effectively in it. By contrast, much mission funding today is invested in short-term mission, which is often very popular. Are these two compatible? What are the strengths and weaknesses of each approach?

2. Jesus spent many years in "ordinary" work and as an ordinary member of the community before embarking on public "full-time ministry." How could that pattern shape ministry and missionary training and service today? How can we best equip Christians for effective witness in everyday life?

3. What contemporary parables and stories could you create to convey gospel truth in your culture?

CHAPTER 3

CONTEXTUALIZATION, INDIGENIZATION, AND SYNCRETISM

Rick Brown

We use the term "worldview" to refer to a person's framework of core beliefs and values. It has been common in the past to treat worldview as one aspect of culture, but this is unhelpful for our purposes. Different individuals in a community can share a common culture yet hold to different worldviews. For example, they might drive on the same side of the road (culture) but have different views regarding the value of compliance with traffic laws (worldview). Except for isolated communities, it is increasingly common to find a diversity of worldviews within the ethnic groups of the world. So I will use the term "culture" in a more limited way to refer to the shared and transmitted social conventions of an ethnic community and "worldview" to refer to the network of core beliefs and values that some people have, whether the whole community shares them or not.

THE BIBLICAL MANDATE FOR CONTEXTUALIZATION

The Bible is a record of revelations intended to reform the beliefs and values of the peoples to whom they were addressed as well as those of peoples who followed them. The biblical authors form and reform the worldview of their readers and hearers by making assertions, by narrating meaningful events, and by revealing the causes, consequences and purposes of those events. This was part of Jesus' mission as well; he said, "In fact, for this reason I was born, and for this I came into the world, to testify to the truth. Everyone on the side of truth listens to me" (John 18:37, NIV). In other words, one of the chief functions of the Bible is to transform the worldviews that people have and bring them into alignment with a single, revealed worldview, which the biblical authors call "the truth" and "the faith." This biblical worldview is theocentric rather than anthropocentric; in other words, it is based on God's purposes, plans and values rather than those of individual people. It is also relational. God's plan for history and for humankind is the development of his Kingdom, and he invites people to become eternal members of his Kingdom by accepting Jesus as their King. This, of course, is very good news for people, but what justifies God's plan is not that it pleases people, but that it pleases God. And this gives singularity to the worldview he has revealed to us.

With regard to culture, however, the New Testament affirms diversity rather than uniformity. Jesus demonstrated this in his own ministry by preaching the gospel to the Samaritans in Samaria (Luke 17:11-19; John 4:5-42) and to the Gentiles in Lebanon and Decapolis (Mark 5:1-20; 7:24-8:10) and the Romans in Galilee (Matthew 8:5-13) without demanding they convert to Jewish customs and identity. He emphasized the value before God of every single culture when he said the gospel must be preached to every ethnic group before Jesus returns (Matt 24:14), and he gave John a vision of the end-time fulfillment of this goal, in which people of every tribe and tongue will praise God (Rev 5:9-10; 7:9-10). A preview of this goal was demonstrated at Pentecost, when the Holy Spirit enabled the disciples to praise God in a multitude of languages (Acts 2:4-11). The implication is that God's Kingdom will not be complete until it includes people representing the full diversity of races, cultures, and languages!

Most of the disciples remained reluctant to invite Gentiles to follow Christ (Acts 11:19-20), but the Lord showed Peter in a vision and by the outpouring of his Spirit that he grants faith and salvation to Gentiles who have not adopted Jewish religious customs (Acts 10:1-11:18). More importantly, he showed James and the Apostles, through key Scriptures and through the manifest evidence of the Holy Spirit, that Gentile believers everywhere should follow the customs of their own cultures rather than adopting Jewish religious practices, although they would need to shun some bad practices (Acts 15:1-35). Paul modeled this policy by planting churches that fit the local culture rather than converting people to the religious traditions of his own Jewish background (Acts 17-28), although he faced severe criticism from traditionalists who wanted uniformity. His ministry team modeled cultural diversity as well by including people from a variety of ethnic groups (Acts 20:4). In his letters Paul emphasized spiritual unity amidst cultural diversity (Col 3:11; Rom 10:12; 1 Cor 12:13; Gal 5:6). In fact, he modeled a kind of diversity within his ministry by adapting his lifestyle (1 Cor 9:20-23) and preaching style[1] to fit the customs of the people to whom he was ministering.

The result of all this was that believers in different cultures had different ways of worshiping and different ways of living out their faith in community with one another. Yet each of these believer subcultures was appropriate for the culture in which it was embedded. In other words, the outward expression of their evangelism, discipleship, fellowship and worship was contextualized to their cultures. They continued to have differences of culture and ethnic identity, but this no longer constituted a barrier preventing fellowship among them, because they shared a common spiritual identity as disciples of Christ and members of God's Kingdom.

---

1   In Acts 22:3 and 23:4, Paul begins his message by identifying with the religious Jews and in particular with the Pharisees, while in general he begins his preaching to Jews and proselytes by citing Old Testament passages, as in Acts 17:2-4. But when Paul preaches to Greeks at the Areopagus in Athens (Acts 17:22-31), he begins by praising their religious concerns and by affirming the principle that all nations should seek God because he created them all from one man (Acts 17:26-27), supported by relevant quotations from two Greek poets (v. 28).

In summary then, the Bible reveals a divine program, mediated by Jesus Christ, that advances God's Kingdom on earth by fostering communities of faith who conform to a single, revealed, theocentric worldview while maintaining diversity of culture, including culturally appropriate manners of worship and discipleship. This program has its ultimate fulfillment in the heavenly Kingdom, where these communities of faith are united in their worship of God and yet are seen to represent every ethnic group, race, and language (Rev 7:9). So the biblical mandate for contextualization is to maintain both the biblical faith and the diversity of cultures by ensuring that in each language and culture the faith is expressed in forms that preserve its meaning and integrity. As a result, we can say that a local church is contextualized to the extent that (1) it conforms to the worldview revealed in the Bible, and (2) it conforms to the customs of their native culture insofar as these are compatible with the Bible. I will argue further below that a local church is syncretistic to the extent that it (1) diverges from the worldview revealed in the Bible or (2) diverges from native customs that are compatible with the Bible.

> The biblical mandate for contextualization is to maintain both the biblical faith and the diversity of cultures by ensuring that in each language and culture the faith is expressed in forms that preserve its meaning and integrity.

DISTINGUISHING CONTEXTUALIZATION FROM INDIGENIZATION

Discussions of contextualization have been muddied by divergent uses of the term. Some missionaries use contextualization loosely as if it were a synonym for indigenization. To indigenize something, however, means to make it conform to local custom (or to put it under local control). One could conceivably indigenize a form of "Christianity" to the point that it has little in common with the biblical worldview, and a number of Western Christian traditions seem to have done just that. To contextualize something, on the other hand, is to adjust its form to a new context so that its meaning is preserved in that context. So *while it is possible to over-indigenize, it is impossible to over-contextualize.* (See box labeled "Exercise in Linguistic Contextualization.")

This account of contextualization conforms with the normal usage of the term in English, where it means to select a manner of speech or custom suitable for a given linguistic or cultural context so that it fulfills the purpose intended for it in that context. For example, an advertising firm may be given the task of increasing global sales of a particular product by creating effective advertisements for it in a variety of locations. The firm may find, however, that it cannot do this effectively with a uniform presentation of the product, not even in English. An advertisement that is effective in California will often fall flat in London, and one designed for Sydney will not always succeed in Nairobi. So the advertising firm has to contextualize its message for different cultures. And when it goes to advertise its message in other languages, such as Hindi, Arabic or Chinese, the contextualization required is even greater.

Failure to contextualize leads to misunderstandings and unintended responses. When Coca-cola was first introduced into China, people misunderstood its name to mean "bite the wax tadpole." The company, however, found a way to write its name that had a good meaning. When Pepsi's 1960s "Come Alive" advertising campaign was imported to Chinese audiences with no re-contextualization, they thought it was promising new life for their dead ancestors.[2]

An Exercise in Linguistic Contextualization	
Suppose you are a county health inspector and you need to inspect a number of sites in a port city. You want to approach each site by first asking to see the most senior administrator present, and for that you want to use the administrative title that is normal for that context. So you need to "contextualize" the title to fit the context. For each context on the left, see if you can find the most appropriate title on the right. Note that some contexts involve geography as well as one type of facility.	
(EH = eastern hemisphere, WH = western hemisphere)	
"May I please speak to speak to the _____."	
Facilities (contexts)	*Titles for people in charge*
1. Anglican church	a. store manager
2. apartment building (WH)	b. master
3. army camp	c. conductor
4. block of flats / tower (EH)	d. commanding officer
5. church (Roman Catholic)	e. guard
6. church (Methodist)	f. site manager
7. church (Pentecostal)	g. charge nurse (UK: sister)
8. convent	h. minister
9. hospital ward / unit	i. pastor
10. house	j. rector (or vicar)
11. monastery	k. rabbi
12. prison (*EH*)	l. head teacher
13. prison (*WH*)	m. head of household
14. school (*EH*)	n. construction foreman
15. school (*WH*)	o. superintendent (super)
16. ship (merchant)	p. abbot
17. ship (naval)	q. residential block manager
18. railway station	r. captain
19. supermarket	s. abbess (or superior)
20. synagogue	t. warden
21. train (*WH*)	u. governor
22. train (*EH*)	v. principal
23. worksite (*EH*)	w. stationmaster
24. worksite (*WH*)	x. priest
Note that it is not possible to over-contextualize a concept, but one can under-contextualize it by using 'manager' in every context, and one can mis-contextualize it by asking for the "captain" of a train or the "warden" of an army camp or the "governor" of a supermarket. Such mistakes characterize poorly contextualized translations, because categories distribute differently in different languages.	

---

2   See http://www.snopes.com/business/misxlate/ancestor.asp.

When church customs have been contextualized to Western culture and then imported into Asian cultures, without re-contextualization, the result can be misunderstanding and syncretism. In other words, under-contextualization breeds syncretism (see Owens 2007, 74-80). An example would be the custom of wearing shoes into the place of worship, setting one's Bible on the ground, and letting unrelated men and women sit next to one another, with the women bareheaded. In some cultures such customs are understood to be acts of impiety and lewdness, leading new believers and even new churches to think that piety and purity are unimportant in the life of disciples. The need is for the church to practice "critical contextualization," as described by Paul Hiebert (see Hiebert 1987, 104-112), so that it can express its faith and can practice its discipleship in culturally appropriate ways that are not mitigated by cultural relativity. This requires a careful analysis of each custom of the culture to see if it is (1) compatible with what the Bible teaches, in which case it should be retained, (2) capable of being made compatible with the Bible, in which case it should be retained in a modified form, or (3) irredeemably incompatible with the Bible, in which case it should be abandoned or replaced. For example, (1) marriage is compatible with what the Bible teaches, but (2) the marriage relationship might need to be redefined for believers, and (3) wife-beating should be abandoned. Indigenization alone will not lead to these conclusions because it lacks a criterion for setting limits; what is needed is critical biblical contextualization.

CONTEXTUALIZATION AS A MISSION TASK

Since Scripture calls for people to re-align their worldview with the Bible in a way that retains customs compatible with the Bible, it therefore obliges missionaries to practice contextualization as well. Darrell Whiteman describes this missionary task as follows:

> Contextualization attempts to communicate the gospel in word and deed and to establish the church in ways that make sense to people within their local cultural context, presenting Christianity in such a way that it meets people's deepest needs and penetrates their worldview, thus allowing them to follow Christ and remain within their own culture (Whiteman 1997).

Whiteman further notes that contextualization is a duty, not an option:

> Contextualization is not something we pursue motivated by an agenda of pragmatic efficiency. Rather, it must be followed because of our faithfulness to God, who sent God's son as a servant to die so that we all may live (Whiteman 1997).

Whiteman presents the incarnational ministry of Jesus as the chief mandate for contextualization. As noted above, however, the Scriptures make it clear in many places that God calls peoples and communities to be transformed into the moral and mental likeness of his Son in contextualized ways that maintain their cultural identity.[3] A first step, as Whiteman notes, is for the Word to "penetrate their worldview," but it seems to me that the ultimate goal cannot be less than full alignment with the worldview promoted in the Bible.

---

3   For a thorough discussion of the biblical mandate for contextualization, see Flemming (2005).

Although the Bible as a whole does not endorse a particular culture or dictate a full set of customs (as does Islam), the biblical worldview does inculcate particular values, and Jesus offers the power of the Holy Spirit to actualize those values in the lives of his disciples. For example, the New Testament does not dictate any particular mode of dress, but it calls for modesty. It does not dictate any particular political system, but it does call for servant leadership. It does not mandate any particular economic system, but it does condemn greed and advocate generosity. It does not dictate certain postures for prayer, if those seen in the Bible are merely reflections of local custom, but it does call for one to pray often to God.[4] It does not dictate particular forms of music and instrumentation, but it does call for one to sing praises to the Lord.

God's program, however, is to save and sanctify his people in the context of community, i.e., through local churches. Ideally these Christ-centered communities will develop a biblical worldview and bring out the best in their host cultures, while shunning practices that conflict with the Bible. In this way they can achieve a contextualization of God's Kingdom in their community.

THE DANGER OF SYNCRETISM

The main threat to contextualization is syncretism. *The Concise Oxford English Dictionary* (11th edn.) defines syncretism as "the amalgamation or attempted amalgamation of different religions, cultures, or schools of thought." We can see in this definition at least two kinds of syncretism: cultural syncretism, which results from mixing elements from different cultures, and ideological syncretism, which results from mixing elements of different worldviews. Since we are concerned here with the interplay of theistic worldviews, we can follow Nicholls in calling this latter *theological syncretism*, while with him we call the other *cultural syncretism* (Nicholls 2004). Given the argument thus far, it can be seen that both forms of syncretism stem from insufficient contextualization.

> Both forms of syncretism (theological and cultural) stem from insufficient contextualization.

CULTURAL SYNCRETISM

Most aspects of church life are culturally determined: the clothes people wear, the kinds of homes and buildings they erect, the way people interact socially, the relationships between the sexes, the way people sit (or stand) during meetings, the way they sing, the instruments they use, the role of reading in their lives, the way they transmit skills and information, and their conventions of music, poetry, song, and art. So if a form of church life is imported or imposed from outside, then this can lead to cultural syncretism in the church. Cultural syncretism disfigures the host culture by needlessly replacing parts of it with elements of a foreign culture. For example, church leaders might lead people to wear foreign clothing, use foreign music, eat in a foreign way, and even use a foreign language. This is especially likely if

---

4   There are Scriptures that endorse kneeling, bowing to the ground, and raising hands in prayer, such as Psalm 95:6: "Come, let us bow down in worship, let us kneel before the LORD our Maker" (NIV) and Psalm 134:2: "Lift up your hands in the sanctuary and praise the LORD" (NIV). The Bible provides several models of prayer posture but does not say they are necessary in order for prayers to be effective.

the leaders are themselves foreigners or have been trained in a foreign country or in a foreign institution.

The local church's adoption of alien customs can make it appear to the host community as a foreign intrusion or even a threat to their culture. It can seem to them that the church does not belong to the community and that members of the community should not belong to the church. Such churches appeal to people who dislike their culture and want something foreign, but they have little impact on the mainstream community. In fact, the community may view members of such churches as outcasts who have rejected their own people and culture.

Many are the Muslim seekers, for example, who have visited an alien church with sincere openness yet have left in disgust because of the cultural syncretism: the people were wearing shoes in the sanctuary and sitting on chairs and benches as if it were a tavern; their Bibles were on the floor; the women were uncovered and mixed among the men, they prayed without kneeling or lifting hands, and they sang "pop" songs with Western melodies, often with foreign lyrics. (The first-century Jewish Christians might have been surprised as well, because their customs of worship were more like those of Muslims.) So syncretistic church culture can put a stumbling block in the way of many seekers.

A second problem with cultural syncretism is that the use of alien lifestyles and languages in the church encourages people to compartmentalize their life and worldview. As a result, when they are at church meetings, they think and act like foreign Christians, but when they are elsewhere in the host community, they think and act like the others. Thus the adoption of foreign or syncretistic culture in the church can lead to double-mindedness and syncretistic worldview. As Whiteman puts it,

> When we fail to contextualize, we run a much greater risk of establishing weak churches, whose members will turn to non-Christian syncretistic explanations, follow nonbiblical lifestyles, and engage in magical rituals (Whiteman 1997).

The main problem, however, with non-contextualization is theological in nature rather than methodological: It conflicts with God's missional program by failing to value what God values, namely, cultural diversity. The adoption of foreign customs into the local church denigrates and disfigures cultures which God wants to redeem and which he wants to have represented in his Kingdom. Thus non-contextual approaches to mission are biblically unsound because they reject part of God's missional plan.

AVOIDING NON-CONTEXTUALIZATION

The solution to non-contextualization is to (1) understand and reject its unbiblical philosophical foundations, (2) understand and reject its psychological foundations, (3) identify and overcome other obstacles to contextualization, and (4) let Jesus be Lord of the local church. Hiebert discusses (1) and (4) quite thoroughly in his aforementioned article "Critical Contextualization," so there is little need to repeat what he has written.

In regard to point (2), the psychological causes, Hiebert repeatedly mentions ethnocentricity as a problem. It seems to me, however, that there are two kinds of ethnocentricity. One stems from naïveté. Cross-cultural missionaries, their leaders, and their supporters may not understand or appreciate the local culture or may naïvely assume that their way of doing things is the only way to do them. The local believers are often naïve as well and assume that the way practiced by the missionaries is the one and only right way. One sees this in traditionally Buddhist countries like Thailand. This can happen even if the missionaries are from another ethnic group in the same country. The second form of ethnocentricity stems from denominational pride and ethnic prejudice; people assume that their way is the best way and they are closed-minded to diversity. Some seek to justify this by saying that Christian unity requires that church life be uniform throughout the world, but what they mean is that everyone else should do church they way they do. Their comfort zone is threatened by diversity and by the uncertainty of seeking God's will for the local church, and so they cling to traditionalism.

As for (3), other obstacles, Whiteman mentions denominationalism; in particular, he cites the expectations of supporting churches and mission executives that churches planted in the field will be just like those at home, and that the pagans will be converted to become just like them.[5] The missionaries themselves are usually more contextual than this, but nevertheless, the contextualization goal of most denominational missions is to contextualize, not just the biblical faith, but their own denominational tradition. As a result, most denominational churchplants retain all of the boundary markers of their parent denomination, but they contextualize the expressions of that tradition.[6] For example many Roman Catholic churches in Africa use local instruments, local styles of song and dance, and local versions of vestments and décor, while retaining the core of their religious tradition. Many Baptist missionaries go further, however, by planting contextualized house churches that are "baptistic" without being replicas of Western Baptist churches; of course, the boundary markers that define their denomination remain in place and are simply contextualized within the new culture.

The second obstacle mentioned by Whiteman is resistance on the part of local church leaders who have been trained by outsiders to do church the way it is done in another culture. Since that way is the only one they know, they can feel threatened if it is questioned. From what I have seen, however, what concerns the leaders of some local churches and denominations is to do church in a way that pleases the donors and missions which fund them. Hiebert notes this problem as well, and in "Critical Contextualization" he calls it "ecclesiastical hegemony" (Hiebert 1997). In addition to that, people need a model for practicing their new faith, and so they imitate the missionaries, including their cultural habits, and the resulting values and practices become normative for their Christian community. Stephen Neill describes the process as follows:

---

5   One of the ironies is that many Western church practices have their origins in pagan culture, as Frank Viola has shown in *Pagan Christianity: The Origins of Our Modern Church Practices* (2002). This does not in itself make the practices contrary to the Bible, but it does make it ludicrous to impose them onto churches in other cultures.

6   For a discussion of boundary markers, see the discussion of centered-set models of church versus bounded-set models in Paul Hiebert, *Anthropological Reflections on Missiological Issues* (1994).

Many missionaries went out with the best intentions of carrying out the declared intention of the London Missionary Society to preach the pure gospel without tying it to any Western forms of organization or polity, but they usually ended by producing a copy, faithful down to the minutest detail, of that form of the Christian faith to which they themselves were accustomed in their own country. For this the missionaries were not entirely to blame; converts are imitative, and it is often they who wish to have everything done in the way which is traditional in the Western Churches (Neill 1990).

A third obstacle is ethnic pride and prejudice, and this is as likely to characterize national Christian subcultures as foreign ones. For example, the bishop of a traditional Christian church in a predominantly Muslim country was asked why he was opposed to contextualized approaches to churchplanting among Muslims. He answered that Muslims did not merely need to be converted to Christ; they needed to be converted to a superior culture. By this he meant the subculture of his own community of traditional Christians. Few Muslims have been converted under the bishop's conditions, yet those remain the conditions under which he will accept them. Elsewhere I have found traditional Christians refusing to accept Muslims who come to faith in Christ unless they disavow their former culture and community and adopt the culture and language of the Christian community. Their bitterness towards Muslims is such that they will accept them only if their lives say, in effect, "Everything about us was bad, and everything we did was wrong. Everything you do is right, and we want to be your disciples." Obviously this approach owes more to ethnicity than to missiology, and more to pride and disdain than to love and respect. It is not very successful.

Point (4), you may recall, highlights the need for local church leaders to look to the Lord Jesus to build and guide their church in accord with his will for them rather than following the example of other churches, especially ones from other cultures.

> Local church leaders need to look to the Lord Jesus to build and guide their church in accord with his will for them rather than following the example of other churches, especially ones from other cultures.

THEOLOGICAL SYNCRETISM

Although the Bible does not endorse any particular culture, it does challenge the worldviews which people hold. It does this by revealing one specific worldview as "the truth" and "the light" and by exposing contrary viewpoints as "darkness." The term "light" is quite appropriate. Just as light dispels darkness, so the truth of God's Word reforms the false beliefs and unfelicitous values found in all human worldviews. The result of this reforming process is that some people in the ethnic group become disciples of Jesus and form church communities with transformed subcultures. Ideally, the worldviews of these disciples will be transformed into perfect harmony with the Bible, incorporating all of the values and beliefs taught in the Bible and eliminating unbiblical values and beliefs. Then the disciples would truly be "the light of the world" (Matt 5:14). In reality, however, there are no Christian denominations that are in perfect harmony with the biblical worldview; all have syncretistic worldviews to some extent.[7] With some exceptions, most Christians have worldviews that are anthropocentric rather than theocentric. Looking at the American church from a missiological perspective, Lesslie Newbigin showed that it was poorly contextualized and excessively syncretistic (Newbigin 1986).[8] By this he meant that American Christians had adopted many elements of the "pagan" worldviews that dominate their society. In most Christian subcultures, the dominant influences are preaching and tradition, with the Bible used as a source of proof-texts to support traditional beliefs and practices. So when converts in Muslim countries are incorporated into a traditional Christian community, they assimilate the traditional values and beliefs of that community, even those that differ from the Bible. So they are left with a syncretism that is both cultural and theological. Of course, if they remain as insider believers, then they risk retaining unbiblical elements of their community's traditional worldview, but that is the case for all believers who live in the world, even if they are not of the world.[9]

God, however, has given us the Bible and his Spirit to transform our hearts and minds. When believers immerse themselves in the Bible and receive good discipling, they grow in their understanding and acceptance of the biblical worldview. So even though they may start off with a worldview that is dissonant with the Bible, their worldview becomes progressively more biblical as they continue to be nurtured with quality biblical input.

THE ISSUE OF MUSLIMS WHO FOLLOW CHRIST

"Essential Christianity," as Charles Kraft calls the biblical faith (Kraft 2005), is a worldview and a relationship to God in Christ rather than a culture. The term "Muslim," however, designates communities and cultures rather than one particular worldview. Just as there are ethnic Jews, religious Jews, nominal Jews, and a whole range of Messianic Jews, so there are cultural Muslims, religious Muslims, nominal Muslims and a whole range of Muslim followers of the Lord Jesus Christ. Many of these latter retain a Muslim identity as members of Muslim families in largely Muslim communities. This is where they feel they belong, as

---

7   Some Western Christian denominations, for example, forbid wine while ignoring gluttony, forbid polygamy but approve no-fault divorce, forbid movies or music or guitars or work on Sundays but accept greed and materialistic values. They hold loyalty to king or country to be as important as loyalty to Jesus. They affirm Jesus as a sacrifice but ignore his ongoing role as Savior and Lord of all. They hope for heaven but live for this life, resisting sanctification. They honor the Bible but rarely read it; the real authority being traditional church teachings and practices. Their views of the world to come owe more to Greco-Roman worldview than to biblical exegesis. The Bible calls the church to be a family and a community, but they practice individualism and Sunday ritualism. The Bible calls them to confront injustice, preach righteousness, and proclaim truth, but they make religion a private matter.

8   Newbigin focuses on syncretism that results from accepting a "modern scientific worldview" that religion is a private matter separate from public life, that science is the only publicly acceptable way to discover truth, and that values must be kept separate from science and truth. As for values, most Western Christians have adopted their culture's values of materialism, hedonism, and individualism.

9   It should be noted, however, that some forms of syncretism are more harmful than others, simply because some elements of the biblical worldview are more critical to salvation and Kingdom growth than are others. For example, it is more detrimental to salvation to deny that Jesus is Lord and Savior (like liberals and Muslims do) than it is to deny the Trinity (like "Jesus-only" Protestants do). It is more detrimental for spiritual growth to reject the divine authority of the Bible than it is to attribute divine authority to both the Bible and to additional writings. So in evaluating the dangers of syncretism, we need to recognize these differences in gravity. In the case of Muslim communities, it may be better to have Messianic Muslim movements that promote the Bible, biblical doctrine, and the gospel of Christ alongside an affirmation of the Qur'an than to have no movement at all.

"insiders" who openly follow Jesus and who study the Bible as the highest authority, but without becoming apostates by renouncing their Muslim heritage.[10]

Most members of Muslim societies are "nominal" Muslims in the sense that clerics do not regard them as true believers. What is required, however, for them to remain within the Muslim community is not that they be true believers, but that they voice assent to the confession that God is one and that Muhammad was his messenger. In some countries and provinces, voicing assent is a legal requirement. So although this is rarely required, nominal Muslims comply with the legal requirements or social conventions. Muslim followers of Christ are divided on this issue, but most insiders will voice assent to this confession if so required, for one reason or another. Here are some examples:

In one country a Messianic Muslim evangelist was taken to court and accused of apostasy, a crime punishable with death. He testified that he was a Muslim who followed Jesus and that he encouraged others likewise, but not an apostate. The judge told him to say the Muslim confession and he did so, including the part that Muhammad was a messenger of God. The judge then asked him to explain what he meant by it. The man answered by saying that at one time there was no Arab nation. There were just tribes who fought and raided one another and worshipped many idols. Then God in his mercy sent Muhammad (SAW) to lead the Arabs from polytheism to monotheism and from tribal chaos to political unity. The judge accepted this explanation and acquitted him. (Not all judges, however, would do that.)

In another case, in a country where saying the confession is a legal requirement for all citizens, the leader of a house church was arrested and accused of apostasy. Again, he acknowledged his faith in the Lord Jesus Christ but denied being an apostate. The police told him to say the confession, which he did. Then he reminded the police of two Islamic teachings regarding the confession: (1) saying the confession is valid only if the person says it with sincerity (*niya*), and (2) only God knows if a person says it with sincerity. The police realized the man was letting them know that he said the confession from duty rather than conviction. Since he had obeyed the law they could not execute him, but they beat him before they let him go. As a result of his wise response, the house church leader was able to stay alive, continue living in the community, and continue his ministry among them.

The actions of these two men are not unusual. They follow a long-standing custom in Muslim societies, namely that everyone has to give lip-service to the confession whether they believe it or not. There are no statistics for the percentage of nominal Muslims in Muslim communities, but it is clearly high in many places, yet all of them have to give lip-service to the confession. When nominal Muslims come to faith in Jesus Christ, they may carry on with this practice, especially if the alternative is death or exile. This has always been the case with secret believers, but secret believers have very limited witness, whereas insider believers are open witnesses to their faith. They hold meetings in their homes for Bible study and fellowship, and they invite friends and relatives to join them. Some of these Bible study

---

fellowships have multiplied at amazing rates. But this is not generally possible if the disciples are secret believers or apostates.

Most Muslim communities have a remarkable degree of tolerance for disciples of Jesus who remain loyal to their community. Messianic Muslims do not apostatize from Islam, with all its history, civilization and culture, and hence they do not shame their family and community or bring misfortune upon them. As a result, many other Muslims in their community want to study the Bible with them, pray with them, and hear their testimonies. It seems to me that this is contextualization rather than syncretism.

CONCLUSION

The Bible mandates contextualization of the biblical faith in each culture so that its meaning remains clear and undistorted while preserving and reforming the culture itself. We can say that a local church is contextualized to the extent that (1) it conforms to the worldview revealed in the Bible, and (2) it conforms to the customs of their native culture insofar as these are compatible with the Bible. A local church is theologically syncretistic to the extent that it (1) diverges from the worldview revealed in the Bible and (2) culturally syncretistic to the extent that it diverges from native customs that are compatible with the Bible or could be made compatible.

Rick Brown, a Bible scholar and mission strategist, has been involved in outreach to the Muslim world since 1977.

QUESTIONS FOR REFLECTION:

1. In your culture, what evidences would you look for to suggest that a church is contextualized in a biblical and healthy manner? What might be some of the main cultural and theological "blind spots"?

2. Rick Brown writes (footnote 9) "it may be better to have Messianic Muslims that promote the Bible, biblical doctrine, and the gospel of Christ, along side an affirmation of the Qur'an than to have no movement at all." Do you agree with this statement? If so, on what grounds? If not, why?

3. In conversation with a friend of another faith, explore what he/she finds offensive, and what he/she finds attractive about the Christian faith as he or she has encountered it. How far are these issues cultural, and how far genuinely theological? If the former, what might you do to help overcome them?

CHAPTER 4

CONTEXTUAL EXEGESIS

The Role of Interpretive Summary
Matthew Cook

Contextualization should happen at every level of the Christian life. This includes every part of the exegetical and theological process.[1] Therefore, motivated by plenary inspiration and contextual exigencies, I urge retaining an interpretive summary as the final step in exegesis (and that which is handed on to either homiletics or theology). Typically a spiritual principle is retained after exegesis, but I suggest that this approaches a "kernel-husk" dichotomy at the exegetical level,[2] loses some of the meaning of the text, and implies against reality that a supracultural proposition can be stated. I believe that this interpretive summary well communicates the contextual understanding of a passage in the exegete's culture and yet maintains fidelity to the nature of Bible and the meaning of the passage.

---

1   Hesselgrave indicates that what I am suggesting is not contextualization at all (1985, 448). "One might argue that in cases where the theologizer himself is a citizen of the third world (and the second and third horizons therefore coalesce) the case is completely different" (454). Rather contextualization is when an exegete from one culture interprets a text for another culture. What is important at West Africa Alliance Theological Seminary (FATEAC) is that the student reflect on an appropriate interpretation and response in his own culture. In one sense we could call that contextualization. In another sense, it is really just good interpretation—that toward which every exegete should strive: a coalescence of the two horizons. Nonetheless, I will continue to use the word contextualization in this paper.

2   While it is impossible to comment on the whole of the kernel-husk debate in contextualization, I am using the larger debate (a gospel core stripped of its cultural husk in order to communicate the former elsewhere) as a model for what many exegetes do in the interpretation process. The larger debate is not over: On the one hand, a supracultural kernel is necessary to support "a careful definition of 'Christianity.' And there is no way, in cross-cultural communication, to achieve any kind of a working definition without carefully distinguishing between its cultural, relative forms and expressions and its absolute, supracultural core—the elements of Christianity that are non-negotiable" (Buswell 1986, 90). On the other hand, Donald Carson asserts that "there is no core of gospel truth in the sense presupposed by von Allmen, no 'supracultural truth' in the sense demanded by Kraft. ….[This core] reduces the locus of non-negotiable truth to one or two propositions such as 'Jesus is Lord' or 'Christ died and rose again', when in fact the corpus of non-negotiable truth embraces all of Scripture" (Carson 1987, 248).

THE SEARCH FOR A SUPRACULTURAL NORM COMMUNICATED BY, THROUGH, OR IN SCRIPTURE

Scripture can communicate to cultures far removed from its own. It was even intended to do so.[3] But Scripture, and how we learn from it, has been oversimplified, overdistilled.

In the 1980s there was a great deal of discussion about the nature of Scripture and revelation. At that point, Nash made a distinction between the propositions which are revealed and the sentences which carry them. Although he did not say that it was the case for him, it was clear that "theoretically, a person could accept propositional revelation but reject verbal inspiration." Verbal inspiration makes explicit "the extent to which God's revelation is conveyed in words, notably the written words of the Bible" (Nash 1982). Those who hold propositional revelation without verbal inspiration lean toward a quasi-Barthian view of Scripture. "By insisting that sentences convey propositions, they locate revelation outside the actual biblical texts, creating a logical gap between revelation and the Bible" (Vanhoozer 1986).

To avoid the position that the text is a witness to revelation, we need to shy away from the idea that any particular text can be effectively communicated through a single proposition or principle. Unfortunately, the goal of exegesis normally continues all the way to shaving off the valuable depth and detail of a text and arriving at a mere "kernel" or principle taught by the text. In their exegetical method, George Guthrie and J. Scott Duvall[4] teach an exegetical process which includes step 10.2: Write an extended paraphrase of your passage in order "to expand your translation and emphasize explicitly what you see as significant in the text... [to provide] your own condensed commentary...[to] capture the passage's meaning in a way that connects with your audience. We predict that you will enjoy this as much as any part of the exegetical process" (Guthrie and Duvall 1998). In this step, it is not a translation which is sought nor (I would suggest against the label offered by the authors) a paraphrase, but an interpretive summary. The exegete is enjoined to produce something that is faithful to the text (with all of its depth) and yet connects to his culture. I agree that this is the most valuable step in the exegetical process. Unfortunately, the authors continue, eventually arriving at step 11.2: list the general principles communicated by the passage ("boiling down the truth"). In that section the following steps indicate that the nuances (depth) in the text do not make the cut: "(1) Does the author state a general principle?...(2) Does the broader context reveal a general principle?...(3) Why was this specific command or instruction given?" (Guthrie and Duvall 1998). This extension is possible by assuming that there is a cultural carrier of meaning which can and should be discarded when the kernel is visible.

---

3   2 Tim 3:16: "All Scripture is God-breathed and is useful for teaching, rebuking, correcting and training in righteousness"; 1 Cor 10:11: "These things happened to them as examples and were written down as warnings for us, on whom the fulfillment of the ages has come"; etc., cf. Knight 1996, 3-13).

4   For other examples, see Fee (2002, 37): "take the *point* (or the several points) of the passage"; Stuart (2002, 28): "decide what [the text's] central issues are"; and the source from which I learned this technique, Kaiser (1981), which lists "principlization" in the index as being discussed on pages 92, 121, 150-63, 194, 197-98, 205, 206, 231, and 236.

THE PROPOSITION OR PRINCIPLE IS NOT CAPABLE TO FULLY REPRESENT A TEXT OF SCRIPTURE

Exegetes have usually not failed in their work to communicate a meaning of the text. Rather, they have been missing the fullness for their culture (perhaps 25% or 2.5% of the text's meaning, depending on the amount of nuance unaccounted for).

When I say that a proposition is not capable of representing a passage, it does not matter that the text in question is an epistolary, narrative, or poetic text. A text cannot be boiled down to a single proposition or principle that may be used in the process of application. There is a depth about a text that cannot be whittled down to this extent. It may be described; it may be put in another context; it may be paraphrased (though with difficulty).[5]

> A text cannot be boiled down to a single proposition or principle that may be used in the process of application.

That a proposition is not capable of summarizing a passage is clear from the semantic parallel. "The linguistic problem is the easiest to formulate. We know that exact synonyms do not exist between languages; idioms are even more challenging to the translator and a literal word-for-word translation will often convey virtually nothing of the originally intended meaning" (Davis 2006). The problem is not limited to curses, puns, and rhymes. Linguists have long taught that there are no exact synonyms. Writers have experienced the frustration in trying to paraphrase another author's work without changing the meaning (Roig 2006). It is often more faithful to the original text to merely cite the other author. In our case, we do not want to merely cite the Bible, nor offer a paraphrase, nor, certainly, a proposition in an attempt to convey the text, but an interpretive summary: one that does not alter the cognitive meaning nor illocutionary force but alters both the genre in which it is written and the target audience who will read it. We need to communicate the text in a new context.

BETTER TO LEARN FROM SCRIPTURE THROUGH AN INTERPRETIVE SUMMARY

This interpretive summary is not an innovation. Before detailing what it is, I want to be explicit about that which it is not. An interpretive summary is not a translation of the text. I agree that translation of the biblical text is very important. It is an indispensable task for contextualization, but it is not the end of exegesis, merely a step. An interpretive summary is not dynamic equivalence in Nida's sense: "The three steps are reduction of the source text to its structurally simplest and most semantically evident kernels, transference of the meaning from the source language to the receptor language on a structurally simple level, and generation of the stylistically and semantically equivalent expression in the receptor language."

---

5   Vanhoozer also is right, in part, that the power and beauty of a text is lost in a conceptual paraphrase and that speech-act theory can help retain some of that intention for which the text was written (Vanhoozer 1986, 74). My proposition would only help communicate those illocutionary and perlocutionary elements by placing this interpretive summary in the target language and culture. Although the value of speech-act theory is not my point here, it is valuable to maintain those various forces—talk about them in the extended paraphrase and make them contextually poignant so that the interpretive summary carries that same force as the text.

(R. Thomas 1990).[6] There is too much interpretive loss in such a method for it to serve as the interpretive summary. Nor are we discussing dynamic equivalence according to Kraft which demands dropping the text down into its equivalent cultural function (Poythress 2006).[7] It is not a paraphrase of the text in the traditional sense. Nor is it a commentary. Nor is it merely what the text meant.

An interpretive summary is a way to communicate the full meaning of the text (with its depth, power, and beauty) in its context (both literary and historical) with all that is comprehended by the exegete at that time in her own context even if there may yet be more depth that has to be understood using the hermeneutical spiral.[8]

This formulation offered at the end of the exegetical process must connect with the readers participating in the context of the exegete. There is no non-cultural step in the exegetical process. Since the interpretive summary will be in the exegete's own words, and perhaps, mother tongue, it will make the crucial first step in contextualization by locating the understanding of the text in the exegete's own conceptual framework. The interpreter has no choice but to use her own social location in formulating her understanding of the text.[9] The end which I advocate would allow the text to draw us into its world (through exegesis) and still communicate that meaning fully in our language, using our concepts. There is no point where the naked supracultural propositions are viewed in themselves. They are always clothed by some culture. The New Hermeneutic has taught us that these supracultural propositions are not even thought because each reading is done from a social location.[10] "From God's point of view, of course, truth may be supracultural....[but] it cannot be communicated supraculturally....We would inevitably couch the principle we thus 'discovered' in some other cultural garb—ours!" (Carson 1987, 249ff).

---

6   This article also makes a significant case for justifying my decision to include dynamic equivalence in this section on exegesis. In fact, dynamic equivalence is more about hermeneutics and exegesis than Nida would have proposed.

7   Kraft's own explanation appears excellent at times (even if a bit overwhelming). Here is one version from Kraft (1979, 135) as seen in Hesselgrave (1985,444):

This approach attempts to see more deeply into language and culture both at the biblical end and with respect to their influence on the interpreter himself. The "context" of which we speak is not simply the literary or even the linguistic context in which an utterance occurs...; it is the total cultural context (including both literary and extra-literary components). And we focus not only on the central message of the Scriptures as expressed in the original linguistic and cultural vehicles (as important as that is), but also on the total process by means of which God seeks to communicate that and numerous other messages (both then and now) via language and culture.

8   I agree with Grant Osborne that there is a spiraling toward the meaning that is to be communicated from the text (1991).

9   While I do not advocate the New Hermeneutic with its strong view of social location, I think that Carson is right when he says that "We human beings cannot escape either our sinfulness or our finiteness; and both are guaranteed to make the matrix out of which our questions emerge different from the matrix of every other human being....Pushed too far, of course, the new hermeneutic must result in the unqualified subjectivity of all knowledge." (Carson 1987, 217).

10   Of course, Wittgenstein was onto this idea long ago by denying the possibility of non-linguistic thoughts.

[T]his summary may look different in each context, i.e., now or a year from now for the same translator and interpreter…as he faces a new context and it will look differently for another interpreter at the same time of the first exegete. So, we will never have two summaries that will be identical. Therefore, in order to come to the depth and width of the meaning of a biblical text we need one another in interpreting it.[11]

But that which is known is set forth in a form that is well understood by the receiving culture—using metaphors that may communicate not just the truth but the power as well of that passage. Metaphors must be used with caution because they often carry connotations in the culture that far surpass the sense in the text at hand. For example, a student wished to discuss "kephale" from 1 Corinthians 11:3-13 but did so using the term "chef" (en français) (Traoré 2006). That might not have been a bad idea if we had not been in the African context where "chef" carries an enormous load of social, relational, and judicial connotations.

The difference this socially located presentation offers from reader response criticism is that the exegetical process can and should be discussed, understood, and justified across cultures or readers.[12] The end results are verifiable in conversation with other exegetes from other cultures.[13] The proposed result would not be something that is incommensurable with other cultures or social locations nor a lowest common denominator meaning. Instead, it would provide a locus for discussing the interaction of words, images, and sentence structures that communicate the meaning of the text. It would also provide the locus for discussing the cultural fit for the reader. Either in the interpretive summary or the subsequent explanation, the exegete could indicate how the images and depth of the text would be effectively communicated to the target audience for which the exegete is doing this interpretation.[14]

> The exegetical process can and should be discussed, understood, and justified across cultures or readers.

Some may argue that this is really just another bifurcation of the text into a supracultural kernel and a cultural husk. Even though Buswell's point is well taken, "But, just because the supracultural core gospel must always be expressed on the human scene in cultural terms and in cultural forms should not necessitate any doubt of its existence or its reality" (1986, 90), I have to respond with the question, "If one can never formulate an expression of it, where or in what sense does it exist?"[15] This is the case for the meaning of the text. I would

---

11   Stefan Hanger, Dakar, Senegal, in personal communication, September 12, 2006.

12   Inherent in this assertion is the rejection of cultural incommensurability which is advocated by some in the New Hermeneutic and in postmodernism. The most trenchant of these is Richard Rorty. The idea of cultural incommensurability is seen in Africa in those who say that Westerners cannot criticize African theology because they don't understand the context.

13   "[T]here is no intrinsic reason why these two Christians should not sit down and, with patient probing, not only learn from each other but be corrected by each other" (Carson 1987, 256).

14   The literature on the fusion of the two horizons is now immense following the groundbreaking work of Anthony C. Thiselton (1980).

15   This interchange reminds me of Kant's noumenon (in this case, equal to "the meaning in itself") and the phenomenon (here taken as "the cultural expression of that meaning"). To complete the analogy: what we are referring to is one phenomenon representing another phenomenon without any access to the noumenon—should it exist at all.

rather refer to meanings (represented in the interpretive summary) that are more or less faithful to the details of the text than *the* meaning of the text. There will be variations in the expression but other cultures and contexts will be able to understand (after due explanation) how and why the interpreter has chosen those modes of expression (vocabulary, models, and metaphors).

There are certainly disadvantages to this proposal: First, it is too much information. An interpretive summary is not easily packaged like a proposition or principle. It is not conveniently preached in Western-modernist propositional preaching style. There is not a neat transfer of the exegetical data to the homiletic gristmill. Second, it is not enough information. This is not sufficient for a contextual theology. Of course, this is *only* the exegesis. More work with other texts will be necessary. But this will allow a good exegetical basis for contextual theology—a lacuna in some proposals.

Exegetes have been making extended paraphrases for years. Why are we suggesting something so similar? Because exegetes, preachers, and theologians typically leave the interpretive summary on the cutting room floor in order to progress to the principle—thereby over-distilling Scripture. I urge them to stop with the exegetical summary and use that in the theological and homiletical process.

AN EXAMPLE: MATTHEW 3:13-17

In order to demonstrate that about which I have been writing, allow me to offer an interpretive summary of Matthew 3:13-17, the baptism of Jesus. I will not, at this point, justify my conclusions because that would require an exegetical analysis. The point here is to give simply the summary that can convey the meaning with some hoped-for depth. I propose the following: Many Christians obey when they can or if it seems appropriate to their level of dignity. John was not qualified to baptize Jesus and they both knew it. Nonetheless, Jesus obeyed in having John baptize him in order to prepare himself. It is in that preparation that the Father was pleased in the Son. This delight of the Father (eudokeo) is mostly seen in passages having to do with salvation. This Son was willing to become man in order to bring salvation to all. The Father was not just happy that Jesus was baptized, but that Jesus obeyed in fulfilling all that God had asked and was, thereby, prepared with the presence of the Holy Spirit, first, to face overwhelming temptation, and second, to accomplish the salvation of the world. We understand and live out more of the willing love of the Son, the difficulty of his time on earth, his purposeful obedience, as well as an example for us to follow in order that we prepare for the mission of the Father in our lives.

Knowing that no interpretive summary is perfect, the point is that an interpretive summary can offer a place for (1) broader explanations of the text and literary context than possible in the supracultural principle, (2) more rapid summary than a full exegetical analysis, (3) incorporation of some theological and contextual insights, and (4) set the stage for the transition for further theological or homiletical reflection.

Let us not boil down the text too far. Let us seek contextual formulation at every stage of the exegetical and theological process for more faithfulness to the Bible.

Let us not boil down the text too far. Let us seek contextual formulation at every stage of the exegetical and theological process for more faithfulness to the Bible.

Matthew Cook, formerly a pastor in the USA, teaches theology in Abidjan, Cote d'Ivoire.

QUESTIONS FOR REFLECTION

1. Matthew Cook says "the proposition or principle is not capable to fully represent a text of Scripture." Do you agree? Much traditional exegesis, preaching and theology has focused on propositions and principles: what would need to change, and how?

2. In your own words, explain what "interpretive summary" means, and give some worked examples.

3. Imagine that you are working in a strongly oral culture, and are keen to disciple some new believers. How would you utilize Matthew Cook's interpretive summary approach? Which Scriptures might you begin with?

CHAPTER 5

A NECESSARILY WARY ENTERPRISE?

North American Evangelicals and Contextualization

Mark Young

Picking up a porcupine is a necessarily wary enterprise. No matter how desirable or important it may seem to pick up a porcupine, our instincts warn us that those razor sharp quills warrant caution.

In many ways evangelicals have viewed contextualization as a necessarily wary enterprise, a desirable even critical task, but one that demands caution. This caution has created tension in our conversation about contextualization in the movement's academic institutions and on the front lines of mission. Even though evangelicals have authored hundreds of books and articles on the topic and thousands of hours have been spent in conferences and forums discussing it, we seem to have made little progress in reducing our angst over contextualization. Most likely this ongoing anxiety has contributed to the noted lack of implementation of contextualization theory now some thirty years since we began to discuss the concept (Kraft 2005, 32).

From the very beginning, conservative evangelicals in North America reacted cautiously to contextualization (Kraft 2005, 22-26). In part their concern was due to the term's formal introduction in the 1970s through the World Council of Churches (WCC), an organization that many evangelicals had grown to distrust (Coe 1976). Furthermore, since some of the most persistent voices for contextualization in those early days were associated with liberation theology in the Latin American context, some evangelicals in North America became even more concerned that the term did not reflect the social and cultural values of the conservative wing of the movement. Viewing liberation theology through the lens of the Cold War, many saw it as a threat to their theology and an assault on the American values of democracy and capitalism. Guilt-by-association sullied the image of contextualization among these conservative evangelicals. In some cases the concept was rejected outright; others saw the need to explore the concept and simply chose different terminology to describe the same process and goal. In my own theological training in the late 1970s, the term contextualization was treated with caution if not outright suspicion.

Even though we can identify sociocultural and geopolitical realities in the 1970s as reasons for caution on the part of evangelicals in North America, we should not dismiss evangelical wariness toward contextualization as solely based on issues of that historical and cultural context. Caution has framed evangelical consideration of contextualization throughout the four decades that we've used the term in mission circles because it seems to challenge deeply held theological values and commitments that have shaped the movement's existence and identity. In particular, conservative evangelicals view contextualization warily because they suspect that it threatens belief in absolute, transcultural truth as revealed in the Bible. That's why evangelicals tend to resonate with a cautious definition of contextualization like that penned by B.J. Nicholls, "the translation of *the unchanging content of the Gospel* of the Kingdom into verbal form meaningful to the peoples in their separate cultures and within their particular existential situation" (Nicholls 1975, 675).[1]

Because evangelicalism does not have an historic ecclesial identity but exists transdenominationally, consistency and continuity in the movement's identity are based on common creedal commitments. Nicholls' language, "the unchanging content of the Gospel," is bedrock dogma for conservative evangelicals.[2] It expresses evangelical belief that absolute truth, valid for all cultural contexts, is revealed by God in the Bible. Furthermore, conservative evangelicals believe that the "unchanging content of the Gospel" is propositional. They seek not just common belief in the gospel but also common language to confess that belief. This commitment is a highly valued legacy built upon the development of creedal formulations dating back to the early church.

If a commitment to the idea of unchanging truth in Scripture and a commitment to common confessional language in expressing that truth fuel the wariness of conservative evangelicals in contextualization theory and practice, perhaps ongoing reconsideration of the nature of theology, theological confession, and Scripture may be needed before conservative evangelicals can more willingly embrace contextualization. Are there ways to discuss these fundamental theological commitments that may energize evangelicals to embrace contextualization more naturally? Yes. Are conservative evangelicals in North America willing to have this discussion? Maybe.

Unfortunately, many conservative evangelicals fear critical thinking and dialogue about these foundational issues. For some, such conversation threatens their personal sense of security built upon an uncritical certainty of belief. For others, the risk to their own professional identity and security is too great. In many ecclesiastical and mission relationships, common confession acts as social power. When membership in a faith community depends upon the assessment of any member's adherence to common confessional language (e.g., signing an organization's doctrinal statement to join or remain in it), vigorous theological conversation is muted because members fear expulsion by those who hold social power over them; yet it is exactly this kind of theological conversation that contextualization demands.

---

1   Italics mine. For further development of this concept of contextualization see Bevans (2002, 37-53).
2   In the early years of the debate conservative evangelicals preferred the term "indigenization" to "contextualization" because of this commitment. See Taber (1991).

Contextualization requires the freedom to explore and risk intellectually without the fear of dire social and financial consequences.[3]

CONTEXTUALIZATION AND THE NATURE OF THEOLOGY

Contextualization requires the freedom to explore and risk intellectually without the fear of dire social and financial consequences.

How could we reconsider the nature of theology and theological confession in order to stimulate more meaningful contextualization? Perhaps Paul Hiebert's application of set theory to a theological consideration of Christian conversion provides a starting point (1994). In a landmark article, Hiebert discussed how four different concepts of a mathematical set affect the way we understand the term "Christian." He postulates four kinds of sets based on the following two variables: (1) the basis for being included in a set and (2) the nature of the boundaries that define the set. For our purposes in this chapter, two of Hiebert's concepts of sets—bounded sets and centered sets—may be helpful for reconsidering the nature of theology and theological confessions.

According to Hiebert, bounded sets are formed on the basis of common intrinsic characteristics. Taxonomies, so typical in Western scientific thought, exemplify bounded sets well. Bounded sets have clear lines of demarcation (boundaries) for inclusion and exclusion depending upon the possession of those intrinsic characteristics that define the set. Something either has those characteristics or it doesn't. Bounded sets clearly demarcate what's outside the set from what's inside it. Therefore, the boundaries of the set define it and become the focal point of attention for those creating and maintaining it.

Whereas bounded sets are defined by the possession of shared characteristics, centered sets develop on the basis of a member's relationship to the center point of the set. In a centered set, boundaries do not determine membership in the set; rather, boundaries emerge and change as members relate to the center of the set. No matter where a member may be spatially in relation to the center, as long as there is a positive relationship to the center, it is a member. A positive relationship is illustrated by a member moving toward the center rather than away from it. The concepts of movement and orientation for set membership imply that affective criteria influence inclusion in the set. Whereas bounded sets are static, centered sets develop dynamically.

THEOLOGY AS A BOUNDED SET

Using Hiebert's categories to reflect on the nature of theology and theological confession, one could argue that conservative evangelicals tend to view both as a bounded set of propositions. Diverse theological and ecclesiastical traditions within evangelicalism select various intrinsic characteristics of the propositions that make up their own bounded set. Common intrinsic characteristics may come from broad theological traditions (e.g., Calvinism and Arminianism) and historic creeds. Ecclesiastical hierarchies, academic guilds, denominational

---

3   Social and economic power influences the development of contextualized theologies and ministries worldwide far more than we care to admit. Exclusion from institutions, agencies, and denominations acts as a powerful restraint on creative thinking and ministry especially when such exclusion means loss of financial support.

and mission leaders, and local religious power brokers—those who believe they possess the set and are responsible to maintain it—arbitrate the inclusion and exclusion of discrete propositions and those who hold them. What these groups all have in common is not just shared confession, but a shared commitment to the value of control. Set boundaries create security and identity for those who control them. When theology and theological confession are viewed as a bounded set, they function as static boundaries of intellectual and social control.

Although theology and theological confession are often assumed to be simply conceptual, in reality they are intensely social and cultural. In reality, evangelical theology as a bounded set of propositions is formed, possessed, and controlled by a confessing community along conceptual, social, and cultural lines. Conservative evangelicals tend to diminish the reality of contextual influences on theology, insisting rather that theological truth is transcultural and theological confession must be as well. Many believe, therefore, that adoption of a bounded set of propositions in diverse cultural settings requires use of common language regardless of context. When conservative evangelicals downplay the personal, social, and cultural dimensions of theological belief and confession, the language of absoluteness and objectivity rules theological discourse and the boundaries of belief are drawn with uncritical certainty. In this approach to theology, contextualization cannot and must not occur.

As noted before, when theology is viewed as a bounded set of propositions, the confessional community (church, mission, denomination, etc.) possesses the set, and focuses primarily on its boundaries in order to determine whether any given proposition is inside or outside the set. Boundary maintenance is considered essential to maintaining the integrity of the set and the identity of the confessional community. Those who propose changing a bounded set risk exclusion from the confessional community that possesses it. In this approach to theology, theological understanding must remain bounded by the propositions of a community's common confessional language as embodied, for example, in a doctrinal statement or creedal confession. The goal of theological discourse, therefore, is to reinforce the boundaries and strengthen allegiance to the community guarding them. In this regard confessional statements serve a magisterial function that often inhibits the development of new understandings.

Historic creeds and confessions of Christian truth create both a sense of unity and continuity for evangelicals. Their role must never be underestimated. However, we must admit that creeds are historic documents expressed through the linguistic forms deemed to best express common understanding and belief at the time and place of their composition. Creeds arose as confessing communities sought to reshape or reinforce conceptual boundaries and group solidarity. Exclusion from the community and, in some cases, even more severe penalties, befell those whose beliefs were deemed outside the boundaries of the set.

Because the truth of Scripture is seen as unchanging, many conservative evangelicals view theological confession as immutable also. For these evangelicals, the boundaries of theological confession have been fixed historically and must remain as they are. The beliefs and the language of belief are therefore static and must be fiercely defended. Unfortunately, a bounded-set view of theology does not invigorate contextualization. In fact, insistence on the perpetuation in diverse contexts of theological language that was crafted in one historic context may inhibit a confessing community's ability to understand the truth embodied by that language originally.

On the other hand, contextualization may demand re-articulation of creedal language in order to preserve common belief across cultures and times. Steve Strauss notes,

> Forms established by churches of one culture and period of history should not be considered the exclusive way that Christians in another time and culture can express the same theological truth. Creeds and confessions are expressions of biblical truth for specific times and places. As such, they unite the universal church around a common history and serve as examples of theology that was both biblical and relevant in the past. But the forms of creeds and confessions will rarely (if ever) be *equal to* the truth they are expressing. In certain cultures and situations a *different* form might be the only way to express the same confessional truth (2006, 118).

For conservative evangelicals to more freely embrace contextualization, theology cannot be viewed as a static, transcultural set of propositions, but rather as dynamic and contextual confessions of belief. The goal of contextualization is to help create understanding of the meaning of the great confessional statements of historic Christianity as a basis for belief. It is the perpetuation of ancient Christian belief—more than the repetition of theological propositions—that drives contextualization. Belief grounds and exceeds confession. Thomas Oden writes, "To say credo (I believe) genuinely is to speak of oneself from the heart, to reveal who one is by confessing one's essential belief, the faith that makes life worth living. One who says credo without willingness to suffer, and if necessary to die for the faith, has not genuinely said credo" (2006). Belief is the source and goal of contextualized theological confession.

THEOLOGY AS A CENTERED SET

In order to encourage contextualization among evangelicals, theology needs to be viewed more as a *centered set of beliefs* than a bounded set of propositions. Membership in a centered set, according to Hiebert, is defined by orientation and movement toward the center of the set. When applied to the nature of theology and theological confession, a centered set perspective illustrates the importance of valuing the center of the set and maintaining allegiance to it. A centered set view humanizes theology and theological confession by expressing the affective dimension of human belief. Membership in the set requires common belief—common valuing and allegiance to the center of the set—not just agreement on common language.

This perspective on theology allows evangelicals to retain the sense of personal security and identity based in belief in unchanging truth revealed in Scripture, while at the same time admitting to the contextual limitations of all theological creeds and confessions. Furthermore, by emphasizing the affective dimension of theological development and belief, a centered set metaphor captures the personal, social, and contextual character of theology. Theological propositions are not disembodied truth statements that are included in the set just on the basis of logical consistency and historic confessional language. In a centered set view, theological propositions are personal (communal) statements of belief in, the value of, and allegiance to the center of the set.

Identifying the center of the set—the focal point of belief and allegiance—becomes the primary task of the confessing community in a centered set approach to theology. Unfortunately, agreement on the center of the set has proven to be more elusive for evangelicals than one would think or hope. For example, many conservative evangelicals in North America have viewed the inerrancy of the Bible as the very center of the set. For example, the Evangelical Theological Society (ETS) made affirmation of belief in the inerrancy of the Bible the sole criterion for membership at its founding in 1949.[4] Conservative evangelicals in North America continue to use statements on inerrancy in this way. However, the elevation of inerrancy as the watershed issue for evangelical identity is inadequate to describe the theological center of the complex and dynamic global evangelical movement today.

Although "core convictions" like biblicism, convertive piety, and evangelism are widely used to identify evangelicalism in North America and Europe, these common characteristics "have never by themselves yielded cohesive, institutionally compact or clearly demarcated groups of Christians" (Noll 2003, 19).[5] Diverse social, institutional, cultural, theological, and personal alliances splinter evangelicals into sometimes more, sometimes less, cooperative identities and entities. Is there a center to evangelical theology? Can we hope to express it? Yes.

At the center of evangelical theology must be belief in the One True God, as revealed in the Bible, who acts to redeem humanity so that all may worship him alone. Belief in, allegiance to,[6] and the worship of the God of the Bible, the One True God—Father, Son and Spirit—reside at the center of evangelical theology. Although various propositional statements about the person and work of our God reveal divergent articulations of that belief, allegiance, and worship, the center of evangelical theology must remain the person and purpose of the One True God as revealed in the Bible. He is the point of reference and orientation for evangelical theology, and thus, the point of reference and orientation for all contextualization.

> When we affirm that the center of evangelical theology is belief in, allegiance to, and the worship of the One True God as revealed in the Bible, we aver that we may not simply make up what we want to believe about the One True God and his work in the world.

When we affirm that the center of evangelical theology is belief in, allegiance to, and the worship of the One True God as revealed in the Bible, we aver that we may not simply make up what we want to believe about the One True God and his work in the world. We believe in and worship the One True God who has revealed himself in human history and mercifully given us the written record of it in the Bible. Therefore, our belief in, allegiance to, and worship of the One True God develops around what Don Carson calls "the turning points of redemptive

---

4   According to the ETS website, the original intent of the society's founders was to form a doctrinal basis for ETS rather than a doctrinal statement or confession of faith. The statement was amended to include Trinitarian language (www.etsjets.org/?q=website_constitution_amendment_announcement accessed October 9, 2008).

5   See also Bebbington (1989, 1-17).

6   Allegiance to the One True God implies commitment, loyalty, esteem, and love.

history" as recounted to us in the Bible. He writes, ". . . however loyal one judges oneself to be to Jesus, it is difficult to see how such loyalty is a mark of Christian thought if the Jesus so invoked is so domesticated and selectively constructed that he bears little relation to the Bible" (Carson 2008).

These "turning points of redemptive history" as described in the biblical record fill out our vision of God as

- the One who has created, sustains and rules over the universe and all that is in it,
- the One who has redeemed sinful humanity from its hopeless and hapless estate through the death of the Son and his resurrection from the dead,
- the One who has privileged and empowered his people by the Spirit to testify of him throughout all the earth, and
- the One who will consummate human history and restore all creation according to his eternal plan.

Whatever else evangelical theologies may include, they must be believed in the light of this essential image of the One True God as revealed in the Bible.

THEOLOGY AS PARTIAL OVERLAPPING CENTERED SETS

Human depravity and finitude limit the scope of all theological knowledge. A centered set approach to theology assumes that all theologies are partial because they are developed by finite and fallen humans in distinct cultural and historical contexts. No single theology encompasses all that can be known about the One True God because no human has exhaustive knowledge of God.[7] Each faith community's theology develops around whatever is deemed necessary to express its belief in, allegiance to, and worship of the One True God. Affirmations and propositions included in one community's set may not be a part of other communities' sets.

If all evangelical theologies are partial and contextual, yet centered on the belief in, allegiance to, and worship of the One True God, *overlapping* sets of affirmations and propositions in diverse evangelical communities emerge. Common belief is not necessarily expressed in common propositions, yet some theologies will share common language. The articulation of common belief must involve the development of contextually appropriate theological affirmations and propositions for each confessional community (Strauss 2006, 18). In order to pursue theological contextualization, evangelicals will have to admit that common belief in, allegiance to, and worship of the One True God may not always share common theological language, even though such should be sought in order to enhance unity of belief and identity. Common beliefs center evangelical theologies, but the trajectories of development in both content and language for each theological set are shaped by the peculiar cultural contours of each context.

---

7   In my classes I draw a large circle on the marker board and ask students, "If this circle represents all that can be known about Christ as revealed in Scripture, how much of this circle does your theological tradition encompass?" Most have never considered that their theological system does not contain all that can be known about God as revealed in Scripture.

CONTEXTUALIZATION AND BIBLIOLOGY

Because bibliology is the watershed issue for many conservative evangelicals in North America, some of whom seem to value agreement on matters of inspiration and inerrancy as highly as the common belief in the deity of Christ and the efficacy of the gospel, a reconsideration of what evangelicals believe about the Bible may be necessary for greater freedom and facility in contextualization. It is not coincidental that initial evangelical wariness toward contextualization occurred during the same decade that conservative evangelicals had publicly reignited the "battle for the Bible" in North America (Lindsell 1976). That battle hasn't stopped and issues of bibliology continue to play a major role in evangelical wariness toward contextualization.

It may be tempting to see contextualization as solely an issue of the interpretation and application of the Bible, but that view may be too limited. Evangelical caution toward contextualization is first influenced by how we view the Bible, then by the question of how we interpret and apply it.

When the term "evangelical" is used in a global sense, it almost always connotes those who make the Bible their "final rule for faith and practice."[8] Evangelicals affirm this identity through the practice of distilling propositions of truth and principles for life from Scripture just about every time we read it. Evangelicals see the Bible as the source of universally true propositions about God and universally valid principles for godly living.

This view of Scripture spurs evangelicals to identify some propositions and principles as "biblical" and others as "not biblical." When propositions and principles are deemed "biblical" in a particular evangelical confessional community, it is assumed that these are universally binding for all who view Scripture as the final rule for faith and practice. Even though we use the term freely, it seems that evangelicals frequently do not clearly articulate what it means when we say that a proposition or a principle for godly living is biblical. What does it mean to say that there are biblical principles for marriage, for child-rearing, for money management, and for dozens of other dimensions of human experience? In many cases "biblical" simply means that a statement, value, or behavior in a given contemporary context resembles selected statements, values, and behaviors found in a text of Scripture. For example, based on Moses' example of delegated judicial authority to selected leaders in Exodus 18:17-23, many evangelicals affirm that such delegation of authority is a biblical principle for leadership. Once we describe a principle as biblical, it is typically considered to be universally valid in all contexts.

Unfortunately, this approach to the Bible often leads to an ethnocentric elevation of the interpreter's values and behaviors as "biblical" based on a selection of those passages in Scripture that more closely mirror already acceptable behaviors in the interpreter's culture. On the other hand, passages that describe behaviors that do not fit the interpreter's own cultural setting are simply ignored. These passages, and the behaviors they describe or prescribe, are

---

8   From "An Evangelical Manifesto" (2008), downloaded from www.anevangelicalmanifesto.com, May 10, 2008, 6.

frequently dubbed "cultural," and are not treated as authoritative for the interpreter's context and faith community. This approach to the Bible arbitrarily elevates some passages to a position of authority for contemporary faith and practice while relegating others to a role that is not. For example, whereas the delegation of responsibility by a leader can be considered "biblical" in those cultures where it fits the interpreter's cultural norms, it may be routinely overlooked as simply "cultural" by those in settings where such delegation does not naturally fit the profile of authority and leadership. In North America we would gladly assert that delegation of responsibility is "biblical," but quickly disavow other behaviors found in biblical texts that offend our own cultural values. For example, few in North America would argue that a father should give his raped daughter, a virgin, to her rapist in exchange for money, even though such behavior is prescribed in Deuteronomy 22:28-29. Deuteronomy 22:28-29, we must conclude, is "cultural" and, therefore, does not create a "biblical" principle for godly living today. The rather arbitrary designation of some behaviors found in the text of Scripture as "biblical" and others as "cultural" is difficult to defend hermeneutically, yet widely practiced.

Once a behavioral principle is deemed "biblical" by one faith community, it is assumed by that community to be universally applicable in every setting, even if it may communicate in a given cultural setting values and beliefs that are inconsistent with belief in, allegiance to, and worship of the One True God. This egregious practice is seen throughout the Church globally, particularly in the areas of marriage, finances, gender roles, and leadership. When we inconsistently apply the moniker "biblical" to some behaviors and not to others, the task of contextualization suffers and those with social power in mission relationships stifle contextualization.

This understanding and use of the term "biblical" is based on a rather limited view of the nature of the biblical text and seemingly does not engage the whole of Scripture. Perhaps it would be helpful to see the Bible as more than a book of propositions about God and principles for godly living. It is, after all, first and foremost a story, coherent and meaningful when read as a whole. The Bible is not just *a* story, however. Evangelicals believe that it is *the* story of human history and existence in a world of competing stories.

> The Bible is universal history: it sets forth a story of the whole world from its beginning to its end. It is the true story of the world, and all other stories are at best partial narratives, which must be understood within the context of the biblical story" (Bartholomew and Goheen 2004).

Chaturvedi Badrinath, a Hindu scholar of world religions, challenged the church in India to go beyond a view of Scripture that limits it to a book of religious propositions and principles.

> I can't understand why you missionaries present the Bible to us in India as a book of religion. It is not a book of religion—and anyway we have plenty of books of religion in India. We don't need any more! I find in your Bible a unique interpretation of universal history, the history of the whole of creation and the history of the human race. And therefore a unique interpretation of the human person as a responsible actor in

history. That is unique. There is nothing else in the whole religious literature of the world to put alongside it" (Bartholomew and Goheen 2004).

When viewing the Bible as the only true story of human history and existence, evangelicals see that its purpose is to reveal, in the radically pluralistic contexts of its origin, the person of the One True God and his purpose for humanity. Every passage, when read within the whole story of Scripture, reveals something of the One True God and how he accomplished his eternal purpose. Each passage can be evaluated in the light of the character and purpose of the whole story, as the revelation of the person and purpose of God so that all may believe. Two questions dominate the interpretive task, "What do these behaviors, values, and teachings reveal about the One True God in that context?" and, "How do these behaviors, values, and teachings contribute (both positively and negatively) to the accomplishment of God's eternal purpose?" The answers to those questions create a foundation for interpreters to formulate principles for godly living based upon serious linguistic, literary, theological, and sociocultural examination of the passages in their original settings. In this way, the entire Bible is viewed as authoritative. Indeed, the biblical text speaks authoritatively to every dimension of human experience. It contains hundreds of characters, stories, and teachings that describe how the One True God was revealed in human history and how he prosecuted his purpose through his people.

On the basis of careful, culturally sensitive exegesis, evangelicals in every context have the privilege and responsibility to develop propositions about the character of the One True God and principles for godly living that contribute to the prosecution of his universal redemptive purpose in their own context. The faith community's task is to confess and to live in such a way that the character and purpose of the One True God is clearly communicated in their context. When they shape their behavior to reveal God clearly and to accomplish his purpose, they can confidently speak of being biblical in their own setting. In this regard, evangelicals face the possibility that some behavior or value that is determined to be biblical in one contemporary setting may not be so in another setting. In other words, we must admit the possibility that discrete behaviors and values that reveal the person and purpose of the One True God in one setting may communicate something very different in another setting. It is the privilege and responsibility of each faith community under the leadership of the Holy Spirit to diligently study the text of Scripture to understand how the person and purpose of God were revealed in the biblical setting and then diligently study their own context in order to bring their own behaviors, values, and teachings under the authority of Scripture.

> The faith community's task is to confess and to live in such a way that the character and purpose of the One True God is clearly communicated in their context.

When read this way, the Bible becomes intensely missional, and the faith community's motivation for creating a true vision of the One True God for their own culture through their beliefs, values, and practices drives the hermeneutical task. "Biblical" then takes on a more expansive meaning that gives each faith community a sense of their privileged role in the grand purpose of God and a dose of humility toward their own cultural limitations in interpretation and application. That gives urgency and rationale to every faith community in the task of contextualization.

WARY BUT NOT FEARFUL

Embracing contextualization with restraint will likely continue as the *modus operandi* for evangelicals from North America. And that's good. Contextualization should be a necessarily wary enterprise for evangelicals. Our fundamental understanding of the nature of theology and the Bible demands caution when formulating beliefs, values, and behaviors for the purpose of prosecuting God's universal, redemptive purpose. But we need not be fearful of contextualization; it is our privilege and responsibility in every context to create a testimony of the gospel that shouts the truth about God and his purpose to a lost world. For us, contextualization is not the end, but a means to the end that all evangelicals must share—the worship of the One True God by all peoples.

Mark Young is President of Denver Seminary, USA.

QUESTIONS FOR REFLECTION

1. Mark Young writes that "conservative evangelicals view contextualization warily because they suspect that it threatens belief in absolute, transcultural truth as revealed in the Bible," and that bounded set theology is a form of social control. Do you agree with this assessment? What do you think constitutes "absolute, transcultural truth"?

2. Living cross-culturally often shows us, perhaps for the first time (and painfully!), that we are selective in which parts of Scripture we regard as authoritative and which as cultural. How is this tendency different from responsible contextualization?

3. How might centred set theology create greater unity and understanding among Christians around the world? How might it create greater disunity and misunderstanding?

CHAPTER 6

MULTICULTURALISM IN THE CHURCH

Why We Need Multicultural Churches
Paul Coulter

The worldwide Christian Church has been multicultural since its very inception, and early local churches, most notably in Antioch (Acts 13:1), expressed this reality through multicultural membership and leadership. However, a number of factors have historically led to the development of ethnic-specific local churches. Firstly, some ethnic-specific churches exist because they are language specific. This is perhaps the most convincing reason for having an ethnic-specific church, as other churches in the host country will not be able to effectively evangelize and integrate people who cannot speak the host language. First-generation immigrants, for instance, whose proficiency in the host language is limited, will probably best be served by congregations that worship in their mother tongue. Secondly, ethnic-specific churches may develop as a sanctuary from domination by the predominant ethnic group in the host country. In an ethnic-specific church, ordinarily powerless people can assert power within the group. This factor was perhaps most evident in the formation of African-American churches in the USA. Thirdly, ethnic-specific churches may develop to preserve cultural traditions. Although cultural preservation may be a natural desire of immigrant communities, it is in danger of superseding the gospel as the driving force of ethnic-specific churches, so that the focus of the church shifts from evangelism and discipleship to the preservation of culture.

In recent decades, however, monocultural churches have found a new ideological justification on the basis that they have the potential to grow more rapidly than multicultural churches. The idea that churches grow best when they target a single cultural group was popularized in the 1970s through the Church Growth Movement that originated in the Fuller Theological Seminary with Donald McGavran. McGavran's *homogeneous unit principle* advocates the utilization of the racial, economic, and cultural separation that already exists in society to enhance efforts at evangelism. He famously claimed that "people like to become Christians without crossing racial, linguistic, or class barriers." Peter Wagner extended this principle to the local church, claiming that a healthy growing church will have a membership composed of basically one kind of people. Advocates of the homogeneous unit principle do not absolutely deny the possibility of truly multiethnic congregations, but believe that they are only possible in societies where integration between ethnic groups is already a reality (as evidenced, for example, by high rates of mixed marriages and shared education) and where church leaders have a specific, rare missionary gift. There is empirical support from churches in both the USA and the UK for Wagner's thesis.

In one sense the history of Christianity has been the story of the interaction between culture and gospel since "there are major cultural issues in the development of every new denomination" (Kraft 1999), but the interaction between gospel and culture is also at the heart of many present challenges facing Western churches. The challenge of multiculturalism is not merely limited to ethnicity, but impinges on differences of "race, color or ethnicity, gender, age or generation, social or economic status, mental and physical well-being" (Milne 2006). Underlying attempts by local churches to include young people in their services or to cross socioeconomic boundaries are fundamental clashes of cultures. If the homogeneous unit principle becomes the determining factor for the demographics of churches, the end result will be churches consisting of narrow bands of people of similar age, economic status and life experience as well as ethnic group. Some may say that this is acceptable so long as the result is growth in the overall number of Christians. However, a growing number of writers express concern that this scenario falls short of the ideal for Christian churches and advocate Christian multiculturalism as an alternative. In the first instance, they argue that the homogeneous unit principle denies the priority of obedience to Christ over loyalty to one's culture:

> While there may be practical and sociological reasons for creating and maintaining Churches that are ethnic specific…(t)he continued maintenance of racially divided Churches …points only to the fact that a large majority of Christians…are probably identifying themselves more with their racial background, with all its cultural baggage, than they do with Christ and the gospel (Hays 2003).

SCRIPTURE AND MULTICULTURAL CHURCHES

McGavran's basic premise, that it is easier for people to become Christians if they do not have to cross barriers of culture, may not stand up to scrutiny under the lens of Scripture. Jesus Christ did not reduce the challenge of discipleship to maximise the number of people who would follow him. On the contrary, he consistently challenged people to count the cost and to realize that following him would involve sacrifice (see, for example, Matthew 16:24-25 and Luke 14:25-33). Milne warns that "the attempt to plane down to a minimum the cost of becoming disciples of Jesus in order to make the commitment more attractive runs into serious difficulty with the terms set by Jesus" (15). Ultimately, the debate between multiculturalism and the homogeneous unit principle should not be settled over which approach will maximize numbers, but which is most faithful to the biblical vision of the church. Milne further writes that:

> It is not our place to adjust the terms of entry to God's community to the point where our contemporaries feel personally comfortable. If Scripture informs us that the community of Christ is by the will and good purpose of God, to be a diverse body, and

that by that very fact it will honour and glorify the Lord and magnify the cross-work of his dear Son, then we dare not set aside that characteristic (154).

The radical nature of obedience to Christ's command to love one another can only fully be displayed in sacrificial love for those who are different from us (a principle illustrated in the parable of the Good Samaritan recorded in Luke 10:25-37). Christians ought to have more in common with other Christians from different cultural backgrounds than with non-Christians from their own background.

> The radical nature of obedience to Christ's command to love one another can only fully be displayed in sacrificial love for those who are different from us.

Our primary identity as humans is to be based on our union with Christ, and no longer based on traditional human sociological connections. Christians of other races are not just equal to us, they are joined to us (Hays 2003, 204).

In other words, the local church does not only aim for equality, but for a radical unity based on shared faith, vision and love.

A second objection to the homogeneous unit principle is that it can become:

> a means of riding rough-shod over the radically inclusive character of the people of God... Church growth theorists are not so much wrong in some sort of absolute way; they are somewhat blind, insensitive and unrealistic (William Abraham, quoted in Fong (1999, 6).

Many other writers agree that to continue to maintain ethnic-specific churches is unscriptural since an ethnic church denies the all encompassing gospel message, and there is no biblical basis for churches segregated along ethnic lines. Gary Parrett writes that:

> Diversity in the church, according to Scripture, is not merely good; it is essential. It is not something to be sought or tolerated; it is a reality we must obey and endeavour to preserve. Indeed, neither the idea of unity without diversity nor the idea of diversity without unity is a biblically viable option (Parrett 2004, 76).

The starting point for understanding multiculturalism in the church should be a biblical theology of culture. The biblical origin of distinct cultures was the confusion of human languages at Babel, and, because of the effect of sin, every culture has both dignity and depravity. In the words of B.J. Nicholls (quoted in Parrett 2004, 53): "Culture is never neutral, it is always a strange complex of truth and error, beauty and ugliness, good and evil, seeking God and rebelling against him." The New Testament, however, brings hope for the reversal of the division of mankind that happened at Babel and the redemption of culture in Christ. It can be argued that the imperative to form multicultural churches originates with the church-planting strategy of the apostles themselves, and particularly with Paul, who pioneered missions beyond the Jewish origins of Christianity to Gentile cultures, but expected the congregations he planted would be multicultural. This vision is particularly clear in Galatians 3:26-29, where Paul proclaims an end to divisions of ethnicity, social status and gender in the body of Christ. Unity and cohesion are not to be based on these things.

Paul's theology places a strong emphasis on reconciliation between God and human beings, and therefore between groups of human beings who were previously divided, with the end-result of a new humanity which finds its identity in Christ. Sugden (2000, 105) writes that:

> The new humanity is demonstrated in the church, not in dissolving ethnicities but in fulfilling them and fitting them into the whole. This is brought about by the reconciling power of the cross. The new humanity demonstrates peace, reconciliation, access to God and to one another, holiness and the dwelling place of the Spirit. The future is with the new humanity, so why not hasten it?

Larry L McSwain (quoted in Milne, 2006, 152) also recognizes the doctrine of reconciliation as a basis for multicultural churches:

> For the church to embody into its structures the separations of race, class, language, or sex is to deny the gospel which reconciles. The church is not a unity of one culture, but a unity amid diversity (I Cor 12:4-11), one body with many members (I Cor 12:12-13), reconciled individuals who live in peace (Eph 2:11-12). The fullest expression of that reality is the church of multicultural persons who worship, serve, and fellowship with each other in the unity of their faith in Christ without the sacrifice of their personal identities.

A third objection to monocultural churches is that they reduce their members' concept of God and his self-revelation in Scripture. Manuel Ortiz warns that, "We limit the greatness of our Lord when we know God only as a local God who speaks our language and understands our conditions alone" (1996, 13). Elmer (1993, 13) writes that:

> There are sound theological reasons for committing ourselves to understand other cultures and appreciate them wherever possible. Making that commitment will unfold for us new and wonderful dimensions of God's character, for our God can be properly revealed only through diversity.

The limitations of monocultural churches are expressed clearly by Vinay Samuel (quoted in Sugden, 2000, 22) when he writes that "a church by itself tends to be blind to its cultural captivity and sometimes practices and proclaims a distorted gospel." Interaction with Christians from different cultures in Bible study can mean that "powerful insights and truths invisible to one culture become accessible through disciples from another cultural background" (Samuel, quoted in Sugden, 2000, 52). When we cocoon ourselves only within our own cultural setting, we run the risk of missing out on answers to many of our own questions that others may be able to give. Eric Law (1993, 55) writes about the dynamics of learning in a multicultural Bible study:

> Depending on the cultural contexts of the readers and the context of the multicultural situation, the same scriptural story may challenge, support, affirm, motivate, or even put down different people. In other words, if scriptural study is shared among people from different cultures, people from one cultural context will be able to hear how people from a different cultural context interact with the same scriptural story.

Engagement with other cultures can also help to reveal the weaknesses inherent in our own cultures and perhaps especially within the Western Christian subculture. In his book *Dynamic Diversity*, Bruce Milne contends that the whole gamut of biblical theology confirms the mandate to form multicultural churches (Milne, 2006, 56). In particular, he lists six major doctrines and their implications:

- The Trinity, which reveals that unity in diversity is the very essence of the Godhead.
- Creation, which teaches us that all human beings are created in the image of God for community.
- The incarnation, which is the ultimate example of love breaking down boundaries.
- The atonement, which establishes reconciliation through sacrificial love as the central tenet of the Christian faith.
- The image of the church as the body of Christ, which teaches us that unity in diversity is both normal and beneficial for the church.
- The eschatological perspective of the glorified community of believers from every tribe and language, which shows us that unity in diversity is God's eternal purpose for his people.

ADVANTAGES OF MULTICULTURAL CHURCHES

Contrary to the claims of the Church Growth Movement, proponents of multicultural churches also argue that they are more effective in mission than ethnic-specific churches. Multicultural churches create an opportunity for a greater understanding of, and commitment to, world mission, as members are able to enlighten others to the situation in their nation of heritage. Cross-cultural missionaries may be much better prepared if they have already been engaged in a learning process with Christians from other cultural backgrounds in their home church. Furthermore, multicultural churches may be advantaged in local evangelism. The world of the 2000s is significantly different from the world of the 1970s in which McGavran developed his theories, not least because of the increasing cultural diversity in Western society, causing Milne to claim that the homogeneous unit principle is outdated:

> Multicultural churches may be more effective in mission than ethnic-specific churches, may create a greater understanding of world mission, and may be advantaged in local evangelism.

> The world in which these justifications of segregated congregations were framed is in fact fast disappearing; the world of tomorrow will be very different, but wonderfully, in the process, it will afford new opportunities to obey God's Word and discover in the process the God-honouring joy and richness of multi-racial, multi-everything church life (2006, 156).

This societal shift has created new opportunities for evangelism and has also led to a change in the attitude of many people who are now attracted by the prospect of knowing and understanding people from other cultures. Ken Fong (1999, 7), whose ministry focuses primarily on Asian Americans, writes that:

> I believe that pursuing a strict homogeneous unit approach blinds us to how an incredibly diverse Christian fellowship that is united around Christ can stimulate the

curiosity of unconvinced persons, particularly Asian Americans… there are mounting numbers of unconvinced Americanized Asian Americans who are drawn to churches that display an uncommon sense of community amid a complex amalgam of generations, cultures, combinations, and accents.

It is likely that Fong's observations will be equally true of people of many ethnic backgrounds, especially those who have migrated, for whom true cross-cultural community will be not only a novelty but something deeply desirable. The other-centred love that binds a multicultural church together will be the very quality that enables its members to reach outward and embrace others who are outside the church community. Being multicultural should help a church not to become inward looking or irrelevant. A community of believers consisting of people from many different cultural backgrounds but transformed by the love of the living God will be ideally suited to reach out to a society of people from many different cultural backgrounds who are hungry for love.

One final benefit of multicultural churches is that they demonstrate how people of different ethnicities and backgrounds can live together harmoniously, a model badly needed in today's fractured world. By contrast, ethnic-specific churches may actually risk reinforcing the distrust and misunderstanding between minority groups and the dominant culture, whereas multicultural churches can spearhead reconciliation. In countries where migration raises acute issues of non-integration, Christians have a special responsibility and opportunity to show how the cross of Christ breaks down barriers. Integration is possible, albeit only by the power of God.

MODELS OF MULTICULTURAL CHURCHES

Based on these theological and pragmatic arguments for multicultural churches, an increasing number of authors argue that all churches should have the ultimate aim of becoming multicultural, especially in those contexts where the population has now become ethnically diverse. There are three main ways in which such multiculturalism may be displayed. Some churches rent out facilities so that a congregation using a different language from the host church can meet; this is not true multiculturalism, but where genuine attention is paid to fostering friendships between members of both host and minority church, this may lead to a second model, that of sister congregations. Here, while some activities are retained separately, there is also commitment to joint services and activities from time to time. Each group has equality, and hosts the other on a regular and intentional basis. The third model, a multiethnic congregation, integrates people of diverse ethnic backgrounds.

This latter is, of course, not easy to accomplish. Intentional inclusivity must permeate every aspect of church life, and will entail a great deal of effort and sacrifice from all cultural groups. Power must be sensitively distributed, especially where one ethnic group is dominant, so that minority groups do not become disenfranchised, as they may well be in the wider society. Leadership needs to be multiracial, even if this appears disproportionately to favor minority groups. Most people will have to surrender some of their cultural preferences, but none should compromise commitment to Scripture as their authority transcending all cultures. Disagreements must be patiently addressed, practicing careful listening, reconciliation, repentance, and humility. The goal is not that everybody should be assimilated into the dominant group's traditional ways, but that there should be enrichment through diversity.

Amongst migrant churches in particular, there are special issues relating to the first generation and subsequent generations. The first generation may never feel comfortable in the language or culture of the host community, even if it is within the same nation (e.g., provincial groups with their own distinct language, moving to an urban center), and emotionally will need the support of their own peer group. For them, the sister church model may be the best option. They will also want their children and grandchildren to retain something of their own ethnic heritage, and a church can offer language classes to assist in this. This is also a good evangelistic tool for reaching non-Christians of that ethnic group in the wider community.

For second and third generations, there is likely to be a greater identification with the host culture, especially in language, and transition into a truly multiethnic church may be much easier. Although the unity of the two generations may suffer in the short-term, the ultimate goal of integration will be better served in existing ethnic-specific congregations by encouraging the next generation to move beyond that and to integrate into a multicultural church. Alternatively, the younger generation may develop services in the host culture's language, and then intentionally work to make this new congregation multicultural and multiethnic.

For theological and practical reasons, any church that claims the name of Christ must actively seek to include people from a wide range of cultural backgrounds, spanning differences of class, generation, ethnicity, and sex, and must aim for integration towards a common "Christian culture" based on Scripture.

> For theological and practical reasons, any church that claims the name of Christ must actively seek to include people from a wide range of cultural backgrounds.

As an example, the Chinese Churches in the UK stand at a crossroads where they must decide whether to remain as ethnic-specific churches or to encourage their English-speaking ministries to become multicultural congregations. Based on the experience of Chinese Churches in North America and research conducted in the UK by this author, British born Chinese are privileged in being able to move between two cultures, and they positively want to be part of multicultural churches whilst still maintaining links with their parents' generation. This can best be achieved by Chinese Churches encouraging their English ministries to develop into integrated multiethnic congregations. For this to happen, leaders must be intentional about it and develop strategies to help their churches move in this direction. Chinese Churches in the UK are ideally positioned to lead the way for the wider church and for British society as a whole. They can, if they choose, become dynamic, vibrant centers of reconciliation where Christ is truly and manifestly all and in all (Eph 4:6).

This is true not only for Chinese churches, or only for the UK. These principles hold for other ethnic groups, and for other parts of the world. God's desire is that his people should be visibly multicultural, demonstrating the reconciling power of the gospel that transcends all human barriers.

Paul Coulter has pastored both Chinese and local congregations in Northern Ireland.

QUESTIONS FOR REFLECTION

1. In your context, are there multiethnic, multicultural, multigenerational churches? If so, what are the main positives and negatives about such a church? If not, what would need to happen to make it come about?

2. Imagine you are an immigrant/refugee non-Christian in an unfamiliar country. What might draw you to a church made up of people from your own background? What might draw you to a multiethnic church?

3. Imagine you are a leader of a monoethnic congregation and become convinced that the Lord desires you to become multiethnic. How would you set about making that change? What difficulties would you expect to meet along the way, and how might you address them?

CHAPTER 7

TREASURES BUT NOT IDOLS

Contextualizing Tribalism and Ethnicity to the Glory of God

Miriam Adeney

"Eleven o'clock Sunday morning is the most segregated hour in America." Whether true or false, this statement has been repeated many times. But racism is a problem not just in America. On other continents, tribalism spews violence.

Given this sad history, should Christians minimize their tribal and ethnic allegiance? As members of God's family, should we de-emphasize our distinctive cultural heritages?

BOTH UNITY AND DIVERSITY

No. Unity and diversity both are part of God's plan. On unity, Jesus poured out an impassioned prayer that we would all be one (John 17). His followers are to be known by our love for one another (John 13:35).

The Apostle Paul developed this theme. "There is neither Jew nor Greek…but you are all one in Christ," he wrote (Gal 3:28). Because Jesus decisively broke down the wall between ethnic groups, we are "no longer strangers and foreigners but fellow citizens" (Eph 2:14-19).

"You are a holy nation…In time past you were not a people, but now you are," the Apostle Peter wrote (1 Pet 2:9-10).

Yet cultures are gifts of God. It is God who created us in his image, endowed us with creativity, and set us in a world of possibilities. It is through using his gifts that we have developed the cultures of the world. As A.A. Stockdale says,

> When God made the earth, he could have finished it. But he didn't.
>
> He left it as a raw material—to tease us, to tantalize us, to set us thinking, and experimenting, and risking, and adventuring. And therein we find our supreme interest in living.

He gave us the challenge of raw materials, not the satisfaction of perfect, finished things.

He left the music unsung, and the dramas unplayed.

He left the poetry undreamed, in order that men and women might not become bored, but engaged in stimulating, exciting, creative activities that keep them thinking, working, experimenting, and experiencing all the joys and satisfactions of achievement (1964, 20).

TAKING JOY IN CULTURE

When I lived for several years in the Philippines, I saw strong families. Warm hospitality. Lots of time lavished on children. Enduring friendships. A heritage of economic freedom for women. The ability to live graciously on little money. Sauces that extended a small amount of meat to many people. An eagerness to share. Skill in the art of relaxation. Lithe, limber bodies. The ability to enjoy being with a large number of people continuously.

These fine traits are not merely products of nature. Every good gift is from above (Jas 1:17) and all wisdom and knowledge come from Jesus Christ (Col 2:3). The beautiful qualities in Filipino culture are gifts of the God who so loves diversity that he creates billions of unique snowflakes, personalities, smells, colors, and even tropical fish.

> God so loves diversity that he creates billions of unique snowflakes, personalities, smells, colors, and even tropical fish.

If God delights in diversity in nature, is it any surprise that he programs us with the capacity to enrich his world with an amazing array of cultures? And what does he want around his throne at the end of time? A beige uniformity? No, he welcomes a kaleidoscope of peoples and tribes and kindreds and nations.

Cultures contain sin and must be judged. But taking joy in our culture is not sin. It is like the joy a father or mother feels for their child. When your child does well, your chest hammers with pride. This is not pride at the expense of your neighbor, who takes joy in his child. No, you are proud simply because you know your child's stories, the sorrows he has suffered, and the gifts that have blossomed. You yourself have cried and laughed and given away years of your life in the shaping of some of his stories. At its best, joy in culture is an expansion of this good family pride. It is a sense of identity, a birthright.

Stories of sorrows and successes constitute a people's history. This is part of their birthright. Jews have their history. Chinese have their history. African-Americans have their history. No one can take this from them. A people's history gives them no ground to lord it over others, but it does give them ground for joy in their own community.

STEPPING BEYOND OUR CULTURE

How much should we value race, tribe, ethnicity, and culture? Our call is complex. God is glorified by unity. God also is glorified by diversity. To his glory, we cultivate both.

That means we delight in our culture, we take joy in it, we are willing to sacrifice for it. But culture is not the last word. Our loyalties do not stop at the edge of our culture. Christians must step out into the margins and bridge between cultures.

This should feel natural. Abraham was commissioned to bless *all* the families of the earth. Moses charged God's people to "love the aliens as you love yourselves." David sang, "May *all* the peoples praise you." Isaiah envisioned God's followers being light to the nations. Paul was propelled by a passion for the unreached peoples. John vibrated with a vision of peoples and tribes and kindreds and nations gathered together around the throne of God at the end of time.

Where I live, there are sixty Russian and Ukrainian churches where immigrants worship. For some reason, an Iranian Muslim began attending one of these. He delighted in debating with the Christians over tea after the evening service. This went on for months. Then a Russian evangelist conducted special meetings. To everyone's surprise, the Muslim came to life-transforming faith in Jesus.

The Russian church began to disciple him. Soon he was bringing other Iranians, and the Russian church was no longer monocultural. To welcome the Iranians, they had to accept changes. Like Christians everywhere, they were called to connect cross-culturally as a matter of course, whether or not they had anticipated this.

SALVATION FOR SMUGGLED CHINESE

Eight years ago, dozens of Chinese people smuggled themselves to the U.S. in ship containers. Most of them died. Those who lived were taken first to hospitals, and then to a government jail in Seattle to await deportation.

Christian Chinese-Americans in the city said to each other, "We must help them, They have no one else. China is angry with them. The U.S. is angry with them. The smugglers are angry with them. Their families are angry with them because now they owe a lot of money to the smugglers."

So the Chinese-Americans petitioned the U.S. government until they were allowed to hold services in the jail. Many of the Chinese prisoners came to faith. They became powerful in prayer. They composed Christian songs and eventually burned a CD. When they were sent to other jails or deported to their home country, they went as missionaries.

Meanwhile, other prisoners began to attend the Chinese services. Although they couldn't understand the language, they knew God was present and knew they needed his help. The ministry team had to diversify in order to serve them. A recent e-mail reads: "For the jail baptism Sunday night, we need pastors who speak Russian, Spanish, Farsi, Mongolian, and Mandarin."

A Chinese believer was deported back to China, but he found no promising future there. An uncle invited him to a Chinese shrimp-fishing village in Ecuador. Here he found a whole town with no gospel.

"Come help me plant a church!" he wrote to the Chinese-Americans in Seattle.

At first they declined, but eventually five Chinese churches in Seattle sent teams that went door to door and shop to shop in Ecuador and established a church that now has thirty members. The five churches continue taking responsibility for prayer and occasional visits and training.

"IF OUR CULTURE IS GOING TO SURVIVE…"

Tribe, ethnicity, and culture are God's gifts. They are treasures. The Chinese-Americans in Seattle loved their culture. They preserved it in their Chinese speaking churches. But they did not idolize it. When called, they moved beyond their culture because of the love of Christ. Similarly, the Russian church preserved their Russian language and culture. But they also welcomed Iranians and accepted the changes that they brought.

> Tribe, ethnicity, and culture are God's gifts. They are treasures. But they are not to be idolized.

On the continent of Africa at the height of the gory conflict in Rwanda and Burundi, students of the Hutu tribe were killed on their campuses by fellow students of the Tutsi tribe. Hutus who managed to escape fled into the mountains. Reaching across the abyss between their peoples, Tutsi Christian students followed the Hutus into the mountains and brought them food and clothes. Later the Christian Tutsis returned with more supplies, even for strangers that they did not know. Because of this, some of their own families rejected them.

When the non-Christian university president heard about this, he made a noteworthy observation. "Our culture is disintegrating," he said. "On our campus there are three types of people: Hutus, Tutsis and Christians. If our culture is to survive, we must follow the example of the Christians" (Brown 2006, 134).

Miriam Adeney is an international speaker, author, and trainer of writers. She teaches at Seattle Pacific University and Fuller Theological Seminary in the United States and at Regent College in Canada.

QUESTIONS FOR REFLECTION

1. What is the difference between ethnocentrism and a godly celebration of our own culture?
2. What practical steps might we take to encourage both diversity and unity in our local congregations?
3. In her final paragraphs, Miriam Adeney tells a story from the Rwanda genocide. How might Christians be agents of reconciliation, transcending cultural hostility, in places or communities known to you?

CHAPTER 8

FRUITFUL PRACTICES IN CONTEXTUALIZATION

Bob Fish and Gene Daniels

Local expressions of faith in Christ have always been in a state of flux as that faith has passed from one person to the next across generations and cultures. The story of redemption has repeatedly broken free from the traditions of those carrying that message to become expressed in new cultural idioms whenever the gospel has encountered new peoples and their ways of life. Lamin Sanneh puts it this way, "The history of Christianity has become properly the history of the world's peoples and cultures, *not simply the history of missionaries and their cultures*" (Sanneh 2008, 56, emphasis added). All this is another way of saying that contextualization has always been a part of the spread of faith in Christ across new frontiers.

Today, one of the leading edges of this 2,000-year-old process is the world of Islam.[1] Over the past few decades, Christian witness among Muslims has steadily grown. A wide range of debate has grown along with that expansion—debate about the degree to which those witnesses should allow local Islamic contexts to influence their ministries. What is beyond debate is the fact that the local practice of faith in Christ is being negotiated at another missiological frontier.

The Fruitful Practice Research team has had the privilege of documenting the ways that God is working in the Muslim world. This article presents some of the research that specifically relates to contextualization. Not all of the fruitful ministry approaches we have studied were highly, or even significantly, contextualized. Yet after examining the work of field practitioners, it is clear that the contextualization of their Christian witness has had a large and positive impact on seeing Muslims turn to Christ and be gathered into communities of his disciples.

---

1   In fact, this is Dr. Sanneh's context. He is the descendant of an ancient African royal house and grew up as a Muslim in Gambia, West Africa. He is now the D. Willis James Professor of Missions and World Christianity at Yale University.

Before we go on, we want to quickly discuss the objectivity of our research model. Maintaining objectivity in scientific research is always difficult. Still, we want to categorically state that it is not the intent of Fruitful Practice Research to promote any contextual model *per se*. The research team includes members with widely divergent opinions. We might fall on different sides of the debate about when contextualization leads to syncretism. However, all agree that our team must study the topic in an objective manner that simply evaluates the impact of contextual approaches and contextualization on fruitfulness. To the extent possible, we have attempted to collect and analyze data in a manner consistent with rigorous quantitative and qualitative methods and hope that we have contributed results that can be utilized by practitioners of any persuasion.

RESEARCH RESULTS THAT REFLECT CONTEXTUALIZATION

After extensive research, our team distilled and summarized our findings into a list of sixty-eight "Fruitful Practices." For the purposes of our research, we have defined a Fruitful Practice as an activity that promotes the emergence, vitality, and multiplication of fellowships of Jesus followers in a Muslim context.[2] For the entire list of Fruitful Practices, see Allen, et al. (2009).

From that list of Fruitful Practices, we have included here those practices that either relate directly to contextualization or have bearing on this topic. They are organized into groups that reflect the cross-cultural worker's relationships in the Muslim society.

RELATING TO SOCIETY

Fruitful workers communicate respect by behaving in culturally appropriate ways
A worker's attitude toward the host culture sends powerful messages. Fruitful workers behave in culturally appropriate ways in major cultural domains such as clothing and food, and especially in regards to hospitality. The key is sensitivity to the local setting, not necessarily wholehearted adoption of local practice.

Fruitful workers relate to people in ways that respect gender roles in the local culture
Gender roles, and the taboos associated with them, are potent issues in the Muslim world. While maintaining a biblical perspective on these issues, fruitful workers strive to understand gender roles in their local context and demonstrate respect for these social norms.

---

2   Fruitful Practice Research is a multi-agency team studying activities that promote the emergence, vitality, and multiplication of fellowships of Jesus followers in a Muslim context. Much of the philosophy behind this project can be found in other articles. (See, for example Allen (2008) and Adams, Allen and Fish (2009).)
The team initially surveyed and interviewed teams from thirteen organizations representing more than 5,800 workers in the Muslim world. From these interviews, the team gleaned 104 potentially fruitful practices. In 2007 we evaluated these practices in a five-day consultation where we conducted more than 100 recorded interviews, collated five detailed surveys, and collected notes from 25 daily discussion groups. Together, this produced responses from more than 300 individuals from 76 organizations, experienced in planting fellowships. Two-thirds of the respondents had witnessed the emergence of at least one Christ-centered community in the Muslim world. The analysis we have conducted on this data was from a mixed-methods approach, combining interviews, focus groups, quantitative surveys, and experience. The result of the research was a list of activities that we have called "Fruitful Practices," which our research subjects felt had significantly contributed to their fruitfulness.

Fruitful workers pursue language proficiency
Workers who are able to freely and clearly communicate in their host language(s) are much more likely to be fruitful. Fruitful workers carefully consider questions concerning language choice, such as whether to use heart or trade language, sacred or secular language. By learning language, they also gain a deeper understanding of culture, making language proficiency fruitful across a number of different dimensions.

RELATING TO SEEKERS

Fruitful workers share the gospel through existing social networks[3]
Group disapproval can be a significant barrier to any kind of social change. Group affirmation can be a significant catalyst that helps many people come to faith. In situations where many are coming to faith, often the impact and spread of the workers' initial witness has been multiplied as new believers share their faith with their family and community.

RELATING TO BELIEVERS

Fruitful workers disciple in locally appropriate and reproducible ways
Disciples are more likely to share their faith and make new disciples when all needed books, tools, and resources are locally available. Fruitful workers avoid relying on discipleship manuals that must be ordered from abroad, electronic equipment that is unaffordable for disciples, or training that is only offered elsewhere.

Fruitful workers help seekers and believers find appropriate ways to identify themselves to their community as followers of Jesus, without imposing their own preferences
Fruitful workers actively help seekers and believers to consider ways to establish their identity in their community by asking them questions that help them consider their alternatives. They avoid presuming or predetermining this identity for followers of Jesus.

Fruitful workers help believers find ways to remain within their social network
Most seekers and believers live in strong webs of existing family, social, and religious relationships. The gospel is more likely to spread quickly when faith travels through these existing webs. Fruitful workers encourage seekers and believers to maintain these relationships, to share their faith journey with family and friends, and to incorporate new seekers and believers into fellowships within those networks.

Fruitful workers encourage believers to follow the Holy Spirit's leading in applying the Bible to their context
Rather than imposing their own application and interpretation on biblical passages, fruitful workers help seekers and believers to ask for God's help as they reflect on biblical truth and apply it to their situation. They encourage seekers and believers to trust that God will answer them when they ask for his help.

---

3   It may seem strange to include this Fruitful Practice in an article about contextualization. However, other sociological, strategic, and missiological considerations aside, to focus on networks is to contextualize to pre-existing social structures, rather than to create new ones.

Fruitful workers deal with sin in biblical ways that are culturally appropriate.

Fruitful workers understand that the biblical principles of correction of sin and restoration, as described in Matthew 18 and Galatians 6:1-2, must be applied within the local cultural context and worldview. In the process of applying biblical teaching, fruitful workers consider local cultural dynamics such as honor and shame, gender roles, community standards, family and clan status, and social standing.

RELATING TO LEADERS

Fruitful workers prefer to develop leaders locally

Fruitful workers prefer to develop leaders as locally as possible. If it is not possible to train leaders in a geographically local setting, then it is more fruitful to train leaders within local culture and local social norms. When leaders are trained outside of the local setting, they can find it difficult to return. The further their training is from local life, the less likely it is that they will return and readjust well.

COMMUNICATION METHODS

Fruitful workers use culturally appropriate Bible passages to communicate God's message

The Bible is central in the communication of God's message, but using it effectively requires cultural insight. Fruitful workers help seekers find the passages that address the issues most relevant to them. The ability to effectively apply biblical truth to the issues of life requires a thorough knowledge of God's word and an ongoing dependence on wisdom from God.

Fruitful workers communicate the gospel using the heart language, except in situations where it is not appropriate

In most situations, the heart language is undoubtedly the best way to meaningfully communicate the gospel. However, in areas where more than one language is in common use, established patterns often dictate when one language should be used as opposed to another. Fruitful workers seek to understand local patterns of language use and plan their communication strategies accordingly.

Fruitful workers share the gospel in ways that fit the learning preferences of their audience

Although people from Western countries rely heavily on written media, people in many other parts of the world are accustomed to oral forms of communication. Good communicators understand the learning preferences of their audience and plan their communication strategies accordingly.

Fruitful workers use the Qur'an as a bridge to sharing the biblical gospel

Certain passages from the Qur'an can be used effectively in sharing the gospel. Discretion is needed, as inappropriate references to the Qur'an may validate a seeker's belief in the divine origin of the book. In general, the use of the Qur'an as a bridge is most advisable when relating to seekers who already know the Qur'an well. Fruitful workers do not dwell unnecessarily on the Qur'an, but use various passages as a bridge in order to share the biblical gospel.

FRUITFUL TEAMS

Fruitful teams adapt their methods based on reflective evaluation and new information
Teams bear fruit when they intentionally evaluate their progress. They change their methods and strategies when necessary. They adapt their methods based on the experience of informed local experts and other efforts to build God's Kingdom.

CHARACTERISTICS OF FRUITFUL FAITH COMMUNITIES

Fruitful faith communities worship using indigenous forms of expression
Fruitful faith communities design their worship using indigenous music and other forms of expression that reflect their cultural heritage, including prayer posture, seating arrangements, or the kinds of food used when sharing the Lord's Supper.

Fruitful faith communities redeem traditional festivals and ceremonies
Life cycle ceremonies (such as weddings and funerals, traditions surrounding birth and death, and festivals that mark various events in a culture's historical identity) are important to the fabric of any society. Rather than abandon all tradition or remove themselves from all association with traditional festivals, fruitful faith communities seek ways to redeem them as an expression of their faith in Jesus.

Fruitful faith communities share the Lord's Supper in culturally appropriate ways
Fruitful faith communities use elements and adopt a method of sharing the Lord's Supper that makes the most sense in their cultural context. In the West, the elements of bread and wine are commonly used. But in many cultures, bread is not available and wine is forbidden. Likewise, there are many ways to distribute the elements, either during a meal or as a separate service.

Fruitful faith communities involve women in culturally appropriate forms of ministry
Understanding that the Lord calls both men and women to participate in ministry, fruitful faith communities seek to involve women in ways that are appropriate for the cultural context. In some areas, this may be limited to hospitality. In others, it may be appropriate for a woman to serve the Lord's Supper or to lead other women in studying the Bible.

Fruitful faith communities equip their members to share their faith in effective and culturally appropriate ways
Believers share their faith in many ways. What is effective in some cultural settings may be counterproductive in others. Fruitful faith communities encourage their members to share their faith and equip them to do so in ways that are appropriate for the situation.

DISCUSSION

In addition to developing these practices, Fruitful Practice Research's collaborative team has analyzed the data from other perspectives, producing other findings that also bear on the subject of contextualization. Their research will also briefly be explored here.

So, what can we learn from these practices related to contextualization that are proving to be fruitful?

CONTEXTUALIZED APPROACHES

We have used the term *contextualized approaches* here to indicate when there is an emphasis on the things we outsiders do, our efforts to be sensitive and appropriate, and the general steps we take in communication.[4] Many of the practices listed above are basic, yet cross-cultural workers often ignore them or do not fully implement them. These "basics" deal with language choice, gender issues, and cultural sensitivity. As Daniels has said elsewhere, "Cultural adaptation is not just a matter of changing the clothes we wear or the foods we eat—it is about attitude. When we respect people and the boundaries of their social norms, it pays rich dividends that they return in the form of trust" (Daniels 2010, 22). The research shows that "Fruitful workers communicate respect by behaving in culturally appropriate ways," meeting local expectations in the areas of clothing, food, and hospitality. Yet they should do so without becoming legalistic or odd.

> "Cultural adaptation is not just a matter of changing the clothes we wear or the foods we eat—it is about attitude."

Gender issues seem straightforward: generally speaking, in Muslim cultures, men should relate only to men, women only to women. Yet for those who understand the culture deeply, there may be subtle exceptions to the principle. In our study, women workers considered sharing along gender lines more important than men did (Greenlee and Wilson 2008). We also found that the cross-cultural workers' value for respecting gender difference "…tapers off markedly with age. This suggests that the respect that comes with age in Muslim societies is so powerful that it trumps some of the taboos related to gender relations" (Daniels 2010, 23). He also mentions an example in which a female worker appropriately taught Muslim men in a family setting. "In this example, we see a female worker teaching men, which would have been unthinkable in public or one-on-one, yet the same practice is fruitful within a family setting. This example reminds us that applying fruitful practices can be counter-intuitive, and workers must carefully learn from their context as they attempt to implement them in their ministries" (Daniels 2010, 23).

IDENTITY AND CONTEXTUALIZATION

Very deep and complicated issues surround the identity of new believers as followers of Jesus. Many cross-cultural workers have come to use the C-scale as the only yardstick for categorizing the level of contextualization of ministry among Muslims. This scale, originally developed by John Travis (1998), describes degrees of contextualization in the domain of religious practice. (It should be noted that Travis designed the C-scale to be a descriptor of how the believing communities identify themselves, not something that outsiders impose on them.) The scale helped to catalyze discussion about contextualization; however, these authors welcome new models of religious identity based on a more subtle and complex sociological,

---

4   In the *Global Dictionary of Theology*, Gener uses the terms "contextualization from without" and "contextualization from within" (2008, 193) to help make this distinction. We are particularly focusing on the former in this section and the latter in the sections on identity and social networks.

spiritual, ecological, and psychological matrix that is currently being developed. In spite of its limitations, and because we lack any other commonly agreed metric, the Fruitful Practice Research team has used this well-known scale to evaluate the relative fruitfulness based on levels of contextualization.

Recognizing that the results represent a small sample size (n=137), Brown, et al., found that "All three levels of contextualization, C3–C5, correlate with the formation of churches, but higher degrees of contextualization appear more conducive to the development of movements. This data should not be interpreted to mean that C5 communities are the ones mostly likely to multiply in all situations; there may well be situations where C3 and C4 are equally effective or more so. Different levels of contextualization might also have different degrees of appeal to Muslims in different population sentiments, in which case the greatest multiplication would come from having both C4 and C5 movements in the same society" (Brown, et al. 2009, 22-23). Brown, et al. concluded that higher levels of contextualization were often associated with the gospel expanding within social networks.

SOCIAL NETWORKS AND CONTEXTUALIZATION

Other researchers within the Fruitful Practice project agreed that there appears to be an association between contextualization and social networks. (This idea is developed in Gray and Gray, 2009a; Gray and Gray, 2009b; Gray, et al. 2010). In Gray, et al. 2010, the authors report that two types of church-planting models emerged from the data: "The first was an attractional model, in which unrelated individual believers are gathered together to form a social network (church) that is separate from existing social networks in the community. The second was a transformational model, in which the gospel is shared within the context of a natural social network, gradually transforming the network towards Christ, regardless of the stage of faith of individual members of the network." They argue that a relationship exists between contextualization and the transformational model.

This relationship does not simply focus on using the right forms that are socially appropriate, but it goes deeper to affect the cross-cultural worker's model of what a church is. This also affects methods of evangelism. They say, "We can see here the relationship between a culturally appropriate way of sharing the gospel and the gospel spreading through social networks. Because the team shared with this woman appropriately, she is able to share her faith appropriately with others in her sphere of influence. The key lesson we can draw from this interview and several like it is that when the message is contextualized at the level of identity and worldview, and is therefore portrayed as something that will strengthen the social network, rather than tear it down, it is more likely to be embraced" (Gray and Gray, 2009a, 26-27).

They conclude, "While contextualization is a highly debated topic in church-planting circles, our analysis of these interviews indicates that contextualization in and of itself is not the chief factor in the formation of church-planting movements. It appears from the interviews we analyzed that contextualization is effective only insofar as it supports a transformational model of church. We also found that contextualization of external practices (e.g., growing a beard) was less important than contextualization at the level of worldview (including language, terminology, group identity, and the application of the Bible's teachings to real life)" (Gray and Gray, 2009a, 28). A significant research program needs to tease out the issues related to contextualization, identity and the transformation of social networks by the gospel.

CONCLUSION

The Fruitful Practices project has gathered, and continues to gather, data in order to discern how the Father is working in our times among Muslims. The principles we are developing need to be set in a framework of reflective practice and stewarding of our experience (Torkko, Adams, and Adams 2009). We cannot naively apply these principles, but we must study the culture in which we are working, and with the Holy Spirit's guidance, seek to implement them as best we can. These principles do not guarantee success. We plant, others water, but God gives the increase (1 Cor 3:6-8).

Bob Fish and Gene Daniels serve with an international agency working among Muslims.

Authors' note: We thank Don Allen, John Becker, and David Greenlee for reviewing the article. E.J. Martin provided editorial assistance which clarified our writing immensely.

QUESTIONS FOR REFLECTION:

1. The authors list fourteen practices which relate specifically to "fruitful workers." Taking each one in turn, how would you set about developing that good practice? What might be involved? What would make it difficult? How would you apply these practices in your own context?

2. The authors list one practice relating to fruitful teams: would you add any others? Then, they list five practices relating to "fruitful faith communities." Taking each one in turn, what biblical support could you cite? What might be some of the difficulties such communities may have to overcome?

3. The authors contrast the "attractional model" (where unrelated individuals come to faith) and the "transformational model" (where an existing social network moves together towards faith). What are the strengths and weaknesses of each model? There are biblical examples of both models: what can we learn from them? What might we do differently in practice and strategically between these two models?

CHAPTER 9

LEARNING LESSONS FROM AN ASIAN CHURCH LEADER

Reflections on Hwa Yung's Theology of Mission

Warren Beattie

Much talk of contextualization is based on models that discuss theory but do not bring the discussion to a more practical level. Within East Asia, one theologian who looks not only at the theoretical aspects of contextual theology but who seeks to bring this theory to bear on the life of the church is Hwa Yung. He has been involved in theological education in Singapore and Malaysia and is currently the Bishop of the Methodist church of West Malaysia. Hwa's theology of mission makes him take account of both the social context and the pastoral needs of the church. As he engages in mission socially and pastorally, he encounters many issues that are essentially issues of contextualization.

This chapter will explore Hwa's missional stance and its implications for contextual theology in the religious and social spheres in relation to the church's pastoral and evangelistic work. Hwa has developed a theology of mission that is contextual. He affirms that themes for contextualization need to be generated by the concerns of local Christians as they focus on issues that are significant for their experience. He emphasizes contextualization from the inside, and the "deep structures" and "root metaphors" (Maggay 2001, 9) that are significant for a largely Chinese church in Malaysia.

A MISSIONAL STANCE THAT ENCOURAGES CONTEXTUAL THEOLOGY

In Asian settings, Hwa reminds us that we urgently need to see mission as "a comprehensive concept" which has "vertical and horizontal dimensions." Mission involves sharing the gospel of Jesus Christ to all. It includes missionaries who have the "calling to cross frontiers to share the good news," but also "evangelism and church-planting, deliverance from diseases and demon powers as well as sociopolitical action for freedom and justice in the world" (Hwa 1997, 43, 57). A robust theology of mission will address the sociopolitical contexts, empower the church in evangelistic and pastoral tasks, and pay due consideration to contextualization, the task of self-theologizing.

For Hwa, theology of mission needs to be formed in relation to the Asian settings and the Christian Scriptures as they are read with Asian eyes. It is in the interplay between the Asian settings and the Asian reading of the Scriptures that Asian Christian identity is formed. This identity is given expression in the Kingdom community which serves as a center of formation for Christian disciples so that they can engage in mission in contextually appropriate ways.

THE CHRISTIAN SCRIPTURES READ BY ASIAN EYES

The Christian Scriptures are central in shaping mission in Asian contexts,[1] as elsewhere. However, there is a tendency for evangelicals in Asia to read the Bible either through the lens of popular spirituality texts from Asia or through academic texts from the West (Hwa 1997, 42-43, 57-58). In an attempt to move beyond these approaches, Hwa affirms the need to develop an Asian Christian hermeneutic and suggests that "Asian Christians must begin to learn to read and understand the Bible from within their own contexts" (Hwa 1997, 224).[2] He advocates a reading of the Scriptures that takes account of the wholistic dimensions of mission found in the New Testament, pointing out that there are many examples in the gospels, such as Luke 4 and Luke 6, which point to a concern for both spiritual and physical realities. In short, even the act of reading the Bible needs to be "wholistic."

DEVELOPING ASIAN CHRISTIAN IDENTITY

Kingdom identity

The concept of the Kingdom is an important theme in missiology. The vision of the Kingdom of God stresses four inter-related themes: Jesus as King; power over spirits and evil; power in the area of healing; and God's reign over human society (Hwa 2002).

Christians have a basic theological identity as children of God[3] and at the same time a cultural identity that depends on their social setting. The dual identity of Christians is formed by their Christian and sociocultural backgrounds. Hwa is concerned about forming the identity of Malaysian Christians so that they are seen as genuinely Malaysian. Mission in the Malaysian setting needs to show that Christians are rooted in society. In countries like Malaysia, with its strong monolithic religious tradition, this dual Christian and cultural identity may well be challenged, but Christians need to deal with the pressures of being Christian in Asian societies whilst at the same time being committed to those societies in a wholehearted way.

> Hwa is concerned about forming the identity of Malaysian Christians so that they are seen as genuinely Malaysian. Mission in the Malaysian setting needs to show that Christians are rooted in society.

---

1   Though the heart of this article is interested in Christianity in South East Asia, the challenges faced by Christians in this region are shared by those in other contexts. However, the distinctive problem for Christians in South East Asia is that theological writings that come to Asia from other places (especially pervasive English language materials from the cultures of Europe, North America, and Australasia) do not necessarily interact with Asian cultural issues.

2   For Hwa, Western interpretations of the spiritual and minjung readings which play down the spiritual, both equally avoid the implications of Scripture.

3   This comes from his reading of the New Testament, e.g., Romans 8:14-17. Hwa observes that Samuel talks of Christian identity as an identity as children of God. See also Hwa's *Mangoes or Bananas* (1997, 197).

The character and theology of the church in places like Malaysia must have a genuinely local flavor. Hwa welcomes the contemporary focus on contextualization and indigenization. Cultures need to be brought to the Kingdom to be Christianized, recognizing that in doing so there are cultural elements to be affirmed and some to be left behind. "What is good and right must be brought into the Kingdom of God to become part of our identity in Christ" (Hwa 1997, 3-7). Hwa uses the concept of the Kingdom of God to discuss the need for Christian communities in Asia to build their identity around the values of the Kingdom of God as well as the values that are derived from their own nation and culture.

A clear sense of Kingdom identity involves:
1. The development of an agenda (Hwa 1997, 19) for Asian Christian theology and mission
2. An engagement in mission in Asian social and religious settings
3. The individual and communal life of Christian discipleship.

In this way the theology of the Kingdom is at the heart of theological efforts to establish the Asian identity of the church because the Kingdom deals with both the spiritual (inner world) and the social realities of life (outer world).

Community of the Kingdom

A "Kingdom identity" means taking seriously the place and role of the church in forming the character of both the individual Christian and the Christian community as well as the dynamic that leads to Christian action at various levels. There are three sets of priorities for the church in Asia: to share in the task of sociopolitical change; to evangelistically proclaim the Christian message; and to develop a greater interest in the pastoral needs of the Christian community in its Asian context, especially as this relates to the distinctive spiritual context of Asia (Hwa 1998, 48-52).

These priorities connect to the theology of the Kingdom of God in that the Christian community must:

> …bear witness to the in-breaking of the kingly rule of God…and in its ministry manifest the signs of the kingdom which would include evangelism and the life-changing power of the gospel in personal life, good works and social transformation, exorcism and healing (Hwa 1998, 48-52).

Pastoral structures and leadership of the Kingdom community

Each local Kingdom community needs to develop leadership, pastoral structures, and pastoral practices which are shaped by Asian Christian identity. For pastoral leadership, Hwa stresses the integrity and Christian character of the church leader who must display the Christ-like qualities of servanthood (Hwa 2004, 30). A lack of balance in terms of attitudes to others, finance, and relationships will diminish the integrity of those in leadership.

Pastoral structures need to facilitate a real interaction between individuals and their Christian leaders. The Wesleyan model of small groups and its successors (Hwa 2002) is seen as offering a possible model that, adequately contextualized for Malaysia, takes account of the real needs of Christians in that country. The widespread adoption of small group strategies has facilitated Christian growth and can continue to offer help with Christian living. Pastoral structures need to help Christians deal with ethical issues in daily life; however, much existing Christian writing does not engage with the specifics of Asian countries. Various small group models can help develop a Christian life that is vital, genuine, and able to equip people to deal with the pressures of everyday life in Asia.

ENGAGING WITH RELIGIOUS CONTEXTS IN ASIA

Recognize the impact of pluralism and religious resurgence

For contemporary Christians in Asia, Hwa would like to develop new approaches in the religious sphere. Most Asians are used to dealing with religious plurality: their experience has been different from that of Christians in Western countries in the past. In most Asian contexts, Christianity has been a minority faith, yet within the constraints of other religious cultures, it has continued to be present and sometimes even to grow. In religiously plural contexts, Christians must be people who understand the religious mind of the other communities such as Muslims, Buddhists and so on. This is important for two reasons: one is to establish Christian identity in the face of the plurality of belief in society; the other is that the outward-looking nature of Christianity means that Christians will want to bear witness to their faith in the light of other religious faiths.

> In religiously plural contexts, Christians must be people who understand the religious mind of the other faith communities such as Muslims, Buddhists, etc.

In a well-known essay, Samuel Huntington affirmed that there is a resurgence of traditional cultures and religions in non-Western societies and this is confirmed in Asian societies today (Hwa 2000, 86). Hwa agrees with this aspect of Huntington's analysis and he believes that many members of the elite in Asian societies are drawn to non-Western values (Hwa 2002b). In the Malaysian context, he considers that the Islamic resurgence brings new stresses for the church there, and it has to learn how to deal constructively with these pressures (Hwa 2004, 86).

Spiritual realities

In Asia, there is an intense interest in the other-worldly dimensions of life. Hwa and like-minded colleagues recognize the need for a greater awareness and understanding of the spiritual dimensions of life as experienced by Christians and those of other faiths.[4] These "spiritual realities" in the Asian religious context (Hwa 2004, 28-30) need to be recognized and appreciated so that Christians can respond to the distinctive needs of Asian peoples in appropriate ways.[5] Christian leaders in Asia would like to develop ways to understand and engage with these spiritual realities (Hwa 2002c, 3-27); they would like to help Asian Christians to relate their faith to the other religious perspectives and expressions of spirituality in Asia. Although at present this remains a partly fulfilled intention and vision rather than

---

4   See Solomon on interest in the "spiritual world" in the Chinese diaspora in Singapore (1992, 48-74).
5   On this theme see Lee (2003).

a reality within evangelicalism (Ng 2002), there are signs of progress, though there are still areas which appear to need fresh theological analyses (Thomas 2002, 126ff).

Evangelicals and religion

Christian leaders like Hwa reckon that evangelicals a) often have a less than biblical understanding of religions and cultures and b) suffer from a weak doctrine of general revelation, including "mastery of Asian cultures and religions which is not often found within the evangelical community" (Hwa 2000, 89). Hwa draws on biblical perspectives to set out contours for the debate about other Asian religions, but uses them creatively and flexibly. He stresses the need to draw on a theology of creation which locates all human beings and their religious beliefs in the context of general revelation and is sympathetic to the possibility of working with others for "the redemption of all creation" (Hwa 2000, 90). However, this does not take away from the need to recognize differences between Christianity and other faiths, especially in the areas of belief in Jesus Christ and the Christian view of soteriology. Hwa sees the need for integrity in this area. He stresses that if there is to be a measure of social transformation in societies which are religiously plural, then the existence of a Christian community which demonstrates the reality of its faith so that it promotes such social change is paramount.

Orientation to spiritual realities

Asian Christians need to re-evaluate their own spiritual context and how they offer pastoral care against this backdrop. Hwa notes that Western theology fails when it encounters the spirit world of Asia. Western-derived theologies, even when they address Asian settings, "do not and cannot engage the Asian world of demonic spirits, astrology, and the occult, as well as the wholism of Asian worldviews…" and as a result "fail to speak with power" (Hwa 2005, 53). They do not engage with aspects of human experience that Western thinking, since the Enlightenment, has found difficult to process.

Also, sometimes Christian workers from outside Asian cultures make very negative judgements about religions and cultures without adequately distinguishing key elements. An attitude of "rejecting non-Christian religions as wholly demonic…often rejects much of non-Christian [cultures] on the same grounds by association.…The net result is that often, only what comes out of the west will pass the test of having no pagan or demonic associations." This results in unfortunate consequences. In the Chinese Christian context, "Christians are often told that acupuncture and the martial arts must be fully rejected because of their pagan demonic associations, without analyzing further as to which aspects are good and redeemable and which are demonic and ought to be rejected" (Hwa 2000, 88). This distorts Asian forms of Christian faith and inhibits the formation of a genuinely Asian Christian identity.

Impact of cultural realities—Chinese religions, festivals and ancestral practices

In interacting with Chinese spiritual life, Hwa notes the need to develop pastoral practices that address adequately the family and community alignments of Asian societies. Chinese social structures put a strong emphasis on the group (more than on the individual), and loyalties to family members and especially to parents are strong. Group emphasis, while sometimes hard to pull away from, can also be an important resource for Christians seeking to align themselves with Kingdom values. If changes need to be made in contrast to the opinions of parents, then the individual will need to find that the local church is offering resources to sustain and support through times of transition and pressure.

> If changes need to be made in contrast to the opinions of parents, then the individual will need to find that the local church is offering resources to sustain and support through times of transition and pressure.

Pastoral ministries are important as they relate to healing and freedom from spiritual oppression. Chinese diaspora Christians are faced with many spiritual realities in places such as Malaysia: the worship of idols, the use of charms, and participation in witchcraft and related occultic practices. Such activities necessitate that Christian leaders think carefully about how they shape Christian experiences of "worship and prayer" and how they develop "prophetic and healing gifts" and how they handle "deliverance from demonic bondage" (Hwa 2002d, 9). There are "felt needs" which also need to be discussed and analyzed and which can explain why Asians make religious choices away from Christianity and see it as irrelevant to their deeply held concerns. Despite signs of progress, these areas appear to need fresh theological analysis in Asia (Thomas 2002, 126ff).

Finally, we need to consider the use of "Christian functional substitutes" as these apply to issues like ancestral veneration, funerals, and cultural festivals. At present, although there is considerable discussion of these social/cultural areas of Chinese Christian life, suggestions for what "functional substitutes" might be are much more tentative.[6]

EVANGELISTIC TASKS IN ASIAN RELIGIOUS CONTEXTS

Proclamation—apologetics and witness

Hwa writes that Christians must "empower the church in the evangelistic and pastoral tasks of calling men and women to repentance and faith in Christ and planting and building churches" (Hwa 1997, 57). Mission has the basic aim to make clear the gospel to people in a way that demands a response which will lead to conversion and genuine and meaningful Christian discipleship. The gospel that is proclaimed needs to be a wholistic gospel: a gospel that takes account of the whole of life and that proclaims Jesus as Lord over all of life—"be it spiritual, psychological or ecological, both now and in the world to come" (Hwa 2004, 31ff).

Additionally, proclamation of the gospel should include engaging in responsible interaction with other religions. There needs to be renewed efforts by Asian Christians in the area of apologetics and its witness to those around it. "A careful and sympathetic understanding of another religious tradition can open up new doors for the communication of the gospel through a cogent Christian apologetic" (Hwa 2000, 89ff). This has clear implications for contextual evangelization in Asia.

---

6   See for example Mary Yeo Carpenter (1996, 503-17).

ENGAGING WITH ASIAN SOCIAL CONTEXTS

Recognize the need for wholistic approach

Hwa makes explicit his interest in the application of Christian faith to social engagement when he writes that Christians are not to be "dualistic but fundamentally holistic" (Hwa 2004, 31-32). The idea of a missiology that is not dualistic, separating out evangelism and social action, but rather wholistic, is widely supported in Asia. Hwa positively endorses this emphasis in mission.[7]

Hwa uses the concept of "transformation" to express wholism in Asian contexts:

> …Many of us lack a theology which helps us relate the gospel to the world and which informs and guides us in positive Christian ethical and sociopolitical action in a sinful world. Put in another way we tend to be pietistic and personal, focusing on personal holiness in private lives and an inward spirituality without a corresponding emphasis on social holiness in public life and righteousness in society (Hwa 1998b, 62-63).

The concept of wholism, therefore, helps the Malaysian church relate to the world of economics, to politics, and to social change.

Social witness and engagement is expressed in a distinctive Christian adoption of values and through a life lived out in society that shows these values in practice. As suggested earlier, a Kingdom theology offers a missional perspective and an action plan for everyday life.

Appropriate social engagement in Asian societies

In Malaysia, resurgent Islam endeavors to make a contribution to Malaysian society, engaging in discussions of modernity and postmodernity. Islam generally takes seriously its social dimensions. "Islam has always insisted on bringing every area of life, including economics and politics, into its ambit" (Hwa 1999, 40). Hwa is concerned that, in the Malaysian context, the church take seriously its responsibilities and not opt out of the sphere of civil society and its concerns.

Grappling with Asian values

The "Asian values" debate is part of the contemporary context of Asian discussion about society. Asian cultures are keen to emphasize traditional and indigenous values and seek to forge a future for themselves using their own intellectual resources and categories. At times, such language can be used to stifle debate, participation, and the freedom of minorities. The debate gives opportunities for Asian Christians to participate through the value system of their faith in the Asian societies in which they live. To do this successfully they need to be aware of the sensitivities which surround the debate and to adopt an appropriate discourse.

The debate about traditional Asian values offers Christians the opportunity of introducing a Christian agenda on values to be contrasted with the Asian agenda of values. A Christian values-based agenda can be drawn from the gospel and the Christian Scriptures. To embrace

---

7   See Hwa on Vinay Samuel (1997, 196-205).

and live out the values of the Kingdom provides a concrete agenda that can be shaped to the different societies in which Asian people live. This is a process of dialogue, not imposition. Hwa points to Matthew's gospel and Jesus' teaching on the Kingdom in relation to Christians being salt and light in society (Matt 5:13-16). He notes too the injunction to Christians to be peacemakers (Matt 5:9). Hwa considers Christian values to include an affirmation of family life, adoption of a specific code of sexual morality, and responsible attitudes to wealth and stewardship (Hwa 1999, 66-70). He notes the long Christian tradition of compassion towards the poor and the sick, especially at times of social upheaval.

Developing social ethics
The contextualization of ethics is another critical area of theology to be addressed in Asian contexts. To date, much of the theological discussion of ethics has been based on Western situations and contexts.

> Much of the way we think about Christian ethics has been largely shaped by modern western Christian thinking on the subject. Christian thinking invariably prioritizes principles over relationships. But how do Christian ethics operate in a culture where the order is often reversed? For example, family ties are so close in many Asian societies that nepotism invariably results. Yet if a Christian fails to take care of family members, he or she is also damned in the eyes of his or her culture. Or again, where is the dividing line to be drawn between a bribe and a gift given in appreciation and to cement a relationship? There is obviously the need for the development of a more culturally sensitive ethics (Hwa 2000, 90).

Christians in Asia need to be aware of the interplay between relationships and principles and seek to interpret biblical testimony in a way that does justice to Asian sensitivities whilst seeking to apply the teaching of the Bible. The area of gift-giving, which Western Christians can find hard to negotiate in Asian cultures, relates in part to the importance of relationships and maintaining positive and harmonious relationships with others. Bernard Adeney's work is a helpful starting-point for helping Asians to think through these issues (Adeney 1995). Although Adeney is Western by birth, he has been based in Indonesia for many years and has a deep understanding of the issues involved. Hwa's commitment to this issue is given greater expression in an article on ethics in a series of essays on Malaysian society (Hwa 2010).

MISSION IN ASIA AND CONTEXTUAL DISCIPLESHIP

Towards contextual discipleship in Asia
The discussion of ethics must include our personal conduct. An appropriate ethical stance includes lifestyle choices, such as the use of personal resources and the commitment to being involved in mission in deeper ways.

In the context of Malaysian society, Hwa draws a picture of churches preoccupied with wealth and money-making. Sometimes popular teaching in the Malaysian church is bound up with the prosperity gospel. Hwa contrasts these lifestyle choices with those of John Sung, who seemed to show less interest in matters such as personal wealth (Hwa 1999, 27-28). For Hwa, the challenge of poverty is a reminder to evangelicals of the need to be engaged in society. He disapproves of evangelicals viewing Christian faith simply in terms of personal piety and hopes that Asian evangelicals will break out of this mold. Hwa is aware that in a society like Malaysia, with its growing economy and increasing opportunity, the prosperity gospel has apparent attractions for some evangelicals (Hwa 1999, 20, 25-26, 44), and he recognizes the pitfalls of this.

In missions, churches can be too ready simply to give money from a distance rather than face the hard challenges involved in a deep identification with other cultures by living amongst them. The desire to give must be tempered by an understanding of local situations and an appreciation of the potentially negative impact of money shared without due regard for issues of dependency. The church must understand the need to identify with others for a genuine encounter in mission. There is often a temptation for wealthy Christians to go into other South East Asian countries for short-term trips and to offer financial resources to help. "O how the people love us" (Hwa 2008, 10). This is a short-sighted, and not always very healthy, strategy. The deeper failure is to recognize the challenges that mission brings for us as individuals if we are to be committed to the long haul. This is not just true for those who move overseas to minister cross-culturally but for those in Asian societies who move to the provinces or to poorer regions.

CONCLUDING REFLECTIONS

A number of significant realities about contextualization emerge from Hwa's theology of mission. Mission in Asia must be done with a clear grasp of God's purposes for the world. These purposes have an integrative and wholistic character and aim to produce the formation of a Christian Kingdom community which lives life in light of the vertical dimension (of our relationship with God) and the horizontal dimension (of our life with others). Against that understanding of mission we need to take seriously the concerns of the specific context in which we find ourselves. For those living in East Asia this means taking account of the social, religious, and cultural influences that Christians face in these societies. These social and religious contexts will shape contextualization no matter our perspective on the Bible itself. The relative priorities that Christians give to aspects of mission will be shaped by context and cannot simply be decided *a priori* on the basis of a reading of the Bible in a vacuum. This is an important point for Asian societies, where issues of social justice, poverty, and corruption make the development of Christian values and lifestyles that demonstrate integrity paramount.

The relative priorities that Christians give to aspects of mission will be shaped by context and cannot simply be decided *a priori* on the basis of a reading of the Bible in a vacuum.

Contextualization means more than simply appropriate ways of responding to the sociopolitical context. It also involves a commitment to understanding and responding to the religious contexts of Asia. Islam shapes Christianity in Malaysia in that it affirms the importance of religious faith being relevant to all of life, and yet it is an environment which does not readily welcome Christian responses in the public square. Hwa encourages Christians not to retreat from these challenges and to privatize faith, but to develop wholistic approaches to mission that address such issues. The religious context means that spiritual realities also need to be addressed. The way in which theology deals with religious practices forms part of the activity of contextualization. Contextualization requires an awareness of religious customs, religious issues, and religious and cultural festivals. Contextualization extends to the apologetic work of the church, which needs greater attention in many Asian societies. The pastoral and evangelistic tasks of the church need to be shaped in relation to specific contexts and specific concerns.

In responding to all these issues, models of contextual theology should not be formulated around Western situations, texts or people—this thought is at the heart of Hwa Yung's thinking. If we hold the Bible firmly in one hand, the other hand should be stretched out to hold on to the community where we live and work: that is our context. Our thinking and theology needs to keep pace with the needs of our context. Christians who live in Asian contexts must seek to build an Asian Christian identity that takes seriously their Christian identity, shaped by the Bible, and their Asian identity, shaped by their Asian contexts. It is only as they hold these two aspects of their identity in an appropriate tension that they will be able to create a genuine Asian Christian identity that will bear witness to the gospel of the Kingdom as a gift for Asia. Hwa Yung is one Asian thinker and church leader who offers real theological insight and practical wisdom about how to do so.

QUESTIONS FOR REFLECTION:

1. In what ways has Western-dominated theology distorted the gospel in your country of origin or country of service, because of its blind spot? What correctives are needed, and how would you try to bring that about?
2. Hwa suggests that in Western theology and cultures principles take precedence over relationships, while the opposite is true in Asia. What are the strengths and pitfalls of each approach?
3. What elements of another religious faith expressed in culture, (e.g., Islam, Hinduism, etc.), could you affirm as evidence of general revelation? How would you support this from Scripture?

PART TWO

CONTEXTUALIZATION AT WORK

CHAPTER 10

A PERSONAL JOURNEY

Chua How Chuang

Not long after my wife Kaori and I arrived in Japan as missionaries with OMF International some ten years ago, a senior colleague told us the following story: A missionary was preaching the gospel in a public evangelistic meeting. Toward the end of his talk he gave the usual impassioned plea: "If you accept Jesus Christ as your personal Lord and Savior, you will have everlasting life. This means that after you die on earth, you will go to heaven where you will live forever." Unfortunately, no one responded to the missionary's invitation. After the meeting, however, an elderly lady came up and expressed her concerns to the missionary. "Teacher, why do you assume that we want to live forever? Besides, I don't want to go to heaven. When I die, I want to be where my ancestors are." I do not know if this story is true, but certainly even in our first term of missionary service in Japan there were more than a few occasions when we encountered variations of that same anecdotal theme—namely, the great difficulty on the part of many Japanese people in understanding the gospel as it is presented to them.

It did not take me long to discover that a key reason for this cognitive difficulty is the clash of worldviews. Most Westerners, raised on Judeo-Christian moral foundations, see everlasting life as a value and consequently assume that everyone wants to go to heaven after they die. However, in a culture deeply influenced by Buddhism the existential reality of life is suffering, and to desire everlasting life is to desire perpetual suffering. This religious mindset is complicated further by the ancestors, who continue to be an indelible part of the Japanese psyche. It is hard to preach about going to heaven when the hearers care so much about where their ancestors are. One of the earliest and most important lessons I learned is the necessity to understand the people that we are reaching—the way they think and make sense of life. I went to Japan with two theological degrees, thinking that I was fully equipped to preach the gospel. It did not take long for me to discover how much more I needed to learn. I might have theological knowledge, but I certainly did not have the necessary cultural knowledge.

One day I had a prolonged conversation with a Japanese man who not only was asking me difficult questions about life and death, but was fervently trying to convince me that Buddhism is true. I was, of course, zealous for the gospel, but I was frustrated that my zeal came to nothing because he just could not make sense of the message that I was trying to share. And since I knew next to nothing about Japanese Buddhism, I was not able to make any connection to help him understand. It was a humbling experience, and since then, I have always kept Proverbs 19:2 in my mind, "It is not good to have zeal without knowledge, nor to be hasty and miss the way." I learned that sharing the gospel in a cross-cultural situation involves not only a truth encounter, but also a worldview encounter. To understand a worldview, it is not enough to just learn about the culture in a classroom setting. What is more important is the need to cultivate a reflective mind-set in our missionary practice as we constantly engage with the people whom we seek to share the gospel with. And of course, this requires time, patience, and a teachable heart.

Besides the worldview barrier, I learned that the difficulty on the part of many Japanese people in understanding the gospel is being reinforced by the prevalent view that Christianity is a Western religion and, as such, it does not have universal relevance. Indeed I have had some interesting encounters in which my Japanese friends expressed surprise when they discovered that I was a missionary. In their minds, all missionaries are Westerners, and they could not quite make sense of how I, as an Asian, could be a missionary. Theirs is, of course, a misconception, but it is not a totally unfounded one. Most of the missionaries working in Japan have been, and still are, Westerners, and the gospel that they bring with them is still colored with a distinctive Western flavor. For instance, many missionaries tend to define sin as "missing the mark," only to experience a stone wall of non-comprehension. This definition, while biblical, is not the only, or even full, biblical explanation of sin. But it is one which is consonant with the Western moral understanding of law and guilt. Thinking Japanese people would often ask, "Why is there a mark? Who sets the mark?" In a communitarian culture like Japan, which is defined less by law and guilt and more by relationships and shame, it is more helpful to utilize the biblical emphases corresponding to the latter when explaining the meaning of sin. I was helped by a Japanese theologian who defined sin as "betrayal of God's love." In my experience, I found that to be more easily grasped by Japanese people than the concept of "missing the mark."

> In a communitarian culture like Japan, which is defined less by law and guilt and more by relationships and shame, it is more helpful to define sin as "betrayal of God's love" over "missing the mark."

It was a revelation for me to discover that we often confuse between our particular cultural understanding of the gospel and the gospel itself. This is a blind spot that afflicts all missionaries, not only our colleagues from the West. To be a reflective practitioner, therefore, means minimally three things for me. First, it means that I need to understand the people whom we are reaching. Second, it means I need to be critically aware of my own cultural presuppositions in my understanding the gospel and to be willing to learn from my Japanese brothers and sisters a different biblical and theological perspective. Finally, cultivating a reflective missionary practice means looking for creative ways of preaching the gospel so that it is culturally understandable without compromising its biblical integrity. My goal as a missionary in Japan is not to build a Singaporean or Chinese church, but a biblical, Japanese church.

Let me end with a personal testimony. Last year, we visited my wife's 93-year-old grandmother in the hospital. The doctor informed us that she could die soon. Grandma was frail and could barely speak. But she looked worried. For years, we had been sharing the gospel with her but she just could not understand what we said. This time, sensing her anxiety, Kaori asked her, "Grandma, do you have peace in your heart?" Grandma shook her head slowly. Kaori then told her that if she would confess her sins and put her trust in Jesus, she would receive the gift of "eternal peace." Kaori held Grandma's hands, and asked Grandma to squeeze her hands if she wanted to receive Jesus as her Lord and Savior. To our delight, Grandma squeezed Kaori's hands. We then prayed with Grandma, asking God to forgive her sins and to give her the gift of eternal peace. While Grandma had difficulty grasping the concept of "eternal life," she found it easy to understand "eternal peace" because it spoke to her condition. Of course, what we shared was not the complete gospel. We did not even know how much Grandma was able to understand. But I believe what Grandma heard was sufficient for her to make a decision to put her faith in Christ. Since then, by God's grace, Grandma's health improved. A year later, this summer, we visited her again. And we were amazed and encouraged to hear that Grandma still remembered the prayer that she prayed last year.

This episode is a huge encouragement to us, not only personally, but also in our ministry as reflective messengers of the gospel. While we seek to obey the Lord's command to make disciples and teach them "everything" he has entrusted to us (Matthew 28:20), we will do well by beginning to look for creative points in the culture where the gospel can make its first and decisive entry.

Chua How Chuang is a Singaporean missionary church planter serving in Japan.

QUESTIONS FOR REFLECTION

1. From Chua How Chuang's experience, why is it so important to enter into another person's worldview, and how might we learn to do that?
2. In much of Asia, Christianity continues to be regarded as a Western religion. How might attention to contextualization help change that perception?
3. In much of the West, especially Europe, Christianity is regarded at best as irrelevant and at worst as a harmful lie. What might be some "creative points in the culture where the gospel can make its first and decisive entry"?

CHAPTER 11

PERSONAL REFLECTIONS ON CONTEXTUALIZATION

Jim Chew

Missionaries from the United States brought the gospel to my grandparents. My father's mother came to Christ in Malacca, Malaya through Methodist missionaries. These missionaries majored on education and started schools. My grandmother's father was keen not only to have his daughters educated in English, but to have a school started in his home. My grandmother was the first convert to be baptized and was also the first local teacher of the Methodist Girls School.[1] Both my paternal and maternal grandparents were "Straits-born Chinese" (or "Peranakan") as they had mingled with Malays and spoke Malay. As I reflect, I am thankful my background has helped me value other cultures.

With exposure to Western education, those converted to Christianity were more than happy to adopt Western patterns while holding to some of their own customs. These would sometimes cause tensions. For example, the selection of a husband for my grandmother would normally be done by her parents. But because my grandmother insisted on having a Christian for her husband, the choice became difficult because there were no eligible Christian men in Malacca. Her father had to journey to Singapore. With the help of missionaries, he met five fine Christian men for his daughters, and my grandmother, the eldest daughter, was matched with the one who was to become her husband. The Methodist archives describe some of these customs which to us today would be quite hilarious (Lau 2003). The Methodist mission through schools bore much fruit. My father, Benjamin Chew, trusted Christ as a teenager through the Anglo-Chinese School when the evangelist E. Stanley Jones spoke.

My mother's side of the family was influenced by Presbyterian missionaries and prominent lay leaders. My parents were also ministered to by Brethren missionaries. When my parents married in Singapore, they were already members of the Brethren Assembly. The churches

---

1   See *My Times Are in His Hands* (1991, 23-25).

that were founded followed the patterns of church governance and liturgical practices of the Methodist, Anglican, Presbyterian or Brethren from England or America.

At an early age, I responded to the gospel through New Zealander J. Oswald Sanders who spoke at my church. I loved my Bible, which was the Authorized King James Version, the Bible used by all congregations. The many Scripture verses I memorized were in the King James. Our leaders prayed using "Thee," "Thou," and "Thy" and we were taught that this was the reverential way to address God. The hymns and choruses we sang were also in "old English." They remain meaningful to me—to this day.

Many Singaporeans, former "Buddhists" (though more accurately, practicing a mixture of Chinese religions) and "freethinkers" (a favorite expression of those who considered themselves broad minded) turned to Christianity as their new "religion." Conversion was commonly viewed as changing religions—often through the rite of baptism when one would sometimes be given a Christian name. Some Christian leaders would scarcely know the difference between true conversion or converting to Christianity as a religion. Christianity in Asia, then and now, is generally viewed as a Western religion. Paul Johnson made the piercing statement that "though Christianity was born in Asia, when it was re-exported there from the sixteenth century onwards it failed to acquire an Asian face" (1976, 410). He explained, "It was the inability of Christianity to…de-Europeanize itself, which caused it to miss its opportunities." Christianity came to Singapore with British colonization. Colonialism, however, was a political issue and not a religious one. I don't ever remember Christians speaking of "cultural imperialism."

The People's Republic of China was proclaimed on 1 October 1949. China began to expel missionaries, and in the early 1950s, the China Inland Mission, later renamed Overseas Missionary Fellowship (OMF), set up its headquarters in Singapore. Churches were to benefit from the presence of many OMF missionaries. "Parachurch" organizations such as Scripture Union, Youth for Christ, and The Navigators also came to Singapore. These groups influenced our churches in Bible reading, teaching, evangelism, and discipleship. Theological seminaries were founded and also had evangelical teachers.

Being English-speaking, I had limited contact with Chinese-speaking congregations. In some Chinese services I attended, the worship patterns and hymn tunes were (except for language) similar to English-speaking churches. Dr. Bobby Sng's book, *In His Good Time,* gives the story of the church in Singapore (2003). Today, there are English-speaking and Chinese-speaking (some in dialects) churches, and also Tamil-speaking and other language groups. However, to this day, to my knowledge, there is no official Malay-Muslim congregation, though there have been some Muslims who have become followers of Christ and are part of a Christian congregation. Would "contextualization" be an issue? I believe so.

During my student days, a university-mate from a staunch Hindu background received Christ. He did not change his name to a "Thomas" or a "John" so common in India. If he did, it would have made it more difficult to influence his family for Christ.

I first encountered the concept of "contextualization" when working with university students in Malaysia. (According to David Bosch, the term "contextualization" was first coined in the early 1970s [1991, 240].) For example, I found some Malay Muslims open to talking about religious things. I knew that it was against the law to "convert" Muslims to any other faith. I thought about the relevance of the gospel to Muslims. I had a conviction that getting them to change their religion to "Christianity" and to join a "church"—adopting a Christian culture— was not the mandate of Christ. However, these seed thoughts were dormant.

I had a conviction that getting Muslims to change their religion to "Christianity" and to join a "church"—adopting a Christian culture— was not the mandate of Christ.

In Malaysia, my wife and I learned the importance of applying the principle of "incarnation" by opening our home, sharing our lives, and having students and young graduates live with us. They came from non-Christian backgrounds. Some students we discipled later ministered cross-culturally (see Bok 2001, also Scott 1970, 203-208).

In the early 1970s, we were sent by The Navigators to New Zealand where we served for four years. At first, it seemed strange to us as Asians to go to what we thought was a "Christian" country. Our "mission field" was primarily the university, where we discipled New Zealanders (and not Asian or international students). In order to identify with these students, I enrolled in a course on campus. Our New Zealand friends helped us learn the culture. Since we spoke English, there was no need for language learning. As in Malaysia, our home became the center for ministry with many coming to Christ. There wasn't a big need to work at "contextualizing" the message. We studied the Scriptures, developed a sense of community among the students, and gave them a vision for their lives—to seek God's Kingdom above all. From New Zealand, young missionary trainees were sent, mainly to Asia, for exposure to cross-cultural missions. Some continued in long-term missions. As missionary sending increased, I realized that missionary preparation and orientation was absolutely vital. On the mission field, missionaries were starting to pioneer ministries among Muslims, Hindus, Buddhists, and Chinese in East Asia.

My wife and I returned to Asia in the mid-1970s. Seeing the need to prepare mission candidates (both from the West and from Asia) for their work, my colleagues and I had long discussions on culture and contextualization. We studied the Scriptures and read books, papers, and articles on culture and cultural anthropology. One textbook was "The Church and Cultures" by Louis Luzbetak. I also read books by Christian anthropologists Eugene Nida (1963), Paul Hiebert (1978), and others, as well as articles in *Evangelical Missions Quarterly*. David Hesselgrave's book, *Communicating Christ Cross-Culturally*, was helpful (1991). I recognized the importance of understanding "worldviews." The concept can be complex as a worldview is a composite of beliefs from one's culture, family, and religion and determines how one views and interprets reality. From this worldview will flow a person's values, which in turn will influence behavior. There can be no behavioral change without transformation within the heart of a person. I observed why missionaries like E. Stanley Jones made an impact because of their understanding of their host culture's worldview. I remember hearing Jones preach on "conversion" defining it as a "change, gradual or sudden, when one passes from the kingdom of self to the Kingdom of God." He was certainly passionate about the Kingdom of God. He wrote, "Jesus was obsessed with the Kingdom of God....The Kingdom of God was the only thing he called good news" (Jones 1968, 153). Surely, that's what we are called to advance among the nations—the gospel of Jesus and his Kingdom.

I strengthened my convictions about contextualization, rooting these in the Scriptures. Jesus Christ, of course, is our prime example. "The Word became flesh and dwelt among us" (John 1:14). All New Testament authors wrote "in context." Paul was constantly ministering contextually and his messages were relevant to his different audiences. For example, his sermon to the Jews in Pisidian Antioch (Acts 13:14-41) was very different from his message at the meeting of the Areopagus (Acts 17:22-31). Contextualization will affect not only our message but our lifestyles and the ways we minister.

In 1978, at a Congress on Evangelism, I presented a paper and spoke on "Culture and Religious Background in Relation to Conversion" (1978). By then, contextualization was becoming a much-discussed concept. The *Evangelical Missions Quarterly* (January 1978) had an issue on contextualization. In January 1978, there was also a landmark Consultation on "The Gospel and Culture." The Willowbank Report on the Consultation is a must-read.[2] One section of the report worth re-reading is on "Missionary Humility." "Ethnocentrism" is an obstacle we face in crossing cultures. None of us can claim to be exceptions! Peter (in Acts 10) is a classic example. Dean Flemming writes about Peter's conversion from his Jewish ethnocentrism. "The 'conversion' of the messenger must come before the conversion of those who need the message"(2005). Humility means taking the trouble to understand and really appreciate the culture of those to whom we go.

> "The 'conversion' of the messenger must come before the conversion of those who need the message." Dean Flemming

In the 1980s, I continued studying the Scriptures with my colleagues on issues of contextualization. We held consultations with mission practitioners ministering among Hindus, Muslims, Buddhists and Secularists. Paul's letter to Galatians was one of the key epistles for our study and discussion, together with the history of the early church in Acts and in subsequent church history with many lessons to learn. A project on "The Scriptural Roots of Ministry" was launched. We were concerned about the purity of the gospel, and with it, the mobility of the gospel to spread in context. Studying the Scriptures was both mind stretching and also liberating. Two key questions were: "What is the gospel?" and "What is church"? On the latter question, Western ecclesiology has highly influenced concepts and strategies of so-called "church planting." Such ecclesiology can be extremely disadvantageous among hostile religious contexts—and this could affect the mobility of the gospel. How does the Bible view the whole matter of "church" and "doing church"?

I took a sabbatical in New Zealand where I had discussions with missionary statesman, J. Oswald Sanders, one of my mentors. As we talked about contextualization and mission issues, he encouraged me to write a book. I wrote *When You Cross Cultures* (1990). I was

---

2   http://www.lausanne.org/willowbank-1978/lop-2.html.

particularly impressed by the example of Paul and his team in 1 Thessalonians 1:5-9 and 2:1-12. They contextualized not just their message, but also their lives and lifestyle. In my book, I mentioned the five stages of cultural communication (owing much to Jim Petersen, who had led a seminar on contextualization) (1990, 8-10).

1. The communicator must first gain "Rapport." He needs to be aware of his own cultural background and free himself from traditions that will inhibit him from relating to the new culture. The continuous learning of the host culture's background is essential. Rapport takes place when the people in the receiving culture say, "I now want to hear what you have to say."

2. The second stage is "Comprehension," which occurs when the receiver says, "I now understand what you have to say."

3. The third stage is for an "Equivalent Response" on the part of the receiver—"It means the same to me as it does to you." What the messenger has communicated makes sense and brings about a positive response.

4. The fourth is "Relevance to Life." The message transforms the receiver's life and there is true conversion.

5. Finally, we see "Mature Colaborship" in the advance of the gospel. The apostolic team has assumed its role and the receivers spread the gospel in context undistorted by cultural traditions. As Jim Petersen states: "The issue in contextualization is the truth and mobility of the gospel…It means taking care that it remains undistorted by the culture of the hearer as it is being received. The Gospel plus anything…becomes a non-Gospel" (1990, 10-11).

In practice, this process can be complex and even messy. One obvious problem comes from one's own traditions. The Council at Jerusalem (Acts 15) had to convene to deal with this problem and Galatians was written because "the truth of the gospel" was being threatened. We see Paul in heated battle with Peter on this issue. James' words in Acts 15:19 are a reminder "that we should not make it difficult for the Gentiles who are turning to God."

My understanding was enhanced by Paul Hiebert's book, *Anthropological Reflections on Missiological Issues,* where he writes about "bounded sets" and "centered sets" (1994, 110-136). Western culture and churches often think and operate as bounded sets with a Greek worldview of reality. Hiebert examines Hebrew culture as a "centered set." This helped me to see the dangers of "Churchianity" (promoting the traditions and forms of church), of promoting Christianity (as a religion), and of not focusing on the Person of Christ.

In the 1980s, more Asians were responding to the challenge of cross-cultural missions, many going as bi-vocational tentmakers to restricted access countries. The lack of missionary preparation and pre-field orientation became evident. In Singapore, mission leaders from eight mission societies met, and under the leadership of Dr. James Taylor of Overseas Missionary Fellowship, formed the Asia Cross-Cultural Training Institute (ACTI). We developed a curriculum, which included Cross-Cultural Living and Ministry, Contextualization, and

Cultural Anthropology. ACTI continues to function well. Its September 2007 publication, *Asian Mission* focused on "Contextualization and the Church."[3]

Churches are growing in Africa, Asia, and in Latin America. When evangelical statesman John Stott was asked about this enormous growth, his response was that the growth was a fulfillment of God's promise to Abraham. When asked how he evaluated this growth, he said, "The answer is, 'growth without depth.'"[4] This speaks again of the importance of laying the foundations of the gospel well. It also emphasizes the importance of establishing our churches, ensuring that true spiritual transformation is taking place. In doing so, I have learned the importance of concepts such as function, form, and meaning. Are the functions and forms relevant as we see the work of God in the growth of faith communities?

Finally, in the past decade, the issue of "C5/Insider Movements" has come to the fore. The concept began with John Travis (a pseudonym) in 1998, who proposed a scale (or continuum), C1-C6, describing six types of "Christ-centered communities" (that's what the "C" stands for) found in Muslim contexts (405-408). "C5" refers to Muslim believers who identify themselves as "Muslim followers of Jesus." I don't intend to enter this debate as many papers have been written on this subject.[5] This issue has generated much discussion, sometimes with more heat than light. Do keep in mind that C1-C6 began as an analytical (and not a prescriptive) tool. It was devised by an American ministering in a Muslim country. My American friends think in terms of matrices and spectra (as an Asian co-worker reminded me). These are helpful. However, Asians, and certainly most Muslims, don't have discussions using such a paradigm. We usually communicate through stories (as Jesus did).

Having met some believers in these "insider movements" whose lives have been transformed, each community would have their stories. They worship God deeply and are seeing the movement of the gospel among their own relational networks. I visualize the ongoing work of the Holy Spirit in their lives. I can't help thinking of the years the Apostle Paul took to see the growth of the church at Corinth (see Chew 2007, 50-63). Similarly, the apostolic ministries among these believers have seen fruit. In one Asian country where race, religion, language, and politics all reinforce each other, C5 seems to work best. My plea is for critics to pray more for these "insider movements" and affirm the work of God. The discussions continue and so must our attitude of being learners.

---

3   Website www.acti-singapore.org (look under "PRESS").
4   *Christianity Today*, October 2006.
5   For further research, see *Evangelical Missions Quarterly*, October 1998, articles by Phil Parshall and John Travis, 404-415; Joshua Massey, "His Ways are Not our Ways," *EMQ*, April 1999; *International Journal of Frontier Missions*, Spring 2000, Volume 17, articles by John Travis, Joshua Massey, Bernard Dutch; John and Anna Travis, "Appropriate Approaches in Muslim Contexts," in *Appropriate Christianity*, ed. Charles Kraft (Pasadena, CA: William Carey Library, 2005), 397-414; Bill Nikides, "Evaluating 'Insider Movements': C5 (Messianic Muslims)," *St. Francis Magazine*, No .4, March 2006, published by Interserve and Arab Vision; *International Journal of Frontier Missiology*, January-March 2007 Volume 24:1, articles by Gary Corwin, Herbert Hoefer, J. Dudley Woodberry, Kevin Higgins; *International Journal of Frontier Missiology*, Volume 24:2 (www.ijfm.org/archives.htm).

Some years ago, I was told that these growing believers from a particular people group did a prolonged Bible study on worship. It would have been a grand study! I often try to visualize the scene in Revelation 5 and look forward to worshipping with these believers in heaven! John Piper's words are a powerful reminder— "Missions is not the ultimate goal of the church. Worship is. Missions exists because worship doesn't. Worship is ultimate…because God is ultimate. When this age is over and the countless millions of the redeemed fall on their faces before the throne of God, missions will be no more….Worship abides forever" (1993, 11). That's ultimate reality!

> "Missions is not the ultimate goal of the church. Worship is. Missions exists because worship doesn't." John Piper

Jim Chew is the Asia-Pacific Missions Coordinator for the Navigators, now living in New Zealand.

QUESTIONS FOR REFLECTION

1. "The 'conversion' of the messenger must come before the conversion of those who need the message" (Dean Flemming). What examples of this can you find in Scripture? What is the implication for your own life?

2. Jim Chew suggests five stages of cultural communication: rapport, comprehension, equivalent response, relevance to life, and mature colaborship. What might these involve and look like in relation to your discipling of someone of another faith, both for yourself and for the other person/community?

3. "The Gospel plus anything…becomes a non-Gospel" (Jim Petersen). What steps do we need to take to try to reduce the "pluses"?

CHAPTER 12

THE TRANSFORMATION OF SOCIETY

Adapting Wolof Values to Touch Society
Adama Diouf, translated by J. Bornman

The transformation of society is the goal of any ideology, religion, government, or business. The founders of African independence who created our African nations desired to change society. Today the NGOs, having seen that governments have failed to transform society, seek to work outside of the government structures. Therefore the deep transformation of society is an old idea, but if we look at history the results are disappointing. History does not show us many successful changes. Some work for a while, maybe ten or fifteen years, but then they fail. The USSR is one example, but there are many others.

As believers in Jesus, we too are working on the idea of a community transformation. Let us not fall in the same traps. The only transformation that has lasted is one that is ignored by historians. Major, lasting, transformational changes occurred during and after Jesus' lifetime for the communities that believed in him.

Beginning with Acts 2 and 6 we can see what happened in the lives of Jesus' disciples and the early church. How did a mixed cultural group find their way to a shared set of values? They started sharing the same goals in life.

Jesus said, "The son of man came to…heal the lame, make the blind see, and set the prisoners free" (Luke 2). The church is the biggest silent revolution in the history of the world. What the church is achieving is what all the great leaders and reformers hoped to create. It is a revolution that is founded on God's Word that uses no violence and perseveres despite all challenges. No other philosophy has given us this. This is something God created. The church is for all times and all places.

It is through the church that we must start to look at how to transform Wolof society. We need to look at Wolof values and see how they fit into this biblical vision of transformation.

First, who are the Wolof? This is not a simple question to answer. The force of wolofization is a great wave that is sweeping across Sénégal.

Five centuries ago the Wolof ethnic group was the smallest in Sénégal. Since 1960 they have become one third of the nation. (This process of wolofization needs to be studied by Christians to discover how we are to respond to this change. However, this does not fit in our discussion today.) The Wolof are a mixed people with influences from Egypt, North Africa, and every other ethnic group in Sénégal. The mixed nature of their culture gives this people a great capacity for communication and effective interaction with any culture. Their values have been tools that have allowed them to achieve influence throughout Sénégal.

According to Ibader Thiam there are seven Wolof values, and four are of greatest value. If Wolof society can be pictured as a table, these four values would form the four legs of the table. I will cite these values and then discuss how we can use these values to evaluate the ways they might be used as a means of transforming society biblically. I Corinthians 9:19-23 says:

> Though I am free and belong to no one, I have made myself a slave to everyone, to win as many as possible. To the Jews I became like a Jew, to win the Jews. To those under the law I became like one under the law (though I myself am not under the law), so as to win those under the law. To those not having the law I became like one not having the law (though I am not free from God's law but am under Christ's law), so as to win those not having the law. To the weak I became weak, to win the weak. I have become all things to all people so that by all possible means I might save some. I do all this for the sake of the gospel, that I may share in its blessings.

If we follow the strategy of this passage we can adopt the Wolof values to get close to the Wolof heart…as long as we don't make the error of following culture instead of the Bible.

WOLOF VALUES: THE FOUR LEGS OF THE TABLE

JOM is the characteristic of honor that helps a person squarely meet any challenge that might bring dishonor to the dignity of the family or the clan. The idea of *jom* invokes courage. *Jom* demands that the individual must not only be part of the clan, but that he must defend his honor and the honor of the clan. When the *jom* of the person is threatened, it is the entire clan that is threatened, and one must react to protect the clan and one's own self. If you don't have *jom*, you no longer have a place in society. You can no longer have a wife. You have turned your back on society. You have failed to defend your community. You are no longer a member of it. You will be excluded by members of the community.

KOLERE puts a person in a position of being unable to betray another person. If I have *kolere*, I can no longer betray anyone. It is the summit of personhood. This is why it so hard to convert a Wolof person to faith in Jesus. Conversion to another religion is a betrayal of *kolere*. A person who has converted feels the worst about losing *kolere* and *jom*. *Kolere* is a link that connects the person to his community. For example, a Tiijaani will feel such a strong connection to his community, that even if he agrees with the Mourides, he can't leave the Tiijaans because of *kolere*. Because of this there are many Wolof Christians that we will never know about because they will never leave their community. Imagine a young soldier who flees, deserts in the midst of battle, and later meets his friends at a dance. This picture gives insight to the way a Wolof person would feel if he left and broke faith with his community. *Kolere* is an extremely important value in Wolof society.

MUŃ is patience in all trials, a silent patience that supports suffering. It is a patience that is full of *kolere*. *Muń* absolutely needs *jom* and *fiit*. Without *fiit* and *jom* you can't *muń*. This value is especially required of women. Without this value in the wife, the household is of little value. The foundation of *muń* is in *baax*. "*Ku amul baax mënal muń.*" Translation: without goodness you can't be patient. Goodness is the essence of *muń*. In trials and conflict, *muń* does not seek revenge. It is not only patience in the English sense, but it is a value that always finds in the end what is good and beautiful. Some think that *muń* is just patience. No, this is the great quality we see in the Wolof woman: goodness and courage that has as its end, forgiveness. I believe that because of this value, Sénégal has been able to avoid great catastrophes.

TERANGA: if there is anything Sénégal is known for, it is this value. Many translate this as hospitality, but it is much more than what we know of as hospitality. *Teranga* is hospitality but with the goal of impressing the guest. It is not just showing hospitality to a friend and it is not something that you have to do, but it is the joy of seeking and finding the happiness of the person you are serving. My grandmother shows *teranga* wonderfully. She always seeks the happiness of those who came to visit her. She always has an extra bowl of food ready in case someone arrives after the meal.

The guest hides what will make them happy, and the host needs to discover what will help that person find happiness. *Teranga* is a hospitality where we are engaged and seeking the happiness of the other person. You who receive *teranga* have to give the impression you don't want what you really want. The reverse of *teranga* is that the guest pulls back and allows the host to give what he or she is able to give. And the other person must insist that they don't need it. For example, if the guest loves *supukanja,* he or she will not show this right away and may even try to hide it. But finally the host will discover what the guest likes and make the best *supukanja* she can for her guest. The whole thing is a game in the best sense and the game continues throughout the meal. They give you the best pieces of meat and push the rice towards you and you must give the impression that you are not wanting any more and push back. This is NOT that they are playing around. When you sense that the rice is diminishing your *jom* must assert itself. *Teranga* always has a two-way sense.

Reflecting on *jom, muń, kolere* and *teranga*: Are these values in contradiction with the biblical text? How can they be affirmed?

COMPARING WOLOF VALUES WITH BIBLICAL VALUES

Are *jom, muń, kolere,* and *teranga* in contradiction with the biblical text? Or can they be affirmed?

Let's consider *kolere*: The celebration of the very first communion is the clearest place we can see this value functioning in a biblical context. Jesus said to his disciples that he was eager to eat with them, and they had been faithful to the end. The eleven all knew the last hours were upon them, and Peter, using his *jom*, says, "I will never leave you." The disciples had used much *muń* to arrive at this point. They had been insulted and mistreated and circumstances had been difficult for them. Jesus said, "I am eager to eat this meal with you." The community connection that makes it impossible to separate from your community was active here, but the disciples did not make it. They broke *kolere*. Only Jesus could go to the cross. Jesus guarded and kept his *kolere*. Jesus, when he returned in John 21, knew how difficult it was for them to have broken *kolere* with him. Jesus says to Peter, "Guard my sheep." Peter suffered greatly because he broke *kolere*. Jesus showed that his *kolere* has no limit.

We could say much about how *muñ* is also is included in the fruit of the spirit. In Numbers 12:3 it is written: "Moïse était un homme fort *patient*, plus qu'aucun homme sur la face de la terre" (Moses was a very long-suffering and patient man, more than anyone else on the face of the earth). *Muñ* is goodness, beauty, and a good end. God had proposed to destroy the people of Israel and make a new people from his descendents, and Moses showed his *muñ* and said, "No."

All of the New Testament invites us to exercise hospitality. This Senegalese *teranga* means if someone comes, you will abandon your bed so that another person can sleep there. If it is time to eat, you quit eating so that your guest can eat. We always say, "Come and eat." "*Ëggsil.*" If you see a Wolof family and they are eating and they do not invite you to eat, you know there is a serious problem. The Bible says in Heb 13:2: "Be not forgetful to entertain strangers: for thereby some have entertained angels unawares."

These types of values function in a community setting. This is not to say that these values don't exist in individualistic societies, but that they take another form. Certainly Wolof believers will face a cultural shock if the church does not seem to have strong community loyalty and values, or when they see evangelism so often focused toward individuals. This culture shock is normal because those who are planting the church today are not of Wolof background. The period of shock that accompanies the planting phase needs to be studied both by the Senegalese and missionaries who come.

The most difficult step for me is how to make the jump from understanding these values into the phase of the transformation of society, through capturing the intent of these values and this society and transforming them for Christ.

CONCLUSION
We must not lose sight of the fact that only the Holy Spirit has successfully achieved the transformation of society, both in Acts 2 and in our day. As we have noted, all human projects of transformation have failed. We need to realize that all our efforts will depend on the Holy Spirit. We need the help of the Spirit and the Word.

> We must not lose sight of the fact that only the Holy Spirit has successfully achieved the transformation of society.

A study needs to be written on the Wolof values, which could be read in the churches and studied by missionaries to see how understanding these values will bring value to the church. If you read the Bible with Wolof eyes, you see interesting things. Here is one example: Jesus is walking with the two disciples on the Emmaus road, and they do not recognize him. When they arrive at their destination, the disciples say that it's dark and invite Jesus to stay with them. But Jesus says, "No, I will go on a little farther." He has shown his willingness to continue on. Jesus really wants his "*supukanja*" but he hides this desire. The disciples are the "*supakanja*" that Jesus wanted to eat, but Jesus in the cultural game gives the impression that he will go farther. The disciples insist, "No, it is dark." Jesus responds to their *teranga,* and the evening ends in a meal. Jesus, even though he respected *teranga,* then broke with its rules. The invited one should not have taken the initiative to pray and break the bread. It is in doing this that the disciples recognize him. This sensitive adaptation of Jesus opens the door for the Wolof to receive the message of the gospel.

The process of urbanization has decreased the strength of traditional Wolof values somewhat in this current day. Imagine the impact on the society if Wolof believers studied God's Word and restored these values to society, but from a biblical perspective. Cassettes and teaching could be prepared, shared, and studied in the church, and even communicated throughout Sénégal on the radio. Imagine the transformation of society when the Wolof people can connect to their traditional values and then be transformed by God's Word and the Holy Spirit to use them the way God has intended.

Adama Diouf is the director of World Vision Sénégal's Christian witness program and director of Mission Inter Senegal.

QUESTIONS FOR REFLECTION

1. *Jom* and *kolere* both relate to absolute loyalty to the community and jealousy for its honor. How should these values be expressed in a Christian community? What might be some of the tensions for a Wolof convert as he tried to express these values crucial to his background in relation to his unbelieving family and clan?
2. How is hospitality understood in your culture? What biblical values are embedded in that understanding, and what needs to be challenged?
3. How do you think the contextualization Adama Diouf describes could lead to the transformation he longs to see?

CHAPTER 13

TOWARDS A CONTEXTUAL THEOLOGY OF THE HOLY SPIRIT

A Case Study from Congo

Ruth Julian

In August 2008 I was given the responsibility of teaching a course on the doctrine of the Holy Spirit at our Bible school in Brazzaville, Congo. As a missiologist, I had taught mission courses at our Bible school, but never a course on doctrine. After receiving the textbook and class notes, I started praying for guidance from the Holy Spirit about how to teach a class about this same Spirit. I knew that I could simply use what had been given me, and the students would finish the course with a basic knowledge of the person and work of the Holy Spirit. However, I also knew that I would be teaching in a culture very different from the one where I had studied the "doctrine" of the Holy Spirit. The culture of my students is rife with ideas and beliefs about spirits as well as experiences that bring these ideas and beliefs into reality.

After much prayer, I decided to put the textbook and the class notes aside, at least at the beginning of the course, and use Paul Hiebert's foundational principles of critical contextualization to guide the class toward a contextual theology of the Holy Spirit.

The students and I had approximately twenty-seven hours of class time together, not much time to develop a contextual theology, but enough time, I thought, for the students to not only learn intellectually about the Holy Spirit but also to experience an exercise in contextual theologizing. I explained Paul Hiebert's model of critical contextualization and told the students that we would be doing an analysis of their culture. For the first week, we were to suspend judgment and simply report to the class the ideas existing in their culture pertaining to spirits and the Holy Spirit. At the same time, I also required them to use a concordance to do a study of spirit and Holy Spirit in the Bible.

As we moved through the course, we continued this exercise of uncovering cultural assumptions about spirits and looked at how these ideas compare to what is revealed in Scripture. We discussed the different ideas in the culture about spirits in general and the Holy Spirit in particular and began to evaluate these ideas based on God's Word. Because several people groups were represented in the class, there was some disagreement about spirits' actions based on cultural beliefs. Many main ideas, however, came to the surface in our discussions, which we were then able to agree upon and use in the development of our contextual theology.

What follows is a condensed version of what the class developed. I have left it in the basic form that we accepted as a group. On the last day of class, I gave each student a copy of this document and asked them to critique it personally. Because of the cultural diversity of the class, there were some critiques and changes on that level. A couple of students were not in agreement that this was how a theology of the Holy Spirit should be presented.[1] Overall however, the students were encouraged that they could study Scripture and their culture to find ways to better understand the Holy Spirit.

> The students were encouraged that they could study Scripture and their culture to find ways to better understand the Holy Spirit.

From students living in Brazzaville, Congo and studying at the Institut Biblique de l'Alliance Chrétienne: Our ideas leading toward a contextual theology of the Holy Spirit.[2]

Ideas that we found essential for our contextual theology on the Holy Spirit:
- It is necessary to be born again and from the Spirit; there is need for repentance and the Spirit (John 3:5)
- The Holy Spirit is in the community (Num 11:26)
- God spreads his Spirit on whom he wants (i.e., God chooses) (Num 11:29; Acts 15:8)
- The Spirit transforms the person (1 Sam 10:6; Rom 8:29; 1 Cor 6:11)
- God can spread his Spirit on any person (Num 11:25; Joel 2:28)
- The Spirit gives the confidence to announce the word of God (Acts 4:37)
- The Holy Spirit sets people apart for service (Acts 13:2)
- The Holy Spirit gives life to the mortal body (that is what gives us the hope) (Rom 8:11; Ezek 37:4-6)
- The Spirit announces justice, uprightness, truth (personal, society) (Matt 12:18)
- The Spirit delivers from all kinds of bonds (Matt 12:28)
- The person who does not have the Holy Spirit does not belong to Jesus (this can be seen by their fruits) (Rom 8 :9)
- The Spirit frees people from the law of the flesh (Rom 8:1, 2)
- The Holy Spirit helps us with our wounded faith (emotional, spiritual). (Rom 8:13, 26)
- The Spirit testifies that we are children of God (Rom 8:16)
- The Holy Spirit produces the fruit of the Spirit (Gal 5:22-23)
- The Spirit gives various gifts (1 Cor 12:8-9)
- Be filled (continuously) with the Holy Spirit (Eph 5: 18)

---

1   One student did not agree that the Holy Spirit could be represented by some of the symbols because they were too limiting. Another student was from another country in Africa and so did not agree with some of the interpretations that the students from Congo gave for the different symbols.

2   The graduating class of 2009.

- The Spirit is essential for mission (Acts 2:2; Matt 28:18-20)

The form for expressing our contextual theology on the Holy Spirit:
As we did our analysis of both culture and Scripture, we began to put together a document that we entitled "Toward a Contextual Theology of the Holy Spirit." Not only did we come up with ideas about a contextual theology of the Holy Spirit, but we also discussed some of the forms that could be used to express theology. Of the many different forms that we could have used (e.g., systematic, narrative, symbiotic, etc.), the students decided to use a symbolic form.

The students considered using the cultural idea of *mbongui* for the Holy Spirit, but after some discussion, decided that the *mbongui* would be better as a symbol of the church. The *mbongui* in Congolese culture is a meeting place in the village where community, sharing, unity, solidarity, dialogue, advice, and instruction take place. The students decided, however, that there were many elements of the *mbongui* that could be used as symbols of the Holy Spirit.

The cultural symbols linked with the *mbongui* and how they can represent the Holy Spirit:
- Fire symbolizes:
  - Love in the *mbongui*
  - Bringing people together
  - Power
  - Purification
  - People sharing (people helping each other)
  - Breaking of bread together / brotherhood / a meal of sharing
  - Comforting and consoling (this takes place around the *mbongui* fire)
  - Equality (everyone is at the same level in the *mbongui*)
  - The fire of the *mbongui* should not die out. People maintain it, they add wood so that fire does not die out
- Palm wine (remember the wedding at Cana) symbolizes:
  - Joy
  - Strength
  - Courage
  - Wisdom
  - Song
- Water symbolizes:
  - Atonement
  - Forgiveness
  - Purification
  - Separation of good from evil
- The cola nut symbolizes:
  - Sharing
  - Unity
  - Solidarity
  - Communion

- The horn or the flute symbolizes:
  - Breath
  - Alerting people
  - Communication
- The broom or the cane symbolizes:
  - Power
  - Authority
  - Word (there is power in the spoken word)
  - Influence
  - Bringing about justice
- The tom-tom (drum) symbolizes:
  - An announcement
  - Communication
  - Encouragement
  - Consolation or comfort
  - Dance
  - Joy
  - Inspiration
- Stories that are part of the education in the *mbongui*
  - Can be used to clarify the Word of God
  - But: 1 Tim 1:4—we need to remove whatever destroys the faith
- *Mbongui* is education
  - Through initiation, of which the *mbongui* is a part, children become adults
  - Through sanctification, which is the work of the Holy Spirit, Christians are moved to spiritual maturity
  - Jesus trained his disciples

Other essential ideas related to the Holy Spirit that are not linked with cultural symbols:
- Conviction—the Holy Spirit convicts people of sin
- Peace—The Holy Spirit gives peace
- Other fruit of the Spirit
  - Patience (older men in Congo are said to have this)
  - Gentleness (mothers in Congo are said to have this)
  - Self-control (fathers are said to have this)
  - Kindness
  - Goodness
  - Faithfulness
- The Trinity
  - The Holy Spirit is God
  - There is only one God
- Spiritual gifts
  - Given by the Holy Spirit
  - Necessary to do mission
  - All Christians have at least one spiritual gift

- One problem related to spiritual gifts is that some people think that some gifts are better than the others
- How can we correct this?
  - Through teaching (make the teaching practical—do not just teach with our words, but also through our actions)
  - The attitude that should characterize leaders is humility.
  - We must teach with love because spiritual gifts without love add up to zero
- Sanctification (see education in the *mbongui*)
- The call to the service

LIMITATIONS AND CONCLUSION

Time was one of the main limitations of this exercise, as the class was only three weeks in length. We could not go in depth in our cultural analysis nor our scriptural analysis. Another limitation was that, being a Bible school course, this exercise was done in an artificial setting where the students came from different churches and different people groups. Therefore, a few students disagreed with the meanings of the various symbolic elements because their people group interprets these symbols in another way. One drawback to doing this exercise in a modular class setting was the lack of follow-up. An additional exercise, but one that was not an option given the constraints of the course, would have been to follow-up on this endeavor in order to see if any of the students used our work in their own ministries.

Despite these drawbacks, I, as one who loves to teach, was thrilled to see the students take the truths about the Holy Spirit and come up with culturally insightful symbols to talk about the work the Holy Spirit does among the church and in mission.

I was thrilled to see the students take the truths about the Holy Spirit and come up with culturally insightful symbols to talk about the work the Holy Spirit does among the church and in mission.

Ruth Julian is a professor at the Alliance Bible Institute of Congo.

QUESTIONS FOR REFLECTION

1. Do you think this is a good way to explore contextualization? What are the strengths and weaknesses of such an approach?
2. Ruth Julian's example leads to a very ethno-specific theology of the Holy Spirit. How do we balance this method of theologizing with something more universal that unites the worldwide church?
3. In your own context, if you followed this method, how would you express a theology of the Holy Spirit? What insights do you discover?

CHAPTER 14

A KOREAN CHRISTIAN MEMORIAL SERVICE

A Case Study
David Tai Woong Lee

The origin of the Traditional Korean Ancestor Veneration (Ancestor Worship) goes as far back as the early Three Nation Period (삼국시대: 1ˢᵗ c. BC-7ᵗʰ c. AD). Originally, the concept of ancestor veneration was known to have been passed down from China. By the fourteenth century AD, after the founding of the Chosen-dynasty (1392 – 1910) with Confucianism as her foundational ideology, ancestor veneration took another turn. It became an intricate part and parcel of the overall political, cultural and social system. Nevertheless it was mainly the royal court, scholars of Juja Sungli Hack (주자 성리학: one of the streams of study of Confucian philosophy) and aristocrats (양반: Yang Ban) who kept the rite until the end of the sixteenth century. Then a major Japanese invasion, known as the Imginwealan (임진왜란) occurred. This is the period that the general public began to observe the rite. By the nineteenth century, a majority of the families began to observe the rites as a part of their annual cultic event. Since this time, it has been so identified with the Korean culture that if one does not observe the rites, one is considered to be uncivilized and ungrateful to the ancestors. This became tantamount to losing human dignity.

Needless to say, a custom as old as ancestor veneration is bound to have many forms and types for different occasions. There is no need to dig deeply into the different types for our purpose here. Nevertheless, we must mention at least two different perspectives on the rite. One view is that ancestor veneration is purely a cultural event to show filial loyalty to the ancestors by the descendents. This view was taken by the early Jesuit missionaries to China, Matteo Ricci (1552 – 1610) being the prime example. Those who hold this view will tend to keep distance from the idea that the rite includes calling in the spirits of the deceased ancestors through the rites. Rather, the people are showing their appreciation to the ancestors for the benevolence that they have shown to the later generations.

At the other end of the continuum lies the camp that believes in worshipping the spirits of the deceased ancestors. In various cases, in conjunction with a shamanistic worldview, they tend to appease the spirits so that they will cause no harm to the family members who are living and instead bring prosperity to the family.

Modern Korean people can be found on these two continuums. Regardless of one's educational background and social status—whether one is thoroughly Westernized or not—one will participate in ancestor veneration of some sort without questions being asked as long as one is a Korean. Every year, at the time of the major festival holidays, such as New Year's Eve in the lunar calendar (설날: Sulnal) and Korean Thanksgiving day (추석: Choo Suk), tens of thousands of Koreans will return to their own family in their place of origin where their ancestors reside. It is a national exodus—the highways are packed with cars going to their home town to pay respect to the parents still living and participate in the ancestor veneration known as Cha Rea (차례).

How many people actually believe that the spirits of their deceased ancestors come and take part in the fellowship of the family members during the rite they perform? It is hard to tell. The ingenuity of the event is, though, like a myth, it seems to satisfy people on all places in the two continuums mentioned above. Thus the event seems to integrate both the living and the dead, the young, and the old and bring a strong sense of solidarity among family members. This is precisely the reason why when the early missionaries—both the Protestants and the Roman Catholics—denounced ancestor veneration as unfit for Christian faith, there was such fierce opposition by family members, particularly parents. One thing is sure, though. With changes in the culture and the spread of postmodernity, there seems to be no sign of diminishing trends for practicing ancestor veneration nationwide. Globalization actually strengthened the need for ancestor veneration among the average Korean family.

It is with this prior knowledge that a case study on contextualization of one of the most sensitive areas of Christian practice will be considered. A Christian memorial service (추도예배: Choo Do Yaebea) will be viewed from the following perspectives: The teachings by the early missionaries, the initiatives taken by the Korean churches, the practice of the memorial service, and finally an evaluation of the contextualization process.

THE TEACHINGS OF THE EARLY MISSIONARIES AND THE RESPONSE OF THE KOREAN CHURCH

The Rites Controversy at the end of the sixteenth century between the Jesuits and the opposing parties in China lingered for almost a century and was the context in which early Roman Catholicism reached Korea in the eighteenth century. Jesuits, including Matteo Ricci who had favored accommodation of the local culture, held their ground to their opponents who had condemned ancestor veneration as unscriptural and unfit for Christians—after a century of internal battle among different orders. In conjunction with political rivalries among different factions, thousands of Korean Roman Catholics were executed for refusing to practice ancestor veneration in the early eighteenth century. Prohibition of ancestor worship by Roman Catholics continued until early in the twentieth century when Pope Pius

XII overturned it (1930s), not to mention Vatican II (1960s) when doors were opened even wider towards the accommodation of the local cultures, including other religions.

When the Protestant mission began in the 1880s nearly a century later, the climate was somewhat different. The Chosen-dynasty was crumbing from both internal disputes and rivalries that sapped the national energy and from external threats from surrounding newly rising super powers, such as Japan, Russia, and the Ching dynasty of China. So when the Protestant missionaries taught the Korean Christians to abandon all forms of idolatry including that of ancestor veneration, there was no opposition similar to what the early Korean Roman Catholics had faced a century before. The majority of the Korean Christians followed this rule of faith concerning ancestor veneration.

It was, however, the Korean Christian laity that initiated a dynamic equivalent form of Christian ancestor veneration as early as in 1897. An article featured in the September (2010) issue of *Bulletin of Korean Christians* claimed that it was Moo Sung Lee, then a member of the Jung Dong Methodist Church, who first offered a Christian memorial service on his mother's memorial date.

> After a long struggle he finally decided to offer a Christian form of memorial service to commemorate his mother's death. Ancestor veneration became a public issue in 1920 among the Korean Christians, being featured in the *Dong A Daily*. Finally in 1934, the General Assembly of the Methodist Denomination officially approved of their constituencies practicing memorial services. Subsequently, the Salvation Army had approved in 1950 and Presbyterians at the end of 1970s respectively (http://Knowledge.godpia.com:8080).

In the last twenty years or so there has been overwhelming consensus that a Christian memorial service is an acceptable Christian practice to replace the need to honor ancestors. This is an excellent example of theologizing from the locality. Not all of the global Christian community may sense the same need. However, for the areas where Confucianism has dominated for centuries, such as Korea, Japan, China and parts of Asia where Chinese immigrants are present, this is the most urgent area of theology. The Korean case is an excellent example of not only contextualization from within, but also self-theologizing.

In the last twenty years or so there has been overwhelming consensus that a Christian memorial service is an acceptable Christian practice to replace the need to honor ancestors. This is an excellent example of theologizing from the locality.

THE FORM AND MEANING OF THE CHRISTIAN MEMORIAL SERVICE

Not all of the questions regarding Christian memorial services have been answered, nor are there elaborate theological treaties on this subject. This is one obvious case where praxis preceded theologizing. The churches have long felt the need, and the laity began to practice it. That settled the matter. It is now owned by the majority of the Korean churches and Christians. There will be only a fraction of ultra-conservative Korean Christians that would refrain from practicing it. What form does it take? And what are the theological assumptions behind the service? The following two different approaches will be taken to answer these questions.

First, let us examine a case study of a Christian memorial service from a local church background. The following is a format suggested by one of the leading Presbyterian churches, the Sarangeui Church, in their website (http://kyungjo.sarang.org/sacrifice/sacrifice_4.htm).

1. Significance:
   Choo-Do Yea Bae (Christian Memorial Service) is worship offered [to God—my insertion] by the remaining family members and friends in order to honor and model the spiritual life of the deceased person(s). Through this service the family members should remember and honor the deceased person and also take this opportunity to encourage one another and strengthen the fellowship and spiritual life among the remaining family members, whereby the participants will gain much benefit spiritually, morally, and even socioethically.

2. Preparations:
   a. Place a picture of the deceased person(s) in room. Light candles and decorate with flowers. (Even in cases when there is no picture of the deceased, Ji Bang—a written word that is supposed to call the spirits of the deceased—is prohibited. One could lay a Bible that was used by the deceased person instead, if there is one.)
   b. The family members could sit around the table and the person who presides could either sit or stand beside the table.
   c. The text for the service, hymnal and some spiritual exhortations that the deceased had given earlier on could be printed prior to the service and distributed to the family members at the time of the service.
   d. If the pastor or the other staff of the church could not attend, one of the family members should lead the service.

5. Content of the service:
   a. Silent prayer (reading of the Scripture, e.g., Ps 23)/reciting of the Apostles Creed
   b. Hymnal (Korean Hymnal No. 514, 543).
   c. Scripture readings
   d. Reciting of the personal history of the deceased (at this time one could include memorable sayings, achievements, character, and any other thing that left a deep impression on the hearts of the family members)
   e. Sermon
   f. Prayer
   g. Hymnal (No. 305 or No. 376).
   h. Benediction or Lord's Prayer

9. Examples of prayers
   "We thank you Father God for giving us the grace of Jesus Christ and the leading of the Holy Spirit so that we could live with faith and hope even in these times of sorrow and hopelessness among dark shadows.

Today is the day that we come together to take part in the memorial service to com-memorate the late _____ who went to be with the Lord in heaven, among family members.

Thou God who forgives our sins, we confess that we were unable to fully comprehend the vision and the aspirations of the beloved, thus were not faithful in making it real-ized. For this we ask you for your forgiveness.

Gracious Father God, we ask you to bestow upon us who are living the heavenly per-spective that has been once held by the dead, so that we could continue to be led by the Holy Spirit in Jesus Christ towards reaching the high vision of following the will of God on this earth. For this we ask you to fill us afresh with your grace. We pray in the name of Jesus. Amen."

Second, a mini-survey has been taken among a limited group of Global Missionary Training Center staff and trainees numbering about fifty-five families. Out of these, responses from twenty-one families have been collected. One can readily see that this survey is not meant to be a thorough study on this subject. It is rather a rough study to show the diversity of the forms and meanings behind the service. It would not be a misrepresentation to say that same degree of liberty and fluidity exists among the whole Korean Christian community in this regard.

1. How many times a year would there be such services performed?
    Majority answered once a year, while the second largest group said four times.

2. On what occasion(s)?
    On the memorial date of the deceased grandparents scored the highest.
    On the memorial date of the deceased parents scored the second highest.
    Combination of memorial date and other major Korean holidays scored the third.

3. What forms have these memorial services taken?
    a. Leader: Most commonly an elder person in the family, such as the father or the eldest son is the leader, followed by church staff (pastor) and lastly family mem-bers taking turns to speak.
    b. Content of the memorial service: By far the most respondents used a similar form to the one presented by the Sarangui Church, but less elaborate; followed by not any particular form of service.

3. What was thought about during these services?
    About the deceased person and consolation of the remaining family members fol-lowed by lessons on how one ought to live in future.

4. When you go to a funeral site and offer a silent moment in front of the deceased per-son's picture, what do you think or pray for?
    Mostly pray for the remaining family members followed by thinking about the de-ceased person and lessons to be learned.

5.   When do you usually perform these memorial services?
     Mostly on the day that the person has died plus major Korean holidays.

In conclusion, the following observations can be noted:

1.   The Christian memorial service has been accepted by the majority of Korean Christians from all traditions. It has now taken a firm position in the life of Korean Christians, and they can proudly claim it as a better way of honoring their deceased ancestors. There is no sign that the general non-Christian public has accepted it as an alternative to their rites. Nevertheless, the general public accepts Christians following a Christian way both in private as well as in public life. Within non-Christian families it is altogether a different story. Often a family will be less generous or even hostile towards their family members who do not participate in the older way. Family members, particularly parents and grandparents, will put up a fierce fight against their relatives who follow a Christian way. On the other hand, Christians can go to the non-Christian memorial service or funerals and simply present a flower or offer a silent prayer standing, while non-Christians will bow down, often on their knees to pay a tribute to the deceased.

2.   There is a wide range of forms practiced by different families among Protestant Christians, from a very unstructured observance of offering a simple prayer to following a more elaborate ceremony such as the one used by the Sarangui Church. All are accepted forms at present.

3.   Worshipping deceased ancestors would certainly be ruled out by most Korean Christians; on the other hand, there is not enough theological basis for Christian memorial services. This is a case where the praxis has preceded the formulation of the theological content. Korean Christians desperately needed the Christian form to substitute for the traditional forms, or else they became outcast from the Korean cultural community. Consensus must be reached among Korean Christians over the theological content of the memorial service. There is still uncertainty concerning the theology of memorial services. As the brief survey indicated, each person is left to him or herself to discover the significance of the memorial service. The Bible gives an adequate amount of teachings on honoring parents, but not much on deceased ancestors.

4.   The global church community can learn from the Korean Christian memorial service. In particular, the Western church might learn about honoring our parents, both living and dead. This is a good example of local theologizing taking place in a different locality among the global church that adds new color, making the church a multifaceted, multifunctional one.

> The global church community, particularly the newly emerging missions both from the East and the West, should not be impatient about finding genuine contextualization occurring in a culture where they have been ministering.

There has been much discussion about contextualization since the 1970s. But as the above case study has shown, actual contextualization requires many trials and errors. In the case of Korean memorial services, contextualization did not happen in one day nor come through the efforts of expatriates. It took almost a century for the Korean church to reach some unification on the practice. The global church community, particularly the newly emerging missions both from the East and the West, should not be impatient about finding genuine contextualization occurring in a culture where they have been ministering. For genuine contextualization to take place is more easily said than done. This is particularly true when one is dealing with subjects that have been organically intertwined with a given culture and that must find adequate Christian forms without disrupting the cultural norms that function as the nerve system of their worldview. For Korean Christians, finding Christian equivalents to ancestor veneration was an example of walking through a minefield of culturally sensitive areas.

David Tai Woong Lee is the Director of Global Leadership Focus, based in Korea.

QUESTIONS FOR REFLECTION

1. David Lee's case study describes a key element in Korean culture and the development of a Christian functional substitute. Why is such a process so vital? What continuities and what discontinuities can you trace?

2. Lee suggests that good contextualization must be done by cultural insiders. Is that always true? Are there ways in which outsiders could contribute appropriately? Why and how?

3. Why and how must contextualization be a continuous process for Christians in every culture?

CHAPTER 15

GUATEMALA: A CASE STUDY

The Evangelical Church and the Influential Animistic Mayan Spirituality

Hector Pivaral

Reflection on the search for contextualized teaching is necessary to reduce the incidences of syncretism within the rural evangelical church. This may be achieved through the development of a curriculum based on four essential themes: To know, to fear, to love and to serve the Triune God. Filtering context through these themes by means of contextualized hermeneutics developed in a community will enable the community to apply it (SEPAL, 2001; Grossman 2002, 130). This article will outline these four themes in the context of Guatemala and provide a mechanism that aids biblical comprehension and ministerial practice. In the work of contextualization it is important to always keep in mind: *The more patent and real the living God is in the heart of the people the more the attitudes of syncretism will decrease, because the animistic beliefs will lose strength.*

RECOGNIZING WORLDVIEW

The indigenous people of Guatemala, which include Evangelicals, Catholics, followers of Christian sects, those that follow the Mayan religion, and the indifferent, is not a community without knowledge of God, Jesus, the Bible and sin (SEPAL 2001, Grossman 2002, 130). All have an idea of these cited subjects, albeit a mistaken one. For example, it is not uncommon that a spiritual guide[1] leads people in general prayers to God or to Jesus, although they may include other divinities, spirits, *naguales* and *abuelos*. They clearly have in their minds that they are heard by a superior spiritual world. Furthermore, it is not uncommon to see someone place a Bible open to Psalm 91 at the head of the bed of a sick person. Why do they do it? To fulfill some possible requirement so that a healing miracle may occur.[2] Everyone is capable of reciting the Ten Commandments and the Lord's Prayer. Finally,

---

1 The generalization includes here pastors, priests, Mayan priests or *ajq'ij, chamanes, zahorínes, brujos,* dancers, witch doctors, *el viejo, el rezador*, elders, ancestors, etc. All of these names are present within the Mayan worldview. See Cardoza and Aragón (1986, 22-23). Also in Pacheco (1985, 61-157).

2 Visit that I made to a family in Pablo la Laguna, Sololá, June 17, 2008.

in any community there is a consciousness of what is good and what is wrong or "sinful." In the villages those who do wrong are judged and punished (Sáenz 2009).[3]

The common knowledge of a spiritual life carries into the educational system. In 2006 the Ministry of Education (MINEDUC) promoted work done by Brazilian Angelica Satiro, *Sueño de jóvenes por la paz/* (2006). This work has a strong syncretist content.[4] Although excellent material to encourage young people to dream and plan, it also exposed them to New Age themes, yoga, transcendental meditation and Mayan spirituality (16, 21, 46, 53). Readers were invited to be guided by a fictitious character or spiritual guide called Maizol. Interestingly, some of the evangelical youth from Puerto Barrios who submitted themselves to this material had serious emotional and spiritual problems. In at least one well known denomination, two young ladies consequently were, or were considered, demon-possessed.[5]

One personal family experience regarding Guatemala's syncretistic tendencies was in 2008, when my daughter (third grade) was asked to find out her *nagual* or spiritual guide by reading the Mayan calendar.[6] My wife and I have tried to teach her to defend herself as an evangelical, but the teachers were a bit bothered and felt we were somewhat fanatical. Not completing this project meant a loss of points for our daughter for that unit of study. Everything worked out well in the end, but our daughter was the only one who expressed a different opinion in the entire school.

Even though there are many pagan elements working among the indigenous and non-indigenous people of Guatemala, it is a community that has heard the gospel. As such, much of the ministerial focus should have a discipleship orientation, using the Scriptures with strong conviction to make known the Triune God and man and his position in creation.[7] All this should be used to intentionally pursue a conversion towards true transformation.[8] In other words, that the unbeliever would come to confess Jesus Christ as his Savior and become part of the family of God and that the believers would overcome their "limiting beliefs" that impede them from becoming integrally truly free in the Lord.

COMPREHENSIVE TEACHING IN THE CHURCH

The principal task in the teaching-learning process is to go deeper in the Word of God in both the Old and New Testaments. Everything in this emphasis on, and study of, the Bible should be transferred to the indigenous as well as non-indigenous church, without discrimination against its academic level, social status, gender and age.[9] In addition, each person should be reached with the Word differently with appropriate techniques, whether

---

3   Lynchings included.
4   More information may be found at http://www.crearmundos.net/quien.html.
5   Report offered by one honorable and well-known person from Izabal in August 2006.
6   This was in the material called *Medio Social.*
7   This action still includes social themes in looking at an integral mission. In regarding the mission of teaching, it should be biblical. See this posture in Donovan (1978, 26) and Padilla (1986, 52, 64, 67, 127).
8   An interesting model of communication and internalizing of the Word is expressed in the work by Steuernagel (2006, 18-19). God is communicated to man through the Scriptures and daily living. If God reveals himself through interpreters, working in context, the gospel will make many free and truly transformed.
9   One should always be conscious of the fact that the work is done with both genders.

by oral methods or other pedagogical methods.[10] The main principle is to focus on who the audience is, how they live, and how they value life so that the message of God comes across clearly and pertinently. All narrative has its comprehensible expression to people, but the ones communicating the message should ask themselves at least three questions: What does the Holy Spirit want to say to each listener? Is the Lord being given room to be the one who expresses himself without adding much homiletical or cosmetic methodology? Can the listener react and participate, giving his opinion and experience on what is being communicated?

> What does the Holy Spirit want to say to each listener? Is the Lord the one who expresses himself without adding much homiletical or cosmetic methodology? Can the listener react and participate with what is being communicated?

It will always be a challenge to share the Scriptures with a fresh approach, imitating the model that Jesus Christ gave (Matt 7:29) and not interpreting it on the basis of the teacher's teachings, but on that of God himself teaching and clarifying it. The teacher or expositor of the Word should take care to not give his or her own opinion, or that of others. Teachers should keep in mind what they have learned in many years of studies and training yet continually discern and allow the Holy Spirit to take control of what is said, expounded, produced or written (Flemming 2005, 234-65). Whatever the medium of communication is, it has to be carried out in a creative manner and with excellence.

With these principles paramount, we return to considering this context to which the message of the Word goes out. There are matters of context which should be taken into account when deciding on the most effective manner of communicating.

WHY SOME PRACTICES OF SYNCRETISM ARE NOT DISCUSSED

There are strange practices within villages or regional churches that are so rooted in the worldview of the people that no one will even consider whether or not the practice is consistent with the Word of God. One could say that there are invisible patterns, but only someone from outside the community with an investigative attitude would notice.

The most common practices are the visits from the spiritual guide, *brujo*, or *hechicero* or *Ajq'ijab*. When there is an accident, one may turn to the *sobador de huesos*—the "one who rubs the bones." Or one may turn to the work of *la traída del alma*—one who brings the soul back (Ixtetela 2001). The *comadrona* is said to have a certain influential power over the

---

10   Unfortunately, there is not enough space here to comment on orality developed by the ministry Contaré (www.contare.org) and Viña Studios (www.viyastudios.org) in Guatemala. See the series of articles by Cerril Montgomery Wingerd, Great Commission Update, Colorado Spring: OCI, #14 al 17. Only one article is seen in http://onechallenge.org/gcupdate/index.php?option=com_frontpage&Itemid=1. Also, visit International Orality Network, "ION" (www.oralbible.com/index.php) which will hold their conference in September. It is worth considering what Rubén Paredes says in "La educación Teológica para sectores marginados autóctonos" in René Padilla (1986: 108-112). In regards to the materials see also in René Padilla (1986: 135-36). Some themes on orality are: Ethnic music, biblical narrative, transmission of the Christian message in the mother tongue, megavoice, cinematography productions, dramatization, etc.

future of mothers and newborns. Those who carry out these activities emphatically say that they possess a special gift which was given to them (part of their destiny or *chu'milal*).[11]

These are aspects that are so natural to the people that, in their opinion, they represent no spiritual danger. The reason given is that they are their own beliefs, part of their identity, of their own nature and are their own medicine.[12] If someone argues against these things, the native responds by saying, "He just doesn't know." This response insinuates that the person that opposes these practices is just an outsider who simply doesn't understand.[13] Furthermore, these matters are left on a very personal and private level. This would only have to do with the individual who has a need to resolve something and with the required person to bring about the solution.

> These are aspects that are so natural to the people that, in their opinion, they represent no spiritual danger.

Each of these practices could be interpreted sociologically as the available means of a group to mitigate pain or suffering or to be able to obtain counsel in order to get rid of fear or "the fright," just as someone from the city goes to the doctor, psychologist, lawyer, etc. But, at the basis of these beliefs lies a strong influence of animism,[14] which is driven by the church's approval of a practice of syncretism.[15]

THE *RECOGEDOR DE ALMAS*[16]

What is known of the "recogedor de almas" or "collector of souls" is the following: When a person has had a bad fall because of some unfortunate accident, a "scare" or "fright" stays

---

11   Something can be seen in respect to this on the home page of *Enlace Quiche*, June 27, 2008: http://www.enlacequiche.org.gt/centros/cecotz/RIQUEZA%20TZ'UTUJIL/curanderos.htm.

12   It is even assured that this is the way the human body works. This continues to be part of the way to explain certain phenomena which occur in the surroundings.

13   For example, the power that even a pastor and his followers attribute to a Mayan altar, at which they do not dare to pray for a demon found there to be cast out. It is a sad fact that some pastors have left the ministry to become Mayan priests.

14   In animism, it is understood that human beings and nature are united and as man has a spirit that protects it, each element in nature has its own life. Everything has a spirit; there is nothing that does not have a heart, soul, and beginning to its life. This means that everything is alive, human beings and animals, plants and springs, clouds and caves, light and wind, hills and valleys, rocks and rivers, pots and pans, intersections and roads, underworlds and supernatural worlds. This includes the fact that the dead coexist with the humans, they visit them. Also, the concept of animism states that nature is governed by souls and spirits comparable to those of humans. See: Roncal, et al. (2001, 35). See also in Cooper (2006, 192-93) and Kraft (2005, 172). Kraft mentions that this is the belief of three-quarters of the world.

15   In the specific case of Guatemala, when a person makes animism part of their Christian faith they fall into syncretism. Syncretism is the diluting and distortion of Christianity by adding other beliefs that go against their basic principles. The religious rituals can continue, but the heart of their faith, as far as the person of Christ and the work of grace, is seen as detracting. In general, syncretism is the union or mix of creeds of different religions. See Grossmann (2002, 5-6). Barbosu comments to Morcan who presents this line, as well as Jennings in Gailyn Van Rheenen (2006, 163-64; 265).

16   This belief is common in San Pedro la Laguna, Sololá. Although this is part of the Tzutujil culture, it is also found in other cultures. Fortuitously, I found out that there is a similar practice in the rural areas of Italy. In http://www.rice.edu/projects/HispanicHealth/Courses/mod7/susto.html described something similar to folklore in Latin America. There is a book on this topic (Rubel et al. 1989). On the home page of ODHAG in the Interdiocese Project report «Recuperación de la Memoria Histórica» *Guatemala: Nunca más*, June 28, 2008: http://www.odhag.org.gt/html/TOMO1C1.HTM states about the matter of fear: "In many of the testimonies, fear is referred to as a fright or sickness that carries with it consequences more than just the moment of the threat

with him because, for a moment, he felt lost and as if the life or his soul went out of him. Therefore, what follows is a period of uncertainty, terror, and loss of peace. The idea that emerges is that the soul stayed in the place of the accident.

Some people are known to have the capacity to solve this matter, and such a person is known as the "soul collector." He can be a witch, pastor, deacon, relative or someone else in the town who has this gift. This person offers his help to the family. He goes to the place where the accident happened at a given time and begins to use a belt or whip to "cause" the soul to move in the direction it should go. In some cases, if the accident occurred in a far-off place, the "soul collector" carries the soul in a vehicle. The objective is to bring the soul back to the person who suffered the accident. This occurs when the affected person finally takes in a deep breath. The thank yous follow and the matter is settled.

Even though this practice cannot be biblically based, no pastor or village leader will discuss this matter. But, some biblical arguments against this practice are:

1. *Only at death does the separation of body and soul occur:* The soul does not leave because of any sudden blow, but only with death (Gen 35:16-21, 1 Ki 17:17-24; Matt 10:28, Mark 8:31-38). Also, a soul does not remain walking around without its body. (1 Sam 19:3-19, Luke 16:19-31).

2. *This is a dangerous belief to put into practice:* This supposed moving of souls would be a practice of animism, wanting to manipulate a spirit (or soul). In other words, it would be witchcraft (1 Sam 19:3-19). God opposes such practices (Lev 19:31, Deut 18:9-14; Matt 7:21-23, Rev 21:8). He who practices this does something forbidden (Lev 20:6-7, Matt 23:13, Mark 9:42-50, 1 Cor 6:9-11, Gal 5:16-25).

3. *In God there is salvation and healing:* The practice of being a "soul collector" is easy to argue against from the Word of God. But while taking a look at the history behind this belief, one should answer the following questions: Why is there so much concern over a fall? Why does so much fear stay around? What can God do about this situation? What can God do to come against fear, terror, and fright? Does God give a solution for this? With the answers to these questions, we can come up with the following strategy: To come to people in love explaining that it is normal that one remains fearful after a fall. And that God is with us at all times, He keeps us and wants us to move ahead through every trial and tribulation. At all times it is fundamental to put our faith in God alone. (Ps 121, 139:1-12, Isa 53:3-6; Rom 8:9-17 and 28-39, 1 Pet 2:18-25, Jas 5:14-15, 1 Jn 4:7-21.) An attitude with a pastoral approach can accomplish a lot. Afterwards instruction should follow (2 Tim 1).

(affecting different organs, psychosomatic health problems, alteration the immune system, pains, and non-specific somatic complaints.) Especially in the Mayan culture, fright is identified as a sickness that is manifested after a violent act or in when the person is vulnerable, and that is necessary to leave the body through curative measures." In January of 2008 I ministered to a family that had a fright after a fall. The irony lies in that it served as an illustration of a bad fall that I had recently in front of their house. The fall I suffered was bad but I got up and brushed myself off. After a moment I told them, "Well, I leave my soul here with you so would you please greet it each morning as you leave." Everyone ended up laughing. They still have not forgotten this and they thank me for clarifying this false belief. Unfortunately, it ended up being a painful and expensive lesson for me. Now may they teach this to others. I for one have personally demonstrated this lesson!

Some concerns remain which I will leave for you: Is it wrong to go and pray in the place where an accident occurred? Is it possible to have a worship service with the person that had an accident inviting their neighbors to come and pray that the fear they have will go away?

A BIBLICAL APPROACH

In general, pertinent curriculum material to be used in eliminating and preventing syncretism in the church should consider three subjects: Our Triune God, the Word of God, and who is man. For lack of space here, I shall take into consideration only the subject of our Triune God. This consists of: knowing, fearing, loving and serving God. Each one of these emphases should consider not only the general concept of the Triune God, but also should include each of the persons of the Trinity, the Father, the Son, and the Holy Spirit.

THE FOUR EMPHASES REGARDING GOD

In expounding this theme, there are a few aspects that should be included: God is one, and as the only Deity* is manifested in three persons: Father, Son and Holy Spirit (Deut 6:4, Matt 28:19, Mark 1:9-11, 1 Cor 12:4-6 and 2 Cor 13:14).[17] In regards to Jesus Christ, it is important to emphasize that he is one with and sent by the Father, is truly human, the Son of God, and truly God, Lord, and Savior (John 10:30, 20:21 and 28, 1 Tim 2:5, Heb 1:1-4, 2 Pet 1:11). Concerning the Holy Spirit, it is necessary to mention that he is the other one that is wholly equal to the Son (John 14:15-31), that he seals believers identifying them as sons of God (Eph 1:11-14). He is the present manifestation of God in the believer and in the church, he gives out spiritual gifts, and he is the one that will convict the world of sin, righteousness, and judgment. (1 Cor 12:1-11). Keeping at least this in mind, the following in regards to the Triune God should be transmitted to a community:[18]

1. *Knowing God:* God is one and is manifested in three persons. He is justice and love and he selflessly gives of himself. He made all of creation with love, made man in his likeness and image, and blessed him to rule over all creation. God has walked with man and woman and has chosen his people to testify of his person. (Gen 1-12, Ps 9:10, 46:10; Jer 9:23 and 24; Matt 28:16-20; John 1:18; Acts 1:8). This teaching strips away at animism and syncretism because it clearly states that everything is subject to God. Creation is not God and is administered by man. Creation does not rule over man nor does it ask man to submit to it.

2. *Fearing God:* God is Almighty and everything submits to him because everything apart from him is created. God as Creator is the only Owner and Sovereign of all and over all. Nothing is hidden from God's eyes, and he judges all things. God is just in protecting the righteous and the weak, and he resists, punishes, and destroys the proud, the violent, and evil with vengeance. True fear of God brings true wisdom to man and he submits himself to God's will (Ps 24; Prov 1:7, 8:13, 9:10, 10:27, 14:2 and 26-27, 15:33 and 19:23; Luke 12:5; 2 Cor 7:1; Eph 5:21; and 1 Pet 1:17-21).

---

17   *Godhead.* As reference, see: Dew (1977). This gives a good summary of biblical passages about the Trinity.

18   The four divisions that follow are based on the passage in Deuteronomy 10:12-13. Note that it is divided in two groups, the first two together and the last two together. Between them there is a transition.

This teaching strips away at animism and syncretism because it shows God has all authority and power. Other powers are nothing before God's power. He judges over all things. To walk in fear and in the will of God brings one to a life of righteousness in all areas. Apart from God, any other deity is identified as false or is uncovered as demonic.

Between the two previous points and the two that follow, it is worthwhile to make a transitional point. It is not enough to merely know and fear God, because even the demons do this (Jas 2:19). Furthermore, the two previous points are demanded by other religions. In turn, the Christian believer goes even further: to love and serve God.[19]

3. *Loving God:* God commands us to love and honor him because only he is worthy of all worship. We want to love God because he loved us first. In spite of the fact that humanity was dead in its sin, by his love people come to be saved and become his children (Deut 6:5; Ps 18:3; John 1:12, 3:16; Eph 2:4-5; 1 Jn 3:1). This teaching strips away at animism and syncretism because people can understand that only God loves and that the demons, disguised as gods and idols, only desire to subdue and trick man. To him who worships only God, there is no worship for idols. Loving God allows for man to be faithful and walk in integrity.

4. *Serving God:* In serving God, he asks us to have the following attitudes: to serve with love, in humility, generously, with a clean heart, and with joy. Serving God is shown when one serves his neighbor with love (1 Chr 28:9; Ps 2:11, 100:2; Acts 20:19; Gal 5:13; Eph 2:10; Heb; 12:28). This teaching strips away at animism and at syncretism because: People understand that when they serve demons and any other principality, it is done so with fear and in slavery. It is infidelity and sin against God when one serves other gods. Serving God is the opportunity that all believers have and not just one person has.

Helping people to internalize these ideas will aid in avoiding attitudes of syncretism because the beliefs of animism will lose strength.

This proposal does not pretend to be exhaustive and can be improved, but it shows how people can be helped to have more biblical and Christian patterns to follow. Helping people to internalize these ideas will aid in avoiding attitudes of syncretism because the beliefs of animism will lose strength.

BIBLICAL COMPREHENSION AND MINISTERIAL PRACTICE

With the help of the Holy Spirit, the believer, when concerned with knowing God's will and serving his people, should know and understand the cultural elements of the community that are contrary to the Word and the gospel. In turn, they should determine the possible cause of their practice and what they are substituting from their worldview. Next, go to the Scriptures to determine what they indicate about the matter. Lastly, elaborate responses to be evaluated in dialogue with the community. (It would be much better if each step of the

---

19   During this transition it is possible to introduce the themes on spiritual battle. See the works by Kraft (2005, 361-74), Moreau, (2006, 47-70), and Hiebert (2001, 163-77).

process could be carried out by several people at the same time.) The resulting fruit of this reflection could become a pastoral theology, both practical and daily, for the context (Padilla 1984, 1-23).[20]

The theological work should uncover what is pagan in the culture and later proceed to take the paganism out of the practice in order to transmit the gospel within their culture. The goal is to make known the only Triune God, the God that loves his creation and man, the work of Jesus Christ, and the action of the Holy Spirit. It is to make the message understandable, not easy to reject, so that it transforms the human creature into a child of God.[21] In this way, the knowledge of God is made "suitable" in the hearts of the people and the attitudes of animism and syncretism lose strength.

As was mentioned in the previous point, the work of understanding the context and giving a response according to the Word of God does not come from just one mind. This should arise from a reflection from the community.

From personal experience, I know of a group of leaders in the Chuj region of Guatemala that came together for almost three years to study the Scriptures and understand how to help their individual churches and communities. Among them were people who were part of a team of Bible translators and who participated in an oral recording project called Megavoice, which is a recording of biblical text in the Chuj language. There are also those who are helping in the production of new written materials as well as of instructive videos for their people.[22] These are the ideal people to carry out an autochthonous theology, because it will be done in their own language, in their territory, in their context, and will immediately be applicable to themselves, their family, their governing boards, their churches, their towns, and their missions.

A PARTICIPATIVE AND REPRODUCIBLE METHODOLOGY

It is desirable that the theology come out of a community of leaders and not from a textbook on theology or from a Bible commentary.[23] The theology should come out of the context, reading, and reflection on the Bible itself, the discussion of the group in affable dialogue and in their native tongue with the help of a master facilitator, all while praying for the loving and glorious assistance of the Holy Spirit.[24]

> It is desirable that the theology come out of a community of leaders and not from a textbook on theology or from a Bible commentary.

The methodology I have taught to the teachers and students of the Chuj PEB (Bible training program) to facilitate the teaching-learning process is the following:

---

20   See also Redford (2005, 227-53) and Driver (1998, 5-12).

21   The best model is to see what each writer did on the Word of God. See Kumar (1979, 33-48); Mathews (1995, 30-44), and Flemming (2005, 25-28, 35-53, 235-37, 264-65, 266-69, 272-77, 288).

22   One of the surprising projects is to translate the films of Deditos', from Viña Studios, to the Chuj language. See an example in: http://www.vinyastudios.org/es/deditos.

23   Although each student in PEB (Bible training program) receives an excellent book for their personal library.

24   It is worth consulting the entire work of Padilla (1986).

Two educational atmospheres must be developed—the community of teacher and students and the exercise of knowledge in the context.

1. *Classroom teaching in order to dialogue:* The adult students and the teacher have a meeting in a church or classroom to acquire clear information, share experiences, dialogue, discuss and discover applications, and celebrate what the Holy Spirit has allowed them to learn in it all. This is the first community that learns, reflects, and discovers better patterns in order to go to others and help them better themselves.

    a. *The teacher imparts his material:* The teacher's previous preparation and what he designed for his course, through dependence on the Lord, is shared or expounded on visually to the student community. This presentation should not be mysterious or exhaustive so that the path is open for dialogue and discussion (see Pazmiño 1995, 123).

    b. *The student interprets what he has heard:* Students take the Word and transfer, in a personal way, the information given by the teacher, through an interpretation or translation (preferably in his native tongue), supporting it with the visuals designed by the teacher.

    c. *The community supports and corrects in a dialogue:* The entire community, including teacher and adult students, participate in correcting and contributing to the new information.

    d. *The teacher compiles the community's applications:* The entire community discovers and supports viable applications to their community based on experiences they have had and includes the new ideas that the Spirit provided from the understanding of the Word.

    e. *End of the course:* Celebrate the gifts of the Holy Spirit acquired in community: The entire community gives thanks and rejoices in what God has given to their minds and hearts for personal growth and for serving others. Finally, they commit their lives and what they have learned to serve the kingdom of God (Freire 1996, 53-57).[25]

6. *What is learned should be carried through to the broader community:* The adult student is now able to serve his own family, his church, and his own people. These are his context for developing projects, practice, and the final acquisition of new experiences.

    a. *The student develops projects:* Before starting an actual project, the student should anticipate and design action plans specifically for where he will serve. He should investigate and foresee needs in order to formulate a plan and consider possible alternate measures to be flexible in every situation.

    b. *The student puts into practice what he has learned:* Knowledge and action will develop when the plan is put into practice. Evaluating circumstances and results

---

25   Herein lies the critical transition and the passing of limits of his situation. The student has received his transformation from the Lord and his mission is to carry it to others.

should be consistent. Also, the student should be consistently seeking to improve newly acquired abilities.

c. *The student brings new experiences to his community:* What the adult student has learned and experienced out of the classroom and in real life becomes part of his own life. This should be celebrated, critiqued, and evaluated. The hope is that these new practices will be his testimony before others and that he can demonstrate how to overcome limited situations.

This process is circular, not linear. In good time it is adapted to reasoning and the experienced realities of life. When the Word of God is studied in this process and its practical use is sought out with the community, its effect is very positive. The truth of the Scriptures becomes part of them. In addition, a critical attitude is developed toward the assumed beliefs and actions of the people.

This manner of teaching, in the context of village life, helps to make *patent and real the living God in the heart of the people* so that the attitudes of syncretism will decrease as animistic beliefs lose strength.

This manner of teaching, in the context of village life, does help to make patent and real the living God in the heart of the people so that the attitudes of syncretism will decrease as animistic beliefs lose strength.

CONCLUSION

The opportunity to change is always present within any people group. But in order to generate a transformation from a life of paganism to one that is completely surrendered to the Lord Jesus Christ, it is necessary to produce teachers with a spirit of service that will be reproduced in others while teaching the truth of the Word of God in the church and the villages (2 Tim 2).

The transition of change is present in each village. But, it is only by raising an atmosphere of conscious critique that the people can be liberated from tradition, from enslaving elements, from rural village culture, and even from the non-Christian attitudes or elements which have been added to the church. When teachers of the Word have a clear conscience and become true disciples following the model of God, of Christ, and even of Paul, they can walk away from denominational doctrines and doctrines of other religions so that practices and attitudes can be primarily formed by the Scriptures, which are inspired by God.

With responsible discipleship, a serious study of the Bible, and the guidance of the Holy Spirit, I know that the living God will become patent and real in the heart of the people. Therefore, the attitudes of syncretism will decrease because the animistic beliefs will lose strength.

Hector Pivaral serves with SEPAL Guatemala, an interdenominational agency supporting pastors and Christian leaders.

QUESTIONS FOR REFLECTION

1. Hector Pivaral describes the traditional animistic practices connected to an accident, and suggests some biblical responses. In your culture—native or host—what animistic beliefs and practices can you identify? How would you challenge a believer about them? What alternative practices might you suggest? How might you use them as a bridge for evangelism?

2. How might you adopt or adapt the hermeneutical method Pivaral describes?

3. Why is it important to have a community, not just an individual, to discern specific beliefs and practices? How might you implement that in your own context?

CHAPTER 16

THE PILGRIM CHURCH NEEDS A NEW HOME

Contextualizing the Church in Europe

Richard Tiplady

What is the purpose of church meetings? Why do we gather together? To sing hymns and songs of worship? To hear the word of God preached? To meet in fellowship with other Christians? At the church which I attended after first becoming a Christian, the minister had a favorite saying; "What does the story of doubting Thomas tell us? Never miss a meeting, you don't know what might happen!"

Evangelical Christians are fond of their statements of faith, yet we frequently work to a far more visible method of calculating orthodoxy, that is, consistent and frequent attendance at church on Sundays, and midweek as well if possible. Catholic professor and Dominican Edward Cleary comments on this; "Latin American Pentecostalism shares characteristics of religion in the United States. Specifically, it places exceptional emphasis on congregational participation and worship attendance as a measure of religious involvement" (IBMR 28/2, Apr 2004, 51). But have we ever in fact stopped to consider why evangelical Christianity functions in this way?

> I have sometimes felt that the real purpose of church services is to enable clergy to count the congregation. This is probably a little cynical, but churches often find their main sense of success in the number of people who attend on a Sunday. Regular church attendance is seen as being a significant test of spiritual health, and church growth is measured in the size of congregations. The importance of Sunday attendance and congregational size can never be underestimated for solid church (Ward 2002).

Mission strategy in recent decades has focussed on the importance of church planting rather than just doing evangelism, that is, combining Christians in new communities for worship, teaching, fellowship, and mission. But church attendance in Europe is in freefall. Year by year, across Europe, congregations are shrinking or closing. Most of those congregations that seem to be holding their own, and the few that are growing, tend to do so because of transfer growth, that is, new members from other churches.

And yet across Europe we find a massive interest in spirituality. In a continent that is generally prosperous, and where even its poor can generally be said not to be starving, there is a desire for something beyond material possessions. People are searching for meaning, for transcendence (something beyond themselves), for identity. But they are generally not looking at churches for this. It is not uncommon to hear people say of themselves that they are "spiritual but not religious," with the church being included in the latter category. All too often, we have created communities where spiritual experience is tied to meetings and membership, as well as participation in a whole host of other institutional activities. The spiritual seeker looks at the social price tag, and looks elsewhere. And this isn't a problem only for those currently outside the church.

> Problems arise when younger missionaries are expected to plant churches according to a model that they themselves find boring and irrelevant. It is not uncommon to find young missionaries whose only motive for attending church is a latent sense of Christian duty, and who come away each week wondering why they bothered to go. Such a situation causes problems at three levels: the personal spirituality of the younger missionary whose faith is weakened, not strengthened, by church attendance; the ineffectiveness of the missionary as evangelist and church-planter (after all, why draw people into a church where you rarely meet God?); and tension and division in the missionary team itself" (Stephenson in Tiplady 2003).

So what is going on, and how might we respond to this?

COMMUNITY AND CHURCH IN PRE-MODERN, MODERN AND POSTMODERN EUROPE

In pre-modern societies, communities were based around land and a sense of place. The parish system served well across Europe as a way for the church to reach all those, rich and poor alike, who owned, lived, or worked on the land in a given place.

The modern era was characterized by a significant change, which affected the way that churches were organized. Emigration, urbanization and industrialization meant that the land and the parish became less important. Community was reconstituted in the expanding industrial cities on the basis of shared culture and shared experience. Class, not place, became the most important signifier of identity. Churches emerged with an emphasis on congregation and club, where people gathered to worship with those who were like them, rather than those who lived in the same village. Working-class and middle-class denominations arose.

The postmodern era changes our ideas of identity and community again. Identity is not based on a common sense of place, since we are all more able to be highly mobile now. Nor is it based on common experience or social class. In his book, *Bowling Alone*, Harvard professor Robert Putnam argues that America's "social capital," a term which refers to "features of social organization such as networks, norms, and social trust that facilitate coordination and cooperation for mutual benefit," is being reduced (2000). He quotes a staggering array of statistics showing that across all types of social association, such as religious affiliation (church attendance), union membership, participation in parent-teacher associations and the number of volunteers for civic organizations such as the Boy Scouts and the Red Cross, involvement has declined in the last fifty years. The title of his book came from his discovery that, while more Americans go tenpin bowling than ever, participation in organized bowling leagues fell 40 percent between 1980 and 1993. This is not a trend that affects America alone. Putnam shows that a decline in the level of social engagement is also evident in Europe. People are meeting together less frequently in organized groups. The cultures of the West are changing dramatically.

LIVING IN EXILE?

In the West, until recent decades, Christians have held a privileged position in relation to European/Western life, thought and society. But things have changed. The social and religious changes described above, along with the growth and spread of secularization since the 1960s, have pushed Christianity to the margins of public life, which is a big change for European Christians after 1700 years of Christendom.

It is not difficult to find examples of the marginalization of the Christian faith in Europe. The draft European Union constitution, which was rejected in 2005 by the voters of France and the Netherlands, was notable for its excision of any mention of Christianity from the history of Europe. The furore over the appointment of Rocco Buttiglione as EU Equality Commissioner is equally noteworthy. A committed Roman Catholic, who had previously made known his views on homosexuality, was not accepted to a post which would include gay rights issues. In England, the BBC broadcast on mainstream TV the show "Jerry Springer: The Opera," despite vocal (and sometimes counterproductive) protests against its portrayal of Jesus as "gay" (i.e., homosexual).

European Christians might want to return to what the Bible has to say about living on the margins, rather than at the center of society. One option is to draw on the Old Testament experience of Israel, specifically the period of exile during the sixth century BC, when Israel experienced a catastrophic loss of security and status.

> This is what the LORD Almighty, the God of Israel, says to all those I carried into exile from Jerusalem to Babylon: "Build houses and settle down; plant gardens and eat what they produce. Marry and have sons and daughters; find wives for your sons and give your daughters in marriage, so that they too may have sons and daughters. Increase in number there; do not decrease. Also, seek the peace and prosperity of the city to which I have carried you into exile. Pray to the LORD for it, because if it prospers, you too will prosper." Yes, this is what the LORD Almighty, the God of Israel, says: "Do not let the prophets and diviners among you deceive you. Do not listen to the dreams you encourage them to have. They are prophesying lies to you in my name. I have not sent them," declares the LORD (Jeremiah 29:4-9).

The first group was exiled from Judah to Babylon in 597BC. The destruction of the Jerusalem Temple—the symbol of God's presence among his people—and the second, bigger, exile happened in 587 BC. In the passage quoted above, Jeremiah is writing between these two dates to the first group, now exiled in Babylon. (False) prophets like Hananiah were saying that their exile would only be for a short time, and that they would soon return (cf Jer 28:2-4, 15-17). Yahweh would not abandon his people, they said, for he had promised them a land of their own. Jeremiah advised the exiles not to listen to this advice, and to get used to living in a new situation.

Jeremiah's message to the exiles in Babylon is equally relevant to us today: stop looking back at the (mythical) lost past, accept the new reality, settle in it and serve God there.

There is some fear and pessimism about the survival of the church and the crisis of faith in Europe. I wonder if we sometimes get similar messages of (false) hope? I have heard, on many occasions, quotes of "I will build my church, and the gates of Hades will not prevail." In other words, God won't let the church disappear in Europe. But Islam obliterated the church in Turkey and North Africa, so there are no guarantees. Jeremiah's message to the exiles in Babylon is equally relevant to us today: stop looking back at the (mythical) lost past, accept the new reality, settle in it and serve God there.

But what might this mean? After all, there were significant changes in post-exilic Jewish religion, compared to pre-exilic Israel. Before, the faith of Israel was centred on the Jerusalem Temple, regular sacrifice, and festivals at which people gathered, such as Tabernacles, harvest, and so on. After the exile, the Jewish faith was centred on the synagogue, Sabbath, and Torah (and the Deuteronomistic History—otherwise known as the history books of the Old Testament—was compiled to explain why the exile happened). We face similar major readjustments on how we live as Christians and do church in the twenty-first century. How then should we live?

EMERGING CHURCH?

A movement of new thinking and practices that seeks to respond to the above questions has well and truly "emerged." It is a diverse and fluid movement, still taking and changing shape, one which has been given a variety of names—"missional church" and "mission-shaped church" are but two, although the above term, "emerging church," is the one most widely in use.

Why "emerging"? Because the ideas and practices are nowhere near fully formed, it is imprecise (allowing room for experimentation and avoiding the restrictions of tight definitions), and because "emerging church" ideas and experiments have sprung up or "emerged" in a variety of different contexts, more-or-less spontaneously and simultaneously.

As a movement, it has its roots in the northern/western European cultural sphere, but not just the Anglo-Saxon one. While "emerging church" ideas and practices are present in the UK and USA, they can also be found in the Netherlands and Scandinavia, and significant early practitioners and thinkers "emerged" in Australia and spread elsewhere. In fact, it's probably wrong to describe it as a movement; it's not that coherent. "Emerging church" has "emerged" through the confluence of different social, missiological, theological, and ecclesiological currents, which are outlined below in turn.

CURRENTS THAT COMBINE IN "EMERGING CHURCH"

1. Changing cultural, religious, and social realities in Europe

"Emerging churches are communities that practice the way of Jesus within postmodern cultures" (Gibbs and Bolger, 44). This is a key assumption behind "emerging church." Just as the "gathered congregation" form of the church emerged most definitively in the eighteenth and nineteenth centuries, when the parish system proved inadequate to service the spiritual needs of urban industrial Europe, so new forms of the church will be needed to reach post-industrial, postmodern European people. "Emerging church" tries to avoid the secular/spiritual divide imposed on the Christian faith by the Enlightenment, emphasizing church as the people of God, not a place to meet. If there is no secular/spiritual divide, then there can be no "holy" or "profane" places. Churches are being intentionally planted in cafés, pubs, and in houses, not just in special buildings.

> In Christendom, the Sunday meeting was the centre of corporate spiritual expression for the community. In a post-Christendom context, a church-meeting focus is no longer indigenous to the culture or necessary to be faithful to the gospel. Instead, the practice of community foundation itself is more central than the church meeting (Gibbs and Bolger, 44).

2. New approaches to missionary outreach in Europe

Michael Moynagh describes "emerging church" as a mind-set rather than a model, a way of thinking about church, rather than simply a way of doing church. This mind-set is "we'll come to you," not "you come to us." This has also been contrasted as "incarnational" vs "attractional," the latter being the more familiar mode of church (i.e., bringing people along to the church building or meeting place). In the "incarnational" approach, we model ourselves on the example of Jesus by going among people and embodying the life of the Spirit in their midst. This is central to "emerging church" ideas about evangelism—existing forms of Christian worship and community do not attract outsiders (and may even repel them). There should be no offence except the cross of Christ.

3. A renewed emphasis on the Kingdom of God (the inbreaking reign of God)

A "Kingdom of God" emphasis is central for many emerging church writers. Mark Scandrette of ReIMAGINE in San Francisco said about his attempts to set up a Gen-X church, "We got the questions wrong. We started out thinking about what form the church should take, as opposed to what the life of Jesus means in this time and place. Now, instead of being preoccupied with new forms of church, we focus on seeking the Kingdom as the people of God." The in-breaking Kingdom of God scandalizes the wealthy, the comfortable and the religious, and lifts up the outcast, the immoral and the rejected. At least, it did in Jesus' day, so why should we expect it to be any different now?

"We got the questions wrong. We started out thinking about what form the church should take, as opposed to what the life of Jesus means in this time and place. Now, instead of being preoccupied with new forms of church, we focus on seeking the Kingdom as the people of God." Mark Scandrette

4. Not "What is the church?," but "What is the church for?"

The quote from Scandrette above shows that "emerging church" is therefore as much about the purpose of the church as it is about the shape of the church. Form should follow function. Emerging church challenges us to rethink our fundamental assumptions about what it means to "be the church" as well as how we "do church." Only thereafter should we create new wineskins, doing things in an entirely new way, for the sake of the spread of the good news of Jesus Christ in Europe. For example, Latin American missiologist Orlando Costas described churchplanting as "penultimate," i.e., it is not the goal and purpose of mission. The purpose of churchplanting is to create living communities of Christians that will work for personal and social transformation in their locality. If this is true, then how does this affect the way we plant churches?

EXAMPLES TO ILLUSTRATE

The above elements may describe the ethos and driving forces behind "emerging church," but missionaries, church leaders, and others rightly ask, "OK, so what does it look like?" Three examples, with their websites (when available) for further information, are given below:

URBAN EXPRESSION (WWW.URBANEXPRESSION.ORG.UK)

A churchplanting enterprise that began in the East End of London (which is urban, deprived, socially and ethnically very mixed, multicultural, and multireligious) and now also active in Glasgow, Scotland. They don't always look like church, and their involvement with their local communities' needs is very deep. Most or all members of Urban Expression are evangelical, but they don't have a statement of faith—they are united by what they call their "Core Convictions" which incorporate:

- their Mission Statement ("Urban Expression is an urban mission agency that recruits, equips, deploys and networks self-financing teams pioneering creative and relevant expressions of the Christian church in under-churched areas of the inner city")
- their Values (relationship, creativity, and humility)
- their Commitments (e.g., "We are committed to following God on the margins and in the gaps, expecting to discover God at work among powerless people and in places of weakness" and "We are committed to being Jesus-centred in our view of the Bible, our understanding of mission and all aspects of discipleship").

THE CROWDED HOUSE (WWW.THECROWDEDHOUSE.ORG)

The Crowded House is a network of missional communities in the cities of Sheffield and Loughborough in England, with a strong commitment to church planting. Their website states that "most of our churches meet in homes. We want to offer a place of belonging. We are committed to *mission through community* (we believe that the life of the Christian family is a powerful apologetic for the gospel) and *communities in mission* (we want to be congregations focused on the gospel and church planting)." The following excerpt from their website illustrates their approach:

> At university someone had tried to get Patrick along to church. What a joke! But was he at church now? He wasn't sure. It had started when a colleague asked him round

for a meal. He was impressed by how Simon and the other people in his house all got on with one another. They'd got talking about life and stuff and they'd invited him to come round again on Sunday. Simon had suggested he come round in time to watch the football. When others arrived later in the afternoon they had all eaten together. They were a real hotch-potch [mix] of people, but Patrick enjoyed the banter [informal friendly talk]. After the meal they had read from the Bible and discussed what it meant. No-one seemed to mind his questions. Now some were playing a board game. A family with young children had just left. A couple seemed to be praying in the kitchen. Maybe this was church. Maybe it wasn't. Whatever it was, Patrick felt strangely at home.

WITTEVROUWENVELD, MAASTRICHT, THE NETHERLANDS

A young Dutch couple, Tjerk and Anneke van Dijk, have moved into the inner-city district of Wittevrouwenveld in Maastricht. Modelling themselves consciously on the Crowded House model above, they have opened their home as a meeting place for a new church-plant. In this broken and neglected community, they "do church" around the dinner table, welcoming the outcast into table fellowship, just as Jesus did. This is not a prelude to becoming a proper church, with a meeting room, chairs and the rest. It is already church, and they hope to multiply this model of inclusive community across the district.

A FEW QUESTIONS

"Emerging church" is not a panacea for the challenges facing the church in Europe today. But as an ethos, an idea, and a movement, it offers us much to consider.

How then should we learn from "emerging church"? How can we participate in the discussions, understand the experiments, learn from the mistakes and success of others, and incorporate them into our own mission strategies and practices? In addition, can we encourage and resource our missionaries with these ideas and practices, and can we contribute to and support the work of others without trying to make it our own?

Richard Tiplady, formerly the director of European Christian Mission UK, is now Principal of International Christian College, Glasgow, Scotland.

QUESTIONS FOR REFLECTION

1. What are some of the difficulties, and some of the bridges, for the re-evangelization of post-Christian Europe?
2. Richard Tiplady suggests that "What is the church for?" is a more important question then "What is the church?" Do you agree? How might you hold both these questions together?
3. Tiplady describes three examples of "experiments" with "being and doing church." What do you think might be the strengths and weaknesses of each? How could they best work side by side with more traditional forms of church? What forms of experimental church would be appropriate and helpful in your culture?

CHAPTER 17

THEOLOGY, CONTEXT, AND THE FILIPINO CHURCH

Melba Padilla Maggay[1]

Students in a theological college in South Africa were given this question in an examination: You are talking to an old man who is a follower of traditional religion. Explain to him why Christians believe in God, and what they believe about him.

In one answer, the hand was the hand of Africa, but the voice was that of Europe: I would say to him, "There are five arguments for the existence of God: the cosmological argument, the ontological argument, the teleological argument, the moral argument, and the argument ex consensus gentium" (Arden 1976).

The above example demonstrates the bizarre results of implanting a theological tradition alien to the culture of a people. The domination of Western theological formulations has led to a situation where in order to speak to their people, Christians in Asia and Africa are taught to answer questions raised by Greek Sophists in the fourth century AD.

Filipinos who live in a culture still awed by the Power that can be clearly perceived in things that have been made are taught to start from the supposition that we are talking to post-Christians long past the age of the mythical and, therefore, must belabor the existence of a supernatural God. We defend the Scripture as if we speak to a scientific rationalist, and not to people who have yet to see nature "demythologized," stripped of the wondrous and the magical.

In a society overwhelmed by poverty and injustice and pressed by the constant threat of political instability, we learn to preoccupy ourselves with trivial theological controversies and such fine points as to whether some scandalously miraculous gifts have ceased and whether in baptizing we ought to dunk or daintily pour.

---

1   This chapter first appeared in *Communicating Cross-Culturally: Towards a New Context for Missions in the Philippines,* ed. Melba P Maggay, ISACC/New Day, Manila, 1989, and is reproduced by permission.

Minds that would normally think in concrete wholes are painfully trained to make distinctions between faith and works, Jesus as Lord and Jesus as Savior, the sphere of the "secular" and the sphere of the "holy." Unable to cope with the fact that people are predestined to be saved and that at the same time many freely will to damn themselves, Western theological traditions insist on presenting the sovereignty of God and the freedom of man as problematic, and this to an oriental people happily able to live with the engaging perplexities of a paradox.

> Western theological traditions insist on presenting the sovereignty of God and the freedom of man as problematic, and this to an oriental people happily able to live with the engaging perplexities of a paradox.

In a culture which puts a great deal of emphasis on interrelatedness, the offer of salvation continues to be cast in highly individualistic terms. Salvation is advertised as a purely private entrance into an other-worldly Kingdom. The formula is to receive Jesus as "personal" Lord and Savior, as if he were merely one's own and no one else's, and as if the act concerned no one else but oneself. An act of commitment is thought to be more genuine if made against a backdrop of family hostility than if it were made against the more congenial environment of consensus. The call for repentance remains highly personal and pietistic, having to do almost exclusively with a beating of the breast over one's sins, and very rarely with one's participation in the collective guilt of unjust structures. Discipleship has been narrowed to evangelism and singing hymns to Jesus, completely divorced from the witness demands of the larger community. God is said to be more deeply experienced in the rarefied heights of solitude, not in the warm and earthy explosion of togetherness. In effect, conversion in our culture has often meant a retreat into further isolation, not a flinging of arms wide open to meet the desolation of the world.

Because the Filipino evangelical church is for the most part a creature made in the pale image of the American Bible belt, it has remained alienated from the surrounding culture. Instead of being scattered again in a deeper way among his people, a convert goes through a kind of cultural circumcision: he renounces an inherited culture of symbol in favor of a more barren intellectualism in faith and worship; he learns to sing of summer and winter, springtime and harvest; quite unconsciously, he borrows the tastes and scruples of the missionary's Puritan conscience in matters of dress and lifestyle. If in the past he has burned deeply over the poverty of his people, he learns to temper his political opinions in a way that ceases to be offensive to the sedate politics of people raised in the soporific opulence of Middle America.

The result of all these is a continuing failure to speak to our people's needs, to discern the prophetic Word, God's message to this particular culture at this particular time.

THEOLOGY RELATIVIZED

It seems that at the heart of the failure to situate the gospel adequately within the context of people is the failure to perceive that we have a faith delivered, not interpreted, once for all. The faith of the Apostles has been infallibly set down for our instruction. But insight into this faith has been and continues to be a struggle, a wrestling of the clear Word through the darker glass of time and circumstance.

It has been said that there is no such thing as the indigenization of theology. If we are talking of the same God, then it must be the same knowledge in all cultures. This fails to take into account the cultural conditioning of our statements about the one God revealed in the Scriptures. There are no "unengaged" readings of Scripture. The exigencies of a particular situation largely control the shape of our interpretations.

For instance, the stress on justification by faith as a legal abstraction has been attributed to Luther's tortured need to be sure that he was saved apart from the rigorous discipline of monastic life. It was natural in the light of what has been called the "introspective and guilt-ridden conscience of the West" that this doctrine should receive a great deal of emphasis at a time when the early Jew-Gentile crisis had faded, "where Paul was concerned about the possibility for Gentiles to be included in the messianic community, his statements are now read as answers to the quest for assurance about man's salvation." (Stendhal 1976). Likewise, the problem of poverty and oppression in Latin America has eventually produced a theology preoccupied with the motif of liberation. "Even twentieth century Protestant evangelicalism with its firm maintenance of the Paul-Augustine-Luther-Calvin axis is more closely linked to the structure of Aristotelian philosophy and Thomist natural theology than many of its adherents care to admit" (Boyd 1989).

While there has been a tendency in recent years to stress the exigencies of a context at the expense of what is obviously given in the text, nonetheless, the history of theological tradition tells us that it is context which serves as the hermeneutical principle in interpreting the gospel. The world, in a sense, sets the agenda. Those who hear in this the ring of relativism and captivity to context have only to exercise some degree of "hermeneutical suspicion" to realize that our socio-historical situations determine the selection of central motifs in the formulation of theologies.

This means that our statements about the Absolute Reality given in Scripture are bound to be limited by the specific structure of the reality that is known to us. Men have no eyes but for those aspects of things which they have been taught to discern, says the psychologist William James. The things we commonly see are those that have been labeled for us. We perceive selectively. And so a culture, because of the peculiarity of its needs and circumstances, may be more sensitive to some insight which may be partially hidden or entirely lost on another.

> A culture, because of the peculiarity of its needs and circumstances, may be more sensitive to some insight which may be partially hidden or entirely lost on another.

It is understandable, for instance, that the Jews of Jesus' day, smarting under the yoke of Roman rule, should pin their hopes on the glorious Messiah of Isaiah 11, and fail to see him as the suffering servant of Isaiah 53. The New Testament talks a great deal of the "power encounter" between Jesus and the spirits, but this has largely escaped the notice of countries dominated by the scientific outlook. Animistic cultures, in contrast, are struck in a powerful way by this liberating aspect of the gospel.

Herein lies the difficulty of knowing the "essence" of the gospel. Theologians speak of a "core" which is non-negotiable and supracultural. If our perceptions are culture bound, how do we arrive at a definition of the "essentials," the universal elements which must always be present if the gospel is to be preached adequately in any given culture? How do we separate the "essence" from the "accidents" of culture?

Obviously, what one culture perceives as the barest essentials would differ from what another culture would consider as an important focus. To the West, the elements surrounding the concept of sin and guilt have for years comprised an acceptable minimum. It was only after the advent of radicalism and the awakening of the church to the problems of the Third World that this was shown to be sadly inadequate. Latin Americans deem unacceptable a gospel that falls short of articulating the economic consequences of a thoroughgoing discipleship. Asians and Africans who expect that anyone speaking of God will automatically concern himself with healing and exorcism tend to see release from demonic oppression and bodily decay as central to the saving message of the gospel.

> To abstract a core of selected propositions and put it forward as the gospel is reductionist: a Greek rather than Hebrew practice of approaching the whole gospel.

It is clear from this that there is not a single theology or formulation which may unabashedly advertise itself as universal enough to cover all of Scripture, or be capable of ready transplantation into another culture. The richness of the gospel story is such that no summary may be said to have captured the message in its essence or entirety; the Bible itself presents four versions of the story. To abstract a core of selected propositions and put it forward as the gospel is reductionist: a Greek rather than Hebrew practice of approaching the whole gospel. We would do better biblically to recognize that existing formulations are but functional summaries of a particular cultural context.

THE WORD MADE FLESH

"As the Father has sent me, even so I am sending you" (John 20:19-27).

How has the Father sent the Son? How has he made himself known?

The answer, quite simply, was to become like us. God in speaking to the human condition exposed himself to the scandal of particularity; the Eternal and the Invisible was made flesh, given a body, a time and a place. He dwelt in the world his hands had made, took upon himself a determinate origin, a history, a culture, and a family. In Jesus, we see God in human context: walking the dusty streets of Jerusalem, hobnobbing with the grimy, sweaty people of the marketplace, eating and drinking and trying to make ends meet with the tools of his trade.

The God of the universe was a Jew. He was of the tribe of Judah, was circumcised, fasted and prayed and went to the synagogue and ritually kept the great national feasts. The transcendent, supracultural God circumscribed himself, daringly and in a mind-boggling way, within the bald specificity of Jewish culture.

At the heart of the effort to root the gospel in the soil of culture is the desire to imitate the Father's sending. The Church is to go out, into the heart of the world, and there "make flesh" the Word. She must "sit where the people sit," participate in their life in a way that touches the raw centers of their needs and fears.

The Incarnation means that the Word must have a body; a community that shall make visible the startling newness of life that Jesus brings. It also means that we must empty ourselves, lay aside the sometimes numbing privilege of being in the know, step down from the glory of our clichés and the splendor of our common places, and learn to eat of the common bread, teach our eyes to see as the world sees and our tongues to speak as the world speaks.

For so long, the gospel has been wrapped in a veil of abstraction, a string of ethereal propositions delivered from the heights of a pie-in-the-sky piety, far above the foul and needy world of men. While there is an historical uniqueness to the Incarnation, we must, like Jesus, breathe the stronger air of the world below, and immerse ourselves in the warm and bracing task of living among men. Anything less than this hides the God who has revealed himself, fully and plainly, in the stark humanity of the Son.

THE TASK BEFORE US

For many centuries, the Spirit has illumined the churches of the West as they struggled to verbalize to themselves the unerring Word in the face of accretions and distortions brought about by tradition and cultural consensus. The resulting creeds and formulations form a valuable part of the heritage of the Church the world over. These may not substitute, however, for the work of discerning what the Spirit says to the rest of the churches in other parts of the world.

Before is the problem of defining at what precise points the Word may be made to cut and heal in our cultural situation. How are we to deal with the many cases of demonic captivity, devotion to miraculous images? How do we make sin and guilt intelligible to a culture whose conscience is highly socialized and at the same time sensitive to ruptures in nature and disturbances in the cosmos? How are we to view the millions of our poor? What is our response to organized injustice? In what terms are we to preach discipleship? What is the specific content of the gospel in our own context?

These are questions that need to be answered if we are to wrestle truly with the demonic at its point of greatest power in our culture. There is a need to break out of thought forms and formulations that do not really speak to the needs of our people. Failure to do this condemns the Filipino Church to a continuing history of incoherence. We run the risk of going on unheeded, mumbling in corners about the meaning of our own symbols.

Melba Padilla Maggay is the founder and director of the Institute of Studies in Asian Church and Culture, Manila, Philippines.

QUESTIONS FOR REFLECTION:

1. In the sovereignty of God, the Church until quite recently has been located most strongly in the West. What are some of the consequences of this that Melba Maggay identifies? How has that history shaped the church in your context, both positively and negatively?

2. In your culture, how can you best explain sin and salvation? Which Bible stories and passages would you seek to turn to? Are there elements of your culture that could provide bridges for understanding these themes? How would you teach (and live!) these truths in very concrete terms if you were, like Maggay, in a strongly communal and shame culture?

3. In the West, even in the church, the demonic is often dismissed as ancient superstition. How would you respond to that? Similarly, poverty is often dismissed as economic and nothing to do with the spiritual. How would you respond to that? How do you think different parts of the world church can help other parts to see the gaps in the way each reads Scripture?

CHAPTER 18

CAN CHOPSTICKS EVER BECOME ROOF-BEAMS?

A Tale from China
Nadine Woods

Every time I picked up *Miss Chopsticks*, I could not put it down. Housework had to wait, and so did e-mails that required an urgent reply. This is a book about three girls who migrated from rural China to work in the city. The original title of the book in Chinese, directly translated into English, would be Vegetables, Water and Tea, indicating the respective parts of the city's service sector in which the girls were involved: a restaurant, a spa and a teahouse (Xinran 2007).

Although the girls are as different as chalk and cheese, they share one similarity; that is, they are country girls, generally despised as utterly useless by the people around them. "While men are believed to be the strong providers, who hold up the roof of the household, women are merely fragile, workaday tools, to be used and then discarded"(1). This is a common view of women in rural China. While men are referred to as roof-beams, women are referred to as chopsticks. In the story, the three girls all come from one family with only female children, and because they are girls, the parents did not even bother to give them proper names. They are conveniently called Three, Five and Six, indicating the order in which they were born.

Miss Three escaped from home when her father planned to marry her to the crippled son of a local government official. She landed in a Chinese fast food restaurant. Three's sheer hard work and talent made it possible for her to hold her job in the restaurant and take home lots of money every year when she visited. By doing so, she won back a lot of respect for her family, who previously felt ashamed because there was no son in the family. As a result, her father decided to send two more of his girls to free them of the drudgery of peasant life. Miss Five and Miss Six were chosen.

The experiences of the three girls in the city were in general very positive. They were treated very well by their bosses and coworkers. They learned to do their jobs well and managed to acquaint themselves with city life, an education they would not have received if they had stayed in the countryside. They also managed to make and save money. The story ends with the happy homecoming of the girls, who became the center of attention in the village. Smartly dressed and cheerful, they have endless stories to tell of city life, which none of the other villagers have experienced. Their elevated status has also helped improve their mother's status in their father's eyes. She used to be seen as a woman who "couldn't lay eggs" because she "couldn't give birth to a boy"(1). When a bundle of money was presented to her by the daughters on their return, the father gestured for her to open it. Seeing the money, the father's eyes "began to redden and he asked, in a weak voice, 'Is it possible that our chopstick girls will be able to hold up our roofs?'"(232). Although it was only a question, not a statement, it made the girls very happy because "these were the words they had been waiting all their life to hear"(232). Happy as it is, the ending still leaves a slightly bitter taste in my mouth. I cannot help asking why women in rural China are treated in such a manner.

Traditionally, China was a society where women were not valued. Men were the core of the family. A woman's position in society and in the home could be summed up like this:

> Let a woman modestly yield to others.
>
> Let her respect others.
>
> Let her put others first, herself last.
>
> Should she do something good, let her not mention it.
>
> Should she do something bad, let her not deny it.
>
> Let her bear disgrace; let her even endure when others speak or do evil to her.
>
> Always let her seem to tremble and fear.

This was supposedly written by Ban Zhao, a well-educated woman in the Han dynasty (as cited in Bujak 2009).

Confucius defined women's roles as kinship roles: daughter, sister, wife, mother, mother-in-law. Women seemed to earn the right to exist only by their networked relationships with men. "In all these roles, it was incumbent on women to accord with the wishes and needs of closely-related men: their fathers when young, their husbands when married, their sons when widowed" (Ebrey 2008). This was part of a code which controlled the behavior and instruction of women. This code consisted of three obediences and four virtues:

The Three Obediences: Obey her father before marriage, her husband after marriage, and her son after her husband's death.

The Four Virtues: She should be righteous, her conversation courteous and understanding, her appearance graceful but not extravagant, her role at home always a supporting role to her husband and children (translated from SOSO, a Chinese website).

There are also many Chinese proverbs which are useful in illustrating how unimportant women were in Chinese culture:

> A woman without talent is a woman of virtue.

It is more profitable to raise geese than daughters.

Changes occurred from the mid-nineteenth to the mid-twentieth century, mainly due to China's contact with the West, including Christian missionaries, technology and science, democracy, and egalitarian philosophies. The low status of women was certainly challenged by the Communist Party when they took over in 1949. Mao Zedong encouraged women to work outside of the home and said that women could hold up half of the sky. While all this had an impact on the status of women, traditional views of women still linger, especially in the countryside. As Ling puts it, "Though China may have taken great leaps forward in official statutes and public pronouncements concerning women, nonetheless, in practice, backed by centuries of history and tradition, the old ways die hard." In the current society, the view of women is also shaped by practicality as well as tradition. Because when a woman marries, it is more than likely that she will leave her own home to go to live in her husband's, we have a saying in China, "Marrying a daughter off is like pouring water out, which cannot be retrieved." It is felt to be a total loss to the girl's family. In a society where there is a lack of social security, especially in the countryside, it is thought better to have a son who can bring in a wife when grown up. The son and his wife can then look after the parents when they grow old and feeble. The one-child policy certainly contributes towards the abortion of many female fetuses. The reason is very obvious: if a family can only have one child, they would rather have a son, who can not only look after his parents but also continue the family name.

In the light of this very pragmatic reasoning, it is vital that we ask who ultimately determines the value of a human being. As Christians, we believe that the Bible holds the truth, and therefore we must align ourselves with God's view on this issue. Every Christian knows that human beings are created in the image of God and that life is given to us by him; therefore, life is of the highest value. We may not feel loved, and some of us, like the chopstick girls, are not loved by the people around us, sometimes including our own families. However, the creator of heaven and earth loves each one of us. "For God so loved the world that he gave his one and only Son, that whoever believes in him shall not perish, but have eternal life" (John 3:16). We only need to think of God's love for us to realize that all human beings, men and women, are loved indiscriminately and treasured by God. Jesus died on the cross for women as well as for men.

God loves us so much that he wants to have a personal relationship with each one of us, including women. John recorded Jesus' encounter with a Samaritan woman for the reader to ponder. In this incident, Jesus asks for water not just from a Samaritan but from a Samaritan woman. As we know, at that time, Jews and Samaritans did not mix, let alone a Jewish man with a Samaritan woman. Jesus' act was obviously controversial to say the least. If asking for water from a Samaritan woman is unusual enough, then engaging her in a conversation is just shocking. Moreover, Jesus knows everything about the woman, her present as well as her past. "The fact is, you have had five husbands, and the man you now have is not your husband" (John 4:18). It dawns on the woman that Jesus might be a prophet, knowing what he knows. The conversation did not end there. Jesus goes on to reveal his true identity to the woman, who then spreads the good news and leads many of the people from her town back to Jesus. We all know this story, but reading it with China's many chopstick girls in mind breathes fresh insight into this old and familiar account. There are important lessons that we Christians can learn from Jesus' interaction with the Samaritan woman.

> We all know this story, but reading it with China's many chopstick girls in mind breathes fresh insight into this old and familiar account.

Firstly, Jesus' love is all inclusive, big enough to include Jews and Samaritans alike. Galatians 3:27-28 states that all of us "who were baptized into Christ have clothed ourselves with Christ. There is neither Jew nor Greek, slave nor free, male nor female, for you are all one in Christ Jesus." Jesus has certainly demonstrated the nature of his all-inclusive love by reaching out not only to a Samaritan but a Samaritan woman. Is our Christian love big enough to cover not just women but women from the countryside, or poor, or uneducated, or marginalized?

Secondly, Jesus knows the woman very well, not only her present but also her past. He knows her background and the fact that she has a bad reputation for having had several husbands. The woman comes to draw water at the sixth hour, which is lunch time, the hottest time of the day, probably to avoid other people. Jesus chooses to arrive at this well at this particular time to talk to the woman. Are we prepared to go out of our way to really get to know the women we want to reach? Of course, we are not omniscient, but are we willing to make friends and spend time with the people around us so that we get to know their present and past to serve them better?

Finally, Jesus is at the well to give out living water to this woman. When the conversation made a spiritual turn, Jesus seized the opportunity to tell the woman that "God is spirit, and his worshippers must worship in spirit and truth" (John 4:24). We have been placed where we are to meet other people's physical and emotional needs, but most importantly we are here to meet people's spiritual needs. While Jesus leads people to himself, we are supposed to lead people to Jesus. I'm very impressed with the bosses of the three chopstick girls in the book. They are all caring city people who nurture, educate, and teach the girls rather than use them as cheap labor from the countryside. The success of the girls has a lot to do with their help. Unfortunately, there are no Christians in this story. If only we could add a chapter where the girls meet Christians, hear the gospel, and come to know Jesus as their personal savior in the city! Then when they go home, they would not only have money and material things to show off; they would also have something much more valuable to share with their family and fellow villagers.

Although people's opinions vary when it comes to migration from the countryside into the cities in China, it seems to be a social trend that nobody can stop. There are certain benefits to migration as Ren Xianliang puts it, "Flowing water never gets sour..." Migration can "liberate the people, the masters of society, and realize human freedom, release human creativity, and restore human dignity. This is the path that leads to our future" (as cited in Wakabayashi 1990, 522). However, if we Chinese do not change our traditional views of women, none of those goals would be achieved for poor rural women no matter where they go. Although God has created women to be different from men, women are certainly not chopsticks in the sense that they are useless. Rather, they are roof-beams in God's eyes. Jesus died for them, and that is how precious they are. Now the question for each one of us is: Are we willing to see women the way Jesus sees them? Are we willing to treat them the way Jesus treats them?

Nadine Woods, born and raised in China, now lives in Singapore.

QUESTIONS FOR REFLECTION

1. "Backed by centuries of history and tradition, the old ways die hard." Why is this so? When contextualization into the culture as it is and the transformative demands of the gospel appear to clash, how should we proceed? When is it right to be counter-cultural? Is this a denial of contextualization?

2. In your culture, which groups of people are marginalized and unfairly treated? Does the church speak prophetically into that situation? What else needs to happen? How does change come about?

3. In some situations, especially those shaped by a strong religious tradition, any challenge to the culture (by Christians or others) may lead to acute persecution. Why? How might you support believers in such a situation?

CHAPTER 19

A CAMBODIAN CHRISTMAS CELEBRATION

Yuzo Imamura

In Cambodia, the Christmas celebration is one of the biggest festivals for every Christian.

In rural areas the church budget is generally tight, so sometimes churches start to collect special offerings for Christmas in April. When I once suggested to a congregation that since the budget was tight it might be better to keep the celebration simple and to omit the feast after the celebration, one church member emphatically said that the Christmas celebration *must* consist of both the celebration (worship, teaching God's Word, dancing, etc.) and the feast after the program.

The Christmas celebration typically opens with Cambodian traditional music flowing from the loudspeakers. A group of ladies come to the stage for the Apsara dance (traditional Khmer dancing). Originally Apsaras were mythical, celestial dancers. These dancers wear the Khmer traditional costume, including crowns, Apsara blouse and skirt, belt, and wrist and ankle jewelry. With each step, a bell on the ankle tinkles faintly. Subsequently, the rowdy-dowdy audience becomes silent and watches the Apsara dancers carefully. Apsara music is traditional and very popular among the Cambodians, but the words for this program have been replaced with Christian phrases. Several missionaries with local leaders gifted in music produced hymn books using traditional melodies. "God is wonderfully good" was the music this particular year, although there are many selections.

The leading dancer stands front and center on the stage while others are behind, in line. Most of the dances are synchronized. Every gesture and motion has a rich meaning. One of the amazing elements is the dancer's movement of fingers and toes. For example, in one dance the fingers stretch out backwards and the toes as well with beautiful, flowing movements of both arms. The whole motion means that flowers and leaves are swirling around and falling. However, some gestures which traditionally describe the Hindu gods, such as *naga* (serpent) are not performed or are replaced by Christian expressions and meanings, such as worshipping God the Creator.

In the final stage of the dance, the Apsara dancers throw white jasmine flowers from their silver cups toward the audience. The children rush to gather these flowers dropped at the front seats and the stage; they see it as great fun. Throwing flowers to the audience means giving blessings from God to the people.

After this, the Apsara dancers disappear from the stage while the tempo of music get faster. The audience offers a big hand of applause at long last.

As a whole, this dance is generally viewed as welcoming the audience, offering God's blessings to the audience (congregation), and as an act of worshipping the Christian God—though most Cambodian Christians do not understand the full meaning of each gesture and motion. The Apsara dance is performed in the all important Christian festivals: Christmas, Easter, and other special occasions.

(Another example of Khmer traditionalism found in Christian ceremony is a karaoke video featuring the Christmas story. This video consists of the Khmer traditional dance performance. In one scene where the angel Gabriel comes to Joseph when he was troubled by Mary's pregnancy, Gabriel's costume is the Khmer traditional angelic one.)

The next highpoint of the Christmas celebration is the nativity play.

In general, the Khmer people are very good at drama and are fond of watching plays as well. Both adults and small kids love to play the different roles and are not shy. Indeed they sometimes enjoy performing extempore.

In most countries the nativity play is taken from Matthew 1 and 2 and usually finishes at the scene where the wise men worshipped the baby Jesus (Matt 2:12), but in Cambodia it usually does not stop there. The play continues to include Joseph and his family fleeing to Egypt for a while until Herod the king dies and they return to the land of Israel (Matt 2:23). In fact, not only does the narrator tell the audience about the order King Herod issued to kill all baby boys, but the actors also act out the event of killing all the male children who are two years old or under. It is, indeed, a horrible scene in the joyful Christmas celebration.

The nativity play, which includes Joseph's family's exodus and their homecoming safe and sound to the land of Israel, resonates well with the Cambodian experience of life in the refugee camp and return to the land of Cambodia.

Why do they do this? One explanation is that the Cambodian people have experienced exodus to the Thai borders as refugees during the Pol-Pot regime and the ensuing civil war, so the nativity play which includes Joseph's family's exodus and their homecoming safe and sound to the land of Israel resonates well with the Cambodian experience of life in the refugee camp and return to the land of Cambodia. The story also enables them to understand God's protection and supreme plan for them in a profound way. Cambodian Christians do not know the exact reason why the nativity play is longer than the usual and when it started originally, but most identify with those extra scenes very strongly.

Through the nativity play in the Christmas season, the Cambodian people are reminded of God's never-ending love and his good plan for them. Through it they bring their praises and worship to the true God.

Like the first Cambodian Christian's comment, Christmas celebrations in Cambodia are a very special opportunity for Cambodian Christians to remember God's great love and to worship the Lord with much thanksgiving.

Yuzo Imamura, from Japan, has been a church planter in Cambodia for many years, and currently leads the OMF International team there.

QUESTIONS FOR REFLECTION

1. In Yuzo Imamura's description, in what two main ways do Cambodian Christians contextualize the Christian story? How might you do this in your own culture?
2. What role do drama and the visual arts play in effective contextualization? What other examples can you describe?
3. Why do you think the Cambodian at the beginning of this story insists that celebrating Christian festivals "lavishly," rather than very simply, is so important? Is that true in all situations? What might be some guidelines?

CHAPTER 20

MAUPAY AND THE BIBLICAL SHALOM

Towards a Full-Orbed Understanding of the Gospel
Athena Gorospe

In 1997, during a sabbatical from seminary, I lived for one year in Northern Samar, one of the poorest provinces in the Philippines.[1] The people call themselves "Waray," which literally means "nothing," and is reflective of the self-image of a people who see themselves not only as having nothing but also regard themselves as insignificant and "nothing." Along with an Asian Theological Seminary graduate who is also a member of my intentional community, we started a student ministry, did research on the state of church planting in the area (Gorospe and Cang 1998, 21-42), and conducted training workshops among pastors and lay leaders. I also held an evangelistic radio program every other Sunday morning. In doing so, I tried to look for a cultural link that would enable me to communicate the gospel effectively. I found a relevant link in the Waray's usage of *maupay* and its conceptual similarities with the biblical shalom.[2]

LINKS BETWEEN *MAUPAY* AND *SHALOM*

The word *maupay* is one of the most frequently used words in Samar. It is the word for greeting: *Maupay nga aga sa iyo nga tanan* (Good morning to all of you), a phrase that suggests a wish for the well-being of the other person. When one is asked, "How are you?" the appropriate response is *maupay* (I am well) or *diri maupay* (I am not well). In the same way, the ancient Hebrews greeted each other with shalom, meaning "May it be well with you." The greeting involves a wish for a person's total well-being.

---

1   In 1992, the Eastern Visayas region of the Philippines (to which Samar belongs) was second only to the Bicol region in having the highest incidence of families in the bottom 30 percent income bracket (National Economic Development Authority, *Coverage of Public Programs on Low Income Families,* 1992). About 80 to 90 percent of families are engaged in artisan fishing or are either upland or lowland farmers, groups that are among the poorest in rural society. The average income per day for a family of six in the Eastern Visayas region is Php50, which is about USD 1.25. See Cramer and Cramer (1992, 7-8).
2   Parts of this paper are excerpts from an earlier article, Gorospe (1999, 27–47).

The most frequent meaning of *maupay*, however, is to have food, to have enough money to meet daily needs, and to have material prosperity. For many families in Samar, the good life—*the maupay nga kinabuhi*—is equated with having enough income for basic household needs. Likewise, the most frequent usage of shalom is in the material, physical sense (Yoder 1987, 11), to the point of economic prosperity.[3] Leviticus 26:3-13 emphasizes the abundance of food and the assurance of security as part of shalom. In Psalm 37:11, shalom is connected with inheriting the land and delighting in its abundance. The prophets' expectation of the future involves Israel going through a reversal of fortunes, including a change from poverty to prosperity.[4]

Maupay also means to be healthy and not to be plagued by sicknesses and evil spirits. It can mean that one is safe and protected from physical harm. In addition, it is used in relation to emotional and spiritual well-being. Similarly, shalom may refer to good health or physical wholeness,[5] preservation from harm, victory in battle, and safety in travel or in conflict.[6] To have shalom can indicate that one is released from the source of one's fear and anxiety and is experiencing psychological and emotional wholeness.[7]

However, *maupay* and shalom are not only used to refer to the physical and emotional state of a person but also to harmonious relationships. A relationship that is *maupay* is characterized by giving and sharing, openness in communication, and plenty of time together for storytelling, eating, and shared tasks. When people gather together, celebrate, have fun, and enjoy, it is *maupay*. On the other hand, a relationship of shalom "exhibits harmonious equilibrium, where there is a balancing of the claims and needs of both parties" (Von Rad 2001, 1:130). Shalom can characterize the relationship between individuals enjoying close friendship.[8] This relationship of shalom can also be applied to political and economic alliances.[9]

When used in relation to persons, *maupay* can refer to character, specifically to desirable moral/ethical qualities. Shalom also contains a moral-ethical sense (Yoder 1987, 16).[10] The moral-ethical meaning of shalom is further drawn out in passages where it is paired with tsedeqah (righteousness).[11] A person of shalom is one who is righteous, lives and speaks in truth, and practices justice. By tsedeqah, what is meant is not so much an absolute ethical norm, but faithfulness to the claims made upon a person by a particular relationship (Von

---

3   Ps 73:3; see also Ps 147:14 where shalom is associated with having the finest of the wheat.
4   Yoder (1987, 12), citing Jer 33:6-9; see also Isa 54:11-14; 66:12-14; Zech 8:11-13.
5   Gen 43:28; Ps 38:3; Isa 38:16.
6   Gen 28:21; Josh 10:21; 2 Chr 19:1.
7   Ps 4:8; Judg 6:23; Gen 43:23; 1 Sam 1:17.
8   The idea of close friendship is expressed in Jer 20:10 and Jer 38:22 where Jeremiah cites that the "men of his shalom" (translated as "close friends" and "trusted friends" in the NRSV) have turned against him (Yoder 1987, 14). Cf. Ps 41:9.
9   E.g., the relationship of Solomon and Hiram (1 Ki 5:12).
10   In Ps 34:14, seeking shalom involves departing from evil and doing good. The "man of shalom" is blameless and upright (Ps 37:37). In Zech 8:16-19, shalom is used to mean true and complete justice. See Healey (1992, 5:206). In several passages, shalom is regarded as the antithesis of wickedness (Ps 34:14; Prov 10:9; Isa 48:22). See Good (1962, 3:705).
11   Ps 85:10, 35:27, Ps 72:2-3, 7; Isa 32:17.

Rad 2001,1:370-72).[12] Among Ancient Israelites, there were certain claims laid upon them by virtue of their membership in the same community. When they fulfill these obligations, shalom is upheld. Similarly, in Waray culture, when a person meets the expectations and exhibits the values of the community (such as welcoming strangers), he or she is considered *maupay*.

Aside from people and relationships, *maupay* can also be used to refer to things. When used as such, it takes on the meaning of being aesthetically pleasing or functional, of being whole, intact, and not damaged. Lastly, *maupay* is used to refer to one's work. When work is done carefully and thoroughly, with expertise and knowledge and concern for people who are affected by what one does, it is *maupay*. A government that is incompetent, corrupt, and insensitive to people's needs is a government that is *waray upay* (not good).

INTERSECTING *MAUPAY* AND SHALOM

The overlap between the meanings of *maupay* and shalom makes it an ideal starting point for sharing the gospel, theological reflection, and transformative action among the Warays. On one hand, the biblical shalom can complete the vision of the *maupay nga kinabuhi*, the good life. On the other hand, the ideal of biblical shalom can be brought into focus by other ideas present in the word *maupay*.

> The overlap between the meanings of *maupay* and shalom makes it an ideal starting point for sharing the gospel, theological reflection, and transformative action among the Warays.

For the Warays, the yearning for *maupay nga kinabuhi* primarily revolves around the needs of the family and the extended family. This aspiration can be expanded to encompass the concerns of the community, the immediate society (the people of Samar or the Samarenos), and the whole nation. Shalom in the Bible does not reside only in individuals, but is also applied to communities and nations. A nation that has shalom enjoys economic prosperity, political security,[13] and lives in fear of God. Just as individuals can experience sickness and need healing, so nations also need to be restored to economic and emotional well-being and wholeness.[14] The longing for the good life needs to be viewed not only in terms of individual families or groups, but also from the broader perspective of the whole people of Samar and the Philippines and can be extended to the rest of the human community.

Among the Warays, it is very important to maintain harmony and to restore previous broken relationships within the nuclear and extended family, the primary group, or neighborhood. However, as mentioned above, it is not only individual friendships and alliances, but also nations and peoples which can relate with each other in shalom. In Ancient Israel, it is common for nations or groups to enter into a "covenant of shalom," to ensure the cessation of

---

12   Thus, an action that is righteous in one relationship may be unrighteous in another one. For example, in the case of Judah and Tamar (Genesis 38), Judah proclaims Tamar as "more righteous" than he is, not that what Tamar did was right, but because Judah failed to fulfill the obligations demanded by his relationship with Tamar (that is, he did not give his son Shelah to her after his son had grown up). See Achtemeier (1962, 4:80).

13   For Ancient Israel, political security means protection from the attacks and conquest of other nations, and freedom from internal strife.

14   See Isa 57:18-19 and Jer 33:6-8 where shalom is connected with the healing of the nation Israel.

hostilities and to enter into an agreement for each other's benefit.[15] Shalom is maintained as each fulfills the mutually agreed upon obligations (Healey 1992, 206). It is in this case that shalom takes on the meaning of absence of war or strife (Judg 4:17; 1 Sam 7:14). In a province with a long history of internal strife between the communist-leaning group New People's Army and the military, the message of healing, just reparation, and promise-keeping, which are involved in making a "covenant of shalom," must be heard and seriously carried out.

Moreover, although the longing for harmony in relationships is a constituent part of *maupay nga kinabuhi*, these relationships are mainly understood in terms of people. The biblical view of shalom expands these relationships to include the relationship of humankind with the land and the whole creation. This is particularly important because, in the past forty years, Samar has undergone massive deforestation due to slash-and-burn farming (*kaingin*) and illegal logging. This has resulted in erosion, flooding, and landslides, especially since Samar is visited by frequent typhoons and has bedrocks that support poor soils.[16] Thus, to complete the vision of *maupay nga kinabuhi*, one must broaden the scope of harmonious relationships from interpersonal to cosmic relationships. The Waray, along with many Filipinos, mainly perceive the meaning of *maupay* as absence of overt conflict. To disagree on an issue, to express feelings of discontent and anger and pain, even if it involves one's basic rights, are not considered *maupay*. The biblical shalom, however, connects shalom with righteousness and justice.[17] Without justice and righteousness, the external harmony that seems to be *maupay* will only be superficial and temporal. The *maupay nga kinabuhi* does not mean a life free from conflicts and opposition, since in seeking for justice and righteousness, which are prerequisites for true shalom to take place, one may encounter resistance and antagonism.

Although shalom, like *maupay*, has strong material connotations, it is nevertheless a religious term (Von Rad 2001, 2:403). Shalom is a gift of God, a favor he gives to his people (Beck and Brown 1975, 2:778).[18] The condition for shalom is the presence of God,[19] which is experienced by those who live in obedience and faith.[20] Thus, one should not divorce materiality from spirituality. In the Genesis 3 story, the loss of shalom in creation was caused by the disruption of the relationship between God and humankind. The loss of shalom in the exile was also caused by Israel's unfaithfulness to Yahweh. Thus, the experience of *maupay nga kinabuhi* can only take place by the grace of God through a restoration of relationship between God and humankind. A right relationship with God is a prerequisite for shalom.

---

15   This is the case between Isaac and Abimelech who entered into a covenant of peace (*berit shalom*), where they agreed that their own people would not harm or molest each other (Gen 26:29-31).

16   From 86 percent forest cover in 1952, it went down to 46 percent in 1978, then to only 10 percent in 1987 (Cramer and Cramer 1992, 14-20).

17   This is clearly expressed in the case of the false prophets who opposed Jeremiah's proclamation of doom. In order to please the king and the people, the false prophets proclaimed peace for Jerusalem even though the people were committing idolatry and injustice. Jeremiah, on the other hand, believed that true peace could only be attained through righteousness and justice (Jer 6:13-15; 14:11-14).

18   See 1 Ki 2:33; Job 25:2; Ps 35:27; Ps 85.

19   Num 6:26; 1 Chr 23:25.

20   For Israel, shalom is a blessing that comes from their fulfillment of their covenant obligations to Yahweh (Deut 28:1-14).

Shalom is a gift, but it is also a responsibility. This implies that one cannot be passive in bringing about shalom. Shalom can only come through a pro-active involvement that would bring about healing, restoration, reconciliation, justice, and righteousness. This is especially significant for the Warays. Waray poetry indicates a tone of resignation to the grim realities of life (Vilches 1980, 69). Cramer and Cramer (27) note a high degree of fatalism in regard to the Warays' output of work. Because of this, the dream for *maupay nga kinabuhi* is not translated into action. The idea that the realization of one's hopes for *maupay nga kinabuhi* is a gift as well as a responsibility will aid toward a more pro-active stance in bringing it about.

On the other hand, the biblical picture of shalom can be expanded and enhanced by the meaning of *maupay*. Although shalom is implicit in the state of creation before sin entered the picture, this idea can be brought into clearer focus through the meaning of *maupay* as applied to objects or things. A thing is *maupay* when it is undamaged, whole, aesthetically pleasing, and functional. These descriptions can be applied to the whole creation before sin entered the picture. It was *maupay*. But the disobedience of man and woman brought discord into the whole created order and chaos ensued. Humankind's attitude of ownership instead of stewardship, domination instead of dominion, exploitation instead of preservation has marred creation so that it is *waray upay*.

Another idea which is present in *maupay* but which is not inherently apparent in shalom is the reference to competent, careful, and thorough work. But if one were to see the work of creation as a work of shalom, then it is possible to extend the vision of shalom to include engaging in work that is purposeful, creative, and for the service of others. *Maupay* as "good and creative work" can be used as a resource to encourage professionalism, efficiency, and service in government and in other fields of work.

SHARING THE GOSPEL

Using the links between *maupay* and shalom as a starting point, I shared the gospel by first talking about the Waray's longing for the good life—the *maupay nga kinabuhi*. In my radio program and weekly student meetings, I took the different aspects of *maupay* and the Waray's aspirations of the good life one by one—good health, economic sufficiency, emotional and spiritual well-being, harmony in relationships, etc.—and then showed how each is expressed and expanded by the biblical vision of shalom.

Through each aspect, I expounded on how our sin and other people's sin have kept us from experiencing the good life that God has envisioned for us. However, Jesus' incarnation, life, death, and resurrection sought to bring us back to a place where we can experience shalom again.

> Using the links between maupay and shalom as a starting point, I shared the gospel by first talking about the Waray's longing for the good life—the *maupay nga kinabuhi*.

Using Genesis 1-11 as a framework and its movement from order to chaos, I showed the effects of sin and the curse, not only in terms of the physical, emotional, and spiritual well-being of men and women, but also in their relationship with God, with each other, and with the whole creation. Although shalom is not explicitly stated in Genesis 1 and 2, we see that the harmony and order of creation express a situation of shalom. In the first creation account (Genesis 1), the completion of God's work of creation and his rest on the seventh day demonstrate wholeness and well-being. The structure of the second creation account (Genesis 2) also shows the movement towards harmony of relationships. There was harmony between God and humankind, harmony between man and the ground in which he tilled, harmony between man and the animals, and harmony between man and woman. In Genesis 3, the disruption of shalom caused by the disobedience of man and woman resulted in relationships of disharmony and alienation not only between man and woman, but also between humankind and the whole creation. Creation became "fractured and scattered, disunited, without peace" (Healey 1992, 207). This movement of return to chaos or uncreation continued in Genesis 4-8 (Clines 1978, 61-79), culminating in the flood account, with the physical creation reflecting the chaos and the violence that already characterized human relationships.

The good news is that the narrative movement in Genesis 1-11 concludes with re-creation: Genesis 9 shows God's commitment to reintroduce order out of the disorder, harmony out of the disharmony. But in Genesis 11, sin and its resulting chaos reoccur, and so the process of re-creation begins again in Genesis 12 through the call of Abraham and the election of Israel.

The coming of Christ—the Prince of Peace (*eirene* in Greek), the bringer of well-being, the restorer of disorderly and disharmonious relationships in the whole creation—culminates this process. As I discussed the different aspects of *maupay* and shalom, I also talked about the different aspects of the salvation that Christ brings. In relation to the lack of physical health and emotional wholeness, I presented the healing work of Christ (Mark 5:25-34) and his gift of peace of mind and heart (John 14:27). Noting the lack of shalom in broken relationships, I also shared about the reconciling work of Christ, especially among people who have long been at war with each other (Eph 2:13-18). In the presence of grinding poverty, I talked about the good news to the poor (Luke 4:18; Matt 11:5; Luke 7:22) and the Christ who was willing to become poor for our sakes (2 Cor 8:9). In the face of environmental degradation, I presented Jesus as the reconciler of the whole creation (Col 1:19-20). Ultimately all of these are made possible because, through Jesus Christ, we can experience peace in our relationship with God (Rom 5:1).

Another narrative movement in the Scripture which was helpful as I shared the gospel to the Warays of Northern Samar is the movement of formation—exile—restoration in the story of Israel. The Exile is a very powerful image among the Warays. Indeed, the loss of a sense of belonging and identity, the feeling that God has abandoned them, the longing for the "land flowing with milk and honey," the awareness of God's judgment upon their sins are familiar experiences of the people of Samar. I remember a student's response while I was teaching in Samar. She said: "We are like the Israelites. We are exiles...in our own land." Perhaps, this is the reason why the Warays are highly mobile and have one of the highest rates of migration. Thus, one of the themes that I emphasized in sharing the gospel is that of homecoming. God makes a home for the lonely (Ps 68:6; cf. Ps 113:9), and through Jesus, we can come home to the Father (John 14:2).

SOME CONCLUDING THOUGHTS

Linking *maupay* and shalom and using this as a key to affirm, critique, and expand the Waray's vision of the good life, *the maupay nga kinabuhi*, is a fruitful way of sharing the gospel among the Warays of Northern Samar. I have seen this bear fruit in my ministry among students and have also seen positive responses from my radio listeners. I have suggested above that sharing the gospel could take the form of a narrative movement of creation—uncreation—re-creation in Genesis 1-11, with an exposition on the work of Christ in relation to re-creation. Or it can take the form of the narrative movement of formation—exile—restoration in the life of Israel, with an empha-

> Sharing the gospel could take the form of the creation narrative: creation—uncreation—re-creation (Gen 1-11), with an exposition on the work of Christ in relation to re-creation. Or it can take the narrative of formation—exile—restoration in the life of Israel, with an emphasis on Christ's role of restoration from our exiled state with God.`

sis on Christ's role of restoration from our exiled state with God. Aside from one's reconciliation with God through Christ, the good news would also include economic well-being, healing, reconciliation, justice, and righteousness as main components of salvation.

Athena Gorospe is Associate Professor in Old Testament at Asian Theological Seminary, Manila, Philippines.

QUESTIONS FOR REFLECTION:

1. Trace carefully the case Athena Gorospe makes for linking biblical *shalom* and Waray *maupay*. In what ways do you find her argument persuasive? Are there any weaknesses that you can identify? How might you use and adapt the connection with *shalom* in your own context?

2. Gorospe describes two narrative movements: creation to "uncreation/chaos" to re-creation; and formation to exile to restoration. How could you develop these in your home context, and your host context if that is different?

3. A sense of alienation and absence of well-being, environmental degradation, and migration: these are all widespread concerns all over the world. How might Gorospe's use of *shalom* and *maupay*, and the "two narrative movements," provide a starting point for an apologetic for each of these big issues today?

CHAPTER 21

NEW FACES OF THE CHURCH IN INDIA

Paul Joshua Bhakiaraj

In India, "*Matta, Pitta, Guru, Devam,*" is an oft quoted maxim. It simply means, "Mother, Father, Teacher, God," and signifies the order of priority that many adopt in their lives. In the Indian view of life, therefore, fidelity to one's family and caste community is of paramount importance. Not only is this the foundation of life as known in the present, but also it represents the route for the life hereafter.

Standing alongside that allegiance lies an equally pervasive perception that Christianity is not an Indian religion, rather it has been forced on India by Westerners. Becoming a Christian, therefore, entails turning your back on thousands of years of religious and cultural heritage, rejecting the role your family plays in your present and future life, and not least jettisoning the caste system on which India's social life is based.

It will be obvious to the reader that these attitudes and practices have far reaching implications for Christian discipleship and for the church.

YESU BHAKTAS

One distinctive approach to negotiating such sensitive issues of fidelity to one's community and membership in an institutional church has been *Churchless Christianity.* Theologically speaking, of course, this is a misnomer. A disciple of Christ is by definition a member of the body of Christ, the church. However, since the phenomenon itself was rather novel, its coinage seems to have made sense (Hoefer 2001, xiv). The term "Non-Baptized Believer" and the term *Yesu Bhakta* (Devotee of Jesus) are also employed to refer to this group of people. An able proponent of this form of discipleship, Swami Muktanand, explains the phenomenon:

> To become a Christian means that one has to leave one's birth community and join another community. It also means that one has to reject one's culture (one's way of life). However, it is not a necessity that to be a follower of Christ one has to become

a Christian. This false teaching has come from the Europeans who saw the Hindustani life as demonic and convinced people that in order to become a follower of Christ one has to reject the Hindustani lifestyle and adopt a European lifestyle....A Hindu follower of Jesus also known as a Yeshu Bhakta stays in his Hindu community practicing his Hindustani culture and giving allegiance to Christ and Him alone (2007).

HOW DO YESU BHAKTAS COME TO BE ATTRACTED TO CHRIST?

It is instructive to note that many come to learn of Christ from their neighbors or by way of attendance at a Christian school. This initial knowledge of Christ through personal relationships can be further strengthened when prayers to Jesus are answered, or healing for sickness is received. Growth in morality and an assurance of forgiveness of sins also figures prominently in the spiritual biography of Yesu Bhaktas. Clearly many Yesu Bhaktas have a deep spiritual experience of Christ; theirs is not a case of syncretism, the practice of praying to all gods, considering them all equal and valid paths to one ultimate goal.

YESU BHAKTAS AND THE INSTITUTIONAL CHURCH

On one hand, if Yesu Bhaktas desire to have a relationship with the church, it appears to be a strained one, yet on the other hand, it seems that many have little connection with the institutional church. One description of this phenomenon is helpful here.

> The businessman does not go to Church, but reads his Bible and prays before a picture in his home. He had studied in a Christian school and thereby learned of Jesus. He has experienced Jesus' help in response to his prayers. He listens to Christian Radio programmes. He celebrates only Pongal. (N.B. Pongal is the three-day festival in January which is primarily a social event involving the whole village community. Many village Christians also participate in the festivities though avoiding the one or two traditional home rituals).

When queried further about the nature and reasons for these practices, the businessman and his friend admitted:

> They fear the reactions of relatives if they are baptized.

> They want to have a Christian burial.

> They attend Christian public meetings, but their wives do not come along.

> They expect Jesus to take them to heaven and to take care of their children.

> They do not feel bad about not being baptized, nor do they feel that God is displeased because of it.

> God expects of them that they lead a decent life as a follower of Jesus.

> They feel they should go to church.

> If they get baptized, they feel that they should then leave going to the cinema, smoking, and other bad habits.

They do not try to persuade their wives to join their Christian faith, as it would only cause conflict in the home and among the relations. Now they are still accepted by their caste people and family members.

The best way to reach their wives would be through Christian literature; if there were Bible women, they could possibly speak with them, otherwise, only prayer for them is possible.

They would not be interested to join a cottage prayer meeting even if it was nearby.

They understood Jesus as teaching us to avoid a sinful life and to do good to others (Hoefer 2001, 5-6).

Such men and women, young and old believers in Christ are legion, but are largely invisible to the general population (see also Wingate 1997, 139-151). They all seem to have in common deep attraction and devotion to Jesus Christ, an allegiance to family and community and a genuine desire to forge a mode of discipleship that will enhance personal and family spirituality but yet avoid the stigma of being considered as outcasts of their community. In seeking to hold together the complex socioreligious context they inhabit and their indisputable devotion to Jesus, Yesu Bhaktas are attempting to forge a fresh form of discipleship, that for some seems attempting the impossible while for others appears even necessary if Christ is to have an appeal in India. Identity that is integrally linked to family and community among other things, finds in the institutional church and all that it represents an existence that robs them of their socioreligious mooring and security, indeed an offence to their sensitivities. Instead of either submitting themselves to this existential violence on the one hand, or on the other being content to remain in their old state, Yesu Bhaktas in their own ingenious manner are seeking a mode of existence that does not shake and threaten family and community anchors but yet allows the deep yearning for the spiritually fulfilling and meaningful relationship with Jesus Christ to flourish. This surely is a significant step that is being attempted.

> Yesu Bhaktas are attempting to forge a fresh form of discipleship, that for some seems attempting the impossible while for others appears even necessary if Christ is to have an appeal in India.

HOW DO YESU BHAKTAS NOURISH THEMSELVES SPIRITUALLY?

Most of the time, Yesu Bhaktas relate to Christ only in their private prayers and meditations. Occasionally they venture to church but try to do so anonymously. For the most part they are on their own, sometimes socially and spiritually. More recently though, Christian radio and TV has become a source of nourishment, for it affords an unobtrusive and perhaps safe way of being fed spiritually.

WHAT IS THE NUMERICAL SIGNIFICANCE OF THIS MOVEMENT?

With regard to demographic distribution of these non-baptized believers, one researcher comments that, "[t]he most dedicated followers of our Lord, then, among the 'other sheep' are to be found among teenagers, the housewives, the high schools educated and the poor, from all caste communities" (Hoefer 2001, 139-151). In Chennai alone:

Statistics have shown that there is a solid twenty-five percent of the Hindu and Muslim population in Madras city which has integrated Jesus deeply into their spiritual life. Half of the population have attempted spiritual relationships with Jesus and had satisfying and learning experiences through it. Three-fourths speak very highly of Jesus and could easily relate to Him as their personal Lord if motivated. In addition to this population we have ten percent who are 'of the fold', formally Christian. It would be fair to say that a good one-third of the Madras city population relate to Jesus fairly regularly and deeply in their spiritual life (109).[1]

It seems therefore that Yesu Bhaktas do not represent a few isolated and idiosyncratic cases; they seem to represent an influential movement.

MINISTERING TO YESU BHAKTAS

Since the discovery of these Yesu Bhaktas, effort has been expended to cater to their needs in relevant ways.[2] Assuming the title of an older movement "Rethinking Christianity," contemporary activists see a lot of promise in these patterns of discipleship. Seminars and practical efforts at contextual witness and contextual forms of worship are being encouraged. Some critical reflection also seems to have been initiated. Recently a whole issue of a journal was dedicated to this movement, where a select group of leaders addressed some of these important issues. The evident "success'"of a Hindu-ized devotion to Christ has prompted them to subscribe to one basic assumption: "I am convinced that the Christian faith will permeate India only as part of Hinduism, what I call 'Christ-ized Hinduism'"(Hoefer 2002). For his part H.L. Richard, another leader, echoes that sentiment when he says, "the Rethinking agenda will never die and western Christianity will never deeply impact India." He goes on to declare, "one of the lessons of history…seems clearly to be that deeply Indian Christianity will not arise from the existing Churches" (Richard 2002, 7-17). It is salutary to note that this deep disappointment with the church is akin to a sentiment one notices among well-known pioneers of Indian Christianity and is perhaps reminiscent of their effort to advance contextually relevant forms of discipleship. In that sense the Rethinking group is to be encouraged, for their motive seems laudable.

However, it appears that in their eagerness for reform, some basic notions are not being sufficiently thought through, and the alternatives being proposed seem to lack a rigour that would, in actual fact, help their case. If the vast majority of the church is painted with the same brush and is thought to have had a negligible impact on the nation, the very notion of discussing alternative shapes to Christian discipleship will probably be superfluous. If Christian presence is so miniscule that it attracts little attention in its own right, why then the effort to rethink its shape? For good or bad, the fact that Christianity is a well known, viable and live option for many in the region is testimony to the impact that it has had on the nation. Like it is often said, though only about three percent of the nation's population,

---

1   It must be noted, however, that the statistics mentioned here have not been made public and therefore this claim could be contested.

2   It must be said that my attention here is devoted to one vocal section of the Protestant effort alone, though there are significant movements in the Catholic Church particularly in Hyderabad and Varanasi.

the impact Christianity has had has been significantly more than its numerical strength will have us believe. The "ferment" that the gospel has unleashed is testimony to the power of a little yeast. It appears then somewhat myopic to declare on the back of that: "The real move toward an indigenous Christian faith can never come from the Christian community. It must grow out of the 'Churchless Christianity,' with the help and encouragement of the church" (15, quoting Hoefer). Strong language indeed. Stressing that point Richard once again notes:

> If the Rethinking goal of deeply contextual discipleship to Jesus in Hindu contexts is to be realised it will surely only be through new movements that are born in Hindu society. The way of contextual discipleship to Jesus in the Hindu world must be through the birthing of Christ centred movements within Indian cultures and communities (16).

This apparent lack of appreciation for the diversity, vitality, and legitimacy of the existing forms of Christianity seems to afford little patience. Though it contributes a great deal to the discussion of contextual discipleship and even offers a possible way forward, if the zeal of the Yesu Bhakta movement, as encapsulated in the comment above, is allowed to overtake its more sober intents, could it eventually end up with no different a fate than its progenitors? Zeal for growth, which is right and proper, is to be tempered with patience and forbearance, a virtue Christ preached and exhibited in his own life. Furthermore, if these leaders have discovered a successful approach that prides itself in its contextual suitability, does it not seem ironic that, in a pluralistic milieu like India, it is promoted as the "only" approach for the gospel to impact the nation?

A COLORFULLY DIVERSE CHURCH

This seems to stand out when compared to the reality one finds in India. As any visitor will attest, a complex diversity and colorful variety exists here. To be sure, this diversity is reflected in the church as well. One finds practices of Christian worship that originate from the first century to many that are of a more recent vintage. Linguistic and cultural diversity and its influences are equally evident in the church and add to that diversity. In such a situation it seems only appropriate to allow for some measure of diversity in the expressions of devotion to Christ. However effective certain forms of devotion are, it seems somewhat prescriptive to advocate that one pattern becomes the only appropriate form of devotion in a context as diverse as India.

However effective certain forms of devotion are, it seems somewhat prescriptive to advocate that one pattern becomes the only appropriate form of devotion in a context as diverse as India.

One recent and encouraging example of the colorful diversity that is found in the Indian church is the movement to Christ from those of Other Backward Caste (OBC) backgrounds. Since the vast majority of India's population are said to be made up of OBCs and

Dalits, this movement could be numerically significant.[3] As observers will attest, this clearly is a contextually sensitive movement and one that bears closer study. The creative manner in which key figures in OBC history and traditions are being appropriated; the attempt to address spiritual, socioeconomic and religio-cultural dimensions of life as experienced by OBCs themselves; and the clear attempt to reform Indian society are all constructive and fascinating dimensions of this movement.

> What is striking is the claim made by proponents of this movement that the church at large has hitherto been unconsciously captive to a Brahminical worldview.

What is, however, also striking for our purposes is the claim made by proponents of this movement that the church at large has hitherto been unconsciously captive to a Brahminical worldview. From the composition of leadership to Bible translation, from theology to church practice, the church has been locked into such a system and is in dire need of liberation. Those reaching the OBCs are rather vocal about such a hegemonical outlook at work in the church and indeed work to break it. For them, therefore, the Yesu Bhakta movement, which espouses that followers of Christ retain such traditional practices, is symptomatic of a continued captivity, which they seek to expose and break. In fact they stress that such practices are obstacles in the path of OBCs and Dalits becoming followers of Christ.[4]

Though very brief, this nevertheless suggests that the Indian church cannot be treated in a monochromatic fashion. On the contrary, it is to be treated as a complex and multidimensional reality that provides a home for people from various backgrounds and traditions, be it religious, cultural, and socioeconomic. From the people movements that transpired in the nineteenth and twentieth centuries, to creative movements like the Yesu Bhaktas, to those who are turning to Christ from OBC and Dalit backgrounds, the church comprises various groups. Their specificity is to be taken seriously and granted a legitimacy that it deserves. Patterns of devotion to Christ are to be situated within this broad framework and cannot be forced into a straight jacket of one particular practice, however Indian and appealing that may be for some.

If, as described in the Acts of the Apostles, Jewish Christians and Gentile Christians struggled yet worked with each other to establish what devotion to Christ meant for them and how that was practiced in the first century, we in India who face similar issues will do well to follow their example. The early church represents an interesting model for what we must attempt today within our own context.

THE WAY FORWARD

Clearly we are observing currently in India unprecedented and significant developments. This is both exciting and daunting. However one looks at it, we cannot escape from the realization that close attention should be paid to these phenomena. We cannot afford the luxury of assuming that conventional "Christian" (read Western?) methods and patterns will alone

---

3   National Sample Survey Organisation (NSSO) put the OBC population in the country at 40.94 percent, the SC population at 19.59 percent, ST population at 8.63 percent, and the rest at 30.80 percent (*Times of India*, Sept 1, 2007).

4   This is based on extensive discussions with the leaders of this movement among OBCs.

suffice in our mission effort. Yet we cannot undo history and all that it represents. Surely a mature and continuing dialogue is necessary for a healthy approach that seeks the welfare of the people concerned as well as the long-term theological and spiritual health of the church. It is indubitable that close study and responsible action informed by astute thinking and fervent prayer will enable and facilitate the building of Christ's church in India.

Paul Joshua Bhakiaraj teaches at South Asia Institute of Advanced Christian Studies, Bangalore, India.

QUESTIONS FOR REFLECTION:

1. What would you affirm and what might you be less comfortable with in Paul Joshua Bhakiaraj's description of the Yesu Bhakta movement? What might be the strengths, and the weaknesses of this expression of Christian discipleship?

2. Look at the list of reasons given by the group of Yesu Bhakta businessmen for refusing baptism and involvement in the institutional church. How would you respond to each of these from the Scriptures? What changes do you think the institutional church in India might need to make in its teaching and practices to respond to some of these challenges?

3. Paul Joshua Bhakiaraj suggests that in such a diverse and huge population as India represents the church may need to have many different forms to reach different communities. What might Christians in those different expressions of the church need to do to build unity in their diversity?

CHAPTER 22

CONTEXTUALIZATION FOR INDIA'S MAJORITY

Robin and Steve Smith

Most people in the world, including those involved in missions, when asked to name the main religion of India would say *Hindu*. However, few really understand the term.

According to the *New Oxford American Dictionary* (2nd ed. for Apple OSX), a Hindu is a follower of Hinduism. The dictionary defines Hinduism in this manner:

> ...a diverse family of devotional and ascetic cults and philosophical schools, *all sharing a belief in reincarnation and involving the worship of one or more of a large pantheon of gods and goddesses*, including Shiva and Vishnu (incarnate as Rama and Krishna), Kali, Durga, Parvati, and Ganesh. Hindu society was *traditionally* based on a caste system. (Emphasis mine.)

According to this definition, then, a Hindu is one who believes in reincarnation, worships one or more gods, and may or may not still cling to the traditional system of caste. This definition is accepted by many people around the world, including missionaries and Indian Christians (members of the established church in India).

Here is our question: what if this definition were incorrect? What if most of the world were wrong about what it means to be Hindu for the majority of those whom we call Hindu? If that were so, then missionaries and Indian Christians would be utilizing erroneous strategies for reaching out to roughly half the population of the subcontinent, about 625 million people.

Before we go any further, let us consider some numbers. This is difficult to do because a complete, caste-based census has not been conducted in India since 1931. However, based upon that census, projections have been made. In 2001, the projections showed that about 80.5 percent of India's population, roughly 965 million people, are Hindu.

In our experience we have found that only a small percentage of this huge number have a faith matching the dictionary definition. Moreover, historically, half of those included in this number did not worship many gods, did not believe in reincarnation, and are still very much trapped in the oppression of caste. Yet, the established church and Western missionaries serving in the subcontinent have consistently reached out to Hindus as if all 965 million share the same beliefs. So, what does it mean to be Hindu? What do Hindus believe? Why have they been so misunderstood? How should we change our strategies for reaching them?

WHAT DOES IT MEAN TO BE HINDU?

Historically, the term Hindu described anyone from the Indus River Valley. It was simply a geographic designation and had no religious connotations. Like an Englishman was from England or a Persian was from Persia, a Hindu was from the area near the Indus River. Also, before 1947 there was no united Nation of India. Instead, for centuries, the subcontinent was divided into various kingdoms and city-states. Each region boasted its own food, its own language, its own religious practices.

Eventually, the British ruled the subcontinent. With their rule came a common language (English) and infrastructure for travel (the railroad). For the first time in history, the educated elite of the subcontinent were able to easily communicate with each other and to travel with relative ease. These educated elite joined together, fought for political freedom, and India eventually became an independent nation. During the fight for freedom, many of the leaders began to use the term Hindu as their rallying point. Hindu became synonymous with Indian nationalism.

It didn't take long for the term Hindu to take on religious connotations, as well. It was a simple transition for the elite to begin applying the term to their religious culture. The tragedy is that the religious culture of India's educated, elite Hindus has always been very different from the religion of the Everyman.

The Hindu elite comprise roughly 12 percent of India's Hindu population. These are India's upper castes. Their faith resembles the dictionary quote provided earlier. In contrast, India's working poor comprise 65 percent of all so-called Hindus. This translates to roughly 625 million people. Their religious practices and traditions are completely different from the elite. They are the low castes of India.

It is important to note that these low castes are not the Dalits (Untouchables) and Tribal peoples who are currently responding in great numbers to the gospel. In the caste system, these low castes sit above the Dalits and Tribals, and below the upper castes. India's low castes continue to remain primarily unreached by the gospel, at least until very recently.

This misunderstanding of the divide between the religion of the upper castes and the religion of the low castes has adversely affected mission in India. How did the established church miss the distinction?

This misunderstanding of the divide between the religion of the upper castes and the religion of the low castes has adversely affected mission in India. How did the established church miss the distinction? Historically, the empowered elite, primarily the brahmins, were the only ones allowed to learn. They were the educated, the historians, and the language teachers. When Western missionaries learned language from the educated brahmins, they learned upper-caste language. When missionaries posed questions of faith, they received elitist, brahmin answers. It didn't take long for missionaries to consider the faith of the brahmin to be the faith of all "Hindus." This misunderstanding has remained in the church, and is as prevalent today as ever.

A Western equivalent of this scenario might be something like a missionary wanting to reach the Native Americans of Central or South America, but instead of asking the illiterate workers about their faith, their language, their beliefs, and their oral traditions, the missionary asks the local catholic priest who leads services in Latin! The analogy isn't perfect, but it does shed some light on the disparity that can exist between religious leaders and the masses. In India, followers of Christ have not understood the difference between the faith of the Hindu elite and the low-caste peoples. Thus, we have not used the right words when speaking with the low-caste masses about Jesus. Instead, we have used brahminical religious terms. The result is, Indian Christians and missionaries have not been able to reach the hearts of 52 percent of India's population, the low-caste peoples.

Consider one real example of this misunderstanding. In today's Hindi Bibles, the word Parmeshwar is the word used for God. It is the name for God that the early missionaries learned from their brahmin translators. It is the only name for God accepted by the established church in India. However, Parmeshwar is a brahminical name for God, and in fact is another name for Vishnu, part of the Hindu trinity which sits at the top of the pantheon! The church has used this name for so long they've forgotten its original connotations, but many of India's low castes know what Parmeshwar represents. For low-caste peoples, Parmeshwar is the god who incarnates to oppress them! It makes sense they would have no desire to read a book about the god who oppresses!

HOW CAN WE SPEAK TO THE HEARTS OF INDIA'S LOW-CASTE PEOPLES?

There is no one way to reach out to this large percentage of India's population. The divide between the lower-caste peoples and elite upper castes couldn't be wider. Yet, missionaries and Indian Christians have consistently tried to reach all "Hindus" using brahminical terms. This must change in order for India's low caste to be reached. In order to speak to the hearts of low-caste Hindus, we must tap into their original beliefs, their own oral traditions, and find bridges to the gospel which are intrinsic to their own religious systems.

There is evidence to indicate that the ancient peoples of India were monotheists. They called God Mahadev, The Great God. They considered him to be the divinely Supreme Heavenly Being, the One and Only Spiritual Source of all that is good and beneficial for mankind. Historically, there was no idol for Mahadev.

Around the year 1000BC, Aryan invaders overpowered the peoples of peninsular India. During their gradual, steady domination of the subcontinent, they corrupted the native peoples' view of God by establishing their own polytheistic beliefs and socioreligious order. Over time, the native peoples began to accept the beliefs of their occupiers and align themselves under this new order, caste. The Aryan conquerors convinced the people that it is God who dictates some to be "served," and others to be their slaves.

The Aryan conquerors comprised a small percentage of the total population, yet they were able to retain domination in two main ways. First, they cloaked their social order in religious terminology, making it easier for the masses to accept. Also, they prohibited all people except themselves from receiving an education. With the passage of time, the Everyman of India became illiterate, ignorant, and finally, the slave of the elite, those in the highest castes.

Today, we call this system Hinduism. Many people think that Hinduism was only tradition-ally based upon the caste system and that today it is simply the worship of many gods and the belief in reincarnation. This is not true. The foundation upon which Hinduism still stands is this: that a small minority of people were created by God to be served and it is the job of the majority, low-caste peoples to serve them.

It is vital that missionaries and Indian Christians understand this foundation of Hinduism. It directly impacts the lives and hearts of all low-caste peoples. In fact, their oppression has been so severe, so entrenched for so long, that at some point they began telling the story of a Deliverer, a King, who would return and rescue them from their misery!

A REDEMPTIVE ANALOGY

The story goes like this: There was once a virtuous king named King Bali. He was a righ-teous and benevolent king. It was a golden age. His grateful subjects dearly loved him, and honored him as their Mahabali (the Great Bali). Over time, Bali's kingdom expanded. Finally, the brahmin gods became jealous. Would they, too, be under Bali's rule? The gods approached Vishnu, "the protector," and asked for help. Vishnu assured them that he would overpower Bali. To do so, Vishnu incarnated as a small person, a dwarf, and approached King Bali's throne as a beggar in need of help. He begged the king to grant him one thing: free land covering the distance of three of his dwarfish steps. Bali granted this small wish. Instantly, Vishnu transformed back into his normal size and shape. With his first step, he covered the whole earth. With his second step, he covered the whole sky. For his third step, he placed his foot on Bali's head, and pushed him down to the underworld. However, pleased that Bali did not try to retaliate, Vishnu granted him the permission to return once a year to visit his subjects.

Why did King Bali not try to fight back? In some versions of the story, Vishnu threatened to place his final step on the heads of Bali's subjects. In order to save them, Bali sacrificed himself. However, even if one leaves out that part of the story, it is implied by the king's very name, Bali, which means "sacrifice."

The most widely anticipated annual festival for Hindus is Diwali. For high-caste Hindus, Diwali is the Festival of Lights, the time when they clean their homes, light lamps, and in-vite the goddess of wealth, Lakshmi, into their homes. In contrast, most low-caste peoples celebrate Diwali by lighting a candle, begging for the misery to be gone, and for King Bali to return.

Linking Jesus to this longing for King Bali (literally, King of Sacrifice) seems to be one of the most effective ways of reaching India's low-caste peoples. The following story is a good example. In order to protect those involved, we have changed names and not revealed exact locations.

Linking Jesus to this longing for King Bali (literally, King of Sacrifice) seems to be one of the most effective ways of reaching India's low-caste peoples.

Suresh Paswan is a low-caste statue carver from an eastern state in India. He is a leader in his community of statue carvers, though his fourth grade education makes him barely literate. About two years ago, we at Truthseekers asked Suresh to carve statues for us of some of India's past social heroes, as well as of the fabled Baliraja. While working, Suresh became exposed to the Message and eventually became a follower of Yeshu Baliraja (Jesus, the Sacrificed King).

Soon after Suresh became a follower of Yeshu, two Truthseekers staff members visited him in his home village. They spoke with literally hundreds of villagers each day, usually until late in the evening. The villagers hung onto these new words about God's Kingdom, and seemed particularly intrigued about Yeshu Baliraja. Yes, they had heard of Baliraja! Their grandparents had told them of this ancient hero-king. He was the one who ruled with justice and integrity! However, in recent years, the brahmin (upper-caste) priests had told them that Baliraja was a demon king and that they could not trust him. The brahmins had said that it would be better for the villagers to give their allegiance to the Hindu pantheon through idol worship rather than worship Bali.

After our staff members spoke with them, the villagers acknowledged they had been tricked. They should not have forgotten Baliraja, and they began to understand that Jesus is the ultimate King of Sacrifice! Today, large numbers of people from Suresh's area, not only his fellow statue carvers, but peoples of other castes as well, are embracing the Message of God's Kingdom as revealed in Jesus—the low-caste peoples' Baliraja. Suresh looks to the Lord to help him shepherd these new believers.

Research is still ongoing. However, from experiences such as this one, we are learning that as Jews in Jesus' day longed for a Messiah to rescue them, so many of India's low-caste peoples long for Baliraja, The Sacrificed King, to return and rescue them from oppression. Interestingly, there is also a King Bali tradition among India's high-caste peoples. They make effigies of Bali out of clay and crush them under their feet, cursing his return. The gulf between the elite minority and the low-caste majority is wide, indeed.

CONCLUSION

We at Truthseekers International in New Delhi continue to research India's history, and the oral traditions of the low castes for more ways to communicate the gospel to them. The longing for Bali is not the only link to Jesus. Physically washing feet and using coconut for communion also speak to low-caste peoples in profound ways. Furthermore, throughout the centuries there have been social reformers, poets, and ascetics who have denounced the oppression of caste and spoken of a God who cares for the downtrodden, carries out justice, and cannot be found in a temple.

We have also found that contextualizing the Message for low-caste peoples starts even with their very name, *shudra*. It literally means slave. Today's low castes are tired of the oppression of the caste system. They are tired of being slaves to the elite. They are angered by the teaching that says their only hope is that the next life will be better. Many are openly rejecting Hinduism, and actively seeking an alternative. When we present Jesus as the One who dignifies humankind, they embrace him. In contrast to Hindu gods, Jesus gave (and gives) worth to all people. His Kingdom is inclusive, not exclusive. Low-caste peoples identify with the socially, politically, and religiously oppressed people found in the gospels. When they hear how Jesus honored the oppressed with his words and actions and that he even ate and drank with them, their hearts leap! Finally, here is a God who dignifies!

Today, many low-caste Indians are embracing the Message of Jesus because they are finally hearing it explained in ways they can understand. We at Truthseekers use low-caste stories, religious practices, and traditions as links to the gospel. We describe Jesus as the True Baliraja, who willingly gave himself for our freedom. Jesus, Yeshu Baliraja, is the only God who humbled himself to serve, not just be served.

There is, however, one very important aspect to note about Jesus being the God who dignifies. For India's low-caste peoples, talk is cheap. If we tell them that Jesus gives worth to people, then we must prove this by our actions. To that end, we at Truthseekers actively stand up for the rights of the poor and oppressed. We hold protest rallies against oppressive government policies. We coordinate protest marches where injustice has occurred. We actively stand side-by-side with India's oppressed peoples. We hold foot-washing programs as a practical means of demonstrating the love of God to people who have never been honored. We have found that backing up our words with action is a key element in opening the hearts of India's low-caste peoples.

We ask that you join us in praying for more people to begin expressing God's Kingdom in ways that India's low-caste peoples can understand. They are, after all, half the population of India. As India's low-caste peoples choose to follow the Great Liberator, it could, literally, affect the entire nation.

Robin and Steve Smith serve with Truthseekers International in India.

QUESTIONS FOR REFLECTION:

1. Robin and Steven Smith believe that there has been a deep misunderstanding about the nature of Hinduism and the nature of the religion of those from the lower castes, with dire effects in seeking to transmit the gospel. Trace the story. How do you think this happened? What might you need to watch out for to avoid falling into the same situation elsewhere?

2. What are the strengths and the limitations of the analogy with Baliraja? How should we build on such stories?

3. Compare this article with Paul Joshua's. Do you think these are complementary or contradictory? Why? What do they tell us about the difficulty of "doing contextualization"? How might those working in very different ways, but with the same goal of winning people to be disciples of Jesus Christ, help each other?

CHAPTER 23

THE GOSPEL AND THE PRACTICE OF HOSPITALITY

Joong-Sik Park

The multicultural congregation I pastored in Cincinnati, Ohio from 1993 to 2000 has been involved in urban ministry in a racially diverse community since the spring of 1998—through a coffee house and basketball ministries. Since the summer of 1999, it has extended the ministry to Over-the-Rhine, the most drug-ridden and crime-ridden area in Cincinnati (where the riot erupted in April 2001, following the police shooting of an unarmed African-American teen). Every Saturday afternoon we met and talked with people on the streets of Over-the-Rhine, seeking to communicate the gospel to them.

Walking around the sections of Over-the-Rhine, with its trash-riddled lots and boarded-up buildings, we often felt overwhelmed by the depth of brokenness and hopelessness among the people and by the vicious cycle of poverty and despair. In the face of extreme human suffering, the practices of evangelism and social concern, though distinctive, were so closely interrelated that they could hardly be separated. Through talking with strangers on the street corners and trying to build friendships with them, we discovered that a great number of them had already heard the gospel and many had once belonged to the church. The good news was not new to them; rather, it had to be proven good and true. Without genuinely caring about them and seeking to serve them as whole persons, that is, without practicing biblical hospitality, we could not communicate God's redeeming love in Christ with credibility. We needed to share our lives with them and to share in their lives. It was extremely challenging, but there was no other way. We came to realize the essential need of hospitality in the ministry of evangelism.

In this essay, I intend to view evangelism in relation to the biblical practice of hospitality. Hospitality is neither equal to evangelism nor simply a means to evangelism; it is a primary context for evangelism, within which an authentic evangelism takes place. Evangelism in the context of hospitality is particularly crucial in the post-Christendom society in which North American and Western European churches find themselves today. In this post-Christian era, the church is no longer in a central position of power and influence, but is rapidly becoming marginal. In his article, "Can the West Be Converted?" Lesslie Newbigin writes that our society is a pagan society. Yet "it is far tougher and more resistant to the Gospel than the pre-Christian paganisms," since it is "a paganism born out of the rejection of Christianity" (Newbigin 1985, 10).[1] As Douglas Hall aptly describes, "It is a society that has some awareness of the enormous gap between Christian theories and Christian practice and that mistrusts easy declarations of salvation" (Hall 1996, 368).

Verbal proclamation of the gospel is an essential dimension of evangelism; evangelism is definitely a word event. It is not, however, solely verbal, as demonstrated in Jesus' incarnation, the paradigmatic event of evangelism, in which the Word became flesh. As Niles claims, "The Christian Gospel is the Word become flesh. This is more than and other than the Word become speech" (Niles 1951, 96). As people hunger for evidence of the life of the gospel, the practice of biblical hospitality compellingly embodies the gospel and makes its witness "credible and inviting" (Pohl 1999, xi). An evangelist is not simply a detached and mechanical communicator. In evangelism, our whole being is to be involved and shared. In the context of hospitality, the gospel becomes vital and visible.

HOSPITALITY AS CONTEXT FOR EVANGELISM

When we practice hospitality, we intend to enter into fellowship with those whom we welcome. Evangelism practiced in the context of hospitality is not simply the sharing of our knowledge of the gospel, but of our lives redeemed, transformed, and sustained by the grace of God. When the Good News is shared, the lives of the witness and the one invited to Christian faith are also to be shared. In this way, hospitality is more than simply a context for evangelism; it is integral to the gospel. In fact, the whole life of Jesus was that of hospitality, as Pohl suggests: "Jesus gave his life so that persons could be welcomed into the Kingdom" (1999, 29). Koenig puts it this way: "When Paul urges the Romans to 'welcome one another . . . [just] as Christ has welcomed you' (15:7), he is revealing something close to the heart of his gospel" (Koenig 1985, 11).[2]

> Evangelism practiced in the context of hospitality is not simply the sharing of our knowledge of the gospel, but of our lives redeemed, transformed, and sustained by the grace of God.

The driving force for evangelism is felicitously described in 1 John 1:1-4, particularly in verse 3: "We declare to you what we have seen and heard so that you also may have fellowship with us; and truly our fellowship is with the Father and with his Son Jesus Christ."[3] Thus, our motivation for evangelism is based, first, upon our own experience of God's invitation to eternal life in Christ, out of our gratitude for God's welcoming of us in Christ to fellowship. Second, our motivation is based upon our desire to invite others into the same welcome of God, into this fellowship, which is not only with God but also with one another. The practice of evangelism in hospitality "both reflects and participates in God's invitation of welcome to

---

1   Newbigin also stresses that "the most aggressive paganism" with which the church has "to engage is the ideology that now controls the 'developed' world'" (1995, 10).

2   Koenig also states in his recent study on the missionary dimensions of the church's eucharistic rituals: "Answering the command to join Christ's mission becomes possible only when we can savor the eager and compassionate welcome that he extends to each of us personally (Matt 11:28f.; Rom 15:7ff.)" (2000, 220).

3   Scripture quoted in the essay comes from the New Revised Standard Version.

all" (Pohl 1999, 172). With this in mind, one of the most important questions in evangelism is whether we are willing to share our lives with others and to share in the lives of others.

In Christian hospitality, the ultimate host is Christ. We, as Christians, do not invite unbelievers to the table of our own resources, but to the table of Christ. And to that table "we come as equals" (Pohl 1999, 158). Niles emphasizes that a Christian is merely a guest at Christ's table. In the Christian's role as evangelist, he or she calls others to come to that table (Niles 1951, 96).[4] Again and again, we are pointed to the way mission is described in Luke and Acts as – what Koenig names – "spiritual-material welcoming." Luke carefully seeks to prove "the essential unity between ministries of the word and ministries of the table" (Koenig 1985, 100). A vivid example is found in Luke 15 where Jesus presents three parables which "are a classic description of what evangelism is" (Niles 1951, 57).[5] These are the parables of the lost sheep, the lost coin, and the lost son. Jesus aptly tells these parables of the lost precisely when he is accused of receiving and associating with tax collectors and sinners and having meals with them: "This fellow welcomes sinners and eats with them" (Luke 15:2). Here is a significant connection between evangelism and the hospitality of shared meals. Evangelism is to be practiced in the context of the welcome table, which is a sign of acceptance, inclusion, and equality.

EVANGELISM IN HOSPITALITY AS A BOUNDARY-CROSSING PRACTICE

For evangelism done in the context of hospitality, an intentional and genuine effort to cross significant racial, ethnic, and socioeconomic boundaries is an essential and integral part. As Koenig states, "The kingdom breaks in on meals and other occasions of welcoming; or it somehow advances through alliances with strangers" (Koenig 1985, 125). Hospitality to the stranger, particularly to the marginalized, is then both intrinsic to the gospel and crucial to its proclamation.

For the early church, hospitality to needy strangers "became one of the distinguishing marks of the authenticity of the Christian gospel," and "a fundamental expression of the gospel" (Pohl 1999, 33,35). The very credibility of our witness to the gospel is at risk when our ministry of evangelism fails to cross boundaries, when it is limited to those who are culturally or racially similar to ourselves. The true nature of the gospel is contradicted when our witness becomes selective and does not reach past racial, ethnic, and other boundaries established by society. But evangelism in the context of hospitality recognizes the equal worth of every person and does not accommodate the gospel to discriminations based upon cultural and socioeconomic differences. Thus, the evangelistic practice of hospitality defies prevailing practices of society and can offer a prophetic witness to the prevailing culture.

---

4   In biblical hospitality, the roles of host and guest are far from being predictable, as well illustrated in the story of Zacchaeus in which Jesus invited him to be his host; host and guest roles are often exchanged or reversed. See Pohl (1999, 121). Stephen Bevans rightly stresses the missionary's role as guest: "It seems to me that if there is one basic attitude that missionaries must cultivate as part of their missionary activity and spirituality, it is this attitude of being a guest" (1991, 51).

5   According to Robert C. Tannehill, "these parables help to define the character of God and the mission of Jesus" (1986, 239).

At the synagogue in Nazareth, Jesus read from Isaiah 61: "The Spirit of the Lord is upon me, because he has anointed me to bring good news to the poor. He has sent me to proclaim release to the captives and recovery of sight to the blind, to let the oppressed go free, to proclaim the year of the Lord's favor" (Luke 4:18-19). Most New Testament scholars agree that, in the brief phrase "to bring good news to the poor," we find Jesus' own statement of his primary mission. The question then is, "Who are the poor?"

The phrase "the poor" should not be deprived of metaphorical meaning, and thus it should not be limited either to the spiritually poor or to the economically poor. However, as Tannehill points out, it first of all refers to those economically oppressed and poor (Tannehill 1986, 64). Green extends the meaning of "the poor" as to embrace not simply economically oppressed but also "the excluded, and disadvantaged," all who are on the margins of society and devalued by society (Green 1995, 84). One of the contributions of liberation theology is the rediscovery of "the poor" as a hermeneutical focus, which leads to a new understanding of the Christian gospel and to a legitimate attention to the priority of "the poor" in mission and evangelism. The emphasis of liberation theology upon "the preferential option for the poor" does not imply that God is only interested in the salvation of the poor, but that "the poor are the first, though not the only ones, on which God's attention focuses and that, therefore, the church has no choice but to demonstrate solidarity with the poor" (Bosch 1991, 436).

The rediscovery of the poor in theology has had significant implications for mission and evangelism. Considering solidarity with the poor "a central and crucial priority in Christian mission," Bosch argues that "once we recognize the identification of Jesus with the poor, we cannot any longer consider our own relation to the poor as a social ethics question; it is a gospel question" (1991, 437). It cannot be denied that Jesus particularly demonstrated his solidarity with the poor and made them the principal recipients of the good news. If the gospel is to be announced credibly, believers should follow the evangelistic practice of Jesus, paying careful attention to the kind of people with whom he associated throughout his ministry. Then, as Costas stresses, evangelism is "to be undertaken from below . . . from the depth of human suffering, where we find both sinners and victims of sin"(Costas 1989, 31).

In the book of Acts, the Holy Spirit keeps urging the church to move beyond its boundaries. In fact, in Acts almost every evangelistic endeavor involves the crossing of boundaries. One of the most significant events in Acts is the conversion of Cornelius. It was the first full-blown encounter between a Christian Jew and a Gentile, with significant implications for the future mission and evangelism of the early church. Here the issue is not the legitimacy of a Gentile mission, but how that mission should be carried out in the face of Gentile uncleanness, which prevents Jews' free association with Gentiles (Tannehill 1989, 135). Throughout the whole incident, hospitality becomes and remains both a pervasive and thorny issue. Thus, in the subsequent episode, when Peter goes up to Jerusalem, the Jewish Christians criticize him for having gone to uncircumcised people and having eaten with them (Acts 11:2-3). Here "the inclusion of Gentiles and table-fellowship with Gentiles are inseparably related" (Gaventa 1986, 121).

It is clear that the Cornelius story is about the social barrier to the Gentile mission. For the Jerusalem church to overcome such a barrier, Peter first has to experience a conversion, learning firsthand that "God shows no partiality" (Acts 10:34). Peter's conversion then leads to the conversion of the church from ethnocentrism to multiculturalism. According to Gaventa, "Indeed, in Luke's account, Peter and company undergo a change that is more wrenching by far than the change experienced by Cornelius" (Gaventa 1986, 121).

Unfortunately, the church in North America in the twenty-first century is still faced with the same kind of challenge—to overcome its ethnocentrism and homogeneity and to reach people of different races, cultures, and economic classes. No Christian could possibly deny that God's love is for all, and that God shows no partiality. Yet many Christians and churches still need to have a conversion experience, as Peter and the early church did, so that they can fellowship willingly and joyfully with persons of different cultures and practice mutual hospitality. For the witness of the gospel, we need intentionally to cross many boundaries established by society and to create relationships with those who are different from us. Any church, which is neither multicultural nor seeks to become so, should carefully examine itself and ask why it has become stuck in a monocultural mode. There is always a danger that the church will pursue "culturally exclusive forms of Christian witness and church formation" that could result in "the pollution of Christian witness with racism, classism, and ethnocentrism" (Guder 1999, 48). However, evangelism in the context of hospitality invites believers to go beyond their comfort zone to meet and form a community with people who are different from them, challenging the prevailing patterns of homogeneous human relationships in society.

> Many Christians and churches still need to have a conversion experience, as Peter and the early church did, so that they can fellowship willingly and joyfully with persons of different cultures and practice mutual hospitality.

Practicing hospitality is quite difficult and arduous. It involves our whole being, not just a part, and demands all we have, not just a portion. It requires "the kind of courage that lives close to our limits, continually pressing against the possible, yet always aware of the incompleteness and the inadequacy of our own responses," and thus deepening "our dependence on, and our awareness of, God's interventions and provision" (Pohl 1999, 131-32). Since evangelism in hospitality is so demanding, we can carry it out only with the guidance and in the power of the Holy Spirit. We also need a witnessing and hospitable community, in which every Christian can be equipped, nurtured, and supported for the self-conscious and intentional witnessing.

Being a witness is at the core of our identity and calling as Christians and as the community of faith; it is not optional. We have to understand it "as defining the entire Christian life, both individually and corporately" (Guder 1999, 55). In D. T. Niles's words, evangelism is "being a Christian," and "a way of the church's life" (1951, 33, 28). Indeed, our motivation for evangelism should be based upon our own experience of God's love for us, and on our realization of the truth that every person is the object of God's love. Without an undeniable personal encounter with Christ and an experience of his grace, one cannot become a witness. Furthermore, without love and the willingness to practice hospitality, our witnessing becomes empty words and vain rituals. It is because evangelism is "a labor of love" (Costas

1989, 18) and a form of participation in the cross of Jesus that biblical hospitality is thus to be seen as an authentic context for evangelism. In a similar context some two thousand years ago, Paul wrote to the Thessalonians: "So deeply do we care for you that we are determined to share with you not only the gospel of God but also our own selves, because you have become very dear to us" (1 Th 2:8).

Joong-Sik Park is pastor of a multicultural congregation in the USA.

QUESTIONS FOR REFLECTION

1. What do you think Joong-Sik Park means by "hospitality"? Why does he claim that it is "a primary context for evangelism"? How would you live it out in your own setting?

2. Are there any differences between hospitality towards "those of the household of faith" and hospitality beyond the boundaries of faith? In your culture, what would be regarded as the practical evidences of hospitality?

3. Park comments that "practicing hospitality is quite difficult and arduous." How do we give ourselves to it without falling into burnout or despair when surrounded by multiple needs and suffering?

CHAPTER 24

HOW CAN WE NOT SING FOR THE LORD?

The Songs of Sudan's Dinka Christians
Isaiah Dau

During the recently ended war in Sudan, there was a powerful song outpouring among the Bor Dinka in response to the gospel message and suffering. These songs, described as songs of suffering and faith, and exceeding 1,500, express a variety of theological and missiological themes. They directly relate to the tension between the upheaval and the destruction of the war and faith in Nhialic (God). Salvific themes such as repentance, faith, deliverance, trust, protection, anguish, fear, complaint, lament,and cosmic conflict between Nhialic and Jok (the evil one) dominate these songs. Composed in nuances familiar to the Dinka heart and soul, these songs reiterate the biblical message and themes in captivating styles. The traditional Dinka culture of song is invaded with a new Christian celebration, producing a powerful mixture of Christian and Dinka dynamics which has led to a massive people's movement and widespread response to the gospel message.

As might be well known, the Dinka are habitual singers with the average person composing and singing from memory between 100 and 200 songs. They always sing proudly of their cattle, especially show bulls. In some cases they sing of anguish, pain and ridicule in a parabolic and figurative language. A proud Dinka youth, showing off his new acquired bull or trying to impress a beautiful girl he loves or just for the love of singing, can sing and entertain a cattle camp or a village for a whole night. It is significant that the Dinka can sing about anything at all at this time of war, pain, and death.[1] They had lost virtually all their cattle, having been displaced from their ancestral land, and were now refugees in *jur* (foreign) land and had suffered many other upheavals as a result of the war. Their *cieng* (culture, way of life) and *dheeng* (dignity and humanity) have been challenged or eroded like never before in many long centuries of resistance to foreign influence. Life as they knew became only a dream of the past, having been largely eroded and impaired. But with all

---

1   The Dinka do not sing at the time of death or funeral. When death occurs in a family, a period of mourning ranging from 6 months to 1 year is observed. Beads and other paraphernalia that allude to happiness are discarded.

that loss, they could still sing. How are we to interpret this? What can explain this strange happening? One thing may explain it: the gospel message has finally found room in the heart and soul of the Dinka, and it has become a valuable part of their life, and they could therefore sing about it.

The *cieng* (the Kingdom) of Nhialic has come and is much more valuable than the *cieng* of cattle and all that the Dinka boasted about in the past. The coming of Nhialic and his capturing of the traditional song culture by his living Word have replaced the cattle wealth on which the Dinka *cieng* and *dheeng* were based. The response to the gospel of Nhialic has thus occasioned the song outpouring among the Dinka. The coming of Nhialic, being now experienced by the Dinka, was predicted in an extremely popular song, which Adoor Juach of the Ngok Dinka composed and sang in the 1950s.

> *Let us turn our hearts to the Truth, Nhialic is coming*[2]
> *The Lord Jesus is coming, smiling at us, my lost people he has found*
> *You will take them to the right hand of your Father*
> *Come; wash our bodies to be lighter like adeet,*[3]
> *Our good Lord surrounds us with his bright light.*
>
> *Jesus Christ has sought and found us to turn our hearts to our Father*
> *To turn our heads heavenward (as in prayer), our Father will hold back our tears*
> *He will write our names in his book for a thousand years.*
> *Show your head, you will not fall; Jesus our Lord, you will not fall*
> *We will receive you to give us life everlasting*
> *Our Dinka mock us (for your sake), the whole nation is bound by fear*
> *They refuse your truth and run to the river to wash (as an act of divination and worship).*
>
> *Anei with Deng and a woman called Anok are among these who run*
> *They slaughtered a bull to no avail,*
> *They slaughtered a he-goat to no avail*
> *I will turn my face (head) to our Father; I will turn my face to Christ*
> *Lord Jesus, come and put in order our devastated house.*

This song was the center of Christian proclamation among the Dinka in the 1950s. The essence of its message is the announcing of the imminent approach of Nhialic. This announcing of the imminent approach of God, as Andrew Wheeler has pointed out, is characteristic of the understanding of the contemporary people's movement amongst the Bor Dinka as

---

2   The charismatic Ngok Dinka evangelist, Lual Ayei, greatly used and popularized this song in his proclamation among the Ngok Dinka as Andrew Wheeler notes. However, he is not the one who composed it. Adoor Juach, whom I had the privilege of meeting in Adong while attending a primary school in the Ngok Dinkaland in early 1970s, composed this song. Adoor Juach, like most Dinka Christians of his time who believed, unfortunately reverted to the worship of *jak* that he had early repudiated. Lual Ayei himself retreated into tobacco and hashish addiction. However, the prophetic impact of his song still stands; Nhialic has truly come to the Dinka at this time (Wheeler 1998:66-68).

3   *Adeet* is a type of plant that grows on the sudd and is used to make a type of light shield that the Dinka use for protection in stick fighting. It is used as storage for tobacco as well as a pillow.

well as among other Dinka groups (Wheeler 1998:67). For Adoor Juach and his generation, this coming of Nhialic was still future and perhaps eschatological. For the generation of the 1980s and 1990s, the coming of Nhialic is a present reality. Nhialic is now here, in our midst, although we did not realize it. The proclamation that Nhialic is now here evokes a powerful sense that he would intervene in the war and bring deliverance from suffering. The presence of Nhialic gives hope and encouragement in the face of death and destruction. Nhialic is here and yet we have not realized it as the following song asserts:

Nhialic has come amongst us slowly and we did not realize it. He is standing nearby, right next to our hearts; he is shining his bright light on us. We ask you, our Father, Great Lord of peace in heaven above, who calls in secret, Who knows the hearts of human beings, our faith is weak; make us strong. So that we stand with firm courage until you reach us without wavering.

Send to us your power, Lord, the Comforter, the Spirit of Truth to teach us the written law. So that we may receive your salvation slowly, slowly, all of us, with no one left out. Then, prepare your coming, when we all have received the knowledge. On that day, you will make the whole world to account; you will make us to account. Men will scream in anguish. Nhialic, let us repent in time, Christ, let your light triumph.

Christ, the King of kings has not disowned us. Because he loved us and died for us. If we have not reached it, if we have not tasted it, how can we wait for it (that is the Second Coming of Christ)? He puts his light in us so that we can wait in faith. And he reveals to us the truth, which is yet to come. The son of man will come like lightning. He will sit in the clouds, glorified by his father. This is the light that darkness can never overcome (Mary Alueel Garang).

The coming of Nhialic is both a present and a future reality to the composer. Nhialic will come and make all people account for their deeds on that Day. End times themes such as the final judgment and future bliss, freedom from suffering and other troubles readily emerge. The prophetic imagery in the Bible and particularly in the apocalyptic books of Daniel and Revelation sparks much interest among the Dinka.[4] According to the Dinka mind, the imagery of judgment and destruction in these books seems to bear resemblance to what is now going on in the Sudan. Thus, the coming of Nhialic connotes blessing to those who believe and judgment to those who do not. This is the message of the two songs we have examined.

SONG OUTPOURING IMPLICATIONS FOR THE CHRISTIAN PROCLAMATION AMONG THE BOR DINKA

But what are some implications of this song outpouring among the Bor Dinka? How do these relate to suffering and faith as experienced by the Bor Dinka? First, the song outpouring

---

4   Though quite alien to Dinka and Nilotic traditional thought, as Marc Nikkel points out, the end time events generate interest among the Dinka not so much because judgment is coming and freedom from suffering is at hand, but because the idea that Jok will be finally defeated and thrown in the fire very much appeals to the Dinka. This is in addition to their insatiable curiosity to discover or explain the meaning behind the imageries (Nikkel 1997:99).

emanates from a deeply seated wrestling with suffering and faith. Both in the first civil war of 1955 to 1972 and in the one of 1983 to 2005, songs and hymns have been the most important medium through which the theological wrestling of the people was articulated. Whether through praise, prayer, dialogue with God, reiterating biblical stories, or searching for the meaning of life in the light of present losses, these songs and hymns clearly express people's struggles and wrestling with suffering.[5] Sometimes, the composers themselves emerge from personal loss and suffering into deep song. Mary Alueel Garang, who composed a good number of the contemporary Bor Dinka songs, for example, emerged from great personal suffering and pain to become the most prolific contemporary Dinka singer. Rejected by her own family and jilted by a man she dearly loved and had a child with, Mary suffered humiliation and disdain beyond what a Dinka girl of her age could possibly bear. On top of all that, Mary lost her only child, aggravating her suffering and leading to a near emotional breakdown. It was in the midst of this upheaval that she became a Christian and experienced God's power in a special way, enabling her to compose many songs that have brought fresh meaning to Dinka Christianity. Most of her songs carry deep and dynamic expressions of the Christian message, suited to the Dinka context. The suffering she experienced seemed to have contributed greatly to the uniqueness and maturity of her songs.

Second, the song outpouring articulates the Christian proclamation in idioms and nuances familiar to the Dinka heart and mind. Because of this, the rural Dinka, in particular, have very little struggle to comprehend or receive the message of the gospel that the songs convey. In traditional society, the song was an important vehicle of communication. The Dinka song culture as such, had its roots in attempting to articulate and convey the religious, social, and ethical issues of life in a firm but non-confrontational way that ordinary speech could not achieve. Through song, vital community values were also disseminated and popularized. The community told its story and shaped its character effectively through song. The oral history of the community was mainly preserved through song and story.

> The song outpouring articulates the Christian proclamation in idioms and nuances familiar to the Dinka heart and mind.

So essential was (and still is) the song culture that every Dinka clan had its own peculiar songs that told its own story and preserved its own identity within the larger context of the Dinka cultural hegemony.[6] It is in this important context that the current song outpouring among the Bor Dinka and other Nilotic groups should be seen and interpreted. If this is done, it may not be easy to divorce the current song outpouring from the people's mass movement and church growth among the Bor Dinka. The song has become an extremely

---

5   Andrew Wheeler notes that Sudanese theology is primarily worked out in hymns and spiritual songs. During the first war, 1955 – 1972, there was song outpouring among the Bari, the Moru, the Zande, and other groups in the Equatoria region as it is now among the Nilotic peoples, the Dinka, the Nuer, and the Shilluk during the recently concluded war. It is interesting to note that in each case, suffering was much more in each of these regions when song outpouring occurred (Wheeler 1998:69).

6   Francis Deng records one of the Ngok Dinka clan songs in his *The Dinka of the Sudan* (1971, 135). This is an example of what we are trying to say here. This song, dating back at least fifteen known generations, had been orally preserved before Dr. Deng put it into writing in 1971 with considerable difficulty due to archaic extant Dinka language.

valuable vehicle of spreading the message of Christ among a people whose *cieng* and *dheeng* are rooted in song. The song has efficiently done what other types of communication could not do because it is articulated in idioms and nuances familiar to the Dinka conscience and sensibility.

Third, the song outpouring provides a basis of identification with and a sense of ownership of the Christian proclamation. The Christian message, expressed in the songs and conveying local, familiar cultural idioms and meanings, is unlikely to be treated as foreign. As mentioned earlier, the Dinka have been resistant to the message for a long time, regarding it as foreign and therefore highly suspicious of its influence. Even when the "strongest and bravest warriors"[7] like Archibald Shaw were sent, the Dinka, as ever, were still reserved, suspicious, and prejudiced against "foreigners of any kind."[8] Out of a dark history of the inhumane slave trade and exploitation grew the Dinka suspicion of and prejudice against all foreigners. The Dinka hardly distinguished between a Turk, an Arab, or an Englishman. They were all the same in his eyes; they were "Turuuk" or 'Aciek"[9] even when they claimed to have come with a message from Nhialic. It took a long time before the Dinka learned the difference between them. The Christian proclamation too could not escape being regarded as foreign, especially after Dinka children who attended missionary schools came home denouncing the Dinka *cieng* and *dheeng* as demonic. The children were then branded Turuuk or Aciek in the same way as their missionary teachers. And although the Dinka put them in "line" at vulnerable times such as when they wanted to marry using cattle, these Turuuk and Aciek were subjected to persistent ridicule and harassment until they established themselves, obtained cattle of their own and lived the Dinka way. For the Dinka, therefore, it was difficult to relate to the Christian proclamation, wrapped up in foreign baggage; there was no point of contact for them to relate to. The church was for *mith ke thukul* (school children), not for *Muonyjang* (men of men as the Dinka refer to themselves). All this has radically changed in the last seventeen years since the song outpouring in the Dinka language became a reality. The Dinka have overwhelmingly received the Christian proclamation that the songs convey. This proclamation is no longer a foreign cultural import; it is conveyed in familiar cultural idioms and nuances that the Dinka can relate to. The song outpouring has therefore created some vital identification with the Christian proclamation and has enhanced a sense of its ownership. The church for the Dinka is no longer for *mith ke thukul* (school children) but *kanitha da* (our church), because we can relate to and identify with it. The song outpouring among the Bor Dinka has thus provided a basis of identification with the Christian message as well as a sense of belonging to the community of believers.

> This proclamation is no longer a foreign cultural import; it is conveyed in familiar cultural idioms and nuances that the Dinka can relate to.

---

7   This is taken from a tribute by Jon Aruor e Thor, Shaw's first convert, at a Diocesan Council and ordination in Juba, 1946. M. Willoughby H. Carey as quoted in Nikkel (1997, 102).

8   See note 224 in the above citation.

9   Turuuk is a corruption of Turk that the Dinka used to refer to the repressive regime of Ottoman Turks who ruled and subjected the Sudan to exploitation (1821 – 1885). The Dinka called the Arab and the British Turuuk as well. Aciek is a Dinka word, which inclusively refers to foreigners who are inventors or creators of such things as aeroplanes and motor cars, which the Dinka see as creative miracles.

Finally, the song outpouring among the Bor Dinka contains a large and influential women's contribution, providing a unique gender balance. Contrary to the Dinka traditional culture, women lead the way in composing and popularizing the new Dinka songs. This is highly unusual in a male-dominated society. The Dinka, like most African peoples, have certain roles that only fall in the male sphere. Composing and singing songs was one such sphere. It is not that women never composed or sang songs at all, but it is that men did it most of the time. For sure, some prominent women in the Dinka traditional society composed good songs, usually when praising her family or letting out a grievance in a ridicule song.[10] But now, the ongoing song outpouring among the Bor Dinka has sparked change and women have come to assume influential traditional roles in the Dinka family and community circles due to the present realities of the war and displacement. With most men engaged in the war, women have taken up responsibilities in the home and the church and have provided exemplary leadership. They lead prayers in the home and in the displacement camps, serve as prominent evangelists, and also care for the wounded and the orphans among the victims of the war. A number of them have become what Marc Nikkel calls "natural theologians" as they provide strong, visionary, and influential leadership in the church and the community (Nikkel 1997:65-66). The Dinka community is coming to appreciate the effective role women can play in promoting the social, religious, economic, and political values of the society. Most Dinka girls are now being sent to schools alongside their brothers, an anathema that the Dinka once detested and rejected. War, suffering, and exposure to other cultures seem to have convinced the traditional Dinka that survival in a harsh world we live in takes more than solely depending on bride cattle wealth, shown to be very unreliable following the 1991 massive cattle raids and losses. Perhaps, education, trade, investment, and other means of making a living are necessary if the Dinka are to maintain economic stability. The women's contribution in the song outpouring among the Dinka is a unique balance in a society which has not always allowed women a proper place. Amidst social, cultural, and religious change, war, and suffering, the Dinka pour out their heart songs to the Lord.

Isaiah Dau is a Christian leader among Sudan's Dinka people.

QUESTIONS FOR REFLECTION

1. What combination of factors made radical cultural change possible, including accepting the Christian gospel?
2. Why do you think great suffering can give rise to great music? What does that tell us about the human spirit? What other biblical or historical examples of this phenomenon can you identify?
3. In your own culture, how might music be used more effectively to teach biblical truth?

---

10   Mary Alueel Garang, the current leading Dinka woman singer, ridiculed the betrayal of the friend who jilted her in a long song in the early 1980s. She did this before she became a believer and composed her current popular spiritual songs.

CHAPTER 25

BELIEVERS IN JESUS AS PARADIGM FOR A RESPONSIBLE PLURALISTIC THEOLOGY

Jonas Jørgensen

Faith and fellowship among groups of Isa imandars, "those faithful to Jesus," flourishes outside the institutional Christian churches in Bangladesh. The implicit theology of these groups can be seen as a form of theology which is neither exclusive nor inclusive, nor pluralistic, but all three at the same time. Thus, through their theology and practice, the imandars express a challenge to institutional Christian churches as well as contemporary paradigmatic Christian theology of religion.

Historically speaking, Christian missions have focused on religious transformation and have often subsumed with this social changes in the life of the converts. In a certain sense, the perspective in this article is the opposite: I want to investigate how a social change—more specifically the changing borders of religious pluralism and de-traditionalization as propelled by globalization—changes the context for Christian theologies and the content of Christian identities.

This article builds upon observations and interviews with Isa imandars, "those faithful to Jesus."[1] Some of the informants were involved in institutional Christian churches, while others consciously disengaged themselves from the same, i.e., they claimed a religious belief in Jesus but at the same time remained outside institutional churches and inside their traditional religious culture of Bangladeshi Sunni Islam. This last group caught my theological attention as they had an understanding of Jesus Christ, salvation, and ethics which

---

1   The fieldwork on which this article is based took place in October and November 2002 in Bangladesh and was made possible by a gracious grant from the Danish/Norwegian foundation Areopagos and from the Theological Faculty at the University of Copenhagen. The article was originally presented to the WEA Mission Commission gathering in Singapore August 2004 but was extensively revised in October 2010 upon a request for publishing. The changes reflect subsequent fieldwork in Bangladesh in January – July 2004 which was sponsored by a grant from the Danish Research Council on Humanities (SHF, now renamed FKK) and which has been reported more thoroughly in my PhD thesis, *Jesus Imandars and Christ Bhaktas,* (published by University of Copenhagen, 2006).

resembled my own, but their practice looked different. In contrast to Cyprian's well-known dictum (cf. Cyprian in Cyprian, De unitate ecclesia VI), they claim to "have God as father without having the church as mother."

TERMS AND METHODOLOGY

By the term Isa imandars, "those faithful to Jesus," I use an emic expression used by a number of Bangladeshi men and women claiming a religious belief in Jesus but at the same time remaining outside the established church. Even if the imandars are defined as Bangladeshi, there seems to be similar phenomena in other geographical and historical eras.[2] By the term "changing borders" I mean the changing landscape of religious life: both the religious pluralism as a consequence of the globalization of religions as well as the modern de-traditionalization where there seems to be a shift in authority from "exterior" to "interior" and where the individual sees it as his or her right to exercise authority over tradition, norm, and ethics (cf. Heelas 1999, 2; Kurtz 1995, 151; Robertson 2000, 65). The term "responsible pluralistic theology" I take to mean a Christian theology which reflects upon the meaning of other religious traditions, i.e. a theology which is formulated in the background of the particularity of Christ as well as on the universality of the revelation in a religiously pluralistic world. To sum up and rephrase my interpretation and claim in the light of this clarification: that the Isa imandars are a consequence of Christianity's globalization and that their practiced faith and implicit theology might be interpreted as an alternative paradigm for a responsible Christian theology of religious pluralism.

The method employed here could be termed "phenomenological in a theological framework" in the sense that it focuses on the experience of the individuals, theological reflection, and social life. In order to ensure an open and dynamic method, unstructured participant observation and semi-structured interviews have been used.[3] In the groups there were a number of similar themes occurring in the interviews and my description is ordered after them. The

---

2   Similar phenomena are known from the history of the church at its geographical and theological borders (cf. Coope 1995), and there seems to be a fair number of these groups today (Higgins 1998; Hoefer 2001). In the Indian theological context this phenomenon is fairly common with representatives such as Kandasamy Chetty, Manilal Parekh, Subba Rao, Keshub Chunder Sen (cf. Rajashekar 1979; Dupuis 1991). What might be common for these groups is parallel experiences, insights, or something more concrete as the common traits mentioned by the Scottish theologian Andrew Walls: "continuity of thought about the significance of Jesus, continuity of certain consciousness about history, continuity in the use of Scriptures, of bread and wine, of water" (Walls 1996). This would mean that it is possible to compare the shape of the faith and fellowship of believers in Jesus at different places and see these groups as an attempt to interpret Christianity in a religiously pluralistic culture.

3   I conducted 24 interviews and a number of more informal conversations through the fieldwork October–November 2002. There was an overrepresentation of men in the groups, even if some few women and children participated in the groups. The average number of members in the groups observed was around 10, mainly male members aged 25-45 years. The leaders among the groups of believers estimated the total number of members to be around 15-20 in their groups. Each of the groups seemed to be rather homogeneous in socio-economic sense, one consisting of lower middle class and another of poor people without education. The leaders among the believers reported different and quite varied numbers of believers from Muslim background, and the conclusion must be that the actual number is hard to determine, just as the leaders' ideal views of organization and the actual forms were often mixed in reporting. I have subsequently spent 7 months in Bangladesh in 2004, deepening my understanding of the *imandars'* situation.

central themes for the believers were the understanding of Jesus, the understanding of the church, social forms outside the church, interpretation of the religious culture and faith of the Muslim majority, and finally their own religious faith and self-understanding. My analysis showed that the experience and interpretation of the believers could be presented around the core category "authenticity" which I will return to after my description. The findings presented here are biased in the way that I had ready access to the male members of the groups but more difficulties finding female informants. Furthermore, I spoke with more leaders in these groups than lay members which might have caused over reporting in some areas.

WHO IS *ISA,* JESUS?

It is common for all imandars that they had experienced the Christological question as central in the transformation from a more or less orthodox form of Sunni Islam. The believers often discussed who and what Jesus was, and a number of the imandars describe themselves as Isa-Muslims through their iman, that is, they were "Muslims-through-Isa" or Jesus. Thus, their Christology was also crucial in their dismissal of the established church! In their discussions, common Christian terms from the larger tradition as well as more untraditional descriptions were mixed, and iman was said to be a "faith relation," a "surrender," a "following," and a "love relation" with Jesus "al-Masih," Messiah.

From their New Testament readings, they affirm Jesus as "messenger of truth," just like Muhammad. Abstract descriptions of Jesus as the "truth," as "man of peace," "innocent," "'word," or "spirit of God" are Christological titles also found in the Qur'an. They reported that in conversation with Muslims they consciously stressed the common understanding of Jesus as "word" or "spirit" and pointed out the personal integrity of Jesus' life and teaching. Significantly, the description of Jesus as Messiah was a common Christological description among the believers from Muslim background. Jesus as "al-Masih," the Messiah, gained a new meaning where the traditional Christian understanding (that Messiah besides being the elected one also is the Savior) meet the somewhat weaker Muslim understanding of what the election of Jesus means. Even if orthodox Muslim theology recognizes Jesus' special significance and closeness to God, it was pointed out that Muslims don't realize the point of his suffering and death: Jesus is not only elected to be a messenger but to be a true Messiah in the full meaning of the word, bringing an unknown closeness of salvation as personified in himself. The messianic title thus describes Jesus' fundamental personal authority as realized divine election and a "standard of life." These attempts for a common Christological understanding could be termed inclusive in the sense that all of these descriptions are acceptable for orthodox Muslims as well as for the Christ-believers from Muslim background and Christians.

But the believers also held a more dynamic interpretation, e.g., when one discussed the possibility of substituting "Muhammad" with "Isa" in the Muslim creed or spoke of Jesus as "rasul-ul-Allah," i.e., "messenger of God." Thus, the notion of Jesus' prophethood emphasizes his embodiment of spiritual and ethical qualities such as non-violence, compassion and vicarious suffering, that is, his "nispap," "sinlessness." Like one of the popular wandering saintly Sufi *pirs* in Bangladesh, Jesus is therefore "spiritually powerful" and able to act as intercessor for the imandar. It is exactly through iman that one binds oneself to Jesus as one's trusted saint, *pir*.

Finally, a fundamental concern among the imandars is that Jesus is "alive"—a fundamental fact which both Islamic and Christian tradition agree upon, according to the imandars. The spiritual power and continuous life of Jesus both depends on and demonstrates the unique relation between Jesus and God. Therefore, Jesus is not just a prophet but the prophet par excellence, it is argued. Even if the conceptualization of Jesus' prophethood emphasizes similarity with Muhammad's as "messenger of truth," Jesus is therefore viewed hierarchically superior to Muhammad on the basis of his spiritual power and continuous life. Thus, the continued humanity and present life of Jesus is seen as a paradigm shift in the relation between God and mankind.

To sum up the Christology of the imandars, they view Jesus as a living saint-prophet who through his intercession and vicarious suffering invites those faithful to him into a regenerative relationship. Put in other words: the normative status of Jesus consists in his personification of the truth criteria for what is human and what is divine, what the meaning of salvation and humanity really is. It is this living prophet-saint that the imandars become faithful to.

BEING AN ISA IMANDAR

A typical meeting in one of the imandars' fellowships, the jama'at, takes place in private homes. On Fridays small signboards outside their houses announced 'Jama'at' and inside furniture was removed and mats covered the floor. The meetings started late afternoon as the last rays of the sun disappeared behind the Dhaka skyline. The imandars were handed copies of the Kitab ul Mughaldesh—the Bible in Musalmani Bangla translation—and a homemade collection of Īsāe-songs. The gatherings usually started with a song, either a translation of a classical Christian hymn or a local composition drawing heavily upon the Bangladeshi style of music known as *baul gan*, "folk song." Reading and especially recitation of long passages in the Kitab ul Mughaldesh was part of every meeting. Zabur, the Book of Psalms, and the apostolic letters were often recited. In veneration of the *kitab*, the "holy book," the Kitab ul Mughaldesh was placed in a wooden book stand in front of every imandar. The leader of the jama'at entitled himself "imam," "leader of the prayer" and would occasionally read aloud a text himself, but he usually restricted himself to preach the sermon, commenting and expounding the texts. There were always common prayers after the sermons. These were carried out in contrast to the highly ritualized mosque prayers, as the imandars did not follow any particular ritual, but everyone was free to pray. From time to time the imandars celebrated communion. The ritual was very simple: they would simply read the well-known verses from I Corinthians and distribute bread and fruit juice.

The liturgy of the jama'at fellowship was explained to me to have the same form as any gathering in a mosque would have had. Some informants spoke about their fellowships as "asylums" and "shelters" with "warmth and growth in divine love" and others spoke about their groups as equivalent to pir-fellowships, groups loosely organized around a saintly "holy man."

WHAT ABOUT THE CHURCH?

The negative background for the imandars' alternative social and religious network outside the Christian church was disappointment over the institutional churches. Believers who had had relationship to institutional churches described them as "childish and naïve," "immature," "a fault," or even with a theological qualification as "a sin." Even if common theological ground for the institutional churches and the believers in Jesus was underscored, from the perspective of the imandars, the churches' fractious character was seen in contrast to Jesus as "personified truth." Furthermore, some imandars were disappointed by the lack of seriousness among believers and claimed that the leaders of the traditional churches lacked moral integrity. At the same time it was felt that institutional churches did not take imandars' spiritual experiences and conversions seriously but tried to control the groups of believers from Muslim background, forcing them to embrace the Western religious culture of institutional "Hinduized" churches.[4]

In their critique, the imandars often focused on the churches' cultural and religious insensitivity in regard to water baptism as entrance to full membership: "Jesus came to change my faith, not my name," as one informant puts it. It is worth mentioning that a baptism in a culturally acceptable form is not opposed by the informants, but it seems to be the equation of the church between baptism and Western religious culture which the believers are opposed to. Rather, baptism is explained as an inner and mystical "binding" of oneself to Jesus as prophet and saint. Membership and salvation does not equate according to the experience of the believers. The ecclesiology of the established churches is ironically described as "the Bible plus this and plus that…I believe in the New Jerusalem." Being a member of the established church is thus felt as resulting in that "you have to tell lies." It is felt that the shape of Christianity in the established churches is neither authentic nor responsible: "God frees from the bondage of law. Now the converts must be freed from the missionaries," one of the imandars concludes.

Another of the informants retold the story about Joseph of Arimathea as an illustration of his own authentic religiosity in opposition to what he termed "the last minute business" of the established churches.[5] The point is clear: the informant sees himself in opposition to the established churches, their lack of "morality" and self-centred interests. Belief in Jesus leads to authenticity for him—but membership of the church

> Belief in Jesus leads to authenticity for him—but membership of the church did not do that.

---

4   An often heard critique among the imandars concentrated on the "Hindu" character of the institutional churches. It seems that this critique refers to the church rituals such as processions, candles, and especially the material religious culture such as pictures in churches which for the imandars resembles a Hindu *puja*. Furthermore, the "Hindu" character of the institutional churches surfaced in the Bengali translation of the Bible with its use of the vernacular Bengali *Ishtar* rather than the Urdu *Allah* as the proper name for "God."

5   "When Jesus said that he was about to die, some wanted to do last-minute business with him. The mother of two of the disciples came to Jesus and asked for the place on the right and left side of Jesus. That is the place of the minister of finances and that of defence….But Joseph of Arimathea put him in his own grave and the resurrection happened in his yard. He became a witness to the resurrection. He got to see the angels and the mother of Jesus came there. Joseph was not spiritual, but knew the people in power. Jesus was condemned both by spiritual and civil law, but Joseph buried him in his garden. Joseph never said a prayer, but he knew the high people."

did not do that. This theme is unfolded in a number of passages, e.g., where one imandar tells about how Jesus rather than churches determines the "duties of life" and another says that "Christ is our standard of living…our ministry is to be genuine," i.e., the fundamental religious duty is to be genuine and authentic. I would argue that their understanding of authenticity overlaps the normative nature of Jesus in two areas: their own individual conversion and submission to God; and rejection of unnecessary "luxury religiosity" which includes the church.

THE RELATION TO ISLAM AND MUSLIMS

The believers from Muslim background generally agreed that Muslims "know something about Jesus," about his life, elected status or "power." At the same time all informants stressed soteriology and Christology as the main differences and mentioned that believers from other religions clearly lacked a Christian understanding of salvation and the meaning of Jesus' death and resurrection: as one informant said, she was wondering why her Muslim friends and family could not see that Jesus was the fulfilment of the promises when it was so clear.[6]

Their understanding of themselves as authentic Muslims gave a key term to the interpretation of the religious culture and tradition they themselves are coming from. When the believers in Jesus observe Ramadan, abstain from certain foods, and lead a moral life, it is their experience that they slowly are accepted as moral persons. The wish to be authentic and moral also affected their relationship to the traditional religious culture. The implicit theological qualification for participation in the religious life of Islam is given by one of the informants saying: "If I go [to the mosque] I will go with respect. If I decide to pray I will pray according to the tradition. I am liberated; I have the word of God inside me." Precisely because faith is interior by nature, it allows the imandar to act exteriorly in accordance with the religious culture where he or she lives—thus hoping to ensure social acceptance. Even though the imandars reported a general acceptance from their Muslim neighbors several of the informants shared stories about social pressure—especially concerning inheritance (some Muslims find it inappropriate that people they see as non-Muslims should inherit property from a Muslim), marriage (who one can marry), and funerals (how one should be buried).

Concerning the dogmatic questions of salvation exclusively through Jesus and the possibility of salvation for believers of other religious background, the imandars were more restricted. Several of the informants were clearly uncomfortable about the question, and they seemed to answer either vaguely or negatively whether it was possible. The few informants who themselves brought up the question about eschatological salvation did so indirectly (e.g., by telling that they prayed for their family members).

A typical way of explaining the significance of Jesus was to argue for the significance of Jesus across the various religious institutions of Christianity, Islam, and Hinduism. Thus, an elderly gentleman imandar explained to me that is was certainly possible to be faithful to Jesus independently of your religious background and that the spirit of Christ is

---

6   "Isa is a theme there [in the Qur'an] and Muhammad says he is the only one who will be coming back. But the Bible says it directly. In the Sura Maria it says that someone Spirit-born will come, but only the New Testament is directly concerned with Isa. Somehow the Muslims don't see but it is easy to know in the Bible" (L).

active in human hearts across institutional religious boundaries. Related to this, a conscious and self-conscious way of speaking about the similarity and difference between themselves and other Christians and Muslims is their emic description Isa-imandar, "those faithful to Jesus," which serves to underscore the difference between themselves and the "Hindu" Christians and the proximity between themselves and ordinary Muslims, "those faithful to Muhammad." Thus, most of the imandars describe themselves as being Muslims but with an important qualification in regard to how they are Muslims: as a Muslim through Jesus or Isa-Muslim,[7] as a true Muslim who has surrendered to God outside the established Christian church[8] or as a Muslim with a new faith.[9] The believers in Jesus thus deliberately choose other descriptions of themselves than "Christian": "I am not a Christian; I gave it up twenty years ago," says one informant. When the imandar becomes faithful to Jesus—not to the Christian church—inner transformation is initiated, and the result is a regenerated Muslim, who in his heart does the will of God by following Jesus' example, the imandars argue. This regenerated Isa-Muslim transcends divisions between institutional Christian churches and Islamic mosques.

According to some of the imandars, this understanding of an interior and unbound regeneration allows for participation in any mosque (or church) because mosque prayers are simply "outward" and only hold relative value. However, in the mosque liturgy a crucial point in which social and ritual identity comes together is the collective confession, tawhid, that is the utterance of the Islamic creed which implies a ritual recognition of Muhammad as prophet of God. According to some imandars they simply stop after the first half of the creed which affirms the sovereign status of God. Instead of adding "Muhammad is the Prophet of God" they silently add "Jesus is the Spirit of God." The theological heterodoxy of this statement is clear and those imandars who argue for such a step also acknowledge that the majority of Muslims do not agree with this substitution. Against this background, participation in namaz prayer in mosques might be described as tolerated rather than welcomed by the majority of Bangladeshi Sunni Muslims.

To sum up the imandars' insights on institutional religious life, the imandars claim that their jama'at practice and emphasis on interior regeneration implies an "overruling" of the institutional missionary churches' emphasis on exteriority as well as the rigid nature of Sunni Islamic religious life and morality.

---

7   "To be Isa-Muslim is not the same as being Christian. 'Are you a *Muhammadi-Muslim* or an *Isa-Muslim*? Why?' This is the point" (C).

8   "I think 'Christian' is a name. I don't need to change my name or religion....As a follower of *Isa* I am 100 percent Muslim. But when I am following Christ 100 percent, I am also a Christian. But I am not following it [Christianity] religiously" (A).

9   "I didn't change my religion; but I changed my faith" (L).

ANALYSIS: ARE THE IMANDARS A VALID PARADIGM FOR A RESPONSIBLE PLURALISTIC THEOLOGY?

In this section I intend to discuss the results of the imandars' theology and practice, and I will restrict myself to point at some lines from the experience of the imandars in relation to three central areas of the current theological debate—ecclesiology, Christology, and relation to other religious traditions—and view them in relation to what the imandars themselves view as fundamental, namely their faithfulness:

FAITH AND FAITHFULNESS

The imandars might imply for our understanding of present challenges to institutional Christian churches as well as contemporary Christian theology of religions. "Iman," "faith," is not just etymologically related to imandars but plays a fundamental role in the imandars' self-understanding as "faithful." According to the emic perspective, faith is not abstract knowledge or belief but must be existential and relational, expressed first and foremost as "faithfulness" towards Jesus as their saint-prophet and savior. According to the imandars, iman denotes personal totality, "heart, mind, and thought," and becoming a Jesus imandar means to fixate one's iman on Jesus, that is, entering a relation with Jesus who as a spiritual master will mediate the divine and transform the believer through sheer presence. What was presented above might be viewed as a description of what this idea of faith as faithfulness means in practice.

As described, a recurring theme in the interviews was authenticity towards oneself and towards the Bangladeshi Islamic religious culture. The imandars' use of "faithfulness" relates to three areas: a) negatively in relation to the established Christian church; b) positively in their iman towards Jesus; and c) in a broader sense by the religious concepts which they share with Bangladeshi Islamic religious culture. These three interrelated areas come together when the believers discuss the question about their own identity, a pressing and unsolved problem with their pending status exposed: Where do they belong? Are these people Muslims or Christians or what are they? The question of belonging is furthermore complicated by their wish to be authentic and the fact that they consciously adopt a Bangladeshi Islamic culture: Even if they are clearly different from traditional Islam, does it mean that they are still Muslims with a twist? Or would it be more to the point to say that they are Christians with a twist in their religious background? They have their own groups and gatherings, they have their own leaders, and they study the Christian Scriptures: all traits which point at a sort of pietistic house group. But at the same time several of them report participation in their traditional namaz prayers in their local mosques. Seen from a theological point of view, the central category in the self-understanding of the believers in Jesus, their faithfulness, raises an important dogmatic question: are they authentic Christians and is their interpretation of Christianity valid? Can their theology be interpreted as a good and successful contextualization or enculturation of Christianity, or is it a bad religious hybrid, a syncretistic form of Christianity? I believe that their conceptualization of Jesus' significance gives an answer to these questions:

CHRISTOLOGY

The way in which Jesus is described does, to a large degree, have counterparts in popular Bangladeshi Islam: the notion of prophet-hood, intercession, spiritual power, moral innocence, and mediation by a *pir* of the divine. For the imandars, to become "faithful" refers to an Islamic theological virtue, and to become a Jesus imandar is a "Bengali style of religiosity—but it has a Christian subject matter, something which becomes clear in the presentation of the imandars' Christology. The meaning of the imandars' Christology transcends the Qur'anic universe, and the notion of a hierarchical superiority between Muhammad and Jesus distances the imandars from Islamic theology. Ultimately, it is their interpretation of Jesus' death as gift and sacrifice which most clearly distances the imandars from the majority of Bangladeshi Muslims and definitely transcends Qur'anic Christology. From my point of view, this ultimately places the imandars outside the Islamic theological universe and within the broader Christian tradition.

According to Christian dogmatics, admiration of Jesus Christ does not necessarily qualify for authentic Christianity. Rather, the effect of this admiration is crucial for judging whether we are seeing Christianity. The imandars' understanding of Christ seemed to be that he was normative for salvation (the cognitive question) but what this meant in practice (the question of salvation of believers from other religious traditions) they were either hesitant or pessimistic about. This point is confirmed by their general Christology: as their prophet-saint, Jesus is savior, innocent, authentic, or standard. These Christological descriptions imply a strong affective dimension of the relation to Jesus which is clearer than the cognitive dimension. This leads me to a short note on the relation between the soteriology and Christology: it is my general feeling that my informants spoke more about the "overwhelming love of Jesus" and of his "innocent life" than they spoke of salvation in forensic terms. Judged from the number of times that the informants mentioned the role of Jesus in the eschatological salvation, this could seem to have less importance as well. An appropriate question would be if their formulations of Christology are due to the more developed affective side of their understanding of Christ and if the weaker cognitive side affects the normative status of Christ?

> According to Christian dogmatics, admiration of Jesus Christ does not necessarily qualify for authentic Christianity. Rather, the effect of this admiration is crucial for judging whether we are seeing Christianity.

To sum up, the imandars are a group of believers who have given themselves over to the vision of Jesus as prophet-saint, savior, and way. The theological shaping of what that means takes place in their jama'at practice, and they articulate that Jesus is true and authentic. Jesus' normative status has an affective as well as a cognitive dimension, and both dimensions are mirrored in the self-understanding of the believers in Jesus as authentic in their interpretation of their own religious background.

ECCLESIOLOGY

The believers are practicing their faith in the crossing between the global and the local, in what Roland Robertson has called the "glocal" (Robertson 1995)—another of these "changing borders." I believe that the existence of the believers as a phenomenon can be best understood and interpreted from the perspective of "changing borders" in the local reception and modification of a global belief. Consequently, I think it is possible to understand why and how these people have become believers in Jesus and interpret their existence in the light of the "changing borders" and new "cultural logics" (Schreiter 1997) where de-traditionalization and individualization are important factors.

In his book *The New Catholicity*, Robert Schreiter points out that there seem to be different "cultural logics" for a theology unfolding in the glocal context: anti-globalization, primitivism, and ethnification (Schreiter 1997, 21). Every one of these three logics tries to protect the local in the meeting with the global, Schreiter claims. I will here concentrate on the last of these three strategies: ethnification. Ethnification becomes a strategy at the time when identity is questioned; in the imandars' case this means both from the side of Christianity as well as from Islam. Schreiter's point is that the cultural logic of ethnification as a social and theological strategy is in opposition to the homogenizing powers of globalization. In relation to the imandars, in the face of the homogenizing powers of a global Christianity or Christian church, their cultural strategy is to underscore their difference. A hybrid or mixture is the normal outcome of this strategy and, in the case of the believers in Jesus, this hybrid is clearly seen when they point at their double belonging in relation to Bangladeshi Islamic culture as well as to Jesus. They clearly mix elements from the two religious traditions and interpret the one tradition in the light of the other. Their understanding of "faithfulness" as a fundamental existential and spiritual concept is also an insistence on the local religious culture in the light of globalized Christianity.

Therefore, globalization might be viewed as the condition, and glocalization as the process which establish the context for the imandars' rejection of the institutional churches. The Christian theological question is now: Is this a viable foundation for Christian ecclesiology? Can the homogeneity of a group be a sufficient condition in a Christian understanding of the communion sanctorum, the fellowship of saints? Now, Christian theology does not claim Western Christianity or Western institutional Christian churches to be unique or normative for faith in Christ—from a dogmatic point of view, only the person Christ can hold that position. Therefore, even if the homogeneity of a group does not seem to be the true criteria for discipleship, I believe that the jama'at ecclesiology taught and practiced by these believers in Jesus might find its place inside a global contextual Christianity.

THEOLOGY OF RELIGIONS

As I have pointed out, the imandars frequently discussed how to be "authentic," "moral," and "respectful"" towards the Bangladeshi Islamic tradition. I see the use of these terms as a way of talking about the relation between their former religious belief and their new interior faithfulness towards Jesus as a fulfilment of their former religious belief. Concerning the majority group of Muslims, the informants seem to have more positive views of single pious persons than the whole group as such. The fact that believers judge persons from other religious backgrounds according to their personal piety ("authenticity" and "morality"), rather than their theology and faith, might be interpreted as an area where the Muslim religious culture affects the believers.[10] As described, the relationship was not totally uncomplicated in practice where the believers in Jesus are still in an unresolved position towards Christianity as well as to Islam, partly continuing mosque worship and distancing themselves from the institutional Christian churches in Bangladesh.

Pushing the question of the evaluation of other religious traditions by these believers, I would term their implicit understanding as "exclusive" insofar as salvation through faith in Jesus Christ is concerned. None of the imandars were optimistic about the eschatological salvation of Muslims apart from faith—or faithfulness—towards Jesus. However, their attitude was also "inclusive" insofar as the use of religious concepts is concerned. Even if the believers' reflections about Christology were not overly intellectual, their positive evaluation of the Bangladeshi Islamic religious culture clearly displays an inclusive understanding of Islam. However, the measuring stick for their understanding was neither cultural nor institutional but personal: that is, Jesus as a person was "standard" and "truth" for those faithful to him as their saint-prophet. The believers could thus be said to express an inclusive praxis through their openness towards individuals of other religious belief. Finally, certain areas of their practice might be viewed as pluralistic, that is as mutually shared. Here I am especially thinking about their uncomplicated adoption of Bangladeshi religious culture. However, none of the informants claimed any sort of pluralism which would resemble the understanding taught by certain theologians of religion who claim an Absolute behind all historical religions. I interpret this as that the believers, in opposition to any abstract form of pluralism, respect a religious tradition which they know from the inside and at the same time acknowledge the differences between this tradition and their own faith in Jesus. An important difference between the pluralism implicitly advocated by the imandars and other types of pluralism is that the pluralism of the imandars means that they are exclusive, inclusive, and pluralistic at the same time but in relation to different areas in the social and cultural context where they live out their faithfulness towards Jesus Christ. This explains why the imandars, in contrast to a more abstract form of pluralism, do not seem to have problems with the traditional Christological formulations (cf. Schmidt-Leukel 1997, 578-79; Dupuis 1997, 386-88).

CONCLUSION

The imandars' theology of religions is not easily classified in the common tripartite model of exclusive, inclusive, and pluralistic theologies of religions. But exactly because of this fact, their experience and theology is valuable for a Christian theology of religions which wants to resist the temptation of removing itself from the lived life of actual believers and retracting to systemic and paradigmatic logical deductions. In contrast to such a disengaged theology, the more inductive and less systematic theology of the imandars holds forth another type of theological ideal and virtue than logics, namely faithfulness. It is on the basis of this personal faithfulness towards Jesus that they view their Islamic heritage not only as a fact but also as enrichment in their faith in Jesus as they are willing to use the insights from their former

---

10   See John Williams' thesis that Islam as a religion is more concerned with what the single believer *does* than what he *believes*. In the same way, claims Williams, do Muslims seldom distance themselves from other groups of Muslims for the reason of wrong theology unless this wrong theology leads to activities which cut off the group from the brotherhood of Islam (Williams cited in Kurtz 1995, 135).

religious commitment in their interpretation of who and what Jesus is. In this they can be said to be what Lesslie Newbigin has termed "responsible pluralists," namely, viewing Jesus as normative savior and true norm for life without having to overtake or discharge other religious traditions in advance. The form of pluralism, which the believers in Jesus hold to, is thus a form which does not take the dismissal but the affirmation of the normative status of Jesus as a starting point; this is pluralistic in the sense that it is both exclusive, inclusive, and pluralistic at the same time. In this perspective, the imandars might be viewed as a paradigm for a responsible pluralistic theology. Their understanding can be said to be more authentic in that it is a lived understanding and because its Christology finds itself within the larger Christian tradition. Thus the imandars give us important clues about the changes that Christianity undergoes as it becomes a global religion lived in multiple religious contexts.

> The imandars give us important clues about the changes that Christianity undergoes as it becomes a global religion lived in multiple religious contexts.

Jonas Jørgensen, General Secretary of the Danish Mission Council, Copenhagen, Denmark, has a special interest in India and Bangladesh.

QUESTIONS FOR REFLECTION:

1. Jonas Jørgensen's paper highlights the complexities of contextualization. In this narrative, what do you see as the marks of an authentic work of the Holy Spirit? At the same time, what questions would you have? How would you respond to those same questions if applied to your own context?

2. Jørgensen suggests that the example of the Isa Imandars may give us a model beyond the classical "inclusive, exclusive, pluralist" paradigm. Do you agree? If so, why? If not, why not? What dangers, and what opportunities, do you see in adopting this model?

3. Why is the institution of the church so often a barrier to the gospel instead of a bridge? In the context Jørgensen describes, what are some of the specific problems cited by the Imandars? What changes would the church need to make, and how, to be both more authentic and also more culturally sensitive? How would this challenge the church in your own context?

CHAPTER 26

CONTEXTING C5 CONTEXTUALIZATION

A Christian Brother

Throughout the Middle East, our foremost challenge and prayer is to see the Kingdom of God reach people of all backgrounds, particularly those of the majority faith, Islam. Expatriate missionaries and national believers and churches are trying to reach Muslims and both are in search of an appropriate and effective methodology in reaching them. As an Egyptian believer from a Christian background, I have been involved in missional efforts in the Middle East, North Africa, and the Gulf for around twenty years, and have been exposed to numerous ideas and strategies for reaching Muslims. One of the most controversial issues I have heard is C5 level contextualization. In Jim Leffel's article, "Contextualization: Building Bridges to the Muslim Community," he describes C5 level contextualization in the following way: "*Believers remain legally and socially within Islamic community. Aspects of Islam incompatible with the Bible are rejected or if possible, reinterpreted. Believers may remain active in the mosque.*" In this level of contextualization, believers continue to read the Qur'an, say the Islamic prayers and the Shehada, the Islamic creed which means "*There is no God but Allah, and Muhammad is the Prophet of Allah.*" I was surprised that this approach was being used, so I began discussing the concept and its effectiveness with a number of Arab Christian and Muslim background believers. The following true story illustrates our impressions and the responses I received.

I was with a group of Middle Easterners in a Western country attending a conference. Our hosts desired to show us special favor by serving Middle Eastern food. They purchased a cookbook with Middle Eastern recipes, read the recipes and selected a few of them, purchased the ingredients needed and cooked the meal, all the while following the recipes to the letter. The results were disastrous. The food tasted nothing like any dish we had eaten in our countries. Perhaps there were some familiar aromas, but the food itself was so different. We did our best to be kind and polite and thanked our hosts for their efforts, but the amount of food left on the table spoke volumes about how we enjoyed the food. Thankfully, the next day our hosts decided to cook food they were familiar with, and we were able to enjoy our meal together.

This true story is humorous when I reflect on the situation, but this is exactly how Arab believers from a Muslim background, as well as those from a Christian background, feel about C5 contextualization. It is simply "out of context." There are a few reasons why we feel this way. First, there is a clear contradiction between Islam and Christianity in many Islamic practices. Prayer is one of them. In C5 contextualization, converts may continue to pray five times a day in the local mosque, perform the same rituals of washing before prayer, facing the east, putting their hands behind their ears, standing up and then bowing down, etc. For many advocates of C5, these practices may signify healthy contextualization. However, these are not neutral cultural practices. They are religious rituals that are in clear contradiction to Christian spirituality. In Christ, we are made pure by his shed blood. In Islam, Muslims try to gain acceptance before God through their actions and strict adherence to Islamic law. This is why they wash before praying and pray five times a day, stand facing east, etc. There is also a strong element of fear that motivates them to do this. In Islam, their salvation is not certain, and the Qur'an makes it clear that eternal punishment awaits those who fall short. To continue practicing Islamic prayer and the rituals associated with it is very confusing, particularly to young believers, and keeps them in bondage to a works-based faith rather than experiencing the freedom and grace that Christ purchased for them.

I asked a particular Muslim-background believer what he thinks about Muslim prayers and C5 contextualization. This gentleman has been a believer for more than fifteen years and has managed to maintain a strong relationship with his Muslim family, though he has been arrested and suffered greatly for his faith. His response to my question was, "I have been a Muslim most of my life and suffered for years under Islamic law. When I came to Christ, I found grace and the opportunity to build a relationship with my heavenly Father. Do you want me to lock myself again under the law and not enjoy the grace of praying any time I desire? Do you want me to live again under the restrictions, laws, and fear attached to Islamic prayer? You, a Christian background believer, can enjoy the grace. How is it that you would deny me that same grace because I am of Muslim background?"

> When it comes to deciding which Islamic practices contradict Christianity and which are acceptable cultural practices, who better to make this distinction than believers within the cultural context, whether they be of Muslim or Christian background?

There are, on the other hand, some practices within the Islamic faith that are completely acceptable as they are rooted in the culture. Taking off one's shoes and sitting on the floor for meetings, for instance, is a sign of respect in the Middle Eastern culture. The challenge is distinguishing between culture and religion in our attempts to contextualize the gospel. Which practices are cultural in nature and which ones are religious? Which practices contradict the principles God gives us in the Bible and which do not? In many cases, a line must be drawn between Arab culture and Islamic practices and beliefs. When it comes to deciding which Islamic practices contradict Christianity and which are acceptable cultural practices, who better to make this distinction than believers within the cultural context, whether they be of Muslim or Christian background?

A second reason I and all other Arabs in the Middle East I have spoken with disagree with C5 contextualization is that it does not discourage believers from reading the Qur'an, but simply tells them to reject or reinterpret passages that are in clear contradiction to the Bible. This opens the door for a great deal of confusion and misunderstanding. It leaves room for the continuation of abusive family behaviors and the denial of human rights, since these are clearly allowed in the Qur'an. Women, for instance, do not have equal rights with men. In court, there must be two male witnesses or one male and two women. Women are considered half the value as men! Consider the Qur'an's clear allowance of husbands to beat their wives, take revenge, act violently, or reject others of different faiths. If we don't draw a clear line around all the teachings in the Qur'an that contradict the Bible, then we run the risk of raising disciples who perpetuate these destructive practices.

Thirdly, when the local church or expatriate missionaries use C5 contextualization to reach out to Muslims in the Middle Eastern context, this can actually prevent them from going deeper into the culture and discovering effective ways of reaching Muslims in our context. If one focuses on adapting the external Islamic practices such as Shehada, praying in the mosque, and other Islamic rituals, they may miss aspects of the culture that are much deeper and closer to the people's hearts. Social relationships, family solidarity, their way of celebrating, being event oriented, showing hospitality and generosity, confrontation techniques, shame and honor, and handling politically hot issues are subjects that are often overlooked when we adopt C5 contextualization. One may assume missionaries understand and have adopted the culture when in fact they are missing the true *heart* culture.

> When the local church or expatriate missionaries use C5 contextualization to reach out to Muslims in the Middle Eastern context, this can actually prevent them from going deeper into the culture and discovering effective ways of reaching Muslims in our context.

Moreover, C5 contextualization is not accepted by Muslims in the Middle Eastern context. Muslims view missionaries and converts using this methodology as a cult. C5 adherents in the eyes of Arab Muslims are neither Muslim nor Christian, but are creating a new religion. This puts up immediate barriers and creates serious questions for Muslims in the Middle East. Muslims do not buy this strategy. Expatriates will be rejected. Muslim background believers will experience even more persecution because they will be viewed as deceptive and cultish. What was intended to be an approach to contextualize the gospel and build a bridge to Muslims actually ends up creating a wider gap and causing great misunderstandings.

Many advocates of the C5 model seek to prove their point by building the discussion around the national Christian churches in the Middle East. They say these churches, though they have withstood Islam for centuries, have failed to bring the gospel to the culture and are separate from the Islamic community. This may be true in some ways, but it does not mean all the churches in the Middle East are not good witnesses. It is certainly not beneficial for the Kingdom of God to dismiss the opinion, perspective, and the developments that have taken place within many national churches in the last decade. Even considering the tens of thousands of Algerians and tens and perhaps hundreds of thousands of Egyptians who have converted out of Islam, the opinion of these existing churches in C5 contextualization discussions has been marginalized because academic voices outside their context label them as

"Christianized." We should instead embrace these believers and national churches as part of the positive equation for advancing the Kingdom of God.

My challenge for those who read this article is to seek firsthand feedback from Middle Eastern believers living in this region as you form your opinion on the issue of C5 contextualization. Do not depend solely on reading the well-researched, well-marketed academic books and articles on the subject, or the statistics taken from other regions where Islam is present and flourishing. Consider a Western believer who visited Morocco and went to visit the largest mosque in all of North Africa, situated right along the coast. He commented to a Moroccan Muslim background believer who was with him, "Wouldn't it be amazing if one day this mosque is full of believers in Jesus Christ, worshiping him together?" The Moroccan believer, who of course had converted out of Islam, replied, "I wish this place would disappear into the sea, for all the lies it told us." This conversation challenged this gentleman to reconsider his previously staunch agreement with C5 level contextualization.

A Christian Brother, unidentified for security reasons, is a pastor and leader in a Muslim context.

QUESTIONS FOR REFLECTION

1. What does this story tell us about the need for great care in developing appropriate contextualization?
2. C5 level contextualization has strong advocates as well as strong critics, and sometimes disagreements are bitter. Why do you think people, all passionate about wanting to see those of other faiths come to worship Jesus Christ, reach such different conclusions? Do you think reconciliation and rapprochement is possible?
3. How should we evaluate when something is purely cultural and when it has religious meaning incompatible with belonging to Jesus Christ?

CHAPTER 27

MISSIOLOGY AT THE MOVIES

The Apostle Paul Meets Avatar
Les Taylor

In 2009 and 2010, Ministries of La Habra, California, promoted conferences concerned with a critical assessment of the *Insider Movement* (IM).[1] Their purpose was that the IM would "no longer be an Evangelical option for Christian missions to Muslims," so it is no surprise that this was convened for "the mutual support and edification of people who oppose insider movements." Although it was claimed that both IM advocates and critics were present, it was also claimed that this event was the "only such gathering in the face of many efforts dominated by insider supporters."[2] Using very strong language, claims were made of the IM being buttressed by "unorthodox, anachronistic interpretations of isolated biblical texts in a way that ignores the overall redemptive flow of Scripture and its principal motifs of covenantal, exclusive faith against the idolatrous religions of the nations"; that these conferences have "unearthed aberrant understandings of Christianity and religion in general. IM methods depend on a view of religion that is sociological and cultural, ignoring the fallen [*nature*] they carry"; IMs ignore "the spiritual dangers of false religion, coaxing Muslims who profess Christ to remain embedded in a poisonous faith system that eventually must corrupt and distort its practitioners"; and there is "dishonesty and duplicity in some groups."

Whenever God does something new, a wake of controversy usually follows: consider the tensions when Peter reported to the initially skeptical Jerusalem elders that the uncircumcised but God-fearing Cornelius, with his household, had received the Holy Spirit (Acts 10 through 15). So it is important that IM's key articulators must continue to pen considered and measured responses to misunderstandings, objections and accusations, as they have been doing (see Corwin 2007; Dorr 2006). I write simply as a critical insider. However, I was privileged to have studied the New Testament under an excellent Pauline specialist and

---

1   For the conference website, see http://www.insidermovements.org.

2   See http://biblicalmissiology.org/2010/10/11/recap-of-the-insider-movement-conference-a-critical-assessment-ii-2010.

missiologist during my three years of theological education. Long before relocating to Muslim Southeast Asia ten years ago, I had seen the following for the first time:

- That just as no one offers water without choosing something to offer it in, no one presents the message of the water of life in a cultureless cup.
- The best choice for the "cup" is the one in which the recipients are most familiar.
- Gentiles no longer needed to first become Jews in order to follow Jesus. Therefore, the New Testament mandated conversion—not proselytism (see Walls 2000, 2004).
- Like Jesus, Paul was a Law-observant Jew (Act 21:20-26) who was called to make known among the Gentiles that the risen Messiah was good news for them as well (Acts 9:15, 18:6, Rom 1:5-6, Gal 1:16, 2:1, 6-9).[3]

I relocated to Muslim Southeast Asia ten years ago. As non-Muslim Europeans, my wife and I were outsiders. Although Travis, in his C-scale (1998), *described* (rather than prescribed) how *Muslims* (not Christians) related to Muslims and Christian communities, we were initially textbook cases of the misunderstandings described by Gray and Gray (2009): that "C4" primarily related to (a) our adaptation of local practices, and (b) retention of local practices by the local believers. In other words, the C-scale presented options for our religious identity, philosophy, or practices (see Gray and Gray 2009, 65). We had joined a team who "did C4." As such, we were not Christians but followers of Jesus. We didn't claim to be Muslims, and my non-attendance at Friday prayers confirmed this.[4] I began keeping a longer beard and my wife wore a headscarf. More importantly, we established a strictly *halal* home and set about the lifelong task of learning language and worldviews. Finally, we (unbeknownst to us at the time) adhered to an attraction model also described by Gray and Gray (2009).

We eventually came to see that for Muslims who accepted what almighty Allah had done through his holy servant Isa Al-Masih, C4 is not a viable option. Even if we believed in extractionist proselytism, neither were the other options further down the C-scale feasible in light of the absence of local Christian communities able and/or willing to assimilate Muslim believers. Like others at the time, we talked in terms of a C5 movement of witnessing Muslim insiders that we might not be involved in ourselves. We also became less frustrated at not having become insiders. As non-Muslim, European outsiders who worked in understandable jobs, spoke local languages, and understood local culture and religion, we had become what I have referred to as *inbetweeners*. We were increasingly at peace with seeing ourselves as following in Barnabas' footsteps of finding and encouraging people more able than him to work with the Gentiles (see Higgins 1998, 115).

> We were increasingly at peace with seeing ourselves as following in Barnabas' footsteps of finding and encouraging people more able than him to work with the Gentiles.

---

3   For more on the issue of Paul's Jewishness, see (Boyarin 1994; Eisenbaum 2009; Langton 2005; Nanos 2009a, 2009c; Segal 1994; Skarsaune and Hvalvik 2007).

4   I have recently heard of the C-scale having been tweaked so as to address workers' needs. This has been renamed the W-Scale.

In this paper, I consider some of the practical, emotional, and ethical issues of IM methodology. I consider such a discussion to be overdue. This paper's two substantive sections bring into dialogue the following. The first is key themes from James Cameron's critically acclaimed and commercially successful 2009 feature movie, *Avatar*. The second is arguments by Jewish Pauline specialist Mark Nanos (2009b) about what the apostle Paul did—and didn't—mean by becoming all things to all people so that by all means he could save some (1 Cor 9:22).

AVATAR, JAKE SULLY, AND HIS NAVI AVATAR BODY

James Cameron's film, *Avatar*, is set in 2154 on the planet of Pandora. Humans have colonized Pandora in order to extract a precious mineral called "unobtainium." Futuristic technology has enabled humans to genetically engineer the bodies of Pandora's humanoid inhabitants (the Omaticaya) by mixing their DNA with those of the humans who remotely operate them. These "avatars" have enabled humans to achieve something that has formerly been impossible: to (remotely) make contact with the giant, athletic Navi, a tribe of the Omaticaya race. Nevertheless, despite this breakthrough, the avatar program has been unable to achieve objectives crucial to their mission, to the frustration of those in charge of— and bankrolling—this mission.

The head of the mission to Pandora, a cutthroat corporate character called Selfridge, exasperatedly complains to the head of the avatar program, Dr. Grace Augustine, "Look, you're supposed to be winning the hearts and minds of the natives. Isn't that the whole point of your little puppet show? If you look like them, if you talk like them, they'll trust you?" Similar sentiments are held by the head of corporate security, an ex-marine called Colonel Quaritch. He declares to the hero of the story, another ex-Marine called Jake Sully who is destined to be the meat in the sandwich between humans and the Navi:

> *Quaritch:* The avatar program is a joke....But we have a unique opportunity here, you and I....A recon marine in an avatar body could get me the intel I need, on the ground, right in the hostiles' camp. I need you to learn about these savages, gain their trust. Find out how I can force their cooperation, or hit 'em hard if they don't.

On the eve of his first contact with the Navi in his avatar body, Jake allows himself to be co-opted by Quaritch into assisting the corporate camp, despite being part of the avatar program. Jake asks whether he is still with Augustine. Quaritch declares, "You walk like one of her science pukes, you quack like one, but you report to me!"

On his first mission, Jake is attacked by a *thanator*, the predator on top of Pandora's food chain. Although Jake escapes, he is separated from his team who are forced to return to the humans' base as night descends. Left alone in the forest, Jake, in his avatar body, prepares to fight for his life in the forest. In the middle of a fight with a pack of *viperwolves*, Jake is rescued by a Navi called Neytiri. The following conversation occurs between the two after Jake attempts to thank her.

> *Neytiri*: All this is your fault! They (the viperwolves) did not need to die.
> *Jake*: They attacked me. How am I the bad guy!?

Neytiri: Your fault! You are like a baby, making noise, don't know what to do. You should not come here, all of you! You only come and make problems.

[…]

Neytiri: (You are) stupid! Ignorant like a child!
Jake: If I'm so ignorant, maybe you should teach me.
Neytiri: Sky people can not learn. You do not see.
Jake: Then teach me to "see."
Neytiri: No one can teach you to see.
Jake: I need your help.
Neytiri: You should not be here.

After a series of interventions by the Navis' deity *Eywa*, Jake is taken to the Navis' base, a place called "Home Tree," to meet with their leaders Eytukan and Mo'at, who are Neytiri's father and mother. Eytukan is furious, telling Neytiri, "I have said no dreamwalker will come here, to offend our home! His alien smell fills my nose." Mo'at intervenes, declaring, "I will look at this alien." She asks Jake, "Why did you come to us?!"

Jake: I came to learn.
Mo'at: We have tried to teach other Sky People. It is hard to fill a cup which is already full.
Jake: My cup is empty, trust me…
Eytukan: […] This is the first warrior dreamwalker we have seen. We need to learn more about him.

In the end, Mo'at instructs a reluctant Neytiri to "teach him our way, to speak and walk as we do." Returning to base, Jake proudly reports to Selfridge and Quaritch, "I'm practically family! They gonna study me. I have to learn to be one of them."

In the missions that follow, Jake sets about learning to "see" like a Navi and speak their language. He recounts, "I'm learning to read the trails, the tracks at the water-hole, the tiniest scents and sounds. When you hear nothing, you will hear everything. When you see nothing, you will see everything. Sometimes I have no idea what she's talking about […] She's always going on about the flow of energy—the spirits of the animals and what not." Later on, he recounts trying to "understand the deep connection the People have to the forest. They see a network of energy that flows through all living things. They know that all energy is only borrowed—and one day you have to give it back." Eventually, he is told that he is ready to undergo his initiation as a member of the Navi. On the eve of his next mission in which he will be initiated, he is confronted by Quaritch.

Quaritch: You're not gettin' lost in the woods, are you son? Your last report was two weeks ago. I'm starting to doubt your resolve. From what I see, it's time to terminate this mission.
Jake: No. I can do this…I've gotta finish this thing. There's one more test—the Dream Hunt. It's the final stage of becoming a man. Then I'm one of them. They'll trust what I say…and I can negotiate the terms of their relocation.

He returns, where the clan chief, Eytukan declares, "You are now a son of the Omaticaya (the race to which the Navi belong)—you are part of the People." At this, all members of the clan press forward, crowding around and putting their hands on Jake's shoulders, back, chest—hands upon hands, until he is connected to everyone. That evening, he takes Neytiri as his lifelong mate.

Unbeknownst to Jake, while this is happening, Selfridge and Quaritch have both lost patience with their carrot policy towards the Navi. They have also lost trust in Jake Sully, their ace card. It is time to use the stick! Although Jake is arrested, he and Dr. Grace Augustine manage to convince Selfridge to allow Jake one last chance. He returns to Home Tree in the middle of a war council to inform the people about two truths that they have hereunto been oblivious to:

> *Jake*: A great evil is upon us. The Sky People are coming to destroy Home Tree. They will be here soon. You have to leave, or you will die.
> *Mo'at*: Are you certain of this?
> *Jake*: They sent me here to learn your ways. So one day I could bring this message, and you would believe it.
> *Neytiri*: What are you saying, Jake? You knew this would happen?
> *Jake*: Yes….At first it was just orders. Then everything changed. I fell in love—with the forest, with the Omaticaya People—with you. And by then, how could I tell you?
> *Neytiri*: I trusted you, Jake!
> *Jake*: Neytiri. Please, I only wanted to…
> *Neytiri*: You will never be one of the People!

SUBVERSIVE MISSIOLOGICAL MESSAGES

For those called to relocate among another ethnic group, language, and religion—to live among and love Muslims—we can relate a number of subversive messages found in *Avatar's* plot.

The first, and most important, is that looking like the Navi was not enough. When Neytiri first encounters Jake's avatar body, she immediately knew he was not a Navi. For one, he was wearing clothes! Jake was referred to in a number of ways: Sleepwalker, demon, and alien. Eytukan also complained that he stunk. Jake was oblivious to all these, spoken as they were in a tongue that he did not understand. The depths of his delusion after his return are demonstrated in his declaration that he was practically family.

Although few dispute the success of future Muslim ministry in Asia being related to the role Asian Christ-followers take, it is naïve to assume that merely looking like Asian Muslims is sufficient. If looking like the Navi was not enough, what is? *Avatar's* second subversive theme is that outsiders must be empty cups that determine to learn to see and speak as insiders. Jake not only stood out because he was dressed in human clothes. According to Neytiri, he knew neither how to see nor how to survive in an environment that the Navi were intimately connected to. Jake was told that he was a baby who didn't know what to do. He was as ignorant as a child! Sky people were also incapable of learning to see. Neytiri's mother, Mo'at, commented how hard it was to teach Sky People who were convinced that their cups were already full. Not only did this uneducated ex-marine accept his need to learn, he was also prepared to do whatever it took to see the world as the Navi did and to speak their language.

There were other things required in becoming a Navi that Jake was unaware of. The third subversive message of *Avatar* relates to the emotional cost of relocating among people whose language one is learning and whose world one is attempting to see. The emotional cost paid by Jake was not only related to deceiving Grace about gathering intelligence for the Avatar program's corporate enemies. The deeper he descended into the world of the Navi, the more emotionally conflicted he felt. I submit there are emotional costs in attempts to become an insider when one's primary allegiance remains with the ones who have sent you. This emotional cost was another reality of Jake's mission that he had been naïve about.

> There are emotional costs in attempts to become an insider when one's primary allegiance remains with the ones who have sent you.

In his increasingly conflicted emotional state on the eve of his initiation, Jake persists in foolishly insisting that once he is one of them, he will be trusted and able to negotiate the terms of their relocation from Home Tree. When he attempts to do this, which forces him to confess his duplicity, Jake experiences what might have been his greatest fear: He is rejected both by his new wife and the tribe that he has grown to love. Those who have seen *Avatar* are aware that Jake would eventually fully become a Navi. In a way that confirms my argument, this required him not only to fight against and kill humans, but to forever leave behind his human body.

BECOMING ALL THINGS TO ALL PEOPLE

Avatar is merely a movie. The same cannot be said for 1 Corinthians 9:22, from the following passage:

> For though I am free with respect to all, I have made myself a slave to all, so that I might win more of them. To the Jews I became as a Jew, in order to win Jews. To those under the law I became as one under the law (though I myself am not under the law) so that I might win those under the law. To those outside the law I became as one outside the law (though I am not free from God's law but am under Christ's law) so that I might win those outside the law. To the weak I became weak, so that I might win the weak. I have become all things to all people, that I might by all means save some. I do it all for the sake of the gospel, so that I may share in its blessings (1 Cor 9:19-23 NRSV).

Jewish Pauline Scholar Mark D. Nanos describes what he refers to as "Paulinism." This is based on the proposition that "the role of Torah to express covenant faithfulness had ended for Christians," with its pillars being the privileging of "gentileness, freedom from Torah and Jewish identity." As Paul did not observe Torah while among non-Jews, ethical compromises are central to Paul's character and Christian ideology (2009b, 2-3). Nanos quotes the exegesis of 1 Corinthians 9:22 by respected evangelical scholar, Gordon Fee:

> When Paul was among Jews he was kosher; when he was among Gentiles he was non-kosher—precisely because, as with circumcision, neither mattered to God (cf. 7:19;

8:8). But such conduct tends to matter a great deal to the religious—on either side!—so that inconsistency in such matters ranks among the greatest of evils. Paul's policy quite transcended petty consistency—and 'religion' itself….How can Paul determine to 'become like a Jew'? The obvious answer is, in matters that have to do with Jewish religious peculiarities that Paul as a Christian had long ago given up as essential to a right relationship with God (Fee 1987, 427-28).

For those looking to Paul's life and teaching for guidance, this position has the potential to assert him as a "hero of many disguises" whose tactics must be excused and defended (2009b, 9). What might be our response to those citing this passage as central to their rejection of Paul and Christianity? Does 1 Corinthians 9:19-23 stand in the way of improving relations between Christians and Jews, if it undermines "truthfulness as a core value, an essential element for the complete trust required in mutually respectful relationships," as Nanos claims (2009b, 10)? For Christ-followers, suggestions that Paul was only Torah-observant "when judged expedient for the purpose of gaining a hearing among Jews," leads to the vexing ethical issue of "serpent-like guile" lying at the very heart of Paulinism" (2009b, 11).

Nanos enquires about the implications of prevailing readings like Fee's. Was Paul deceitful, hypocritical, and concerned with expediency over principle? Was this not something he condemned in others—most notably Peter in Antioch (Gal 2:11-21)? Did Paul disguise his convictions and compromise truthfulness for expediency when moving among different groups in order to be successful? Would this not have subverted his own teachings: that those circumcised when they were called should remain in this state (1 Cor 7:17-24)? Would this have represented Paul misleading his listeners into responding to his message into a religious affiliation incompatible with their convictions and lifestyles? Having joined, would people adopt this same strategy of "misleading others to win them to the gospel" (2009b, 3)? Would this not have been impracticable? Would Jews and non-Jews not have ultimately learnt of Paul's "contrary behavior when among other parties subscribing to opposite propositional truths, whether witnessed directly or received via rumors" (2009b, 4).

Drawing on the work of Paul Gooch (1978), Nanos considers two explanations of 1 Corinthians 9: 19-23, which I consider below.

LIFESTYLE ADAPTABILITY OR RHETORICAL ADAPTABILITY?

Suggestions that this passage advocates what Gooch refers to as "lifestyle adaptability" are resoundingly rejected by Nanos: Paul did not outwardly mimic behavior, so as to appear to share the values of those whose trust he wished to gain for the sole purpose of "saving some." Paul's apparent tricking people into believing that "the message he proclaims does not subvert the rational basis or convictional value of living in a particular way," has been commented on by many (2009b, 15). However, few have explained, or even discussed, allegations of inconsistency or dishonesty as Nanos attempts.[5]

As if readers needed to be convinced, Nanos points out more problems with this extant explanation by asking the following questions: Did non-Jews understand Paul to worship their gods? Among Jews, did Paul mislead them into believing that he upholds the propositional conviction of Torah-based behavior as enjoined upon Jews by God? Would those who accepted his message be shocked upon discovering that they have joined a community that has renounced Torah? Would they have agreed to adopt Paul's "chameleon-like expedient behavior" in order to trick more Jews? Would these not have created a "spiral of duplicity, with long-range deleterious results for their psychological and spiritual as well as social well-being should they remain "Christians" after finding out the truth" (2009b, 16)? How could Paul become a Jew? Wasn't he one already? Similar problems are encountered if the phrase "under law" is interpreted as referring to proselytes. Would Gentile idolaters have been made aware that becoming Christ-believers in response to Paul's message would result in no longer behaving in the manner he has mimicked among them? Similarly, would Torah-observant Jews have been made aware that becoming Christ-believers would mean no longer behaving in the manner he mimicked among them?

In short, conclusions of ethical inconsistency or hypocrisy are difficult to escape if 1 Corinthians 9:19-23 is viewed as describing Paul's lifestyle adaptability. Paul did not change his behavior as he switched from one group to another. This would have suggested his preference for subversion over mounting an outright challenge that could be defended (which might have been justified as being in service of the greater good). Suggestions that Paul emphasized expediency versus principle also contradicts Paul's insistence that this should never happen—despite the suffering which might result.[6] Paul taught against proselyte conversion in his letter to the Galatians. By doing so, he took the principled route by denying circumcision to those wanting it—despite the risk of losing them. For Gentiles seeing occasional Torah-observance as legitimate and expedient, they would have indeed been relegated to an inferior position: they were both unable to play the Jewish card, and circumcision had been denied them. Lifestyle adaptability would have also been tactically ineffective for Paul. His duplicity would have alienated more than it had attracted (2009b, 39).

The practical and ethical inadequacies of interpreting 1 Corinthians 19-23 as lifestyle adaptability necessitate alternative explanations being sought. Nanos argues Paul to have referred to his "rhetorical adaptability." In other words, he varied his speech to "different audiences: reasoning from their premises, but not imitating their conduct in other ways." His views were therefore expressed in "vocabulary and by way of models and examples that

---

5   Some of the few exceptions include (Barram 2005 and Langton 2005).
6   See 1 Cor 4:10-16; 6:7, 12-20; 8:7-13; 9:1-27; 11:27-34; 15:30-34; 16:13-14, and Gal 1:6-10; 4:17-18; 5:7-12; 6:12-13.

are calculated to persuade." From the premises or worldviews of Paul's audience, he led them to conclusions based on another set of premises or worldviews (2009b, 40, 41).

In contrast to lifestyle adaptability, "each party has an opportunity to understand the message in their own terms," and to "challenge the arguments presented (if they so choose), or to proceed to be convinced being fully aware of any cost that might be involved" (2009b, 37). In 1 Corinthians 9: 13-23, Paul was not describing his "adoption of conduct representing his various audiences' convictional propositions." His "evangelistic tactic of rhetorical adaptability" was something that a Torah-observant Jew like him could do when speaking to (a) lawless Jews, (b) those upholding different *halakhic* standards, and (c) non-Jews of any stripe. If this was the case, Paul can not be accused of duplicitous conduct, dishonesty, or inconsistency (2009b, 18).

Between 1 Corinthians 8 to 10, Paul does not become knowledgeable to the knowledgeable in the sense of lifestyle adaptability. His rhetorical adaptation is based on his empathy for the weak and desire to communicate this empathy to the knowledgeable. Having begun with reminders that (a) there is only one God, (b) idols are nobodies (8:4-6), and (c) food offered to them can be eaten (8:8; 10:19, 23, 25-26), he then leads them to a very different conclusion. First, as the demons associated with these idols are real (10:19-22) they are not to eat any food known to be dedicated to idols, like Jews. Although idols do not represent gods, flee from idolatry—or pay the price for not doing so (10:1-23). The only food that can be eaten is that known to have *not* been offered to idols (10:14-33) (2009b, 21-22).

> Paul thus moves them from non-Jewish premises, since they are not Jews, to very Jewish conclusions, since they are Christ-believers, which represents a Jewish (communal, philosophical, religious, moral, etc.) way of being in the world—even for non-Jews. Paul leads these non-Jews to the same conclusions to which he would lead them if he was addressing Jews, arguing many of the same essential points (2009b, 22).

This was the way that Paul became like a non-Jew to his readers. If they had been Jews, he would have appealed directly to Torah to discuss this matter. "We would have seen him instead becoming like a Jew, rhetorically, which would have been quite natural for him, since he was a Jew" (2009b). Although "becoming as" has been misconstrued as imitating, mimicking, or pretending to be, alternatives are suggested: "reason/argue like/as/in the manner of," or amplified, "reason/argue (from the premises of) like/as/in the manner of," or "reason/argue (for truth claims) like/as/in the manner of" (2009b, 34). Thus, "Paul reasons with, relates to, or engages Jews as (if he was) or like (in the manner of) a Jew, and so on. In this rhetorical, or discursive sense, Paul could actually become like—or even become—everything to everyone" (2009b, 25).

What are examples of Paul's rhetorical adaptability? In Acts 17:17-31, Paul did not start by denying the reality of the gods revered by his listeners—despite criticizing representations of the divine. The idol designated by them as "Unknown God" need no longer remain unknown. Far from introducing a new god (as was common at the Areopagus), he discloses the identity of the One true God that they *were* ignorant of (v. 23) but have now heard about from his own lips. Paul quotes no Scripture, but does quote their own poets (v. 28). Nanos paraphrases Paul saying "I became (i.e., reasoned) to the idolaters as [if I was] an idolater." Paul's message to them was within their own premises in order to gain them to Christ. Upon arriving in Thessalonica in Acts 17:1-3, Luke describes Paul proceeding immediately to the synagogue where, on three consecutive Sabbath days, he argued from the Scriptures that Jesus was the Messiah. This was his custom (v. 2). These would have made little or no sense to the philosophers at the Areopagus. Both these are examples of Paul's rhetorical adaptability (2009b, 25-28).

Unlike lifestyle adaptability, if Paul was describing his rhetorical adaptability in 1 Corinthians 9:19-23, there is no moral compromise. Nanos suggests that such an interpretation of 1 Corinthians 9: 19-23 is capable of functioning as a guideline on how to evangelize people of other faiths:

> Inter-faith dialogue also involves learning the premises and cultural worldview of the other, but for very different reasons. It seeks to understand the other on their own terms, and to successfully explain one's own premises and worldview in cross-culturally intelligible terms in order to advance mutual respect and beneficial relationships going forward. (2009b).

Consistent with the pastoral approach in this letter, 1 Corinthians 9: 19-23 describes Paul's evangelistic tactic of adapting rhetorically. He was not an ex-Jew who inspired "moral dishonesty, hypocrisy, inconsistency, subversion of principles for expedience, and practical shortsightedness" (2009b, 42).

PERSONAL REFLECTION AND PASTORAL CONCERNS

There might be legitimate concerns at the ethics of some non-Muslims seeking to play a role in an IM. I consider many are unaware of certain decisions being impractical and coming with emotional costs. I furthermore suggest this being no worse than people who make no attempts to adapt their lifestyle. My treatments of *Avatar* and 1 Corinthians 9:22 have included provocative comments open to being misunderstood. As such, before suggesting some implications of my arguments, I wish to clarify my position on a number of issues. I reiterate that I am a critical insider of the IM. I regard many of the principles on which it is based to reflect the insights of New Testament scholarship associated with the new perspective on Paul. Present-day debates between the IM and its interlocutors also resemble those between the Judaizers and the Hellenists described by historians of the earliest Christian movements (Dunn 1991, 2008). Social scientists who have studied some of these confirm these resembling other vital new religious movements (NRMs) and global Christianities (Jørgensen 2008, 2009).

Although reverting to an extractionist proselyte model is theologically incoherent, it is also impracticable in our context. Nevertheless, my present position has moved far from when I "did C4." In other words, I see new ways that I, as a non-Muslim European outsider who becomes an inbetweener, can be used by God to bring about the people movement that our team is prayerfully laboring towards. There is a need for the thinkers and communicators to offer considered responses to allegations or misunderstandings of intentional unethical deceit. I am certain that these might include acknowledgements of widely diverging positions on issues of disclosure. I would hope that this would, at the very least, concede that there are unforeseen ethical, emotional, and practical problems with the methods of some. I am sure that some may cite Jesus' warning that he was sending his followers like "sheep among wolves" and that they needed to be as "shrewd as snakes and as innocent as doves" (Matt 10:16). Would they also point out Paul's rhetoric occasionally being subversive: if Jesus was LORD, and the Son of God, then Caesar wasn't (Rom 1:1-4, 10:9)?

Outsiders relocating to live as aliens and strangers for the sake of the gospel planning to *intentionally* deceive locals with claims that they are no different from them should be informed of the approach's (a) emotional costs, (b) practical limitations, and (c) of superior alternatives. I reiterate the important caveat that this may not be an issue for those with no competing loyalties with Christian family members, sending churches, or mission agencies. These might also be non-issues for those who come from a Muslim background.

As someone who has only recently begun to appreciate the inadequacies of the attraction model, I am sure that some are surprised by suggestions that contextualization involves more than playing dressup. Although there is no doubt in my mind that Asian Christians who live and love cross-culturally among Asian Muslims have an advantage over Europeans, they should not naïvely assume that looking like Asian Muslims is all that is required. They have to learn how to see the world as a Muslim does and to speak as they do. Even those speaking the same language may need to cease speaking Christianese when talking about faith issues—such as saying "Alhumdulilah" instead of "Praise the LORD." They should be warned of, and mentored through, their inevitable time in "social quarantine" during which they will be sized up by their hosts who wait to see what sort of influence they will be. In most contexts attempts at becoming an insider should be replaced with contentment at being some sort of inbetweener, as I have argued elsewhere. Where this is a problem, concerns at being labeled as a missionary might be mitigated by contributing in some way to their local community which will demonstrate being interested in more than just religion. Reminders about Paul's rhetorical adaptability might encourage newcomers in their lifelong adventure of language study and learning to see the world like those they have lovingly relocated among. Looking like locals is nice, but speaking and seeing like them is essential. Through the latter, all can be all things to all people so that some may be saved.

Les Taylor, an anthropologist, social scientist and church planter, spent ten years in a Muslim context.

QUESTIONS FOR REFLECTION:

1. Les Taylor concludes that his role must be as "an inbetweener." How does his analysis of *Avatar* support that conclusion? What do you think are the strengths and weaknesses of being "an inbetweener"? How would you apply this in your context?

2. Taylor contrasts *lifestyle adaptability* with *rhetorical adaptability*. Can you illustrate these two with examples from your own context? Are there boundaries on each of these, beyond which you lose biblical faithfulness? Give examples.

3. Taylor describes his own journey in approach to contextualization. In your own experience, are you developing in understanding and praxis? If so, what has led you to change, and how has it impacted how you engage in ministry?

CHAPTER 28

THE KONKOMBAS AND THE PROCESS OF CONTEXTUALIZATION

Ronaldo Lidório

The Konkombas are an ethnic family with four main distinct subgroups, found in the northeast of Ghana and in neighboring Togo. In general they are patrilinear, polygamous, animist, often fetishist, with strong links with totemic animals, especially among the Bimonkpeln. In their social organization the clan is the principal cell group, with one of the elders acting as chief of each community or village. There is no cohesion between ethnic groups, each of which has its own totem—an object, plant or animal—which demands a particular type of sacrifice.

There are several categories of social roles, such as scholars, advisors, and listeners (who simply hear problems), as well as well-demarcated spiritual categories, such as healers, dreamers, and witch doctors. The fear of death is the main subject of their songs and stories. To die at a good old age, with wives, children, and a history of noteworthy deeds, is the aspiration of every man and a condition for becoming an ancestor. The Konkombas are known as Tiwoor aanib (people of the forest) because they prefer to live in more distant regions. In the popular imagination they are aggressive warriors, but in fact they are extremely hospitable and loyal. In their own estimation, the greatest shame is lying, and greed is the greatest sin. The greatest virtue is to honor their parents when they are old and remember them when they are gone. The children are brought up by everyone and there are no orphans. The clan cells are the base of their strength and social organization.

Since 1994 my wife and I have been involved in the task of evangelizing the Bimonkpeln ("men who live") in the region of Koni in northeast Ghana. From 1995 onwards we witnessed a period of rapid growth in the Konkomba Bimonkpeln church, so that by 2006 there were twenty-three churches and several thousand members. So far we have been able to give biblical training to five evangelists as well as thirty elders. Another sixty elders are being trained by the evangelists, who are teaching Christian life courses. In all, eighty-seven leaders are playing an active part. Only the five evangelists are supported by the churches to work fulltime.

The Konkombas make up a family of ethnic groups which have to be reached individually. The linguistic and cultural differences between the groups mean that they consider themselves bibiil, or cousins. The first language in this family to receive the New Testament was the Lichabol (of the Bichaboln group); they now have the complete Bible. In 1994 we began translating the New Testament into the Limonkpeln language. We prepared literacy primers, and by the year 2000 there were over 500 adults able to read in their mother tongue. By that stage we already had some books of the New Testament translated, and we finally concluded the initial translation in 2002. In October 2004 the completed New Testament was given to the church in a great service of celebration, where believers from all the twenty-three churches were present. This translation was done by a whole team of workers. Five Konkombas labored for several years, especially in the initial stages of gathering information, and more helped in the last stages in testing the text in the community. One, Dambá, is now in charge of the distribution of the New Testament and heads up the literacy program.

From the beginning, our aim was to plant churches among the Konkombas. The decision to focus on the translation of the New Testament came when, in the early stages of the church, we started discipleship training meetings with believers from each of the villages that had been reached. They would be the future leaders. Each month they came from their villages to spend a weekend with us in Koni, a central village, where we lived. There we would teach them the Word and, since there was nothing written in the local language, each believer would learn some verses by heart to pass them on to his group when they got home. A woman called Aadjo came from Kadjokorá, one of the furthest villages, four days walk away. That weekend she stayed with us, learning the Word, and memorized, like all the other believers, thirteen verses. The weekend over, she started on the four-day walk home. But after two days, she found she had forgotten one of the verses. So she turned round and came straight back to us—were we surprised to see her! When she explained why she had come, she said, "The Word of God is too important to let it fall by the roadside." She learned the verse again, rested that night, and the next day set off again for home.

This incident was what made us decide to start straight in on Bible translation, in a less informal way. The church was right behind us in this decision.

MISSIONARY PERSPECTIVE

Looking at it from a missionary perspective, we can see seven essential factors behind the rapid growth of the church among the Konkomba-Bimonkpeln.

PRAYER COVER

We knew of a considerable number of Christians and churches in Brazil that were committed to praying for the Konkomba-Bimonkpeln from 1993 onward. During the years of greatest church growth in the ethnic group, there was also in Brazil a growing interest in praying for the people. Outside Brazil, the WEC recruited many intercessors, especially in the final years of the New Testament translation project. My mother, Euza Lidório, who heads up an intercessory prayer movement in Brazil with over 600 groups meeting weekly for prayer, gave special space to the Konkombas in her prayer guide bulletin. On several occasions we saw a close connection between an awakening of interest on the part of the Brazilian church to pray for the Konkombas and a following surge in the tribe's acceptance of the gospel.

We are convinced that this prayer movement on behalf of the people is directly linked to the growth of the church in the region.

We saw a close connection between an interest on the part of the Brazilian church to pray for the Konkombas and a following surge in the tribe's acceptance of the gospel.

CULTURAL AWARENESS

Our approach to the Konkomba-Bimonkpeln people was based on a good overall awareness of their culture, and we believe that in this way we reduced risks of nominalism or syncretism arising during the presentation of the gospel. Three methods of cultural evaluation were used, which we called "Anthropos" (ethnographic analysis, with a certain ethnological emphasis), "Pneumatos" (phenomenological analysis), and "Angelos" (ideas for developing an applicable theology). Together, these analyses were the key to preparing a list of twenty-seven points of biblical teaching which needed to be expressed in a clear, culturally relevant way in order to effectively communicate the gospel.

In the Konkomba-Bimonkpeln universe there are no distinctions between religious and non-religious, sacred and secular. There is no separation between spiritual and material, body and soul. Religion is part of all of life: working, feeding, making war or making love, giving birth or resting. To be born into Konkomba-Bimonkpeln society means following a set of rituals and ceremonies which make up tribal life. There are no atheists. Everyone believes in the spirits, be they evil or amoral (there are no good spirits). All believe in the fetishes represented by mountains, trees, rocks, or man-made objects, idols made of wood or stone; all believe in the totems represented usually by different animals, and in Satan—*Kininbon*—lord of all the evil spirits; and all believe in the souls of the departed ancestors, who demand respect and sacrifices and threaten punishment. To offset this depressing universe, everyone has heard of *Uwumbor*, a God of time long past and distant dreams, who no longer relates to the people.

They say: "Uwumbor doesn't want to be God in our tribe any more." They believe this has happened because of a grave offense registered in the people's cosmogony. The story is that, at the beginning of time, Uwumbor created a family that lived on an island. They had a good and happy life, especially because the *pacham* (the blue sky we can see) was low down and could be touched by someone who could climb a tall tree. Uwumbor allowed the man to cut off a bit of the sky every day, because there was plenty of meat there for the family to eat. For many years they lived happily, and the man climbed a tree every day to cut off a piece of the *pacham* and bring some tasty meat for his family. One day, however, the man began to think when he was up in the tree how sad it would be if that sky disappeared and there were no more meat. So he decided he would carve off some huge pieces of sky and throw down plenty of meat for the family. The woman warned him that there was too much meat, but he paid no attention. He went on carving, and when he finally came down he saw there was far more than they could eat that day. Next day, a great amount of the meat had gone bad, and he realized that he had done wrong. Just then Uwumbor arrived on the island to talk with the family, as he did from time to time. But when he saw the meat, so much more than he had allowed, rotting on the ground, he became very sad, and called the man a "greedy man," and then went far away, never to return. He also took with him the *pacham* with all its meat, so that is why we can still see the blue sky, but very far off and out of reach.

This cosmogony made us decide to use *Uwumbor* as the name for God and to develop the elements necessary for a biblical theology of creation, sin, fall, and redemption. Besides this one, another dozen cosmogonies and over a score of anthropogonies helped us to realize what sort of worldview the people hold in relation to their universe. We believed we had the base we needed to communicate the creation and fall as described in Genesis.

Cosmogonies and anthropogonies helped us to realize the worldview the people hold in relation to their universe and gave us the base we needed to communicate the creation and fall as described in Genesis.

This systematic observation of the culture paved the way for developing a communication of the gospel that was applicable to the people's lifestyle, and also helped to alert us to problematic areas where syncretism could arise.

DELIBERATE EVANGELISM ON A LARGE SCALE

We believe the scale and extent of evangelism is as important as the quality. In a biblical church-planting process we always need to remember that the centrality of the Word defines the faithfulness of the Mission. In other words, we do not choose our methods simply because they produce the desired results, but because they are based on God's Word and vision. However, this does not eliminate the need for large-scale evangelism. Constant, intensive evangelism is fundamental in any church-planting process, and deliberate effort is needed to make sure it is not neglected.

From 1993 until 2005 we believe that about 100,000 Konkombas (mostly from the Bimonkpeln ethnic group, but also some Bikuln and Bisachuln) heard the gospel message, either through the agency of the missionaries, through the Konkomba leaders, or the Konkomba believers in general. The most common form of evangelism was to get people to meet in the principal villages and then tell them the story of Uwumbor, God, starting from Genesis.

As we were dealing with a culture that has a vast cosmogony, a messianic profile, and a rich historical tradition, we began our gospel presentation with God, his character and attributes. Although we presented him as being just, loving and merciful, the attribute that most caught the attention of this spiritist, totemic, animist people was his power. Many times they would ask us if it was clear in "God's story" (the Bible) that he was mightier than Grumadil, the amoral spirit who was most feared in the region. Grumadil was the one they prayed to most; even though, in the people's view, he was not to be trusted, it was not safe to go against him.

So large-scale, deliberate evangelism was our constant practice, going from village to village with gatherings great and small. Each new convert joined with us on the next evangelistic outing. The evangelistic activity involved public preaching in the center of each village, loud enough for all to hear, whether they wanted to or not.

It was on one of these occasions that Mebá was converted. He was the witch doctor in Koni and known as Grumadil's keeper. It was *kinyiang*, a Konkomba rest day, and Mebá was sitting in the shade of a tree near his hut on the western edge of Koni. We knew him simply as the witch doctor, feared by the people, who played a leading part in the "sacrifice nights," when dozens of animals would be sacrificed in one night to Grumadil and other fetishes at special times in the year. We had had little personal contact with him: his isolated, aloof style of life as a witch doctor kept him apart. But we had heard that he had sacrificed his own grandson when he first arrived in Koni.

There he was, seated beneath the tree. We had already explained the gospel twice to his clan and family in his hut, although he never came out of his room while we were speaking to the rest of his family. But at least he heard us and never stopped us from coming to his house. He was a man who liked to talk a lot, but that day he was quiet and thoughtful. I was taking a bath in the hut where we lived when a boy came running and said: "Something is happening to Mebá." Everybody ran to see and soon a little crowd had gathered around. The man was leaping, dancing, and shouting. He looked at all the crowd, moving from one side to the other as though he wanted to say something. I joined the throng, thinking that something terrible must have happened to him, like having been bitten by a snake or attacked by someone. As I looked at him, I wondered if he was under some evil influence.

They asked him, "Mebá, what's happening?" He answered joyfully, "There's something new inside me. I started to think and understand what they are saying about Yesu Kristu. He really is God's son, he really is God's *mantotiib*. He really is our hope of seeing Uwumbor one day. But what I realized today, what had been my only fear ever since the gospel began to make sense to me, is that Yesu Kristu is stronger than Grumadil. There is nothing to be afraid of!"

His words were like arrows to the crowd. A witch doctor, keeper of Grumadil, saying that the God of creation, Uwumbor, is stronger! It was something they could never have imagined. He said nothing about me or anybody else or any particular message he had heard. He was having an intense experience with God, and I felt the Lord was taking away all his fear at that moment. "There is nothing to be afraid of," he kept on repeating. And the theme of his message, right up to the present time, is that Uwumbor is stronger.

All our evangelism, telling the gospel story—sometimes beginning from Genesis, was aimed at presenting Christ. The basic elements in this evangelistic process were the following: (a) the Creator God, loving, and greater than the spirits; (b) fallen humanity, far from God; (c) the Creator's desire to rescue humankind, with a universal plan for all peoples; (d) Jesus, God's plan, God's Son, God incarnate; (e) Jesus, his death, saving humanity, his resurrection, being among us; (f) the Holy Spirit, sent to stay and guide the church, is among us; (g) the Church, God's plan for fellowship and strength, and for right worship that pleases God; (h) mission, the believer's responsibility to pass on what he knows and has experienced; (i) hope, Jesus' return, heaven is our home.

DEVELOPING AN AUTOCHTHONOUS CHURCH IDENTITY

When we plant churches, we are assuming that the local church is the most efficient, self-sustaining, and long-lasting means of communicating the gospel in a given area, be it a suburb, a social class, or a culturally defined ethnic group, because:

1. It generates a demand for the communication of the gospel in a culturally understandable way;
2. It gives local expression to the Kingdom;
3. It doubles the missionary effect: churches plant churches.

For all this to take root, the church (starting from the local congregations) must be encouraged to develop its own biblical identity and to understand that they are not simply reproducing an alien model, but that their church is the result of a gospel that is above culture and time, a message for all peoples in all generations, including themselves.

We tried to resist the temptation to go it alone. After Mebá was converted and brought his family with eleven children with him, we started a joint effort to make sure that we were together in every step of the way, whether in gospel preaching or in studying the culture in order to better communicate biblical teaching to the new believers. We determined to include the new converts in the process of evangelizing their own people, in the study of the Word to teach their own neighbors, in decisions about meetings, services, liturgy, visiting the sick, answering the challenges of the witch doctors and so on, and this proved to be an extremely fruitful attitude. It is not enough to develop a contextualized biblical ecclesiology. It has to be done with the full participation of the people.

I want to stress this point. Looking back, we can see today that many mistakes, some of them serious, were avoided because we developed our biblical theology and evangelism alongside the local people, the first converts. Despite their limited understanding of the gospel at the time, their contribution to the process of communication (and their discernment of the sacred and profane in the local worldview) was a real strategic help. I remember once how I spent several days studying the different drumbeats used in the tribe; I was trying to see if any of them were used exclusively to call on the demons, or for ancestor worship, or in the animistic purification rituals. One day Mebá, seeing what a hard time I was having, simply commented: "You want to know which are the bad beats? It's easy, just ask any Konkomba child and he can show you."

> Despite their limited understanding of the gospel at the time, the local believers' contributions were a real strategic help.

THE CHURCH'S INVOLVEMENT IN SOCIAL ISSUES

Medical assistance, help with education, drilling wells for clean water—all this activity gained for the fledgling church much more than the sympathy of the tribe. At a later stage, teaching in the mother tongue was another important activity. In this way the church became involved with the social issues of the community and was kept from becoming an alienated institution. These social activities received plenty of attention, especially in the areas of health (on average 3,000 people a year received treatment), education (formal schooling for children and literacy classes for adults in their own language), and drilling for water. All this served as experimental confirmation for the type of socially interactive culture that watches to see if words are confirmed by deeds. In the Konkomba universe, as elsewhere, it would be impossible to understand a Christ who only loves the soul and pays no attention to the visibly suffering body.

One very positive result came from this social awareness. At the outset of our work, when the first converts came to the Lord Jesus, the Konkomba-Bimonkpeln wanted to exclude them from community life. Some were driven from their homes, and others were deprived of the right to take their turn on the yam plantations. But these human issues of sickness, hunger, and thirst created a point of coming together unitedly. When as a church we undertook some social action, such as drilling a well, we always did it as a church initiative, but together with the local community. We would seek a meeting with the chief of the village and with the council of the elders; quite often, the village witch doctor would also be present. A group from the church would show the human need, the possible solution, and the need to work together. As the social projects went forward, we saw the resistance to the church fading away. And the message of Christ was better tolerated.

I can still remember the day when we all met in the village of Koni to try out the recently drilled well. There was an air of expectation. As all had played a part in the project, believers and unbelievers, it was a project that interested everyone. As the water started flowing, Labuer, one of the leaders of the Koni church, began to speak about Jesus as the water of life for everyone. There were happy shouts from all and, perhaps for the first time, no public opposition to the message of Jesus. The church had broken down a social barrier in that village.

> When as a church we undertook some social action we always did it as a church initiative, but together with the local community.

INVOLVEMENT OF THE NEW CONVERTS IN PREACHING AND TESTIMONY

As soon as they were converted, these new believers were involved in some sort of work which meant they had to witness to their new birth. We believe this strengthened them, and in an oral culture it is really important to speak of anything that deeply affects one's life. This also meant that the preaching of the gospel was multiplied.

Kidiik was a new convert whose testimony was outstanding. Since childhood he had been prepared to become a keeper of the family fetishes, an important position in the religious life of the people. He had been brought up by one of the local witch doctors, far from his parents, and learned all the skills of manipulating things natural and supernatural. He became a young man set apart, feared by all. He was somewhat timid, of slender build, and spoke with a slight stutter. After his conversion Kidiik witnessed for Christ in many places, always exposing the deceit of the spirits. He spoke about the techniques used to manipulate and deceive the spirits in order to win favors for people. He spoke too about the rituals used to make people sick and about the meaning of the sacrifices that were demanded by Grumadil. All this provoked a strong reaction against him, and he received various threats. At the time we even asked him not to reveal publicly the details of the witch doctors' rituals. But looking back today, we can see that Kidiik's boldness in taking part in the evangelistic meetings made a tremendous contribution to the people being able to overcome their fears and start to seek the power of God. That young convert made a real difference in the first years of preaching the gospel among the Konkomba, and his readiness to use any favorable situation to witness was good for him and for the gospel.

CONCENTRATION ON DISCIPLING LEADERS

We believe that when we seek to evaluate the growth of a church we should not count the number of believers, but the number of those who are involved in discipleship. We believe that, in an embryonic church, a meeting of six people for discipleship is more important than sixty people meeting for a weekly service. As soon as the first converts came to the Lord in 1993, we began the work of discipleship. Of the five Konkomba-Bimonkpeln pastors, four are fruit of those first two discipleship groups. On average we spent two years of twice-weekly meetings with each one in this formal training. Informally, we were always working together.

Later, as the churches grew, and as we concentrated on taking the gospel to new places, we did not establish adequate patterns of multiplying in-depth discipleship, and this led to problems. Believers did not have the maturity to deal well with local issues. They had a tendency to go to extremes or else do nothing.

MISSIONARY PERSPECTIVE: CONTEXTUALIZATION

Sin is cultural, and shows itself in culturally defined ways. Therefore, in the church-planting process it is essential to have biblical answers for human problems. This means having in one hand a good awareness of the culture and its implications in confrontation with the gospel, and in the other hand the Word of God systematically studied for answers for every situation. So we sought to identify the areas of possible conflict with the culture and began to study what the Word had to say on each question, developing "biblical theologies" applicable in each context. By "biblical theologies" I mean systematic and thematic Bible studies which could encourage firm Christian attitudes in the maturing of the church and the understanding of the gospel.

> We sought to identify the areas of possible conflict with the culture and began to study what the Word had to say on each question.

It is important to start such study early on, when the process of evangelism is more community based, because the roots of syncretism usually appear in the initial stages. They come as a result of spaces left empty because we have not taught the Word as God's answer for a given situation. In our case the life situations most liable to cause conflict for the Konkomba-Bimonkpeln people were on the occasions of births, weddings, funerals, and the yam harvest festival.

BIRTHS

The Konkombas believe that an evil spirit can attack and kill children when they are still small and defenseless and that since these spirits have access to people by their names, they put off naming the child so as to protect it during the first months or years of life. After about a year, the name is given to the child, in the presence of all the family. However, this is only a temporary name, not permanent. Again, the idea is to protect the child, this time deceiving the evil spirit. The child's name could be changed two or three times. Only the parents know the child's true name, which they have decided in a whispered conversation between themselves.

Christian converts adopted the practice of naming their children in a public church service, where the leaders would gather to pray to God for the protection of these little ones. The names, still proverbial in character and culturally acceptable, now represented what God was doing in their midst at the time before or during the birth. The names were given about three months after the birth, since the Konkombas do not take their children out of the house when they are very small. These names are permanent because they are no longer afraid of the children being killed by evil spirits, believing that God is our protector. Twins, which are taboo in the Konkomba culture (usually the second to be born was sacrificed), were now accepted and received their names like any other child.

WEDDINGS

Traditionally, Konkomba weddings are arranged by the families involved in order to guarantee partnership between clans or family groups. When the powerful spirit Grumadil arrived, making Koni the center of his worship for several decades, one of the biggest differences he made to daily life in the tribe was his insistence on "exchange weddings," a feature of the Ewe and Bassari cultures. Only young men with sisters could marry, exchanging their sister for the sister of another young man.

In this way marriage became a symbiotic relationship of two couples in parallel. If one marriage didn't work out, the two would be dissolved and the sisters would return to their parents' homes. As the years went by, this custom produced a culture of unstable and fragile relationships with very many separations. Even happily married couples were always afraid that they would have to separate if the parallel marriage broke down.

The converts reinstated the custom of marriage by dowry, a part of the Konkomba culture which was socially relevant. They rejected "exchange weddings" as being originally an Ewe custom, not Konkomba, the cause of all sorts of family dysfunctions. In the traditional Konkomba culture there is no fixed wedding ceremony at a set date, as the tribe has a cyclical rather than a linear concept of time. So the church held the weddings in special services in which the Lord's blessing was invoked upon the new family, following the same cyclical perspective. We divided the whole process into parts that were culturally acceptable, four parts in all. The physical union between the couple would take place after the last of these four parts and after the dowry had been given to the bride's parents by the groom, in accordance with a complicated set of rules involving respect, material value, and relationships. It might be, for example, a plantation of yams, household goods preferred by the mother-in-law, or a quantity of good-sized yams, the amount agreed beforehand by both parties. A church elder would accompany the whole process, advising the parties involved. The clan elders would also be heard, but always with the church elder present.

FUNERALS

The dream of every Konkomba is to die at a good old age, with many children and a huge crowd dancing at the funeral. In fact, funerals are the best attended and best planned of all the tribal feasts.

When someone dies, the family has to fulfill a series of obligations to make sure that the spirit of the departed does not stay forever in the power of Grumadil. The local witch doctor, at the right moment, would indicate how many animals must be sacrificed for the funeral to be acceptable. This meant that the Konkombas would spend their working lives for the one purpose of getting a sufficient number of cows, goats, and chickens, looking after them with great care in case they died suddenly. We should note that in this tribe, as in many parts of Africa, the funeral is the most important social ceremony and determines the situation of the departed in the afterlife.

These sacrificial animals became progressively scarcer and disappeared from daily life. So the meat eaten by the tribe was more commonly monkeys, rats, and bats, leaving the best for Grumadil at the funeral feasts.

To confront this situation, the church adopted a style of funeral with no space for invoking the spirits. The cultural act in itself kept its social importance, bringing the family together, washing the body before burial in a crouching position in a deep, round grave. However, some aspects were abolished on the understanding that they were of animistic significance: the presentation of the body to the children, the isolation of the widow—who would normally pass a week without eating or bathing—and the breaking of gourds at the moment of burial. Instead of music invoking the fetishes, the church composed hymns speaking of the reality of life with God after the believer's death. Exhaustive teaching was given (repeated to each new convert) about the biblical doctrine of life and death and the sure hope that is ours in Christ. The church seems to be settled and well-grounded in this subject, which was one of the most sensitive points of the culture.

YAM HARVEST FESTIVALS

As soon as the yam harvest is gathered there is a celebratory festival with much demonic influence; usually many people become demon-possessed, led by the local group of witch doctors. This moment is looked forward to all year long, as it is believed the spirits can bless or curse the harvest, bringing abundance or hunger. Once again, it was Grumadil who was the center of attention, as his keepers published his demands for sacrifice in order not to write off the harvest.

The church was not blind to the human and cultural importance of the harvest. As well as being a central aspect of the culture, it also defined the survival of this agricultural people. The believers suggested that we bring the first yams to a special service of prayer, thanking the Lord for the harvest and asking his blessing for next year's crop. This idea won great acceptance with the people, who year by year would bring their first fruits with joy and thanks to God. Thousands of yams are donated to the church in this festival and kept (they can be buried and keep for up to a year) to supply the needy and sick, widows, and the full-time evangelists.

Clear biblical teaching was given to combat the idea that there are specific spirits, coordinated by Grumadil, to bless or curse each plantation. Other ideas combated were: the protective fetishes that needed to be set up in each plot; the ritual washing of the first yam harvested to exorcise any possible evil spirit; the "prayer trees" planted systematically along the east side of each plot; and the food offerings left by these trees at every monsoon season for the *watiir aniib,* a Konkomba type of dwarf, "a people of small stature, with red eyes and white skin, who live in these places and are always asking for food and threatening to destroy our plots." The converts did not despise these things as mere figments of popular imagination, but dealt with them by prayer and the teaching of the Word to give assurance to those who worked daily in the fields. Often we would have services in the fields and make pastoral visits to those who worked there.

ECCLESIOLOGICAL PERSPECTIVE: THE INNER LIFE OF THE CHURCH

There are some points in formal cross-cultural communication which are absolutely funda-mental in the church-planting process. I would like to mention some of these in light of our experience of local church growth among the Konkomba-Bimonkpeln.

The message is communicated in the language of the people, Limonkpeln. From the various dialects around Koni, we chose what we called "domestic dialects," spoken in the home. We avoided using the commercial dialects, although they had a richer grammar, because they are used as a second language. The songs were written in this local Limonkpeln language, always by the local converts. As far as possible, we avoided Twii songs—Twii is a language spoken more in the south by the Ashante people. Music and dances were used in the church services as culturally appropriate, but we took great care not to encourage syncretism, especially in the early days when the liturgy was being defined as a form of worshipping God.

It was made clear to the people, right from the start of our preaching the Word, that the gospel would mean cultural changes. We stressed this in order to avoid syncretism and unrealistic ideas of what church would be like. They were taught that changes to the culture were not necessarily non-cultural, provided they were decided by the society, under the influence of the Word which is above culture. Every culture has freedom to choose changes on the basis of their re-reading of their own customs and their sincere conversion to the Lord Jesus.

In the post-translation process biblical truths were explained to the people using the items from the cultural context, sto-ries, myths, proverbs, and songs to ensure what we might call an applicable understanding—something that could be understood in their culture and applied to their style of life.

> It was made clear to the people, right from the start of our preaching the Word, that the gospel would mean cultural changes.

Local leadership was a major emphasis from the start in order to build a better bridge of com-munication. Often the young church elders could explain biblical ideas and their cultural implications better than we could.

Liturgy and theology were applied as a result of biblical exposition, not the other way round. In about 90 percent of cases the local church members, especially the elders, suggested relevant applications of biblical concepts in the people's practical life. In only a few cases a strong mis-sionary intervention proved necessary. Our missionary work was focused on Bible exposition in the local dialect and facilitating these groups and discussions.

This outpouring of God's grace has resulted in a people with positive attitudes in general towards the gospel and a church with healthy growth. In particular, there is a love for God's Word, perseverance under persecution, and boldness in evangelism.

At the same time, there have been problems and errors. For instance, in focusing so much on developing leadership from within, we inadvertently reinforced ethnic identity at the expense of fellowship with the wider church in Ghana or beyond. We also made some mistakes in relation to the use of drums and particular rhythms, excluding some that did not in fact have animistic connotations. We delayed too long in instituting the Lord's Supper in the churches we planted. We did not adequately teach a biblical theology in relation to war and ethnic conflict, a serious problem in that area.

CONCLUSION

If I could add just one thing more, it would be to stress the importance of being flexible in studying the patterns of communication. Since we cannot have complete access to the culture before we arrive in a new area, we have to learn as we live with the people and as we work and preach the Word. This means we need to continually review our principles, revise our teaching, rethink our terminology and concepts, and always listen to whoever is beside us. We need to pray for a humble heart so we do not lose the flexibility that every missionary needs in order to face the challenge of contextualization. We must fight against the tendency to jump to our own hasty and rigid conclusions.

And we must never lose sight of our aim: to communicate Christ in a way that is soundly-based theologically and understandable in the culture, so that Christ is welcomed, not as a foreign God for people who live far away, but as God at home with them and with us.

Ronaldo Lidório is a Brazilian Presbyterian pastor who has been a church planter in Ghana and in Brazil.

QUESTIONS FOR REFLECTION:

1. Ronaldo Lidório tells the traditional story of *Uwumbor* and the decision to use this name for God. What are some of the advantages and pitfalls of adopting and adapting a name like this? Many cultures have creation stories. In what important ways do these differ from the biblical creation story? What would you need to pay special attention to so as not to end up with syncretism?

2. Why was the conversion of Mebá so significant? Which particular elements of Konkomba culture are challenged and which affirmed, through this event? What are some of the biblical truths that emerge from this story?

3. Lidório describes some of the new ways believers developed to mark "rites of passage." In your own home culture, and in your host culture, how are these events marked? How do Christians approach them distinctively from unbelievers? What elements in general culture can be incorporated?

CHAPTER 29

YANOMAMÖ DEATH RITES

Michael Dawson

The first death I witnessed with the Yanomamö was around 1962 or 1963. It was when Yacuwä's grandfather died. Bautista, Yacuwä's uncle, ran into our house, urgency marking his features.

"My father is really bad off," he panted. "Come quick!"

We all ran over to their leaf hut. Even as a child I wanted nothing to do with medicine, but I could not stay away as the sick old man was my best friend's grandfather. Yacuwä was standing off to one side crying. The women of the village were all there wailing. As they wailed, they took their tears and rubbed them on their cheeks making a thick black crusty sign of their grief on their cheeks. I stood beside Yacuwä as he cried and tears streaked down my own face. I began to cry with him. The grief in the small hut was suffocating.

Dad knelt in the dirt beside the vine hammock of the old man. He almost had to shout to be heard above the wailing.

"Father," he shouted. The old man feebly opened his eyes. "Can you hear me, father?" Dad shouted again. The old man nodded. "Father, when you said you believed on Jesus, were you sure?" Dad was yelling right in the old man's ears. Slowly the old man nodded again.

"Yes," he said in a voice so low I could barely make out what he was saying. "When you told me about a man who was God that had made a way to save me from the fire, I hung my desires on him, and they are still hanging on him."

A short time later the old man died. I stood with Yacuwä as we watched the men build the funeral pyre. Carefully selecting logs that would burn hot and long, they placed them on the bottom. They built up the sides the same way my ancestors had built up the sides of their log cabins. They started a fire in the center of the pyre while they worked. While the fire was being fanned into a roaring blaze, they continued to build up the sides. By the time the sides were finished, the fire was burning hot.

The cries of the mourners were such that I could barely hear myself think. Suddenly it rose even more in volume. I looked over to the house just in time to see them coming out with the old man's body suspended from his ragged vine hammock. They ran up to the fire and threw hammock and all onto the fire. Quickly the body was covered by firewood. The mourners continued to dance and scream around the fire. Yacuwä also wailed his grief. His face was screwed up, his eyes tightly closed as if he could shut out the sight of the burning body. The heat from the fire was intense. I put my arm around his skinny little shoulders and cried with him. As the fire died down, we moved over to an old guama tree. Climbing the tree, we sat on a branch watching the fire burn down until there was nothing left.

This was the first death I had experienced and I was saddened beyond words. I had called the old guy "old man father" just like Yacuwä had, and he was gone now. Yacuwä and I were as close as brothers, and I was afraid now that his grandfather was gone, his parents would come and take him away.

After the cremation, the bones were carefully gathered by sifting through the ashes, painstakingly finding every bone fragment and placing them in a basket made for that purpose. When they were satisfied that they had gathered every piece of bone, the basket was hung above the hearth of the family of the old man. Runners were sent out to surrounding villages and even to far away villages where the old man had relatives, or the village had allies.

As soon as everyone that had been called arrived, they gathered to grind the bones into a powder. They cried and wailed almost as much doing this as they did when they were actually burning the body.

A four or five foot section of a tree had been hollowed out and hardwood poles cut to about six foot lengths, highly decorated. Two guys were selected. Both had decorated themselves by putting the snow white down of a large hawk in their hair. On their arms were colorful armbands made from the head feathers of the curassow bird. In between the band and their arm they had pushed the long blood red tail feathers of the scarlet macaw sticking up. In their earlobes one guy had bright toucan feathers, and the other one had the bright indigo blue of the small moi bird. Their bodies were painted red with heavy black jagged lines. They emptied the basket of bones into the hollowed out tree, then taking the long poles, they methodically began to grind the bones up accompanied by the wails of the mourners.

The ground up bones were then placed in large gourds and left near the hearth of the person who died. Now it began to get a bit ugly, as the different villages and relatives tried to decide how to divide up the powdery bones.

Everyone of course wanted some, but some of the relatives were against giving certain people some, as they said they did not like the deceased for some reason or another. Accusations went back and forth, but finally all the bones were given out.

In the case of this old man, there were already believers in the village when he died, although they were in the minority. Bautista did not want to have anyone drink his father's bones, but he was only one of many brothers, so he was not strong enough to enforce his wishes. Little gourds full of the ground up powder went up and down the river to all the villages where the old man had relatives. Then during the next years each village or family group hosted a bone drinking ceremony with their portion of bones.

THE BONE DRINKING CEREMONY

This first death I observed was of a very old man, but if the man that had died, or was killed, had a young son, it would be during the time of drinking the bones, that he would be repeatedly told who was responsible for his father's death, always with the understanding that as soon as he was old enough he would lead a raid to avenge his father's death. If he was just a young boy, care will be taken to make sure that enough of the powdery bones are left in a gourd so that once he gets old enough to participate in the bone drinking ceremony he will have his father's bones to drink. It will be right after this time that he will be expected to participate in a raid to avenge his father's death and also avenge all the suffering he had to endure growing up without a father.

The bone drinking ceremony is possibly the single most important event in the Yanomamö's calendar. When their plantains are harvested and hung up to ripen, the men will go on an extended hunt. Everything they kill will be smoked and preserved to take home. During the time the men are out, every evening and all night long, the women will sing and dance to assure the men of a successful hunt. This is a time of very loose morals, as any man that has stayed home from going on the hunt will take advantage of as many women as he can.

Then, on or about the day the hunters return, the invited guests begin to arrive, normally camping out a short distance from the host village. Preparations are careful, as it could be that the bone drinking ceremony is only a ruse to get them to come and ambushes are not that uncommon.

When the returning hunters are still a short way from their village, they will stop to allow each hunter to paint himself, usually trying to represent some spirit or animal. When they are ready, their imminent arrival is heralded by two of the youngest members of their party. Decked out in all their feathered finery, waving bright yellow new palm branches, they will burst into the village, dashing madly in and out everywhere with great shouts of greeting and encouragement from everyone in the village. Once they have alerted the entire village to the hunters' arrival, the warriors will make their grand entrance. They whirl around in a colorful mass, each one dancing to his own beat and rhythm based on the image of the animal or spirit he is representing. In spite of the fact that each is doing his own dance, viewed together it has a certain cohesiveness that is hard to describe but fascinating to watch. Finally, each returns to his own hearth.

With great noise and fanfare the visiting villages begin to make their entrance. Most of their actions are to prove how invincible they are and how strong they would be if attacked.

After everyone has arrived, the gourd of powdery bones is brought out and mixed with large pots full of ripe plantain drink. This is stirred in until the bright yellow of the plantain takes on the dark brown color of the bones. Full gourds are then passed around and amidst the wails and cries each participant drinks. During this time, alliances are struck to go on raids and try to avenge the person whose bones they are drinking.

During the day most of the men inhale their drug called ebena. Pretty soon most of the men of the village and their visitors are dancing and chanting with their individual spirits that only in their drug induced state they can see. The ones more attuned to the spirits learn new songs or chants from their hecula, or spirits. They will sing these chants, and the onlookers will do their best to learn the song, so it can be sung later on that night.

During the evenings, the women continue to gather for singing and dancing, with each song getting more and more suggestive. They begin to egg each other on, and soon they engage in wild multiple promiscuity without restraint. Later on in the night, it is the men's turn. Bands of men will go right up to any man's hearth and pull any women they want. If the woman's husband is angry, he does not show it, but gets his revenge by going and dragging some other woman out of the village for himself. This orgy goes on all night. Most of the time, it is a contest between visiting and host villages, leading to many fights later on. When it is time for the visiting village to depart, there is an explosion of violence. First there is name calling which quickly escalates into fighting with fist, club, machete, axes, and sometimes shooting.

Alliances that have been forged over their common grief are suddenly in danger of falling apart. Wise leaders know the best way to get over mutual hostilities is to somehow direct them at a common enemy. Plans are brought forward to go on an avenging raid against an enemy village so that the anger the warriors feel over their women's honor can be directed elsewhere.

MOVING TOWARDS A CHRISTIAN TESTIMONY

One day, I went up to the village of Carawana to encourage our good friend and seminary student, Juan Carlos, who had lost his son a couple of weeks before. His son had also been one of our students. We had been told the bone drinking ceremony was going to be held the next week, and we were hoping to get up there before it took place. But we got to Carawana only to find that the hunters had already returned from the extended hunt and the village was preparing for a large bone drinking ceremony the very next day.

As we walked into the village, there was a large crowd of mourners at the hearth of Juan Carlos. Antonio went straight there. He got down on his knees and hugged Juan Carlos. "Don't cry" he told him. "Your son is in heaven right now." The crowd quieted down to listen to what was being said by this visitor. "My friend, Juan Carlos, you and your wife will see your son again," Antonio went on, "the Bible says that when a believer dies, he is already with God. You are sad, that is our lot to be sad since Adam sinned, but we are told not to grieve like those who have no hope. You and your wife have both asked for Christ's salvation, so your eyes will one day see your son again. This is our hope!"

Juan Carlos slowly nodded his head. He got up and came over to us and we all hugged him. He led us to the area next to their hearth where his son had built a meeting area with some benches so they would have a place for their church services. The crying started up again, and we hung our hammocks quietly as the entire village wailed their grief over the loss of their young man.

"I'll come and talk to you later," Juan Carlos told us. We nodded. He returned to the mourners. That night around seven in the evening he and his wife came back over to where we had our hammocks hung. They sat quietly listening as each of us talked about our life in Christ and the hope we have. His wife started crying softly as I read the verses which tell us about the living not leaving the dead behind, but that the dead in Christ shall rise first and we shall meet the Lord in the air. I was surprised to hear first Juan Carlos, and then his wife, tell us that they were doing okay, God was making their hearts strong, even though they were sad; they knew their son was in heaven with God.

Juan Carlos also told us. "My friends, I am a believer and yet I am all alone here. All the men in this village, we are related. I have brothers, uncles, cousins, and everyone of them claims my son. Now I know we don't have to drink my son's bones for him. But my village will not hear of doing anything else in this matter. I am only one voice. What will drinking my son's bones do to him?" From the intense grief on his face it was obvious he was afraid his actions might somehow cause his son to be cast out of heaven. I told him: "My friend, nothing anyone can do can effect your son now. He is gone from this body, his bones are only bones. Your son is in heaven. God will make him a new body." He smiled his thanks.

I wish I could take each of you through the experience in that village. The wailing, the chanting to the demons, the sheer volume of sound all night long made it impossible to sleep. In spite of the fact that Christ died to give life, few of the Yanomamö have embraced the gospel, so the depths of their despair was something palatable. Early, still dark, the cacophony rose in volume, the morning was split with the sound of shotguns firing, and the wailing increased in intensity as the invited villages began to arrive. Each warrior was painted to represent some animal or spirit. They danced and whirled around the village, their bright colors in sharp contrast to the continued sounds of wailing. It went on and on. In every Yanomamö funeral the mourners always carry some piece of the dead person's earthly possessions. Even in this there is a certain pecking order. The most cherished possessions of the person are carried by the closest of kin. In this case the closest was the mother. What a testimony to me when I saw what she was carrying. There wrapped in the large envelope we had given him was his Yanomamö New Testament and his song book. In the midst of so much grief, the boy's testimony showed bright and clear.

In this work with the Yanomamö there have been many occasions to have to say goodbye to friends as they pass from this life to the next one. And for the Yanomamö, death is so final, so it has been hard even for the believers to really get the victory over death that the Bible promises us. But slowly as they mature in the Word, we are seeing a breakthrough.

Two months ago, our oldest old man died here in the village. Myself with three of the Christian men of the village were up in another village for a Yanomamö summit hosted by the New Tribes Mission for the Yanomamö workers in Venezuela and Brazil, so we were not here when the old man died and was cremated. However, they did wait until we were home to dispose of the bones.

He had called his family around him and told them he was in truth going home, as his Father had sent his "beings" to get him. He seemed amazed that no one could see the beings he was trying his hardest to point out. But that was not his real message. He told his sons to really follow the Lord with their whole hearts. "Teach your children, so they might follow after you," he kept stressing. He laid out how he wanted his body to be handled after he was gone. "Don't go and get all the people from other villages, just cremate my body and bury the bones. Do not even grind them. Just bury them. Don't let all my relatives from other villages that don't know the Lord come here and try and take my bones."

The sons tried to do all he had asked them to do, although with a man as well known and liked as this old man was, there were people showing up on their own without waiting for an invitation, but it truly was a celebration of life rather than wailing of death down in their house this morning. We all gathered and sang songs while the hole was being dug right in under the old man's hearth for the small box holding the bones that they had asked my son Ryan to build. After the hole was dug, Alfredo, the old man's grandson read the precious verses from 1 Thessalonians 4:13-18. When he was finished, Timoteo read Hebrews 2:14-15. What a different scene than I had pictured in my mind as to what would happen when the old man died.

He had been the headman and was a very respected leader in the village. Many times in their old way, when someone like him dies, it is enough to cause the entire village to move as no one wants to be reminded of where he lived. As a matter of fact, he was known as "Coshilowäteli." (Because he was the headman, he assumed the name of the village.) This is the reason they will burn a village down and move, because they don't want to say the name of the village any longer. So I wondered how the Christians would handle this death.

In Yanomamö culture, personal possessions are never passed on, but are destroyed when they dispose of the bones. So I was surprised to see Octavio, the old man's oldest son, walking around with his father's spear. This was even more surprising as one of the old man's names was "Spear" so that would make it even more of an item to be disposed of as quickly as possible. But Octavio walked out in front of everyone, and slowly got every one's attention. Holding up the spear, he waited until even the old ladies at the back had quieted down a bit. "We are doing things differently here. My father became a new person many years ago. He at one time was a fierce warrior, but after he accepted Christ, he changed. He no longer went on raids to kill, but he went on many trips to share his new life in Christ. Now, we are here because my father is not with us any longer. He has gone on ahead. One day, we that have the same new life that he had, will meet him

"We are doing things differently here. My father became a new person many years ago. He at one time was a fierce warrior, but after he accepted Christ, he changed."

again. God's Word says we will meet our loved ones in the air, with Jesus. Well, I believe that. So if my father has just gone on before us, I am not going to destroy his stuff. I am going to keep and cherish this spear of his. When I die, I am asking my son to keep it, because I want to remember my father. I want to remember the great change that God made in his heart. My father loved God! He talked to him all the time. Now, he can talk to him face to face. I am very happy for my father. His last years here, he suffered. Well, he is not suffering now. Children," he said turning to the choir, "sing Number Thirty-nine in the songbook."

I could not believe it. We had already sung some songs, "I Shall Know Him," "Amazing Grace," "Sweet Bye and Bye," but this song, Number Thirty-nine, was almost too happy! It is a song called "In My Father's House." We all sang it at the top of our voices, and what a sound!

FINAL REFLECTION

Later on, I was speaking with Bautista (whose father's death is described at the start of this article) about this. I wanted to know what had led him to make a break from their cultural way of dealing with death. While I had been in the village when all this took place, I was only a kid and wanted to hear from him what had really happened and what his thoughts were to make him start on such a drastic change.

He told me that after he became a Christian, God's Spirit began to deal with the way they handled and thought of death. "To us Yanomamö, death is so final, we no longer want to even be reminded of our loved ones who have died. But God's Word says that our life in Christ is one of hope and confidence in our future with him. If this is truly the case, then, in our everyday lives, we needed to begin to show this hope and confidence especially to our non-believing relatives. When I first began to think we needed to change, my relatives were shocked and horrified that I was going to desecrate our loved ones by not drinking their bones. But God's peace and calm through his Holy Spirit in my heart showed me that I was doing the right thing. He gave me the confidence to stand in spite of much opposition. Slowly the other Christians found the courage to stand with me. Now in my village, we don't drink the bones of our loved ones, but after the body has been cremated, we gather the bones and bury them, knowing that one day, at the sound of the trumpet heralding Christ's return, we will be reunited with our loved one. Death has truly lost its sting, as God's Word tells us. But I do need to say, not all of the believers have made this break. Down through the years I have seen many of my people wrestle with this issue. I see that the ones, who after they get saved, make a clean break away from the bone drinking ceremony, which I might add, in our legends was taught us by Satan, well, the ones that make a clean break have strong testimonies and mature in the Lord, whereas the ones who refuse to make a stand, or can't for one reason or another, never go far in their walk with Lord."

"The ones that make a clean break have strong testimonies and mature in the Lord, whereas the ones who refuse to make a stand, or can't for one reason or another, never go far in their walk with Lord."

Mike Dawson was raised among the Yanomamö tribal people, Brazil, and returned as an adult to continue to serve them.

QUESTIONS FOR REFLECTION:

1. Between the start of this article, at the time of Michael Dawson's childhood, and the conclusion, years later, Bautista has changed his mind and practice in relation to death. Why? Why does he say that a complete break with bone drinking is so important? Why are death practices so crucial an issue to engage with in contextualizing the gospel in almost any culture?

2. By contrast, Dawson comforts Juan Carlos when he says that family and group pressure means that he cannot prevent his dead son being subjected to all the traditional practices. How would you reconcile this with Bautista's position? What can we learn about culture change from this?

3. How would you tell the gospel story in the culture Dawson describes?

CHAPTER 30

A DISCUSSION OF CONTEXTUALIZATION ISSUES FOR PERSONNEL WORKING AMONG MUSLIM PEOPLES

An International Agency

PLEASE NOTE: This document is a new version of a company-specific one previously done, and may at certain points read somewhat awkwardly as a result. Modifications have been made to make possible its wider distribution and use, something requested by a number of ministry friends. The WEA Mission Commission preserves the anonymity of the international company that has sent us this document.

INTRODUCTION

In a period that extended almost a year, this paper was written and revised many times in a process that included multiple reviews and feedback by a committee of nine, an international leadership team, a community of over 200 workers among Muslims, and finally, by the company's Board of Directors. It is offered now to other friends in the prayerful hope that it will be a useful tool and provide helpful insights for ministry among Muslims. It is not intended as a permanent answer to all the issues addressed, but is a statement of how we understand things currently. We anticipate and will celebrate improvements to it in the years ahead as we minister together.

There is obviously much more that could have been said on the subject of contextualization generally, as well as more specifically on contextualization in Muslim contexts. We encourage each reader to engage further with both topics and commend the appendix that is attached to this paper as a good place to start, particularly on the subject of form and meaning. To a large extent the contextualization issues most at debate in ministry to Muslims have to do precisely with those ancient twins.

The questions that arise often boil down to what forms are useful and permissible for the sake of maintaining cultural identification and continuity with one's community without conveying meaning that is not intended and unbiblical. The underlying commitment of this paper is that in all cases the purpose of using or not using particular forms is to minimize misunderstanding and/or unnecessary offense, and to convey meaning accurately – not to ensure that any offence, which the meaning itself might evoke, should be removed. The specific affirmations listed below are expressed with this thought in mind, and with a primary goal of upholding a biblical approach to contextualization.

WHERE THE APPLICATION OF GENERALLY ACCEPTED CONTEXTUALIZATION PRINCIPLE HAS RESULTED IN CONTROVERSY IN THE CONTEXT OF MINISTRY AMONG MUSLIM PEOPLES

Key Principle: Whatever is biblically permissible and culturally appropriate sets the boundary for what is acceptable in the contextualization of Gospel communication and church practice among any people.

The primary source of the differing viewpoints today regarding contextualization in the context of Muslim ministry is over the application of this principle. The dividing line is over just what is biblically permissible. In years past the lines were drawn quite clearly, but they unfortunately looked far too much like the culture and church practice of the West. As a result, missionary efforts were often limiting Gospel penetration. Too long ignored were the perfectly appropriate and biblically permissible stylistic and cultural patterns that existed among the various Muslim peoples.

With the passing of time the wisdom of more thorough contextualization has become almost universally accepted and the fruitfulness of the shift seems apparent. More believers from Muslim backgrounds exist today than are recorded in the entire prior history of the world. Though some may disagree, it is not unreasonable to assume that at least part of the means God used to achieve this increase are more contextualized approaches to Gospel communication and discipling. The question now with regard to contextualization is, "How far is too far?"

CAUTIONS FOR DISCUSSING THE ISSUES

Ad hoc ergo proctor hoc roughly interpreted, "cause and effect cannot be reversed." Just because a person has been genuinely saved by God, it does not follow logically that the means employed are equally desirable, reproducible, or to be emulated (e.g., Nebuchadnezzar).

As it relates to MBBs[1]—a large number of conversions doesn't automatically mean that the strategy is biblically warranted, or that it is sustainable.

While the views of insiders are essential and of great value, some would say, "Only insiders can legitimately weigh in on the conversation about what is appropriate contextualization and application of biblical truth." If this argument were true it would logically follow that no one could disciple anyone coming from a different religious/cultural background.

Some seem to argue that the choice is only between extractionism (taking believers out of their culture) or believers in Jesus continuing to remain Muslims. Many others believe and have shown that there is a middle way that communicates cultural respect and adherence to mores, but does not affirm adherence to Islam. The discussion is properly framed as a continuum of positions.

PARTICULAR ISSUES

Issue #1: We praise God for his work of bringing many Muslims to faith in Christ, leading them on fresh paths in their journey of faith. We see or hear descriptions of the varied self-identity and theological beliefs of these brothers and sisters in Christ. Our current response is not intended as a judgment on the path that they are pursuing. Rather, it is a guideline to assist in the discipling of Muslims to become Christ-followers.

Issue #2: Cross-cultural workers are people of influence and must realize that they will be asked their views on all kinds of issues, contextualization ones included. It is important that they speak gently, but honestly, properly handling the Scriptures, and not leaving the impression that unbiblical practices and beliefs are in fact biblical. This is very different than cross-cultural workers telling Muslim background believers (MBBs) what they must do. MBBs, like all believers, are accountable to God for their own choices and level of obedience. It is important that cross-cultural workers also speak with humility, acknowledging that what has historically seemed biblically clear has sometimes been shown generations later to have been drawn from a very limited selection of Scriptures, and that we have a great deal to learn from our cross-cultural brothers and sisters in Christ.

Issue #3: Many MBBs maintain their identity as Muslims early in their conversion and sanctification process, continuing to participate in all that means (in terms of mosque attendance and faith affirmations) while clarifying Gospel faith issues and as a means to maintain a platform for sharing the Gospel with their friends. This is understandable, but we do not believe that this should be encouraged as a normative and permanent state. Those who chose

---

1 Muslim Background Believers (MBBs) is the term most commonly used to describe individuals of Muslim background who have come to faith in Christ, and whose primary identity is as a follower of Christ. It implies being genuinely born again and results in changed belief and life. Newer terms that some prefer are BMBs (Believers of Muslim Background) and CMBs (Christians of Muslim Background). MBs (Muslim Believers) is a narrower term preferred by still others to describe followers of Jesus who also choose to maintain their identity as faithful Muslims. Some like the term MJFs (Muslim Jesus Followers) for this group. For the purposes of this paper we are using MBBs to describe all believers in Jesus Christ as Savior who come from a Muslim background whether or not they continue to identify themselves as Muslims.

to remain self-identified as a "Muslim"[2] should be encouraged to communicate verbally and by their actions that their primary identity is as a follower of Jesus Christ.

Issue #4: Transitions toward maturity in Christ may take an extended time, but they should always be in the direction of greater understanding of who Christ is as Lord and what He has done. Such transitions may be either individual or community-wide in nature. As believers grow in their sanctification it will be in the direction of greater confidence in the authority of the Bible as God's inspired Word. Other venerated books may continue to be used as evangelistic tools to point others to the Bible and the revelation of the Messiah that it provides, but the Bible alone will increasingly be recognized as the authoritative source for truth, spiritual growth and instruction.

Issue #5: Some MBB's may follow Christ secretly and also continue to identify themselves as Muslims because of certain death or severe persecution if they were to reveal their faith in Christ. We are sympathetic to this circumstance, and see a decision to do so as a matter of personal conscience before the Lord. We embrace these brothers and sisters as part of our family in Christ and pray they would be freed from their situation so they can more openly live as salt and light in their community.

Issue #6: Given the intended purpose (as a declaration of common belief) and implied meaning of reciting the *shahada* (or creed) within the context of the Muslim community we do not believe it is biblically permissible for believers to recite it. We believe that the creed elevates one to the status of a biblical prophet and more, who contradicts biblical teaching in the "divine revelation" he conveyed, especially on the person and work of Jesus Christ. This one is also generally viewed by Muslims as the "seal of the prophets" (the final and most authoritative one), thus raising him to a superior position in his prophetic role to that of the Lord Jesus Christ. While this man was certainly important as an agent of change in Arab and Islamic history, we do not believe he was a prophet of special revelation directly from God, though he communicated some truth.

Issue #7: It is recognized that the mosque is a unique worship/teaching center for Islam. It is recommended, therefore, that apart from truly exceptional circumstances[3] MBBs not be encouraged to continue in the mosque as regular participants beyond a transitional time following their turning to faith in Jesus Christ, as it no longer represents his/her spiritual commitment. Other Muslims may also observe the MBBs continued participation in the mosque as deception. At the same time, it is understood that some MBBs will choose to continue in the mosque while they are becoming grounded in their biblical understanding and spiritual discipleship, as well as to avoid societal ostracism.

---

2   Some, for example, argue that "Muslim" means "one who submits" and thus could technically refer to Christians. In most contexts, however, the term would almost universally be understood as one who follows the teachings of Islam.

3   This might include those very rare situations, for example, where the mosque is little more than a community center where there is little expectation that all would participate in the usual Muslim worship rituals, or where an Imam has become a believer in Christ and is now teaching the Gospel.

Issue #8: We recognize that legalism is common in Muslim belief and structures with salvation ultimately based upon good works, the adequacy of which is determined by God himself. We do not affirm this and firmly believe that salvation for anyone, including Muslims, comes solely by grace through faith and trust in Jesus Christ as Lord and Savior. We would agree that anyone who puts their trust in Him for salvation should be warmly received as brothers and sisters in Christ.

Issue #9: We recognize the reality of new believers embarking on a process that will lead them to a fuller understanding of biblical truth. The true change will begin in the heart and true believers will proceed to evaluate and adjust as necessary their cultural habits and worldview beliefs. This will often result in an outward identity that ties them to the surrounding Muslim culture and community in unique ways—still seen as authentic members of their culture and community, but different because of their trust in and obedience to Jesus Christ. Their identity should progressively and necessarily include a close identification with other followers of Christ around the world. Fellow Christians should not be overly critical as this transitional process takes place in another believer's life, but should graciously accept them as brothers and sisters in the faith.

Issue #10: Due to the great diversity of the Muslim world, a single approach toward the self-identity of Muslim background believers simply cannot be recommended for all contexts. Historical coexistence with Christianity, legal requirements, national attitudes toward religious pluralism, and the wide range of Muslim attitudes toward Islamic orthodoxy are all factors greatly affecting the feasibility of believers in Jesus Christ being able to faithfully follow him and still call themselves "Muslims" in some fashion. There is, likewise, no overriding necessity for anyone to use the term Christian or Christianity to identify himself/herself if that misleads hearers as to what one truly believes or how one lives.

Issue #11: Some recent Bible translations for Muslim languages have decided to use, or are debating the use of, dynamic, meaning-based and receptor-oriented translation of *ben elohim* and *huios tou theou* instead of traditional literal translation as has been used in most English Bible translations which render these as "son of God." We acknowledge that the intent of such new approaches in translation is to assist readers to actually understand the original meaning, but we strongly encourage translation of the phrase as literally as possible because: (1) there is a depth of theological meaning in the phrase that could otherwise be lost; and (2) the term "son of God" is already known worldwide and such a change may be viewed as changing the very Word of God, which Muslims have historically accused Christians of doing. In light of this we think it far better that a footnote or a preface be used to make clear the attendant meaning of expressions like "son of God" within the text.[4] In the event that our company is engaged in a translation project with other Evangelical organizations in which the majority believe an opposite tack should be taken (replacing a literal "son of God" equivalent with another term), but still explaining the usage choice in a footnote or preface, participation and/or endorsement will be at the discretion of regional leadership.

---

4   In the case of audio presentations of the Scriptures explanations will likewise need to be incorporated.

Issue #12: It is a matter of high priority that a believer's words and actions should always take into account how the people in the context will likely interpret them.

Issue #13: Meeting together regularly for worship and fellowship is one of the essentials of healthy spiritual life, and greatly enhances a follower of Christ's sense of identity. We encourage all believers to actively participate in this practice.

Issue #14: Participation in biblically permissible Muslim practices (e.g., avoiding pork and alcohol, no dogs in homes, fasting during Ramadan) is an option that MBBs and cross-cultural workers will often want to avail themselves of as a means to identify and maintain good relations with the wider Islamic community.[5] One should seek to communicate, however, as appropriate opportunity arises that it is not about earning salvific merit with God.

Issue #15: Distancing oneself from the stereotypic and non-Christlike excesses of nominal Christianity is of course understandable in Muslim contexts. However, religious identity is also a statement of community belonging. We therefore think it is deceptive, unethical and not biblically permissible for Christians to convert to Islam in order to win Muslims to Christ.

Issue #16: The Gospel has both personal and societal implications, and cannot therefore be viewed in only personal transformation terms. We encourage MBBs to have as much involvement as possible in bringing the light of Christ to address the larger spiritual and social needs of their community.

APPENDIX: A BRIEF OVERVIEW OF CONTEXTUALIZATION

The issue of contextualization among Muslim-background followers of Jesus can best be addressed within a wider discussion of how to approach contextualization in general. *Contextualization* here refers to how believers in Jesus Christ think, express themselves, and live out their faith within their own particular context. A *context* is the unique and complete sociocultural environment that surrounds every human being. It includes culture, religious/theological background, economic, social, and educational background, gender, the historical era and each individual's personal circumstances. A context can be very broad (e.g., the "African" context), but can also be narrowed to any level of specificity (e.g, Ethiopia, Ethiopian Somalis, Ethiopian nomadic Somalis) to the point of speaking of the context of each individual (e.g., a particular Ethiopian, Somali, nomadic woman). Contextualization touches every aspect of a person's living faith: formal theology and confessions of faith, ethics, rituals such as worship and music, methods of instruction, language and translation, and outward religious symbols (e.g., church architecture, wearing a cross). Contextualization should go deeper than believers' outward behaviors and symbols, penetrating all the way to their worldview.

---

5   It would also be important to make sure MBBs are aware that these practices are matters of Christian liberty, carried out in order to remove unnecessary barriers to the Gospel in that context, but not commanded in the Bible.

Evangelical Christians in general, and our members in particular, believe that the Bible is God-inspired Scripture and is their ultimate source of authority. It is the primary basis for both their beliefs and how they live out their Christian faith within their context (i.e., the Bible is their primary source for contextualization). The Bible not only claims to be God's Word, his revelatory message to the people to whom it was addressed. It also claims to be God's revelatory message for all peoples in all cultures in all historical eras (Romans 15:4; 1 Corinthians 10:6, 11; 2 Timothy 3:14-17). As such, it is more than a collection of "successful local theologies" of God's people in the past. It was written so that people from all contexts can understand its essential truths and to provide the primary source for belief and behavior for all believers in all contexts today (2 Peter 1:3). No one context is particularly privileged in its ability to understand the truths of Scripture; all can have adequate understanding, but none will have exhaustive understanding, of any of the truths of Scripture.

Though believers from all contexts can understand the essential meaning of Scripture, readers of Scripture will inevitably be affected by their contexts. Context increases awareness of some aspects of the text and decreases awareness of other aspects of the text. Context also shapes the way readers will understand and express the truths of Scripture. Because no individual believer or Christian community will have an exhaustive understanding or perfect expression of biblical truth, it is important that believers from all contexts humbly and continually learn from one another. Believers from younger churches can learn from older churches, but believers from older churches can also learn from younger churches.

> All believers have the right and privilege of studying the Bible for themselves and finding their own ways of expressing biblical truth in their lives and worship.

Though they can learn from older churches, all believers—including followers of Jesus from younger churches, such as those in Muslim contexts—have the right and privilege of studying the Bible for themselves and finding their own ways of expressing biblical truth in their lives and worship. It is important that they understand how the universal church has understood and applied Scripture in the past, such as in the creeds and confessions of the church. However, these communities of believers can and should shape their own biblically based theologies (while remaining congruent with the theology of the universal church) using language and forms most appropriate to their context. These theologies may even, in the end, use fresh terms and models to describe core theological concepts, such as the nature of the triune God and the person of Jesus Christ. They will also, if they are truly biblical, make clear that Islamic faith and Christian faith are two very different and largely incompatible religions. Islam as a religion does not reflect biblical belief or practice in following the one True God.

The process of contextualization regularly wrestles with issues of form and meaning. What should believers in the new context do with the old cultural and religious forms and symbols? Should they be retained, filled with new meaning, adapted into some new-but-familiar form, or completely discarded? For example, should Muslim followers of Jesus continue to call themselves "Muslims?" Should they continue to bow in prayer five times a day? Likewise, to what extent should the forms of the Bible or the churches in other contexts be adopted, or to what extent should believers look for new, more culturally appropriate forms?

For example, should Muslim followers of Jesus refer to God as "the Trinity?" To answer these questions, we must understand the varied relationship that forms can have with their underlying meanings.

On the one hand, insisting that a particular form always carries the same meaning across culture and time reflects a naïve view that cannot be maintained in real life. For example, a kiss, walking hand in hand, a wink, or comparing a person to a particular animal all carry different meanings in different contexts. On the other hand, maintaining that any form can freely be substituted to communicate the same meaning is equally simplistic: it ignores the historical connection between forms and their meaning and the control that social groups maintain over symbols. For example, wearing a ring on the fourth finger of the left hand is a form that, in the North American context, carries the meaning that a person is married. It would require a major shift in historical direction and social expectations for this form to take on a different meaning (e.g., that a person was simply wealthy or liked jewelry) or to substitute a different form to communicate the same meaning (e.g., that all married people wear a certain color of clothing). "The relationship between meanings and forms varies according to the nature of the symbol" (Hiebert 1989, 109).

Paul Hiebert has suggested that the relationship between form and meaning is best understood in terms of a continuum (1989). At one end of the continuum, form and meaning are sometimes *arbitrarily linked*. This is, perhaps, best seen in linguistic forms. The sounds to represent the idea of a canine mammal may be "dog" (in English), "perro" (in Spanish), or "wesha" (in Amharic). There is nothing that inherently connects any of these sounds to the idea of a canine mammal; the connection is purely arbitrary. Sometimes form and meaning are *loosely linked*. Some connection exists between the form and the meaning, but the link might be disconnected, especially in cross-cultural communication. For example, many agricultural societies link land and fertility with being female and link battle and violence with being male. However, these connections would not be made in every culture. Sometimes form and meaning are *tightly linked*. Though the two are not completely equal, it would be difficult to discard the form without in some way affecting the meaning. Bowing or falling prostrate is closely associated across cultures as signs of submission or reverence. Finally, form and meaning are sometimes *equated*. For example, when a minister in the USA says, "I now pronounce you husband and wife," or when the vows are exchanged in certain other contexts, the words spoken (the form) actually create a new relationship between a man and a woman.[6]

Understanding that the meaning of symbols can be connected in different ways has several implications in contextualization. First, before old cultural or religious forms are maintained or filled with new meaning by followers of Jesus, they must understand both the meaning of the form in the local context and how tightly the form is connected to that meaning. If it is tightly connected, it may not be possible to give the form new meaning, but if it is loosely connected, it might be possible for the form to take on new meaning. For example, in some contexts it might be possible for Jesus followers to continue to call themselves

---

6   The preceding two paragraphs are adapted from Strauss (2006, 143-44).

"Muslims" or worship using forms that are used by the Muslim community, but still fulfill biblical imperatives for belief and behavior. However, in another context the connection between the form "Muslim" and its original meaning might be so connected that believers in Jesus could no longer use that name and retain their distinctive as Jesus-followers. Second, before new forms are introduced from other cultures, it is important to understand how closely the form and meaning are connected in Scripture, and what the meaning of that form would have in the new context. For example, describing God as "Trinity" in a Muslim context may imply that there are three gods, and that one of them is the Virgin Mary. However, the word "Trinity" is never used in Scripture, and there might be superior ways of describing the biblical truth of the threeness and oneness of the Godhead that would more accurately communicate biblical meaning in a Muslim context. Finally, understanding the varied relationship between form and meaning affects issues of translation. Translators must understand both how closely connected a particular biblical form is to its meaning and the implications of any form used in the target language. For example, before translating huios tou theou into any language, the translator must understand the meaning of the term in the original biblical context and the possible understandings of any proposed translation ("Son of God," "Messiah of God," "Child of God," etc.) in the target language.

Written by associates from an international agency serving in sensitive Muslim areas.

QUESTIONS FOR REFLECTION

1. The authors differentiate between broad, local, and individual variations in culture. How should this affect our practice of evangelism and discipleship? What biblical examples are there which illustrate the broad, the local, and the individual?

2. What principles and process would you follow to decide which old cultural and religious terms, forms, and symbols can be retained and invested with new biblical meaning? How far can an outsider, in say a pioneering context, reach accurate conclusions? Sometimes, after a period of time, it is possible to "reclaim" some former cultural pattern (e.g., the use of drums in African worship). Who decides, and on what grounds?

3. The authors highlight how older churches can both teach and learn from newer churches, and the opposite way round. Give some examples of this from your own experience. As the global church becomes more excitingly multicultural, how can we draw on these spiritual riches in our own church and Christian community? How might we all be changed?

PART THREE

FINAL OBSERVATIONS

CHAPTER 31

POSTSCRIPT

Rose Dowsett

Contextualization is a crucial task for the church in every place and in every generation. It is not to be dismissed as a current fad, a trendy concern for those who like debating theological brainteasers. At its heart, contextualization is about making God and his Word visible, audible, and comprehensible, in every corner of our world and whatever the distance in time and culture and worldview from the worlds of the Old and New Testaments. Our goal is that the Triune God should be recognized, worshipped, and served by all peoples, for his glory and their good, now and into eternity.

With the incarnation of our Lord Jesus Christ as our model, we long to reflect the truth and grace of God in word and deed and character—to become visual aids that demonstrate both the loveliness of our Lord and Creator and the truth that he reveals.

We do not for one moment wish to suggest that if only we could get it right, everybody would automatically respond in repentance and faith. Most of the Old Testament prophets, declaring God's Word, were rejected. The prologue to John's Gospel tells us poignantly of the Lord Jesus himself who "was in the world, and though the world was made through him, the world did not recognize him. He came to that which was his own, but his own did not receive him" (John 1:10-11). The gospels show us many occasions where that rejection was played out. The rest of the New Testament shows the same experience, over and over again. The Apostle Paul could point to the darkness of the fallen mind and the hardness of the human heart, preventing people from turning to the Lord however clearly the truth might be communicated (see for example Rom 1:18-23; 2 Cor 4:2; Eph 4:17-18). And, were it not for the grace-filled, life-bringing ministry of the Holy Spirit, nothing that we did or said would lead to people being born again into newness of life.

All the same, we are called to build bridges for the gospel and to use every godly human means to tear aside all unnecessary barriers. Since all people are made in the image of God, however defaced that image has become, we will always seek for any point of connection, any bridge of language or cultural value across which the gospel may travel. Since God has created human beings to relate to himself, few people manage completely to suppress their awareness of the spiritual; that awareness may show itself in following some other religion or philosophy, but often there is some point from which to lead instead to the truth as it is in Jesus. There may be awareness of a supreme being who needs to be appeased. There may be a longing to be set free from moral failure. There may be patterns of prayer or sacrifice. There may be words and concepts to invest with new meaning.

This means that we are called to ongoing diligent study of the Scriptures, always seeking to understand first of all what they meant in the original context within which they were given, and then seeking to understand how that transposes accurately into today's world. And it means we equally have to be diligent students of the culture into which we are trying to communicate God's unchanging truth. Neither the study of Scripture alone, nor the study of culture alone, will lead to God-honoring contextualization: both are needed, though Scripture will always be the final arbiter of truth or error, right or wrong. Sometimes living in another culture will challenge our understanding of some part of Scripture, some belief held. We are not infallible in our reading of Scripture, and we need the humility to revisit our assumptions, in case we have been mistaken. Contextualization can be wonderfully faith expanding but also sometimes unnerving.

> Here are men and women from all around the world who have sought to be authentic disciples of Jesus Christ, to make disciples, and to see the Lord building authentic Christian communities.

In these essays we do not claim to have found all the answers, or even that every idea or practice described is indisputably right. Rather, these essays show something of the struggles, the failures, the frustrations, and the apparently helpful solutions found, from specific contexts and in relation to specific issues. Here are men and women from all around the world who have sought to be authentic disciples of Jesus Christ, to make disciples, and to see the Lord building authentic Christian communities. Many of them write from cross-cultural ministry, others are working within their own culture. Some write from situations where they are surrounded by another world religion, hostile to the Christian gospel. Whatever the context from which they write, all would describe themselves as learners-on-the-way, eager to be increasingly effective and fruitful for the glory of God. All have proved the gracious mercy of God that wonderfully blesses the bumbling, fumbling, imperfect service of those who love him.

Together, from the Mission Commission, we hope that our stories will encourage you in your discipleship and gospel ministry in your context. We bring these essays as a love offering to our Lord, with the prayer that they may serve the global church as we press on in our generation to make Christ known, and so that the gospel may be understood and received with joy and faith.

Grace and peace.

Rose Dowsett
Scotland, May 2011

REFERENCES

Achtemeier, E. R. 1962. Righteousness in the Old Testament. *The interpreter's dictionary of the Bible*. Nashville, TN: Abingdon 4:80.

Adams, E., D. Allen, and B. Fish. 2009. Seven themes of fruitfulness. *International Journal of Frontier Missiology* 26(2): 75-81.

Adeney, B. 1995. *Strange virtues: Ethics in a multi-cultural world*. Leicester, UK: InterVarsity Press.

Allen, D. 2008. Eyes to see, ears to hear. *From seed to fruit: Global trends, fruitful practices, and emerging issues among Muslims*, ed. J. D. Woodberry. Pasadena: William Carey Library.

Allen, D., R. Harrison, E. Adams, L. Adams, B. Fish, and E. J. Martin. 2009. Fruitful practices: A descriptive list. *International Journal of Frontier Missiology* 26(3): 111-22.

Arden, D. 1976. *Out of Africa, something new*. London: United Society for the Propagation of the Gospel.

Barram, M. 2005. *Mission and moral reflection in Paul*. New York: Peter Lang Publishing.

Bartholomew, C. G. and M. W. Goheen. 2004. Story and biblical theology. *Out of Egypt: Biblical theology and biblical interpretation*. Grand Rapids, MI: Zondervan.

Bebbington, D. 1989. *Evangelicalism in modern Britain: A history from the 1730s to the 1980s*. London: Unwin Hyman.

Beck, H. and C. Brown. 1975. Peace. *The new international dictionary of New Testament theology*, ed. C. Brown. Grand Rapids, MI: Zondervan 2: 778.

Berger, P. L. and S. P. Huntington. 2002. *Many globalizations: Cultural diversity in the contemporary world*. New York: Oxford University Press.

Bevans, S. B. 2002. *Models of contextual theology*. Maryknoll, NY: Orbis.

———. 1991. Seeing mission through images. *Missiology: An International Review* 19:51.

Bok, D. 2001. *The Navigators in Malaysia: The first twenty-five years*. Malaysia: Navigators.

Bosch, D. 1991. *Transforming mission: Paradigm shifts in theology of mission*. Maryknoll, NY: Orbis.

Boyarin, D. 1994. *A radical Jew: Paul and the politics of identity*. Berkeley, CA: University of California Press.

Boyd, R. 1972. The philosophical context of Indian Christian theology. *Indian voices in today's theological debate*, ed. H. Birkle and W. Lucknow: LPH/ISPCK/CLS.

Brown, L. 2006. *Shining like stars: The power of the gospel in the world's universities*. Nottingham, UK: InterVarsity Press.

Brown, R. 2008. Muslims who believe the Bible. *Mission Frontiers,* 30/3:19-23. http://www.missionfrontiers.org/2008/04/pdftoc.htm#brown.

Brown, R., B. Fish, J. Travis, E. Adams, and D. Allen. 2009. Movements and contextualization: Is there really a correlation? *International Journal of Frontier Missiology* 26(1):29-32.

Bujak, C. 2008. The woman's role in Chinese history. Review of *Between worlds: Women of Chinese ancestry* by A. Ling. New York: Pergamon Press, Inc: 1990. http://www.geocities.com/CollegePark/Field/8368/Background.html.

Buswell, J. O. III. 1986. Review article: Conn on functionalism and presupposition in missionary anthropology. *Trinity Journal* 7 NS: 90.

Cardoza, L. and L. Aragón. 1986. *Guatemala: Las líneas de su mano.* México: FCE.

Carpenter, M. Y. 1996. Familialism and ancestor veneration: A look at Chinese funeral rites. *Missiology* 24:4: 503-17.

Carson, D. 1987. Church and mission: Contextualization and third horizon. *The church in the Bible and the world,* ed. D. Carson. Grand Rapids, MI: Baker.

———. 1991. *The gospel according to John.* Leicester, UK: InterVarsity Press.

———. 2008. *Christ and culture revisited.* Grand Rapids, MI: Eerdmans.

Chew, J. 1987. *Culture and religious background in relation to conversion.* Paper presented at Congress on Evangelism for Malaysia and Singapore.

———. 1990. *When you cross cultures: Vital issues facing Christian missions.* Singapore: The Navigators.

———. 2007. Mission and spirituality: Lessons from I Corinthians. *The soul of mission,* ed. Tan Kang San. Selangor, Malaysia: Pustaka Sufes Sdn Bhd.

Clines, D. 1978. *The theme of the Pentateuch.* Sheffield: JSOT Press.

Coe, S. 1976. In search of renewal in theological education. *Theological Education* 9: 233-43.

Cooper, M. 2006. Post-Constantinian missions: Lessons from the resurgence of paganism. *Contextualization and syncretism: Navigating cultural currents,* ed. G. Van Rheenen. Pasadena: William Carey Library.

Corwin, G. 2007. A humble appeal for C5/Insider Movement ministry advocates to consider ten questions. *International Journal of Frontier Missions* 24(1): 5-22.

Costas, O. E. 1989. *Liberating news: A theology of contextual evangelization.* Grand Rapids, MI: Eerdmans.

Cramer, S. and E. Hauff-Cramer. 1992. *Samar: Development issues and analysis.* Quezon City, Philippines: UCCP.

Daniels, G. 2010. Describing fruitful practices: Relating to society. *International Journal of Frontier Missiology* 27(1): 21-26.

Davis, D. 2004. On not translating Hafez. *The New England Review* 25:1-2; 310-18. http://cat.middlebury.edu/~nereview/Davis.html (accessed September 5, 2006).

Deng, F. 1971. *The Dinka of the Sudan.* New York: Holt, Rinehart and Winston, Inc.

Dew, D. S. 1977. *The godhead.* http://www.dianedew.com/godhead.htm (accessed June 29, 2008).

Donovan, V. 1978. *Christianity rediscovered.* New York: Orbis Books.

Dorr, D. 2006. An extended conversation about responses to the September-October 2005 Mission Frontiers. *Mission Frontiers* (1):16-23.

Driver, J. 1998. *Contra corriente.* Guatemala: Semilla.

Dunn, J. D. G. 1991. *The partings of the ways: Between Christianity and Judaism and their significance for the character of Christianity.* London: SCM Press.

———. 2008. *Beginning from Jerusalem.* Cambridge: Cambridge University Press.

Dupuis, J. 1991. *Jesus Christ at the encounter of world religions.* Maryknoll. NY: Orbis.

———. 1997. *Towards a Christian theology of religious pluralism.* Maryknoll, NY: Orbis.

Ebrey, P. 2008. Background essay: Women in traditional China. http://www.askasia.org/teachers/essays/essay.php?no=1.

Elmer, D. *Cross-cultural conflict.* Downers Grove, IL: InterVarsity Press.

Eisenbaum, P. M. 2009. *Paul was not a Christian: The real message of a misunderstood apostle,* 1st ed. New York: Harper One.

Evangelical Manifesto Consortium. 2009. *An evangelical manifesto.* www.anevangelicalmanifesto.com (accessed May 10, 2008).

Fee, G. 1987. *The first epistle to the Corinthians.* Grand Rapids, MI: Eerdmans.

———. 2002. *New Testament exegesis: A handbook for students and pastors,* 3rd ed. Louisville KY: Westminster John Knox.

Flemming, D. 2005. *Contextualization in the New Testament: Patterns for theology and mission.* Downers Grove, IL: InterVarsity Press.

Fong, K. U. 1999. *Pursuing the pearl: A comprehensive resource for multi-Asian ministry.* Valley Forge, PA: Judson Press.

Gaventa, B. R. 1986. *From darkness to light: Aspects of conversion in the New Testament.* Philadelphia, PA: Fortress.

Gener, T. D. 2008. Contextualization. *Global dictionary of theology,* eds. W. A. Dryness and V. Kärkkäinen. Downers Grove, IL: InterVarsity Press.

Gooch, P. W. 1978. The ethics of accommodation: A study in Paul. *Tyndale Bulletin* 29: 111-12.

Good, E. M. 1962. Peace in the OT. *The interpreter's dictionary of the Bible.* Nashville, TN: Abingdon Press 3:705.

Gorospe, A. and C. Cang. 1998. Church planting in northern Samar evangelical churches: A case study in assessing training needs. *Phronesis* 5.2: 21-42.

Gorospe, A. 1999. Maupay nga kinabuhi: A starting point for theological reflection among the Warays of northern Samar. *Phronesis* 6.1: 27-47.

Gray, A. and L. Gray. 2009a. Paradigms and praxis (Part I): Social networks and fruitfulness in church planting. *International Journal of Frontier Missiology* 26(1): 19-28.

————. 2009b. Paradigms and praxis (Part II): Why are some workers changing paradigms? *International Journal of Frontier Missions* 26(2): 63-73.

Gray, A., L. Gray, B. Fish, and M. Baker. 2010. Networks of redemption: A preliminary statistical analysis of fruitfulness in transformational and attractional approaches. *International Journal of Frontier Missiology* 27(2): 89-95.

Green, J. B. 1995. *The theology of the Gospel of Luke.* Cambridge, UK: Cambridge University Press.

Greenlee, D. and P. Wilson. 2008. The sowing of witnessing. *From seed to fruit: Global trends, fruitful practices, and emerging issues among Muslims,* ed. J. D. Woodberry. Pasadena: William Carey Library.

Grossmann, R. 2002. *Interpreting the development of the evangelical church in Guatemala: Year 2002.* Thesis of DM. Wake Forest, NC: Southeastern Baptist Theological Seminary.

Guder, D. L. 1999. *The incarnation and the church's witness.* Harrisburg, PA: Trinity Press International.

Guthrie, G. H. and J. S. Duvall. 1998. *Biblical Greek exegesis: A graded approach to learning intermediate and advanced Greek.* Grand Rapids, MI: Zondervan.

Hall, D. J. 1996. *Confessing the faith: Christian theology in a North American context.* Minneapolis, MN: Fortress.

Hays, J. D. 2003. From every people and nation: A biblical theology of race. *New Studies in Biblical Theology* 14. Leicester, UK: Apollos.

Healey, J. 1992. Peace. *The anchor Bible dictionary,* eds. D. N. Freedman et. al; 6 vols. New York: Doubleday 5: 206.

Hedlund, R. 2000. *Quest of identity.* New Delhi: ISPCK.

Heelas, P., S. Lash, and P. Morris. 1999. *Detraditionalization.* Malden, MA: Blackwell Publishers.

Hesselgrave, D. J. 1978. *Communicating Christ cross-culturally.* Grand Rapids, IL: Zondervan.

————. 1985. The three horizons: Culture, integration and communication. *JETS* 28/4: 443-54.

Hiebert, P. 1978. *Anthropological reflections on missiological issues.* Grand Rapids: Baker.

————. 1987. Critical contextualization. *International Bulletin of Missionary Research* 11/3 (July): 104-12.

————. 1989. Form and meaning in the contextualization of theology. *The Word among us: Contexualizing theology for mission today,* ed. D. Gilliland. Dallas: Word.

————. 1994. *Anthropological reflections on missiological issues.* Grand Rapids. MI: Baker.

————. 2001. Spiritual warfare and worldview. *Global missiology for the 21st century*, ed. W. Taylor. Ada, MI: Baker Academic.

Higgins, K. 1998. Encountering Muslim resistance. *Reaching the resistant: Barriers and bridges for mission*, ed. J. D. Woodberry. Pasadena: William Carey Library.

Hoefer, H. 1991. *Churchless Christianity*. Madras: GLTC&RI.

————. 2001. *Churchless Christianity*. Pasadena: William Carey Library.

————. 2002. Jesus, my Master: Jesu Bhakta Hindu Christian theology. *International Journal of Frontier Missions* 19(3): 39.

Hrangkhuma, F. 1998. *Christianity in India: Search for liberation and identity*. Dehli: ISPCK.

Hwa, Y. 1997. *Mangoes or bananas: The quest for an authentic Asian Christian theology*. Oxford: Regnum Books.

————. 1998. The mission of the church. *Renewal in the Malaysian church*, ed. D. Ho. Petaling Jaya, Malaysia: National Evangelical Christian Fellowship.

————. 1998b. The role of the church in Vision 2020. *Modernity in Malaysia: Christian perspectives*, ed. Ng Kam Weng. Kuala Lumpur: Kairos Research Centre.

————. 1999. *Beyond AD 2000: A call to evangelical faithfulness*. Kuala Lumpur: Kairos Research Centre.

————. 2000. Towards an evangelical approach to religions and culture. *Transformation* 17/3 (July): 86-91.

————. 2002. Endued with power. *Truth to proclaim: Gospel in church and society*, ed. S. Chan. Singapore: Trinity Theological College.

————. 2008. Kingdom identity and Christian mission. *Mission Round Table: The Occasional Bulletin of OMF Mission Research* 4/2 (December): 3-12.

————. 2010. *Bribery and corruption: Biblical reflections and case studies for the marketplace in Asia*, ed. Soo Inn Tan. Singapore: Graceworks.

Ixtetela, R. 2001. La traída del alma. *Tzijonik, cuentos del Lago*. P. Petrich and C. Ochoa Garci. Guatemala: Editorial Cholsamaj/IRIPAZ.

Johnson, P. 1976. *A history of Christianity*. New York: Atheneum.

Jones, E. S. 1968. *A song of ascents*. Nashville and New York: Abingdon Press.

Jørgensen, J. A. and J. Adelin. 2008. *Jesus imandars and Christ bhaktas: Two case studies of interreligious hermeneutics and identity in global Christianity*. Frankfurt: Peter Lang.

————. 2009. Jesus imandars and Christ bhaktas: Report from two field studies of interreligious hermeneutics and identity in globalized Christianity. *International Bulletin of Missionary Research* 33(4): 171-76.

Kaiser, W. Jr. 1981. *Toward an exegetical theology: Biblical exegesis for preaching and teaching*. Grand Rapids, MI: Baker.

Kim, S. C. H. 2003. *In search of identity*. New Delhi: Oxford University Press.

Knight, G. III. 1996. The Scriptures were written for our instruction. *JETS* 39/1 (March): 3-13.

Knitter, P. 1987. Toward a liberation theology of religions. *The myth of Christian uniqueness*, eds. Hick and Knitter. Maryknoll, Orbis.

Koenig, J. 1985. *New Testament hospitality: Partnership with strangers as promise and mission.* Philadelphia, PA: Fortress.

———. 2000. *The feast of the world's redemption: Eucharistic origins and Christian mission.* Harrisburg, PA: Trinity Press International.

Kraemer, H. 1962. *Why Christianity of all religions?* Plymouth, UK: Latimer, Trend and Co.

Kraft, C. 1979. *Christianity in culture.* Maryknoll, NY: Orbis.

———. 1999. Culture, worldview and contextualization. *Perspectives on the world Christian movement,* 3rd ed., eds. R. D. Winter and S. C. Hawthorne. Pasadena: William Carey Library.

———. 2005. *Appropriate Christianity.* Pasadena: William Carey Library.

Kumar, A. 1979. Culture and the Old Testament. *Gospel and culture,* eds. J. Stott and R. Coote. Pasadena: William Carey Library.

Kurtz, L. R. 1995. *Gods in the global village: The world's religions in sociological perspective.* Thousand Oaks, CA: Pine Forge Press.

Langton, D. R. 2005. The myth of the "Traditional view of Paul" and the role of the apostle in modern Jewish-Christian polemics. *Journal for the Study of the New Testament,* 28(1): 69-104.

Lau, E. 2003. Malacca's first Chinese Methodist wedding. *Methodist Message* (June). Singapore: The Methodist Church.

Law, E. H. F. 1993. *The lion shall dwell with the lamb: A spirituality for leadership in a multicultural community.* St. Louis, MO: Chalice Press.

Lee, M. 2003. New paradigms of partnership in the Asian context. Unpublished paper for the Asian Missions Association, Moscow (September 11).

Lindsell, H. 1976. *The battle for the Bible.* Grand Rapids, MI: Zondervan.

Luzbetak, L. J. 1970. *The church and cultures.* Techny, IL: Divine Word Publications.

Maggay, M. 2001. *Jew to the Jew and Greek to the Greek: Reflections on culture and globalization.* Manila: ISACC.

Massey, J. 1999. His ways are not our ways. *Evangelical Missions Quarterly* (April). http://www.EMQonline.com.

Mathews, E. 1995. Yahweh and the gods: A theology of world religions from the Pentateuch. *Christianity and the religions,* ed. E. Rommen and H. Netland. Pasadena, CA: William Carey Library.

McGavran, D. 1970. *Understanding church growth.* Grand Rapids, MI: Eerdmans.

Mills, S. L. 1998. The hardware of sanctity. *Embodying charisma: Modernity, locality and the performance of emotion in Sufi cults*, ed. P. Werbner and H. Basu. London: Routledge.

Milne, B. 2006. *Dynamic diversity: The new humanity church for today and tomorrow.* Nottingham: InterVarsity Press.

Montgomery, R. L. 1991. The spread of religions and macrosociological relations. *Sociological Analysis* 52: 37-53.

———. 1996. *The diffusion of religion: A sociological perspective.* New York: University Press of America.

———. 1999. *Introduction to the sociology of missions.* Westport, CT: Praeger Publishers.

Moreau, S. 2006. Contextualization, syncretism and spiritual warfare: Identifying the issues. *Contextualization and syncretism: Navigating cultural currents*, ed. G. Van Rheenen. Pasadena: William Carey Library.

Nanos, M. D. 2009a. The myth of the "law-free" Paul standing between Christians and Jews. *Studies in Christian-Jewish Relations* 4(1): 1-21.

———. 2009b. Paul's relationship to Torah in light of his strategy "to become everything to everyone" (1 Corinthians 9:19-23). Paper presented at the New Perspectives on Paul and the Jews: Interdisciplinary Academic Seminar. http://www.marknanos.com/1Cor9-Leuven-9-4-09.pdf (accessed October 23, 2010).

———. 2009c. Rethinking the "Paul and Judaism" paradigm: Why not "Paul's Judaism"? Paper presented in 2009. Lund University, May 7, and Linköping University.

Nash, R. 1982. *The Word of God and the mind of man.* Grand Rapids, MI: Zondervan, quoted from K. Vanhoozer, The semantics of biblical literature: Truth and Scripture's diverse literary forms. *Hermeneutics, authority, and canon*, ed. D. A. Carson and J. D. Woodbridge. 1986. Grand Rapids, IL: Zondervan.

Neill, S. 1990. A history of Christian missions. *A history of Christian missions,* 2nd ed., ed. O. Chadwick. London and New York: Penguin.

Newbigin, L. 1985. Can the West be converted? *The Princeton Seminary Review* 6:36.

———. 1986. *Foolishness to the Greeks: The gospel and Western culture.* Grand Rapids, MI: Eerdmans.

———. 1995. *The open secret: An introduction to the theology of mission,* rev. ed. Grand Rapids, MI: Eerdmans.

Ng, Kam Weng. 2002. Interview by Warren R. Beattie (June 20). Kuala Lumpur, Malaysia.

Nicholls, B. J. 1975. Theological education and evangelization. *Let the earth hear his voice,* ed. J. D. Douglas. Minneapolis: World Wide Publications.

———. 2004. *Contextualization: A theology of gospel and culture.* Vancouver, BC: Regent College Publishing.

Nida, E. A. 1963. *Customs, culture and Christianity.* Suffolk UK: Tyndale Press.

Niles, D. T. 1951. *They may have life.* New York: Harper and Brothers.

Noll, M. 2003. *The rise of evangelicalism: The age of Edwards, Whitefield, and the Wesleys.* Downers Grove, IL: InterVarsity Press.

Oden, T. 2006. *The living God* (Systematic theology: Vol. 1) Peabody, MA: Hendrickson Publishers.

Ortiz, M. 1996. *One new people: Models for developing a multiethnic church.* Downers Grove, IL: InterVarsity Press.

Osborne, G. 1991. *The hermeneutical spiral: A comprehensive introduction to biblical interpretation.* Downers Grove, IL: InterVarsity Press.

Owens, L. 2007. Syncretism and the Scriptures. *Evangelical Missions Quarterly* 43(1): 74-80.

Pacheco, L. 1985. *Religiosidad maya-kekchí alrededor del maíz.* San José, Costa Rica: Escuela para Todos.

Padilla, R. 1984. Hacia una hermenéutica contextual. *Revista Encuentro y Diálogo* 1:1-23.

Padilla, R., ed. 1986. *Nuevas alternativas de educación teológica.* Grand Rapids, MI: Nueva Creación.

Parrett, G. 2004. The wondrous cross and the broken wall. *A many coloured kingdom: Multicultural dynamics for spiritual formation,* eds. E. Conde-Frazier, W. Kang, and G. Parrett. Grand Rapids, MI: Baker Academic.

Pazmiño, R. 1995. *Principios y prácticas de la educación cristiana, una perspectiva evangélica.* Miami, FL: Editorial Caribe.

Piper, J. 1993. *Let the nations be glad.* Grand Rapids, MI: Baker Books.

Pohl, C. D. 1999. *Making room: Recovering hospitality as a Christian tradition.* Grand Rapids, MI: Eerdmans.

Poythress, V. 2005. Presentation on translation techniques. http://www.frame-poythress.org/Poythress_courses/WivesWeekendSeminary/W13Types.ppt (accessed September 5, 2006).

Putnam, R. 2000. *Bowling alone.* New York: Simon and Schuster.

Rahner, K. 1976. *Grundkurs des glaubens.* Freiburg: Herder.

Rajashekar, J. P. 1979. The question of unbaptized believers in the history of mission in India. *Debate on mission,* ed. H. Hoefer. Madras: Gurukul Lutheran Theological College.

Redford, S. 2006. Appropriate hermeneutics. *Appropriate Christianity,* ed. C. Kraft. Pasadena: William Carey Library.

Richard, H. L. 2002. Rethinking "rethinking": Gospel ferment in India among both Hindus and Christians. *International Journal of Frontier Missions* 19(3): 7-17.

Riis, O. 1999. Modes of religious pluralism under condition of globalization. *MOST Journal on Multicultural Societies* 1:1. New York: UNESCO. http://www.unesco.org/most/vl1m1ris.htm.

Robertson, R. 1995. Glocalization: Time-space and homogeneity-heterogeneity. *Global modernities,* eds. M. Featherstone, S. Lash, R. Robertson. London: Sage.

———. 2000. Globalization and the future of "traditional religion." *God and globalization: Religion and the powers of common life,* Vol. 1, ed. M. Stackhouse. Paris: Trinity Press International.

Roig, M. 2006. Avoiding plagiarism, self-plagiarism, and other questionable writing practices: A guide to ethical writing. http://facpub.stjohns.edu/~roigm/plagiarism/Paraphrasing%20highly%20technical.html (accessed September 5, 2006).

Roncal, F., B. Muñagorri and F. Cabrera. 2001. *Filosofía universal y maya.* Guatemala: PRODESSA.

Rubel, A., C. O'Nell and R. C. Ardón. 1989. *El susto, una enfermedad popular.* México: Fondo de Cultura Económica de México.

Sáenz, E. R. 2006. The communities in the Sololá region practice common law. *Aplican 75 latigazos a delincuente.* http://www.prensalibre.com/pl/2006/mayo/12/141374.html.

Sanneh, L. 2008. *Disciples of all nations.* Oxford: Oxford University Press.

Sátiro, A. 2006. *Sueño de jóvenes por la paz.* Guatemala: MINEDUC.

Schmidt-Leukel, P. 1997. *Theologie der religionen.* Berlin: Ars Una.

Schreiter, R. 1997. *The new catholicity: Theology between the global and the local.* Maryknoll, NY: Orbis.

Scott, W. 1970. Training Malaysian leaders. *Evangelical Missions Quarterly* 6(4): 203-8.

Segal, A. F. 1994. *Paul the convert: The apostolate and apostasy of Saul the Pharisee.* New Haven, CT: Yale University Press.

SEPAL. 2001. Proyecto Josué/SEPAL Database. Guatemala: SEPAL.

Singapore Youth for Christ. 1991. *My times are in his hands: A biography of Dr. Benjamin Chew.* Singapore: Singapore Youth for Christ.

Skarsaune, O., and R. Hvalvik. 2007. *Jewish believers in Jesus: The early centuries.* Peabody, MA: Hendrickson Publishers.

Sng, B. E. K. 2003. *In his good time: The story of the church in Singapore, 1819-2002,* 3rd ed. Singapore: Bible Society of Singapore, Graduates Christian Fellowship.

Solomon, R. 1992. *Living in two worlds: Pastoral responses to possession in Singapore.* Peter Lang: Frankfurt.

Soso. n.d. http://wenwen.soso.com/z/q68440857.htm?rq (accessed June 25, 2009).

Stendhal, K. 1963. The Apostle Paul and the introspective conscience of the West. *Harvard Theological Review* 56: 199-215.

Steuernagel, V. 2006. *Hacer teología junto a María.* Buenos Aires: Kairós.

Strauss, S. 2006. The role of context in shaping theology. *Contextualization and syncretism: Navigating cultural currents,* ed. G. Van Rheenen. Pasadena: William Carey Library.

Strauss, S. 2006b. Creeds, confessions and global theologizing: A case study in comparative christologies. *Globalizing theology*, eds. H. Netland and C. Ott. Grand Rapids, MI: Baker.

Stockdale, A. A. 1964. God left the challenge in the earth. *HIS*: 20.

Stuart, D. 2002. *Old Testament exegesis: A handbook for students and pastors*, 3rd ed. Louisville, KY: Westminster John Knox.

Sugden, C. 2000. *Gospel, culture and transformation.* Oxford: Regnum Books.

Taber, C. R. 1991. *The world is too much with us: 'Culture' in modern Protestant missions.* Macon, GA: Mercer University Press.

Tannehill, R. C. 1986. *The narrative unity of Luke-Acts: A literary interpretation, Vol. 1: The gospel according to Luke.* Minneapolis: Fortress.

———. 1989. *The narrative unity of Luke-Acts: A literary interpretation, Vol. 2: The Acts of the Apostles.* Minneapolis: Fortress.

Thiselton, A. C. 1980. *The two horizons: New Testament hermeneutics and philosophical description.* Grand Rapids, MI: Eerdmans.

Thomas, J. 2002. Issues from the Indian perspective. *Deliver us from evil: An uneasy frontier in Christian mission,* ed. A. S. Moreau, et al. Monrovia, CA: MARC.

Thomas, R. L. 1990. Dynamic equivalence: A method of translation or a system of hermeneutics? *The Master's Journal:* 153. http://www.tms.edu/tmsj/tmsj1g.pdf (accessed August 12, 2006).

Tiplady, R., ed. 2003. *Postmission.* Carlisle: Paternoster Press.

Tippett, A. 1971. *Bibliography for cross-cultural workers.* Pasadena: William Carey.

Torkko, L., L. Adams, and E. Adams. 2009. Stewards of experience. *International Journal of Frontier Missiology* 26(4): 159-63.

Traoré, T. 2006. L'Homme et la Femme devant Dieu d'après 1 Cor 11:2-16: Une étude exégétique et ses implications théologique pour l'égalité entre l'Homme et la Femme dans le contexte africain aujourd'hui. Memoire presented before the FATEAC on July 1.

Travis, J. 1998. The C1 to C6 spectrum: A practical tool for defining six types of "Christ-centered communities" found in the Muslim context. *Evangelical Missions Quarterly* 34(4): 407-8.

Vanhoozer, K. 1986. The semantics of biblical literature: Truth and Scripture's diverse literary forms. *Hermeneutics, authority, and canon*, eds. D. A. Carson and J. D. Woodbridge. Grand Rapids, MI: Zondervan.

Van Rheenen, G. 2006. *Contextualization and syncretism: Navigating cultural currents.* Pasadena: William Carey.

Vilches, M. I. 1980. The image of Waray in his poetry. *Filipino thought on man and society,* ed. L. N. Mercado. Tacloban City, Philippines: Divine Word University.

Viola, F. 2002. *Pagan Christianity: The origins of our modern church practices.* Gainesville, FL: Present Testimony Ministry.

Von Rad, G. 2001. *Theology of the Old Testament,* 2 vols. Louisville, KY: Westminster John Knox.

Wakabayashi, K. 1990. Migration from rural to urban areas in China [Electronic version]. *The Developing Economies* 28(4): 503-23.

Walls, A. 1996. *The missionary movement in Christian history: Studies in the transmission of faith.* Maryknoll, NY: Orbis.

———. 2000. Eusebius tries again: Reconceiving the study of Christian history. *International Bulletin of Missionary Research* 24(3): 104-111.

———. 2004. Converts for proselytes? The crisis over conversion in the early church. *International Bulletin of Missionary Research* 28(1): 2-7.

Ward, P. 2002. *Liquid church.* Peabody, MA: Hendrickson Publishing.

Whiteman, D. 1997. Contextualization: The theory, the gap, the challenge. *International Bulletin of Missionary Research* 21(1): 2-7.

Wingate, A. 1997. *The church and conversion: A study of recent conversions to and from Christianity in the Tamil area of South India.* Delhi: ISPCK.

Wingerd, C. M. *Great Commission Update* 14(7). Colorado Springs: OC International.

Yoder, P. 1987. *Shalom: The Bible's word for salvation, justice, and peace.* London: Spire.

Xinran. 2007. *Miss Chopsticks.* London: Chatto and Windus.

INDEX